The Bible Story Handbook

A Resource for Teaching
175 Stories from the Bible

JOHN H. WALTON & KIM E. WALTON

CROSSWAY
WHEATON, ILLINOIS

The Bible Story Handbook: A Resource for Teaching 175 Stories from the Bible

Published by Crossway
1300 Crescent Street
Wheaton, Illinois 60187

Cover design: Brand Navigation

First printing 2010

Printed in the United States of America

Trade paperback ISBN: 978-1-4335-0648-2
PDF ISBN: 978-1-4335-0649-9
Mobipocket ISBN: 978-1-4335-0650-5
ePub ISBN: 978-1-4335-2329-8

Library of Congress Cataloging-in-Publication Data

Walton, John H., 1952–
The Bible story handbook : a resource for teaching 175 stories from the Bible / John H. Walton and Kim E. Walton.
p. cm.
Includes bibliographical references.
ISBN: 978-1-4335-0648-2 (tpb)
1. Bible stories—Study and teaching. 2. Christian education of children. I. Walton, Kim. II. Title.
BS546.W35 2010
220.9'505—dc22 2010008043

Crossway is a publishing ministry of Good News Publishers.

"An excellent resource for anyone teaching or preaching the Bible. While written for teachers of children, the Waltons provide clear and accurate exegetical understanding of the major stories of the Bible that will strengthen any teacher or preacher."

Craig Williford, President, Trinity International University

"For too long, Christians have been taught Bible stories as stand-alone episodes that provide moral instruction and encouragement based on imitating human characters in the stories. John and Kim Walton provide welcome correction! The opening chapters show us the *real* reason for teaching Bible stories—the revelation of God himself—and the big picture of the Bible, into which all the individual stories must fit. Not only teachers of children but anyone who uses Bible stories to teach others should examine his or her use of narrative passages by the guidelines in this book."

Starr Meade, Christian school and home school teacher; author,
Mighty Acts of God and *The Most Important Thing You'll Ever Study*

"Wow! What a resource! The Waltons provide us with an invaluable tool for the person who teaches the Bible to anyone of any age in any context. The Waltons focus on the biblical story, keeping it God's story, making God the hero of every story, just as the original writers intended. This work is a gift to Sunday school teachers, curriculum writers, and parents who want informed, rich perspectives on the stories within the biblical metanarrative. The Introduction alone provides a vital background for reading the Scriptures. For a scholar like John, with his expertise in Old Testament studies, and someone with the experience of Kim to corroborate on a work of this magnitude is a timeless gift for the teaching ministries of the church of Jesus Christ."

Scottie May, Associate Professor of Christian Formation and Ministry,
Wheaton College; co-author, *Children Matter*

"Ted Ward once asserted that 'Christian education is neither.' For generations, the church has outsourced responsibility for Bible learning and faith development to curriculum publishers. However, responsible publishers have never presumed that their material can be much more than introduction to the Bible. If Christian education is impoverished, the church, not the publisher, is responsible. This book looks like a curriculum. It is not. It is a description of a method, with abundant examples, that may assist congregations to become 'hermeneutical communities' exercising responsible use of Scripture as they design learning experiences for the people of God."

Linda Cannell, Academic Dean, North Park Theological Seminary

"In an effort to make the Bible relevant to children, too often curriculum writers and parents have focused on the wrong issue, which does violence to the text as they seek to make it relate to children. Bible scholar John Walton and his wife, Kim, have responded with this volume that speaks directly to the well-intentioned but nevertheless abusive use of the Bible, offering succinct insight into biblical stories, helping parents and teachers find the actual meaning of the text to enable responsible teaching. I highly recommend this excellent book for those who want to teach the Bible insightfully to children and to adults. They help us all to take the text seriously, letting it speak as God intended."

Perry G. Downs, Professor of Educational Ministries,
Trinity Evangelical Divinity School

"All too often we who teach children have come to the Bible with an agenda. We come with a lesson in mind and then search for a Bible story that might be used as a sort of 'proof text' for the lesson with nary a thought of the real intent of the passage. This is a wonderful resource for parents and teachers to help them remain true to the biblical text while providing valuable help in communicating truth to children. It can be used as a supplement to classroom curriculum or as a guide in teaching children in the home. I recommend this book to everyone who understands the importance of clearly and accurately communicating God's Word, especially to the youngest of God's family."

Diane Jordan, Director of Children's Ministry, College Church,
Wheaton, Illinois

Contents

New Testament

Acknowledgments

Nearly every lesson in the New Testament benefited greatly from *Zondervan Illustrated Bible Backgrounds Commentary: New Testament*, edited by Clinton Arnold, and the *IVP Bible Background Commentary: New Testament* by Craig Keener. For the parables, we relied heavily on the expert analysis of Klyne Snodgrass in his compendium *Stories of Intent*. We here acknowledge our dependence on them and highly recommend them to teachers.

Why Do We Teach Bible Stories?

Everyone has a story.[1] Our lives are a collection of stories that we share with others to tell people who we are. Our stories concern our past, our present, and our future. When we first meet other people, we communicate a part of our story to begin to "get to know one another." As we become better acquainted, we tell more of our story and hear more of our friends' stories. When deep relationships develop, we want to learn every detail of the story of the one who means so much to us, for through this process we grow to know him or her intimately. When asked whether we know a particular person, we demonstrate our knowledge by identifying something of that person's story. It might be, "Yes, he is from Montana," or "Yes, she works for the law firm down the street." We know people and are known by them through stories.

God also has a story, found in the Bible, by which he has made himself known to us. If we want to know God fully and intimately, we will immerse ourselves in his story. If we want to lead others to knowledge of God, we will tell them God's stories beginning in their early childhood. By knowing God's story, we come to know what he is really like and how we might expect him to act.[2] As with an intimate companion, we want to hear every part of the story again and again.

God tells us his story so that we can understand him; he could have simply given us a doctrinal statement or a list of his attributes, but this would not have been sufficient. "God is good"—fine, but how does that goodness play out in specific situations? Does God's goodness mean that his actions will always seem good to me? If we had only a list of attributes, we would not have a very good idea of how these work out day by day. But stories! With these we can see how God's qualities are demonstrated in perfect balance, governed by his wisdom and holiness, in numerous situations. God tells his story through human authors. This is what we mean when we say that the Bible is "inspired"—God-breathed. The Bible is not ultimately valuable because it gives people ideas about what God is like. Everybody can offer their ideas, but why should we believe them? The Bible is unique because in it God is telling us his own story. We can rely on the accuracy of its portrayal of God and accept it as an authoritative portrayal if we believe that it comes

[1]Sections of this article have been adapted from J. H. Walton, L. D. Bailey, and C. Williford, "Bible-Based Curricula and the Crisis of Scriptural Authority," *Christian Education Journal* 13 (Spring 1993): 83–94. Used by permission.

[2]Tim Stafford, *Knowing the Face of God* (Grand Rapids, MI: Zondervan, 1986), 194–201.

from God, for God does not misrepresent himself. We might call it God's authorized biography.[3] By affirming this authority of the Bible, we likewise affirm its right to speak to us. Not only does it have the right to speak, but it is right when it speaks. We are not free to tinker with the picture of God that the Bible gives. We cannot pick and choose the parts we like or don't like. If we accept the whole, we leave ourselves no room to second-guess God or to believe that we could do better if we were God.

When we affirm the authority of the Bible we also affirm our readiness to submit to it. This means that we accept unflinchingly the story of God and picture of God presented in the story. If we embrace the Bible's story and picture of God, we say that we believe it. God's story is not something that we can keep at arm's length; if we accept the Bible as God's own account of himself, we will also understand that he has made us to be in relationship with him and to be like him. If we truly believe this, God's story will change us. If we are unwilling to change, we don't truly believe.

We tell Bible stories so that students of all ages can know God better. As they come to know God through his stories, they will know better how to be in relationship with him and how to imitate him in their lives. This means that our primary concern in teaching any story from the Bible is to explain what the story tells us about God. Unfortunately, the curricula taught in our churches often are not written with this in mind. Consider the following example:

> As usual, Sunday morning had been hectic—dropping off kids to their classes, getting the baby settled in the nursery, trying to find five different people concerning one thing or another, not to mention trying to make islands in all of this for productive learning and reflective worship. But now the family had finally gathered around the table for Sunday dinner. This was important family time for distilling the most positive and significant aspects of the Sunday morning experience.
>
> "What was your story about today?" I ask my three-year-old.
>
> "Cain and Abel," he answered. I began to feel concern, wondering how such a sensitive story would be presented to three-year-olds.
>
> "Well, what did you find out about Cain and Abel?"
>
> "God made their bodies" came the nonchalant reply. I quickly affirmed the truth of this but pressed for more.
>
> "What did Cain and Abel do?" I queried, probing to find out how the issue of sacrifice had been handled.
>
> "They didn't do anything," was the reply.

[3]Perhaps even an autobiography with ghost writers.

As it turned out, my son had been neither forgetful nor inattentive. The story card sent home confirmed that (thankfully) neither sacrifice nor treachery had been discussed at this tender age. The point of the lesson was, "God gave us bodies." I was left to muse about what this curriculum was indirectly teaching my son about interpreting the Bible when stories were manipulated in this way. He was being raised in an evangelical church that used an evangelical curriculum, but would he learn how to interpret the Bible properly if the curriculum that shaped his education often ignored the actual teaching of the text and manipulated the stories for its own purposes? What was he taught that morning from Genesis 4 that conveyed the authoritative teaching of God's Word?

What he learned was true, but that is not enough. The issue here is not just truth; the issue is authority. The lesson ("God made our bodies") was biblical, but did the lesson carry the authority of the Bible? To answer this question, we have to ask whether it was the author's intention in Genesis 4 to teach that God made our bodies or whether that was simply something that the curriculum wanted to convey. The Bible, as God's Word, teaches with authority and demands the reader to submit to its authority. What we teach as human beings, be it valuable, sincere, challenging, and/or true, does not carry the same authority. Using a Bible story means nothing if it does not commit the curriculum or teacher to teaching what the Bible teaches in the story being used.

> Our task is to enable God's revealed truth to flow out of the Scriptures into the lives of men and women [and children] today. . . . To expound Scripture is to bring out of the text what is there and expose it to view. . . . The biblical text is neither a conventional introduction to a sermon [or lesson] on a largely different theme, nor a convenient peg on which to hang a ragbag of miscellaneous thoughts, but a master which dictates and controls what is said.[4]

If the Bible is used only as a jump-off point for one's own educational objectives, the Bible's authority is bypassed; if a passage is not being used to teach what the Bible is teaching, the teacher stands only on his or her own authority. In truly Bible-based lessons, the purpose of the biblical passage must guide the lesson development process. The focus of the story, the teaching aim for the unit or lesson, and the application must all grow out of careful interpretation of the passage. Teachers must hold educational considerations, such as developmental issues and teaching methodology, in proper relationship to the teaching of the text. This means that some passages of Scripture

[4]J. R. W. Stott, *Between Two Worlds* (Grand Rapids, MI: Eerdmans, 1982), 138–39.

will be inappropriate for younger age groups (e.g., Cain and Abel for three-year-olds) because of their focus; likewise, certain concepts one might desire to teach may not be presented in Scripture in a form appropriate to all ages.

There are many valuable things we can learn from a given passage of Scripture, but not all of them are things that the Bible is trying to teach.

> The first task of the interpreter is . . . the careful, systematic study of Scripture to discover the original intended meaning. It is the attempt to hear the Word as the original recipients were to have heard it, to find out what was the original intent of the words of the Bible.[5]

Only the things that Scripture intends to teach carry the authority of the text. For example, we can learn much about leadership by studying Nehemiah. In the end, however, there is no indication that the author of Nehemiah was preserving and presenting his material so that readers could be instructed in leadership. Because of this, the authority of Scripture is not being tapped when leadership is taught from the book and life of Nehemiah.

Leadership is an important quality, one worth learning about, but one may just as well learn about it from the lives of Abraham Lincoln or John Calvin. There is no special merit in learning it from Nehemiah simply because his story is in the Bible whereas the others are not. The Bible is unique because it teaches with the authority of God; in the case of Nehemiah, we learn, among other things, that God fulfills his promises of restoring the city of Jerusalem and that he sovereignly carries out his plan through Nehemiah's submission. God used Nehemiah's leadership, but that does not mean that Nehemiah's was the best possible leadership, approved by God in every way. Nehemiah's success does not authorize his example as a biblical model for leadership. The model itself has no authority. If, above anything else, we tell Bible stories to convey the Bible's authoritative teaching to students, then our focus should not be on Nehemiah's leadership.

For someone to claim biblical authority for his or her teaching, he or she must use the Scripture as the author intended it to be used. If the teacher desires to equip children to submit to the Bible's authority, the teacher must model a proper method for identifying what the Bible, in its authority, teaches. Too often the teaching objectives are rooted in issues that the text is not really addressing. We cannot legitimately impose a grid on the text in order to extract a desired lesson that the Bible (in that place) is not teaching.

---

[5]Gordon Fee and Douglas Stuart, *How to Read the Bible for All Its Worth* (Grand Rapids, MI: Zondervan, 1981), 21.

> A text cannot mean what it never meant. Or to put that in a positive way, the true meaning of the biblical text for us is what God originally intended it to mean when it was first spoken.[6]

We can only attach authority to a lesson that the text is intentionally teaching; the reader must look to the text to determine what that teaching is. This last statement is methodologically important. Too often we assume that if the principle we want to teach is demonstrably biblical, then it is legitimate to teach it from any passage, even where it is, at best, a vague tangent. Yet this approach damages our ability to hear the text. If a teacher intends to be Bible-based in his or her approach to a text, it would be disappointing if he or she did not teach what that text was teaching. The authoritative teaching of Scripture must be a major part of the teaching objectives for each week.

Some would object to this, saying that we must be more creative to make the text relevant for our day and for the lives of the students. This implies that the text is somehow sterile and obtuse and that curriculum writers must identify appropriate application. We must tread carefully here, for we cannot apply a passage unless we properly interpret it. We will not find the significance of the passage by asking, "What does it mean to me?" (inviting all sorts of random associations and personalized reflections), but by asking, "What are the present-day implications of what the biblical author meant?"

> We want to know what the Bible means for us—legitimately so. But we cannot make it mean anything that pleases us and then give the Holy Spirit "credit" for it. The Holy Spirit cannot be called in to contradict himself, and he is the one who inspired the original intent. Therefore, his help for us will be in the discovering of that original intent, and in guiding us as we try faithfully to apply that meaning to our own situations.[7]

Much modern-day biblical teaching demonstrates the popular notion that application must involve action. We all know that something must be put in practice to be learned and remembered, but it is not unusual for this idea to be taken to what might seem the next logical step: if some teaching is to be relevant and practical, it must be able to be put into practice in the short term—today, tomorrow, or at least sometime this week. This approach is too short-sighted, however, for we know that worthwhile pursuits frequently require a long-term perspective. Years of training are often necessary

[6] Ibid., 27.
[7] Ibid., 26.

to prepare for a particular profession. If someone wants to be an athlete or musician, he or she must be willing to invest long years of practice. People do not train for a marathon in one day and then run it at the end of the week. When we imply that godly living through biblical interpretation has to be accomplished in the short term for it to be practical, we devalue it and diminish its chances of success.

Biblical application cannot be limited to "action points" for the coming week (though if there are some, that is fine). More importantly, we have to think about "belief points." Much biblical teaching involves belief; as we learn stories, our belief should be affected. If our belief is affected, our behavior should change. If our belief has not been affected, then any change in our behavior is likely to be superficial and temporary. We learn what to believe not just so that we can act on it this week but so that we have it firmly in our minds to draw on at need. Pianists do not learn scales so they can perform scales. Instead, as the scales become second nature they can apply the principles of the scales to much more complex pieces. They have to learn the scales well enough that their fingers know them without thinking, because in a performance they do not have the luxury of thinking about each note or sequence.

Application is much the same. We learn what we should believe so that right beliefs become part of us. We may then draw upon them at need. Much of the Bible, then, is intended to give us belief points. Furthermore, we may now recognize that the focus of these beliefs that we are learning is God. We are not learning an ethical system, though informed belief of God should result in a sound ethical system. The Bible is about God, and we should have as our desire to know him and to be like him.

We must realize that the Bible's teachings about God convey certain implications for us. We cannot be exposed to God's character without response. What in my life must change? What attitudes must be adjusted? How does my worldview need to conform? These are the questions of application for adults. Often for children it is not a matter of changing, adjusting, or conforming but of developing a worldview centered on a well-informed picture of God. Teachers and curricula must use the stories of Scripture to inform the child's perspective in age-appropriate ways, but they still must allow Scripture to speak rather than squeezing it through educational grids.

We want our students to be conformed to the image of Christ and their behavior to have been embraced as a way to imitate God. We accomplish this by helping them know God better, not by telling them that they should obey because Abraham obeyed. The text is relevant because it reveals God to us and thus enables us to understand what he desires from us.

The Bible is intrinsically relevant to everyone because it is God's self-revelation. To neglect or ignore the authoritative teaching of the text as the author intends it is to take the first step toward relegating to the text an irreversible irrelevance. It is only relevant insofar as it is authoritative. We dare not think that we can bypass its authoritative teaching and somehow improve its relevance. Even if we could, it would be too great a cost to pay, if authority were sacrificed.

We tell stories from the Bible so that students will:

- learn God's stories
- know God
- come to know God better and therefore know better what to expect from him
- learn what to expect of God so that they know how to respond to him
- learn to respond to God so that they come to understand what it means to be imitators of God
- learn to be imitators of God so they can be in ever closer relationship with him
- come to be in ever closer relationship with God so that they will know how to serve him and be his representatives—salt and light in this fallen world

This whole sequence is important; if we try to race to one part or another without laying the foundation of what has come before, we will foster instability and confusion in our students.

Is There a Right Way or a Wrong Way to Use Bible Stories?

Many parts of the Bible, especially the ones we often use for Bible stories, are narratives. Narrative always shows us characters; some we admire, others we despise, but all play a role in the story. In narrative we engage the concerns of life through the characters and the events that surround them. Such encounters inevitably prompt us to think about our own lives, situations, and decisions. In these ways narrative can impact us, shape us, change us, motivate us, and inspire us.

Biblical narrative does no less, for in this way it is like all literature. The biblical narratives are not different from other narratives because of anything distinctive about their mode of storytelling. "Scriptural" narrative is not necessarily better narrative—its characters purer or more highly developed, its complex levels of interaction with the life and mind of the reader somehow more sanctified. The stories of the Bible are "Scripture" (rather than just narrative literature) because their pages reveal God and thus carry authority. Through the narratives (as well as the other genres) we receive an utterly true picture of God, the primary actor in the narrative of the world he made for the people he loves. If we teach only the elements of narrative, we degrade the Bible to the status of literature (only). When we teach the God of the Bible, we elevate the Bible and honor it as Scripture. A Bible story can be used incorrectly if we fail to move beyond the narrative and the normal function of narrative to arrive at the message that makes the text authoritative Scripture.

Failure to clearly see the scriptural agenda compromises one's ability to convey this depiction of God through curricula and teaching. Instead, the Bible, particularly the Old Testament, is often treated as merely a tool for developmental and behavioral objectives.

> "Bible stories" tend to be weighted too much on the anthropocentric. Biblical narrative all too often is searched for moral examples that can be followed or shunned, as the case may be. Biblical history thus is dissolved into a number of instances of human conduct, moral or immoral. The historical context within which the events are placed by the biblical author tends to be ignored. When a straight line is drawn from "then" to "now," the uniqueness of the biblical events as instances of God's self-revelation is in danger of being overlooked. The nuances of meaning placed in the biblical account by the inspired authors fail to get their due, for everything turns around the supposed "lesson." Biblical events tend to be lifted out of their redemptive historical context by being made into timely paradigms of moral behavior.[8]

When we use a text such as Genesis 41–46 to teach that Joseph is a good example of how God wants us to treat others in competitive situations, we violate the integrity of the narrative. The students miss the central teaching of the narrative section, which concerns the providence of God. Sometimes this may result from genuine puzzlement over the meaning or significance of the text. Other times it merely demonstrates how thoroughly our commitment to developmental and behavioral issues eclipses our commitment to sound

[8]Marten Woudstra, *The Book of Joshua*, New International Commentary on the Old Testament (Grand Rapids, MI: Eerdmans, 1981), 4.

hermeneutics, sometimes compromising how clearly we convey the authority of the text.

This must change. The Bible does not intend to focus our primary attention on Abraham, Jacob, Moses, Joshua, Hannah, David, Nehemiah, Esther, Mary, or the disciples. These are the bit players; God is the focus. When we apply the Bible to our lives only through the role models we find in the characters, we miss out. The message of Daniel 1 is not that since Daniel ate healthy food, you should eat healthy food too. Such an emphasis is not teaching what the Bible is teaching. When this approach is used, human wisdom masquerades as God's authoritative word, and in the process we can easily miss what the Bible is really teaching. In this Daniel passage, for instance, the point is the sovereign protection of God. Sunday school lessons must not focus on the human actors at the expense of God's self-revelation.

This is not to say that Scripture's teaching has nothing to do with the human characters. The authors of the Bible note Abraham's faith and Job's righteousness. Though we certainly desire to emulate these commendable examples, they must not take the focus off God. Each of these narratives seeks to reveal something about God. The characters are the witnesses that testify to God's work, in their lives and circumstances, to his nature as he interacts with them, and to his plan. They point us to him; that is their role. The problem with teaching about the "heroes and heroines of the Bible" is that the hero of the Bible is God. All people have flaws, even at their best. We dare not obscure the view of God to elevate human heroes.

If a teacher uses the biblical narratives to accomplish his own educational agenda and never gets down to what the Bible is actually teaching in its use of those stories, then the teacher cannot claim that his lesson is Bible-based, for such lessons have no biblical authority. For instance, if a teacher decides to use the story of Hannah taking Samuel to the temple to teach that we should be happy to go to church, what has she achieved? The relationship between the Bible story and the objective is oblique at best, for the experience of Samuel going to the temple in that context has no correlation to the children's experience of going to church. Furthermore, the intent of the narrator of that section of Scripture has nothing whatever to do with teaching about going to church. As a result, the lesson has no basis in the Bible and carries no intrinsic authority. Worse still, in teaching the lesson this way, what has the teacher conveyed to the students about the use of Scripture in their own lives? The model they observe has suggested they may use the text indiscriminately, twisting Scripture to support something that may be true but is not taught in that particular passage. Curriculum is at least partially to blame for this sort of distortion that persists among adults, for they are merely imitating what their teachers have consistently modeled.

When, for example, a "behavioral grid" is placed on the text, it may be used to teach a biblical virtue such as obedience. It is natural, then, to begin by looking for a story to teach obedience. The difficulty arises when there is no commitment to use only a passage that intends to teach obedience. As a result, lessons may end up using the story of Joseph being sent by his father to find his brothers and build an entire lesson around Joseph obeying his father. In the same way, the story of the feeding of the five thousand is used to teach that children should share (like the little boy who shared his lunch, John 6:9), and the narrative in which Abraham and Lot divide the land (Gen. 13:9–12) is used to teach that children should give others first choice. While obedience, sharing, and graciousness are commendable virtues that need to be taught, they are not the subject of these texts. Therefore, these lessons model a faulty method of interpretation that suggests we can ignore what the text is actually teaching.

Another flawed approach to interpretation, evident both in Sunday school lessons and in the church at large, suggests that rather than having a single meaning, a given text may teach many different principles, and that the interpreter is responsible to continually bring to light more of these innumerable principles. For example, a teacher freely uses Daniel 6 (Daniel and the lions) to teach primary-school-aged children about worship but just as readily uses the same passage to teach third and fourth graders about courage, and fifth and sixth graders about responsible action. This handling of Scripture threatens biblical authority. All principles are not equally valid. Though we might be able to learn innumerable things from a passage, the passage is not teaching everything that anybody sees in it.

One need not have a seminary degree to discern what the biblical passage is teaching. It is often stated in one form or another by the author, or it can be deduced from his selection, arrangement, or emphases. Where it is not clearly stated, there may be differences of opinion, but as long as one is attempting to identify the authoritative teaching of the text using the material within the text, it is not hard to capture the general thrust.

Teachers must not allow the Scripture to become static and abstract. Certainly curriculum is designed to make the Scriptures come alive in the life of the receiver. Sunday school curricula ought to help people think theologically—to ask, "How ought we live in the world today in light of the gospel?" The curriculum serves as a bridge between the Scriptures and the learner by illuminating the meaning of the biblical text and helping the learner discern its implications for everyday life.

Unfortunately, many so-called Bible-based lessons often mismanage the text at the point of application. In attempting to connect Scripture to life, an inattentive writer may fail to distinguish between the meaning (author's original intended meaning) and significance (the relationship between that meaning and the world of the reader) of the text. Lessons too easily jump from "What does the text say?" to "What does it mean for me?" without first asking "What did the author intend to convey?" For example, a lesson from Esther observes that Haman's negative feelings determined his actions toward Mordecai. The application focuses on how students should treat people they don't like—try to understand others better so they will be more able to love them. The lesson jumps from the action of the narrative to the context of the learner without reference to what the author intended to convey. This is an erroneous approach to Scripture, one that is responsible for much of the endemic misuse of the Bible in contemporary Christianity.

> Basic to perceptive application is accurate exegesis. We cannot decide what a passage means to us unless first we have determined what the passage means. To do this we must sit down before the biblical writer and try to understand what he wanted to convey to his original readers. Only after we comprehend what he meant in his own terms and in his own times can we clarify what difference that should make in life today. . . . Application must come from the theological purpose of the biblical writer.[9]

People have learned to think that in order to make the Bible relevant, it is acceptable, necessary, or even desirable to subject Scripture to our "grid." For example, a teacher might use Jonah's poor attitude toward the Ninevites to warn students against the evils of prejudice—an issue that the text does not address. The forced "relevance" of this application misses the ever pertinent point of the narrative—God's compassion toward sinful people.

Such a handling of Scripture is at worst an insult to God, for it seems to imply that what he has revealed of himself is irrelevant. The teacher's task in application is to recognize and communicate Scripture's relevance rather than to make Scripture relevant. It is unnecessary to generate role models, invent typologies, or extract hidden mysteries to create an artificial significance.

[9]Haddon Robinson, *Biblical Preaching: The Development and Delivery of Expository Messages* (Grand Rapids, MI: Baker, 1980), 90–91.

Conclusion

Teaching that is truly Bible-based must not merely use Scripture but must allow the text to set the agenda, to speak for itself. Sunday-school teachers must commit to the same careful handling of Scripture that an expository preacher uses to prepare his sermon.

Is there a "wrong way" to teach a Bible story? Indeed there is. If we set our own agenda above that of the text, we are teaching the story wrongly. If our teaching does not align with the authority of the text, we have strayed from what is most important to the inspired author. It is not important to the author of John 11 (the raising of Lazarus) that Jesus had friends. It is not important to the author of Exodus 3–4 (the burning bush) that Aaron is willing to help his brother. It is not important to the author of John 6 (the feeding of five thousand) that the boy shared his lunch. If we teach these things, we are telling the story wrongly because we are substituting what we want to teach at the expense of the biblical author's message. A story is told rightly when we can confidently claim that it represents the intention of the author and the authority of the text.

As we have worked with teacher training and curriculum evaluation over the years, we have noticed five common fallacies that draw a lesson away from scriptural authority:

1) ***Promotion of the trivial.*** A lesson is based on a passing comment within the text (Josh. 9:14, they did not consult the Lord), a casual observation about the text (Moses persevered by repeatedly appearing before Pharaoh), or even a deduction from the text (Joshua and Caleb were brave and strong). We are not teaching the Bible properly if we teach virtues that the specific text does not have in view.
2) ***Illegitimate extrapolation.*** The lesson is improperly expanded from a specific situation to all situations. For example, Exodus 3–4 shows that God commanded Moses to do a hard thing and helped him do it, but the lesson taught from the text is that God will also help you do a hard thing—anything of your choosing. In such cases, we pass by the teaching of the text in favor of what we want to say, thus neglecting biblical authority.
3) ***Reading between the lines.*** Teachers or students read between the lines when they analyze the thinking of the characters, speculate on their motives, or fill in details of the plot that the story does not give. When such speculations become the center of the lesson, the authority of the biblical teaching is lost because the teaching is supplied by the reader rather than by the text.

4) ***Missing important nuance.*** This occurs when the lesson pinpoints an appropriate message but misses a connection necessary to drive the point home accurately. It is not enough, for instance, to say that God wants us to keep his rules; we must realize that God has given us rules to display his character and to show us how we ought to respond to him in our actions.
5) ***Focus on people rather than on God.*** The Bible is God's revelation of himself, and its message and teaching are largely based on what it tells us about God. This is particularly true of narrative (stories). While we tend to observe the people in the stories, we cannot forget that the stories are intended to teach us about God more than about people. If in the end the final point is "We should (or shouldn't) be like *X*," there is probably a problem unless the *X* is Jesus or God. Better is, "We can learn through *X*'s story that God . . . " The tendency to focus overly on people also shows up in questions such as "Who are the Goliaths in your life?" The text is more interested in "Who is God in your life?"

The third commandment warns us not to take the name of the Lord in vain. Interpreters often read this as a warning against profane language or insincere oaths made in God's name. While we should avoid these actions, the command is more concerned that we not abuse God's authority by appropriating it for our own purposes. If we were to use someone's credit card to make purchases without his approval, we would be guilty of misusing his financial authority. If we present something as God's Word when it is not, we are misusing God's name. Students of the Bible expect their teachers to present the authoritative teaching of God's Word as given by the inspired authors. If we substitute this teaching for some idea we think is important, students don't know the difference. We are then violating the third commandment because we have attributed God's authority to what is really only our own idea.

FAQ

1) Aren't you getting a little too picky about what we teach?

One cannot be too careful when dealing with the authoritative Word of God. When we teach the Bible, we are teaching more than simple truths—we are explaining what God's Word teaches. We must distinguish that from our own agendas. The same faulty methodology that results in slight deviation from the text can also result in serious abuse. We all know that there are abuses; we have to develop methods that will help us identify what is abuse. This calls for careful discernment and consistent criteria.

2) How can we be confident about identifying what the biblical author intended to teach?

Our confidence comes from careful method as we deal with the biblical text. We believe that God is an effective communicator and that the authors the Spirit used were therefore enabled to be effective communicators.

3) If I follow your suggestions, I will be letting go of a lot of teachable curricula that can guide children toward right behavior. Why should I do this?

The reason such a choice should be made is that teaching the Bible cannot afford to become just good education with sound objectives. We have a responsibility to submit to the Word of God by teaching the lessons behind which it places its authority. You can teach good behavior but pick your stories wisely; teach it because of who God is, not because of how some character acted.

4) If what you present in this book is correct, then there are a lot of misguided curricula out there. How can this be so?

Many curricula and teachers who seek to teach the Bible have a clear idea of education and biblical values, and they do an excellent job at incorporating those elements. But many are less certain about exactly what to do with biblical narratives—particularly those of the Old Testament. It takes education and training to learn the methodology and develop the expertise to identify the authoritative teaching from the Bible, and those with this background often choose other career paths.

5) Are there any good curricula available?

"Good" and "bad" are not simple labels. Many of the curricula have been developed by competent educators who know children well and who know how to execute a lesson. Furthermore, they are godly people with a good grasp of biblical values. In this book we are leaving those matters in their competent hands. We focus particularly on the issue of how to get to the Bible's authoritative message. Curriculum houses are usually not well equipped to succeed in this area. They have people to check the theology, and that is good. But methodology is another matter.

The Big Picture of the Bible

When we tell Bible stories, we should always contextualize these stories within the Big Picture of God's plan as it is revealed in the Bible.[10] This Big Picture answers the question, "What is God's purpose for our world and what part does the Bible itself play?" Some people might think that the Big Picture is Jesus or salvation from sin. These are certainly important elements of the Big Picture and central to the Bible's message, but is there more? Perhaps as we consider the nature of the Bible and the themes that permeate its pages, we can fill in this "Big Picture" a little more.

The Bible is God's self-revelation, and, as such, it enables the reader to know God more fully. This process, however, is not intended to merely expand the reader's knowledge. We know God by experiencing his attributes. While there is some virtue in being able to list God's attributes, those attributes must become the framework of our worldview. Our perspective on ourselves, our society, our world, our history, our conduct, our decisions—everything—should be knit together by an informed and integrated view of God. The Bible's objective is not transformed lives, though knowing God should transform one's life. The Bible's objective is not the adoption of a value system, though a value system would certainly be one outcome of authentically knowing God. The Bible is not a collection of role models, dusty hymns, and obscure prophetic sayings—it is rather God telling his own story.

This story of God begins with creation. The text is more concerned with the beginning of God's plan than the beginning of the world. God made everything just right to set his plan in motion. In that sense, creation is simply the introduction to history. God initially assures his sovereignty by the act of creation. While this effectively denies any claim to sovereignty by other deities, the purpose of the text is not to argue against the pagan polytheism of the day. Rather than denouncing other deities and refuting other worldviews, the Old Testament offers its breathtaking view of the character and sovereign action of the one true God.

The Old Testament is only secondarily concerned with the political or social aspects of history. Instead, the narrative recorded in the Old Testament is primarily interested in God's revelation of himself to people in the past.

[10]Much of this article is adapted from Andrew Hill and John Walton, *A Survey of the Old Testament*, 3d ed. (Grand Rapids, MI: Zondervan, 2009), 21–24. Used by permission of Zondervan.

This observation is illustrated in the names of God that permeate the pages of Scripture. These names portray God as holy, almighty, foremost of beings, the cause of all that is. Yet he is also a God who hears, sees, and provides. The habitual rebellion and feeblemindedness of humankind stand in sharp contrast to the patience and grace of God.

Just as creation flows into history, so history flows into prophecy. God's plan was initiated at creation, progresses throughout history, and will continue until all is accomplished. By seeing God's plan worked out in the past (the Pentateuch and the Historical Books) and projected into the future (Prophetic Literature), we can begin to appreciate the unfathomable wisdom of God, who is worthy of praise and worship (Psalms and Wisdom Literature). Therefore, we should view the Old Testament, and indeed the whole Bible, as a presentation of God's attributes in action. We can know who God is and what he is like by hearing what he has done and intends to do. This is a "theocentric" approach to Scripture—God is at the center of it all and therefore ought to be our focus as we study and teach his Word. Once we know who he is and what he is like, the appropriate responses should be worship, commitment, and service.

The Plan: God with Us

What is this plan that spans the scope of creation, history, and prophecy? We find it communicated throughout the pages of the Bible. From the beginning, God planned to create a people among whom he could dwell and with whom he could be in relationship. We should not suppose that he *needed* a place to live or that he had some psychological need for companionship. His plan emerges naturally, expressing his character as a creative, relational, and gracious being.

This plan is reflected in the initial setting of Eden, where God's presence existed in what we might call a cosmic temple; in this garden he placed people who could be near him and who could come to know him. God's plan was disrupted by the entrance of sin through human disobedience—what we call "the fall." Humans thus destroyed their relationship with God and forfeited the privilege of being in God's presence as the first couple was driven out of the garden.

The rest of the Bible recounts God's program to restore his presence to his people and enable them once again to share a relationship with him. We can offer a brief overview by identifying the seven stages of God's presence.

Stages of God's Presence
Eden
Covenant
Exodus (Burning Bush/Sinai)
Tabernacle/Temple
Incarnation (Immanuel)
Pentecost
New Creation

In the account of the Tower of Babel (Gen. 11:1–9) we find the people engaged in a project that attempts to reestablish God's presence on earth. The tower was provided as a means for God to come down and take up his residence in the people's city and receive their worship. Unfortunately, this initiative was motivated by a flawed conception of deity, a conception which displeased God (for more information see pp. 49–52). The next chapter of Genesis introduces God's own initiative as he establishes a covenant with Abraham. Through this covenant, God purposed to reveal himself to the world (explained in the next section). He chose one family among whom to dwell and with whom to develop a relationship. This second stage is the first step of the reclamation project and involved revelation and relationship.

God's presence reaches a new level as he appears in the burning bush to Moses to reveal his name (i.e., his character and nature) and the next step of his plan (i.e., deliverance of Israel from Egypt). His presence is demonstrated through the plagues and temporarily evidenced in the pillar of cloud and fire. It finally descends to the top of Mount Sinai, where he indicates how his people can be in relationship with him (the Law) and preserve his presence (the rituals and other instructions regarding the tabernacle).

In the next stage God actually initiates a means to establish his presence on earth. The tabernacle is a place of God's dwelling, and many aspects of its design invoke the images of the garden of Eden. By keeping the law and observing rules of purity, the people can enjoy relationship with the God who has come among them. This stage of God's presence eventually transitions to the temple built by Solomon, where it resides through the remainder of the Old Testament. The momentum of God's program, however, suffers a serious setback when the rebellion of the Israelites finally causes God's presence to leave the temple, which is consequently destroyed by the Babylonians (in Jeremiah and Ezekiel). With their exile from the Promised Land, the Israelites lose the covenant benefits, and their relationship with God hangs in the balance.

Though they eventually return to the land and rebuild the temple, the next stage of God's presence comes in the pages of the New Testament, as God sends his Son, Jesus, in human flesh (the incarnation) to reside with humanity (Immanuel, God with us) as a sort of human tabernacle (John 1:14). Through Christ, God's presence thus becomes available in a whole new way, and the relationship is made available at a whole new level—Christ has paid the penalty for sin and provided a permanent mechanism that allows us to be in relationship with God.

Though Christ ascended to heaven after the resurrection, he promised that his presence would not be taken from us: he sent the Comforter to take his place. Thus the coming of the Holy Spirit at Pentecost marks the beginning of yet another stage in the availability of God's presence—now within his people—and a relationship based on the indwelling of the Holy Spirit. Consequently, God's presence resides in his people, both individually (1 Cor. 6:19) and corporately (1 Cor. 3:16)—we are the Temple. The veil that restricted access to God's presence has been torn (Ephesians 2); relationship is now available to all who seek it.

The final stage remains in the future; it is described in Revelation 21:3, "Behold, the dwelling place of God is with man. He will dwell with them, and they will be his people, and God himself will be with them as their God." In the new heaven and new earth (Rev. 21:1) there will be no temple because "its temple is the Lord God the Almighty and the Lamb" (Rev. 21:22). God's throne will be in the city (Rev. 22:3).

Consequently, we would conclude that the Big Picture focuses on access to God's presence with the people he created (eventually through Christ and the Spirit) and relationship with God (made possible through Jesus and guaranteed by the Spirit). We are "saved" not only from our sins but into a relationship with God. The promise of eternal life assures us that this relationship will not be broken by death. Relationship is the goal, salvation is the means, and eternity is the scope. We should focus more on the goal and less on the means and the scope. Our approach to the stories of the Bible ought to focus on how each one helps us to understand God and his plan better.

Old Testament

1. God Created Light (Genesis 1:1–5, 14–19)

Lesson Focus

God is the creator; all things were made by him.

- God made our world to function by time.
- Light and the heavenly bodies regulate time.
- God has brought order to our world.

Lesson Application

We know that we have a great and powerful God by the world that he made.

- God is the master and creator of our time.
- The sun, moon, and stars do his bidding, so we believe that God is in control of our world.

Biblical Context

The book of Genesis tells us how God prepared a place for the people he created and how he has entered into relationship with them. Genesis 1 reveals that God ordered the world so that it would be just right for people and also determined to live among them. God began to order the world for people by creating time. Verse 1 is most likely an introduction to the story, and verse 2 indicates that the story begins when there was no order; however, the presence of God's Spirit also indicates the potential for development.

Interpretational Issues in the Story

Light and time (Gen. 1:3–5). In Genesis 1:5 God calls the light "Day" and the darkness "Night." Thus, we learn that day and night are the creative focus, since they are named. God has spoken a *period* of light into what had previously been darkness (v. 2) and named the period of light "day." This rotation of periods of light and darkness (day and night) constitutes time. We see then that nothing material is created on day one. It is a function—time—which shows God bringing order to his world. This is why it is important to see that in verse 2 the account begins without order (not without matter). Though material is inevitably involved, the focus of the narrative is function, not material.

"Good" (Gen. 1:4, 18). The word *good* can have many connotations. Here it refers not to moral goodness but to functionality—it worked just right.

We know this because that which is not good (Gen. 2:18) is simply not yet fully functional, rather than morally corrupt.

Evening then morning (Gen. 1:19). This reverses the way we would say it, but only because the account starts with darkness (v. 2); God then introduces the period of light to set up regular transitions. The first transition from the period of light to the period of darkness is evening.

Sun and moon created after light (Gen. 1:3–5, 14–18). Many have noted the apparent problem of light being created on the first day and the bearers of light on the fourth day. Even young students might ask this question. In our view, days one through three involve the establishment of the major functions by which the world operates (time, living space, weather, and vegetation/food). In contrast days four through six install functionaries. Functions are prioritized over functionaries in the order rather than following a material chronological order.

Background Information

Ancient audience. Genesis was written in the ancient world to an ancient audience, even though it contains truth for all. Nevertheless, it talks about the world in the terms that were important then. The point is that this is not a scientific account.

Separation. Since separation was an important creative activity throughout the creation literature of the ancient world, it is no surprise to find it so often in Genesis 1. To separate things from one another is the first important step in giving them individual roles.

Signs and seasons. The heavenly bodies provided signs for the agricultural calendar and for orientation in travel. Most parts of the world do not have four seasons. The seasons referred to in the biblical text are agricultural seasons (plowing, planting, harvesting) and the seasons of the religious calendar.

Mistakes to Avoid

Do not try to turn this into a science lesson, for such an emphasis misses the point entirely. Science today explores the natural world. Biblical faith affirms that everything we call "natural" is the handiwork of God, but that does not mean that we need to convey the handiwork of God as expressed in the Bible in natural terms (e.g., "Here is where God did the Big Bang"). Speak of the Bible's message in the Bible's terms: God set up and designed our world to work the way that it does. He did this for the people he would create. He set up time and put us in time. He controls time.

God's act of speaking is important because it shows his control. But the fact that "God spoke and it happened" leaves a lot unspecified: what God speaks could come about instantaneously or gradually; what God speaks could come about in startling, unexplainable ways or in ways that can be tracked and understood step-by-step. All of it is the work of God. Teachers should avoid trying to resolve the question with the opinion that the response was instantaneous. The length of the day is, of course, disputed, but there will generally be no need to get into this issue for elementary-school-aged children. Our commitment should be to focus on what the text is focused on rather than mixing in our opinions on controversial issues. The message of Genesis 1 is that God is the one who made our world work.

2. God Created the World around Us (Genesis 1:6–13)

Lesson Focus

God is the creator. All things were made by him. No one but God could create the world.

- God made our world to function with weather.
- God provided places for us to live (dry land).
- God created ways for food to grow.
- God has brought order to our world so that we can live in it.

Lesson Application

We know that we have a great and powerful God by observing the world that he made.

- We believe that God has set up the weather under his control.
- We believe that God provides food for us by the way the earth works.

Biblical Context

The Genesis story is about God entering into relationship with people whom he created to be in relationship with himself. Genesis 1 shows how God created an environment perfectly suited for human habitation. The first three days are about the major functions that characterize the world around us: time, weather, and food. God designed the world with all that humans need to survive and thrive.

Interpretational Issues in the Story

Expanse (Gen. 1:6). Understanding this word presents one of the most difficult issues in the chapter. The King James translation, "firmament," followed the Latin interpretation of earlier times, conveying the idea that the sky was solid and held back waters. This interpretation was widely believed until just a few centuries ago. We know differently now, but that does not change the language of the text, which reflects an ancient worldview derived from appearances. But there is no need to get into this issue or fret about it. In the story-telling it is sufficient to talk about the sky. The point is that God set up weather mechanisms, regardless of how they are described. The "waters above" simply describe the source of precipitation (the sky) in nonscientific terms. Remember that the Bible tells about creation in relationship to how people thought about their world in ancient times. The "waters above" are not the clouds, mist, and fog, and the "firmament" is not invisible. In the ancient world they believed that the rain was held back by a solid sky.

Separated and gathered (Gen. 1:6, 9). Separating and gathering were acts of creation in the ancient world, because in this way distinct identities were set up. The focus is on order and function.

"According to its kind" (Gen. 1:11). This comment is not intended to give botanical taxonomy but to indicate that God set up a world where everything reproduces itself rather than something random growing. A plant grows and drops seed, and the same thing grows again. In this way farming can take place and food can be grown.

Background Information

Waters that were above. In the ancient world everyone believed that since water came down (in the various forms of precipitation) there must be water up above the sky. If water is up there and doesn't come down all the time, something must hold it up. As a result, everyone in the ancient world believed that the sky was solid and held back heavenly waters.

Mistakes to Avoid

Do not try to turn this into a science lesson, for such an emphasis misses the point entirely. Science today explores the natural world. Biblical faith affirms that everything we call "natural" is the handiwork of God, but that does not mean that we need to convey the handiwork of God as expressed in the Bible in natural terms (e.g., "Here is where God did the Big Bang"). Speak of the Bible's message in the Bible's terms: God set up and designed our world to work the way that it does. He did this for the people he would create. He set up time and put us in time. He controls time.

God's act of speaking is important because it shows his control. But the fact that "God spoke and it happened" leaves a lot unspecified: what God speaks could come about instantaneously or gradually; what God speaks could come about in startling, unexplainable ways or in ways that can be tracked and understood step-by-step. All of it is the work of God. Teachers should avoid trying to resolve the question with the opinion that the response was instantaneous. The length of the day is, of course, disputed, but there will generally be no need to get into this issue for elementary-school-aged children. Our commitment should be to focus on what the text is focused on rather than mixing in our opinions on controversial issues. The message of Genesis 1 is that God is the one who made our world work.

3. God Made Animals (Genesis 1:20–25)

Lesson Focus

God created each animal according to his special design and purpose.

- Animals are part of God's plan for the world.
- God gave the animals the ability to multiply and fill the world.
- Each animal reproduces the same kind of animal.
- God made animals of all sorts to serve different purposes.

Lesson Application

We believe that God is very wise from the special way he made each animal.

- We believe God's wisdom is expressed in the diversity of creatures.
- We believe God's wisdom is expressed as we observe how each animal is designed for its environment.

Biblical Context

The book of Genesis tells us how God prepared a place for the people he created and how he entered into relationship with them. Genesis 1 shows how God created an environment perfectly suited for human habitation. The first three days relate how God set up the major functions that we experience as we live on earth (what we would describe as time, the water cycle, and the plant cycle). Days four through six explain the roles and positions of those who inhabit the cosmos. The text does not indicate why God created animals to fill our world but affirms that he did, whatever his purposes.

Interpretational Issues in the Story

"Let the waters swarm . . . let birds fly" (Gen. 1:20). Here the language focuses on the realm God is filling but does not express the mechanisms God uses.

Great sea creatures (Gen. 1:21). In the ancient world people believed in creatures that represented a threat to the ordered cosmos. The book of Job describes such creatures and speaks of God's control over them (Job 40–41); Psalms occasionally speaks of God's victory over them (Ps. 74:13–14). Here in Genesis there is no conflict between God and these creatures—they are just another of God's works.

"According to their kinds" (Gen. 1:21, 24). This comment is not intended to give zoological taxonomy but to indicate that God set up a world where creatures would be able to reproduce to populate their space.

Background Information

Domesticated animals were essential for the life and survival of ancient peoples. The birth of sheep and goats enlarged the herd and provided for another season of supply (milk, meat, and clothing). Sometimes they viewed wild animals as threats associated with chaos; at other times they saw them as simply mysterious. In all cases, the animal kingdom reflected God's provision and wisdom.

Mistakes to Avoid

When discussing the animals, some might be inclined to suggest that prior to the fall there were no predators. Such a conclusion might be supported by the idea that all was peaceful and harmonious, with lion and lamb living side by side (from passages such as Isa. 11:6–8). Further evidence might be that all was good and that there was no death. These are all arguable. When the apostle Paul writes that death came by sin, he was addressing the question of why *humans* are subject to death. Death came to humans because they were cut off from access to the tree of life. However, Paul had not suggested that death was absent from the rest of creation. There is death involved as cells regenerate, as plants drop their seed for new to grow, as animals eat plants, when fish eat flies, and when birds eat worms.

There is no place to draw the line here to rule out predation. A lion eating a zebra is in principle no different from a fish eating a fly. We need not think that the situation described in Isaiah 11 is a replication of what it was like before the fall. There is therefore no biblical support for the absence of predation before the fall. The food chain is one of the significant ways that God ordered the world in which we live. When God declared the world "good" he was saying that it functions just right for us, not that it operates by perfect moral principles. Gravity is not moral, nor is the animal kingdom.

4. God Made People and God Made You (Genesis 1:26–30; 2:4–7, 18–24)

Lesson Focus

People are the most special part of God's creation because they are made in his image.

- God made all of creation for people to use and enjoy.
- God put people in charge of the world.
- God intends people to represent him and serve his purposes.
- All people have been made in the image of God and must be treated with dignity.
- The first people God made were Adam and Eve.

Lesson Application

God made you special. You are important to him.

- Because we all are made in God's image, we must respect one another.
- Since we are God's representatives, we must treat the world as his, not ours.
- Because we are made in God's image, we each have a part to play in God's kingdom.

Biblical Context

The book of Genesis tells us how God created humans and then entered into relationship with them. In Genesis 1, God creates an environment perfectly suited for human habitation; during days one through three, God set up the major functions that we experience as we live on earth; during days four through six, he appointed roles and positions for those who inhabit the cosmos. God established all the operations of the world for the benefit of people. God's blessing in these verses defines human roles and privileges. In Genesis 2 God set up relationships as the nature of humanity is discussed. Humans are related to the ground, and men and women are inherently related to one another.

Interpretational Issues in the Story

"*Let us make . . . in our image*" *(Gen. 1:26)*. We might be tempted to read these plurals—"us"—through our modern Christian perspective and think of the Trinity. The Israelites had no revelation or knowledge of the Trinity, but these plurals meant something to them (possibly discussion in a heavenly assembly). Because there are other strong possibilities it would be best to avoid planting the Trinity interpretation in children's minds. Focus on what it means to be in God's image.

"*Image*" and "*likeness*" *(Gen. 1:26)*. Make sure students understand that these words do not suggest physical similarity to God. God has no physical body, but we are his representatives in physical form. Many have suggested that being made in God's image consists in our ability to think and to be aware of ourselves and of God and to do anything that animals cannot do. More likely, the abilities humans have are not how we are made in God's image but rather the tools God has given to humanity so that we can serve in God's image. We might best understand being made in God's image as the role we have as God's representatives and vice-regents. We are not worthless slaves to God, but we are accountable to him.

"*Be fruitful and multiply*" *(Gen. 1:28)*. It is important to note that even though this is grammatically an imperative, it does not mean it is a command. Imperatives can serve various functions in Hebrew. Here it is identified as a blessing, and as such it is a privilege, not an obligation.

"*Subdue . . . have dominion*" *(Gen. 1:28)*.This does not give people the right to abuse or exploit the world. Instead, God has charged us with bringing the world under our control (a role that is seen in early times in domestication of plants and animals and more recently in development of science and technology). Like God, we should be just and wise rulers.

Plants given for food (Gen. 1:29). This cannot be used as a defense for vegetarianism, since in Genesis 9:3 God permits the eating of meat.

"*Formed . . . of dust*" *(Gen. 2:7)*. This is a statement about all humanity (Adam is not only the name of the first man; it is the Hebrew word for *human*). We are all made from dust and that is why we all return to dust

(Gen. 3:19). Genesis 2:7 is not a comment about chemical composition but about the nature of humans.

Adam's rib (Gen. 2:21). The word often translated "rib" is not used anywhere else in the Bible to describe anatomy (but it is often used in architecture to describe things such as the two doors of an entryway). It can also refer to one of two sides (note how we speak of a "side of beef"). Adam notes that Eve is both his bone and flesh. God takes one side of Adam and builds it into a woman. This is not an issue of anatomy; it is an issue of the nature of the ultimate relationship between man and woman (as Gen. 2:24 indicates). All womankind is made from one side of all mankind.

Background Information

Image. The ancients believed that an image (including an idol) carried the essence of that which it represented. These cultures believed that the deity accomplished its work through the idol. Furthermore, kings set up images of themselves in places where they wanted to establish their authority. So, since we are in God's image, he accomplishes his work through us, and we are representatives of his authority.

Human role. The ancients believed that people were created to be slaves to the gods and that they were responsible to provide for the needs of the gods (food, clothing, housing). The God of Genesis has no needs and created people to serve him, not as slaves but as vice-regents. They don't take care of God's needs; he takes care of theirs.

Mistakes to Avoid

When teaching this lesson, it might be tempting to focus on any number of contemporary issues, such as ethnic and gender diversity, tolerance, and ecological care. These are related to this text, so it would be appropriate to mention them, but they are not the main point and should not replace the main point. The foundation for our social and ecological responsibilities is found in who we are in relationship to God. It will be a challenge to communicate the idea of human dignity to younger children. The term *special* is often misunderstood and overused, but something like that will have to suffice for the younger ages.

Genesis indicates that God made people special, but it emphasizes how people as a whole are special in comparison to all God's other creations since only people are made in the image of God. The text does not talk about the individuality or uniqueness of each individual. Genesis does not affirm that individuals are unique and special—that is American talk. The "wonderfully made" language of Psalm 139 applies to all humans and stresses what is common to humanity, not what is different from one person to the next. It is true that God made us, but the material nature of our bodies is not in view in Genesis. The dust is not a chemistry statement and "rib" is not an anatomy statement. If we want to keep our attention on what the text is doing, we can talk about how God set up functions and relationships. Any number of aspects about the wonders of the bodies God gave us could be legitimately brought in as part of this lesson. Our responsibility as teachers is to prioritize what the text prioritizes and use other aspects secondarily as illustrations.

5. The Garden of Eden and the Fall (Genesis 2:8–17; 3)

Lesson Focus

Adam and Eve disobeyed God and experienced the consequences.

- God gave people rules and responsibilities.
- God considers obedience very important.
- God has not given up on us.
- God continues to care about people even when he must punish them.
- Disobedience caused people to lose access to the presence of God.

Lesson Application

We should obey God.

- When we are serious about God, we will be serious about doing what he asks.
- We must not allow our own reasoning to persuade us to ignore what God has said.
- Our sinful nature is a result of Adam and Eve's disobedience.

Biblical Context

The Genesis story is about God entering into relationship with the people he created. He began by creating us to be in relationship with himself. This account concerns how people broke away from that intended relationship and sets the stage for the rest of Scripture, which recounts how God reestablishes relationship with mankind.

Interpretational Issues in the Story

"Eden" (Gen. 2:8). Technically speaking, the garden is not Eden but is adjacent to Eden, where God's presence is. Note that in 2:10 the water flowed from Eden through the garden.

"To work it and keep it" (Gen. 2:15). Word studies suggest that these activities are priestly tasks rather than landscaping or gardening tasks. The garden is sacred space because of its proximity to God's presence, and people serve him there.

"Tree of the knowledge of good and evil" (Gen. 2:9). Word studies suggest that this tree is associated with mature wisdom (see Gen. 3:6; 1 Kings 3:9). There is nothing wrong with wisdom, but it must be acquired in appropriate ways at appropriate times. The tree is not something arbitrarily chosen at random for a test of obedience—the fruit actually gives wisdom comparable to God's (Gen. 3:22).

"You shall surely die" (Gen. 2:17). This refers to physical death—spiritual death was not a concept in the Old Testament. It does not suggest that death will be immediate; rather, the wording indicates that they will be doomed to die. This destiny is sealed when they are cast from the garden and prevented from eating from the tree of life.

"Serpent" (Gen. 3:1). Though there may be good reason eventually to connect the Serpent to Satan, the Old Testament never makes this connection, and those in the Old Testament era would not have understood the Serpent as such. It would be advisable, therefore, to leave that issue to the side and speak of the Serpent as the one who persuaded the people to disobey. It thus represented evil.

"Her husband who was with her" (Gen. 3:6). Lest we place all the blame on Eve, note that Adam was with Eve during the entire temptation.

"God walking in the garden in the cool of the day" (Gen. 3:8). The translation here is very difficult. Teachers should avoid making too much of the time of day and likewise avoid suggesting that this was a regular occurrence; the text does not suggest that.

"On your belly you shall go" (Gen. 3:14). While it is possible that the narrator is depicting the Serpent as originally having legs, this is not the only viable interpretation. Another is that the narrator is distinguishing between a serpent raised up to strike and one that slithers away.

"Bruise your head . . . bruise his heel" (Gen. 3:15). The two verbs translated here as "bruise" are the same Hebrew word, but it suggests a broader concept of "strike." The heel strike of a poisonous serpent is just as lethal

as the head strike by a human. The verse does not clarify who will win. The point is that there will be ongoing conflict in which people will be tempted to do evil (and will often succumb) but will still be able to resist. Evil had not won, but neither was this a onetime occurrence.

Multiplied pains in childbearing (Gen. 3:16). The text speaks of conception in the first phrase and childbirth in the second. Since conception is not physically painful, the verse is probably referring to anxiety, not just pain. This interpretation is well within the range of the word used. In many ways, the anxiety connected with the whole process is more significant than the brief labor pains at the end. Anxiety results from all the uncertainties: Will conception be possible? Will mother and child both survive? Note that this is not called a *curse.* Instead of thinking of the anxiety as an additional punishment, we should consider it to be the inevitable result of death, to which humans are now subject.

"Cursed is the ground" (Gen. 3:17). The word used for *cursed* here indicates that something is removed from God's protection or provision. In the garden their food had been provided for them. Now the ground will not show the same favor of God's special provision.

Made garments (Gen. 3:21). This shows God's care for them. The text makes no suggestion that God used this act to teach them about sacrifice.

"Cherubim" (Gen. 3:24). The cherubim are not angels; they are composite creatures that guard God's presence. These creatures likely look more like griffins or sphinxes than the chubby infants of medieval art. In this passage they are preventing access to the tree of life in their characteristic role of guarding that which is sacred.

Background Information

Garden. Gardens in the ancient world regularly adjoined the sacred space of temples, as well as royal palaces; they symbolized the fertility that flowed from the presence of God.

Serpent. Serpents were understood in the ancient world to be wise as well as threatening. Their wisdom concerned issues of life and death; at times they were also connected with sacred trees.

Mistakes to Avoid

Most of the mistakes in teaching this story come from traditional understandings of the story that are not particularly supported by the text. (We have alluded to many of these in the interpretive comments above.) If we are interested in focusing on the authority of the text in its context, we will avoid making the following suggestions:

- Adam and Eve were responsible for gardening.
- The tree was just a random test to see if Adam and Eve would obey.
- God was referring to spiritual death as the punishment.
- The Serpent was Satan.
- God came and walked and talked with them every day.
- Serpents had legs.
- Genesis 3:15 is the first reference to God's plan for a Savior.
- God cursed women with labor pains.
- God gave instructions for sacrifice when he made them skin garments.

These suggestions are not necessarily inaccurate, but they are at best arguable, and the text does not clearly support them. Our commitment is to teach the text.

6. Cain and Abel (Genesis 4:1–16)

Lesson Focus

Once sin entered the world, it quickly spread and worsened.

- God continued to relate to people even after he drove them from his presence.
- God received gifts from people and expected that they would relate to him in certain ways.
- God was willing to give Cain a second chance, but he was not willing to overlook Cain's sin.
- God holds people accountable for their attitudes and their actions.

Lesson Application

With sin, one thing usually leads to another.

- When we allow sin to occupy our lives, it grows.
- We should respond when God gives us the opportunity to make things right.
- Often sin begins in our attitudes before it results in actions.

Biblical Context

The Genesis story is about God entering into relationship with the people he created in his image. He began by creating us to be in relationship with himself. This account concerns sin spreading from an initial act of disobedience (Adam and Eve) to an act of murder. The first eleven chapters of Genesis continue to trace the increase of sin alongside the continuing evidence of the blessing (e.g., in the genealogies people continue to "be fruitful and multiply" and begin the process of subduing and ruling [4:21–22]).

Interpretational Issues in the Story

Cain's offering (Gen. 4:3). The text makes no suggestion that Cain's offering was unacceptable because it was not a blood sacrifice. Even Abel's offering does not refer to blood—he offers the fat parts of the animal. The word used for their offerings occurs most often in Leviticus as a reference to grain offerings. The most likely reason Cain incurred God's displeasure was that he did not bring the best of his produce. Cain's problem is apparently in his attitude, as the conversation that follows indicates.

Cain's mark (Gen. 4:15). We simply do not know what this is.

Background Information

Blood offerings. Blood was usually offered to deal with offense; such a sacrifice would involve the whole animal, not just the fat parts. Blood rites were not common in the ancient world and do not appear in the Bible until the period of the exodus and Sinai. The fat parts (suet) were inedible and were typically offered as a gift during a ritual meal before the meat was eaten.

Mistakes to Avoid

Hardly anything in this story is appropriate for young children. Acceptable and unacceptable sacrifice and the murder of a brother are not matters easily discussed with a young audience. One curriculum that we encountered many years ago used this story to teach that God made our bodies. While this truth is easily affirmed, it is not what this story is teaching. I suspect that since the objective of this particular curriculum was to work through Genesis, the writers did not want to skip the story, so they told it (without much detail) and then shifted the focus to something entirely different. That approach is not recommended, because it uses poor principles of application for the biblical text.

Likewise, we would be mistaken to use the story as if it were teaching the importance of blood sacrifice. Abel's offering did not include blood, nor was Cain's sacrifice rejected for the absence of blood. Most importantly, the sacrifices they offered are not designated as those dealing with offense, the normal situation in which blood would have a role.

Finally, this is not a story instructing us on appropriate (in this case, inappropriate) family relationships. Obviously conflict and violence are to be avoided, but the narrative is provided to show the advance of sin.

7. Noah (Genesis 6:9–9:17)

Lesson Focus

God destroyed the people on earth because they were evil, but he saved Noah and his family because Noah was righteous.

- God's judgment was just because of the widespread influence of sin.
- God noticed, valued, and rewarded Noah's righteousness.
- God's grace is evident even in his acts of judgment.
- God maintains order in the world, and God can also undo the order that he has established.
- God recognizes the inherent sinfulness of people.

Lesson Application

We should obey God.

- How we act is important to God, and he notices.
- Our sin makes God sad.

Biblical Context

Genesis tells the story of God's entering into relationship with the people he created in his image. He began by creating us to be in relationship with him. Genesis 1–11 traces the increase of sin alongside the continuing evidence of blessing. This account concerns the spread of sin and the resulting violence evident in all humanity.

Interpretational Issues in the Story

"*Noah walked with God*" *(Gen. 6:9).* Not many in the Old Testament are described in this way, so it is a notable commendation. Nevertheless, it is difficult to give it further clarification. He is also described as being righteous and blameless. These are descriptions that compare him to others who lived at that time; they do not suggest that he is perfect in God's eyes or without sin.

The extent of the flood (Gen. 7:19–20). The universal language clearly indicates that this is an account of general, widespread destruction. There is no need to get into a detailed debate about the extent of the flood.

"God remembered Noah" (Gen. 8:1). When Hebrew uses this verb, "remembered," in connection with God, it reflects his action on the person's behalf; Noah had not slipped God's mind.

"The mountains of Ararat" (Gen. 8:4). The text does not refer to a single mountain but to a mountain range.

Background Information

Flood stories from the ancient world. We know of flood stories from the ancient Near East that predate the earliest estimates for the writing of Genesis. These stories—the tale of Ziusudra, the Atrahasis Epic, and the Epic of Gilgamesh—share many similarities with the biblical account but also differ on numerous points, large and small. These show a widespread tradition of a massive flood but do not suggest that the biblical authors simply picked up and revised the mythologies from their world.

Chronology. When we add up the numbers in the biblical account of the flood, we can conclude that Noah was in the ark for about one year. We do not know when the flood took place. On the science end, there is no archaeological evidence for the flood, and geological evidence is controversial. From the Bible side, we cannot simply add up genealogies, because genealogies are known to have gaps (note the genealogy of Jesus in Matthew). Archaeological data go back to about 9000 BC with no break that could be attributed to a wide-scale flood. There is no reason for this discussion to be part of the lesson for kids.

Mistakes to Avoid

The flood account too often is used to let the students have fun with animals; we should resist this tendency. Very young children may not be ready for exposure to the wide-scale death and destruction inherent to the flood story. If this is the case, the best strategy is to omit the story until they are older, because if we tell the story without the judgment aspect, we will be unfaithful to the biblical account. Another potential distortion occurs if we do not balance judgment and grace. The story features both, and to be faithful to the story, both must be acknowledged. Often in the telling of the story of the flood we bring in details that are traditional but have no foundation in the text. Such traditions include:

- People ridiculed Noah for building the ark.
- Noah traveled around collecting animals and preaching to people.
- Noah could have brought others onto the ark or would have tried to do so.
- There had been no rain prior to the flood (the lack of rain is mentioned in Gen. 2:5–6, but there is no reason to extend that from the time of Gen. 2:5–6 all the way to the time of the flood).
- It took 120 years to build the ark (one interpretation of Gen. 6:3; but even if that does speak of the time until the flood that does not mean that Noah began building the ark at that time).

None of these ideas should be part of the lesson or perpetuated, since they are not in the biblical text.

8. Tower of Babel (Genesis 11:1–9)

Lesson Focus

God was displeased when the people tried to regain his presence in their own way by constructing a tower that would allow him to come down and be worshiped in the adjoining temple. In the ancient world this worship would have entailed the people's meeting the needs of deity (food, clothing, and housing) with the expectation that the deity would then favor and bless them.

- God does not desire people to anticipate his needs and try to meet them, for he has no needs.
- God will carry out his plan for his presence to be established in his way and in his time.
- God is dishonored when people elevate themselves at his expense.

Lesson Application

We should not think that God is like us.

- We cannot make God what we want him to be.
- We cannot manipulate God in order to fulfill our wishes.
- We cannot dictate the terms of relationship with God.
- We do not meet needs that God has—he has no needs.

Biblical Context

Genesis tells the story of God's entering into relationship with the people he created in his image. He began by creating us to be in relationship with him. Genesis 1–11 traces the increase of sin alongside the continuing evidence of blessing. This account concerns the last in a series of escalating sins. The violence of society brought the flood; here a new problem has arisen as people develop incorrect conceptions of God. At the plain of Shinar, we see the first instance of people thinking about God in human terms and trying to reestablish his presence (lost at the fall) by their own initiative.

Interpretational Issues in the Story

Men moved eastward (Gen. 11:2). This does not necessarily indicate a migration of the whole world population; it may only involve some from the line of Shem, since the other lines were dealt with in Genesis 10, and the latter part of Genesis 11 will focus on Shem's line. It is common in Genesis for the author to extend the lines of those that he was not as interested in before going back and telling the story of those he *was* interested in (so Cain's line was extended, then the author backtracked to Seth; Ishmael's was extended, then the author backtracked to Isaac; Esau's was extended, then the author backtracked to Jacob).

Plain of Shinar (Gen. 11:2). The story took place in southern Mesopotamia, known as Sumer.

"Tower with its top in the heavens" (Gen. 11:4). This refers to the building of a ziggurat (see below in Background Information), not the building of a tower so high that it could reach God. Such towers were a major feature of the temple complex and were made for God to come down and establish his presence in the adjoining temple. They were not for people to use to go up to God.

"Make a name" (Gen. 11:4). While people may well seek through arrogance and pride to make a name for themselves, those need not be the only motivations. The ancients considered it very important to do something that would allow them to be remembered in future generations. Doing so could be as simple and innocent as giving birth to the next generation. Therefore, it was not necessarily pride that led these people to want to make a name for themselves. So rather than noting a contrast between the people's trying to make a name for themselves and God's making a name for them, it is more to the point to think of them as desiring to make a name for themselves *instead* of making a name for God. This tower was connected to a temple, as such towers always were, and temples were designed to honor a deity. In

the ancient world, the temple was also a place where people could meet the needs of deity so that deity would reciprocate and meet their needs. This text says that their motivation was not to honor God but to bring prosperity and honor to themselves. We could explore our own motivations when we build beautiful churches—is it to honor God or ourselves?

"Lest we be dispersed" (Gen. 11:4). Families never want to be separated, so it is no surprise that the people did not want to disperse. The building project relates to developments in urbanization that would allow a larger population to exist in one location. If they were successful in building this sacred space and God came down to establish his presence and bring blessing to the people, they would enjoy the prosperity God's presence brings and not have to scatter to find sufficient food. It is no sin to want to avoid scattering—the problem was in their chosen remedy.

Nothing impossible (Gen. 11:6). This indicates only that their actions have crossed a threshold so that they had no inhibitions to prevent them from developing further degrading ideas about the nature of God.

"Confuse their language" (Gen. 11:7). Confusing the language brought an end to the cooperative effort that had led to this building project. This remedial action did not eliminate the problem (which continued in the Mesopotamian religious system), but it registered God's displeasure and paved the way for his decision to work through one nation and one language group—a plan brought out in the next chapter, as God makes a covenant with Abraham.

Background Information

Early cities. In these ancient times the city was not a place where the population lived but a secured area that contained public buildings, mostly the temple complex. The most prominent building in the city/temple complexes of southern Mesopotamia was the ziggurat. Unlike pyramids, these had no inside; they were built to support the outside stairway, which was meant to provide a way for deity to come down, enter the adjacent temple, and receive worship. This worship involved the assumption that gods had needs that people could meet. These towers were considered links between heaven and earth, built for the convenience of deity. They were not for people to go up but for God to come down.

Mistakes to Avoid

There was no disobedience here. We cannot consider the builders as having disobeyed God's mandate to be fruitful and fill the earth because scattering is not the same as filling. Scattering is geographical expansion; filling is numerical growth. The blessing in Genesis 1:28 allowed people the privilege and ability to fill the earth; it was not a command or an obligation, so it could not be disobeyed. In the blessing, people fill the earth by being fruitful and multiplying; the people were having no trouble doing that.

The teacher should be careful not to turn this into a lesson on human pride. We may not rule out the element of pride, but it is not the emphasis of the story. Like everyone throughout the history of the world, the builders were anxious to make a name for themselves; this goal was achieved in appropriate or inappropriate ways. The concern in the text is that the people were more interested in their glory than in God's and more interested in establishing his presence for their own benefit than because he is worthy. Finally, the teacher should resist presenting this incident as the origin of all languages; it could be, but it could also be just a reference to the diversification of languages in Shem's line.

9. The Call of Abraham (Genesis 12; 17:1–8)

Lesson Focus

God promised Abraham that he would give him the land of Canaan and many descendants and would bless the nations through him. God kept his promise through Abraham's son Isaac.

- God initiated a relationship (through the covenant) so that he might give people correct information about himself.
- God has always desired to be in relationship with the people he has created.
- God makes promises and keeps them.
- God is able to overcome any obstacles that seem to get in the way of his promises.
- God has a plan and is in the process of carrying it out.

Lesson Application

We can believe what God says. God always keeps his promises.

- We can trust God.
- We should be patient as we wait for God to work out his plan in his time.

Biblical Context

The Genesis story is about God's entering into relationship with the people he created in his image. He began by creating us to be in relationship with him. Genesis 1–11 traces the increase of sin alongside the continuing evidence of covenant blessing. In Genesis 12–50 the author turns our attention to the covenant. The blessing in Genesis 1–11 ("be fruitful and multiply") becomes a promise to Abraham ("I will make of you a great nation"). Through the covenant, God revealed himself to and through Abraham and his family. Each narrative shows either how the covenant was progressing (in terms of land, family, or blessing) or how God was in the process of overcoming obstacles to the covenant, whether perceived or real.

Interpretational Issues in the Story

"Go from your country" (Gen. 12:1). As God asked Abraham to leave his land, his family, and his inheritance, he also promised to give Abraham a land, make him into a large family, and give him a legacy (blessing).

"Famine in the land" (Gen. 12:10). Very soon obstacles arose. They could not stay in the land, they were not able to have a family, and the blessing of God seemed nonexistent.

Name change (Gen. 17:5). The ancients believed that a person's name was tied up with his or her destiny. When God changed someone's name, it was an act of authority as he exercised his control of that person's destiny.

Background Information

Abraham's travels. The text offers no rationale for why Abraham ended up in Haran before going to Canaan, the land that will become Israel. Some have suggested that the principal god worshiped in Ur was the same one worshiped in Haran, but that is just a guess. In Mesopotamia most travel followed the rivers. If Abraham and his family followed the Euphrates, Haran was quite a bit out of the way, and this would have necessitated an 80-mile detour. If they followed the Tigris, the turn west would have taken them through Haran, a convenient stopping point.

Sacrifices prior to the law. The instructions for sacrifice come in Leviticus when Israel was in the wilderness. All the religions of the ancient Near East had a sacrificial system, so Abraham would have offered sacrifices in Ur even before the Lord called him. These sacrifices would have been what Leviticus later calls "burnt offerings," and they would have invoked God's presence when making petitions. Here, the sacrifices might also have been made to invoke God's presence in this new land that Abraham had come to.

Famines and Egypt. Agriculture in Canaan is dependent on rainfall, while in Egypt it is dependent on the regular flooding of the Nile. As a result Egypt did not usually experience famine at the same times Canaan did. In most sections of Canaan the normal annual rainfall is barely at subsistence level, so it would not have taken much to drive its people into drought and famine conditions. The standard strategy was to move temporarily to Egypt.

Abraham and Yahweh. Joshua 24:2 tells us that Abraham and his family had not worshiped the one true God all along. They would have worshiped many gods.

Circumcision. Circumcision was practiced by other peoples in Abraham's world. It was often used as a rite of passage to adulthood. God chose this familiar practice but turned it into a rite of passage into membership in the covenant community.

Mistakes to Avoid

Resist drawing ethical or behavior standards from the lives of the characters. These narratives are given that we might know God better, not that we might be like Abraham or Sarah. Genesis 12 is not telling us to leave family behind to follow God. Though these passages describe the behavior of the characters, we should not conclude that such information was included so that we might learn lessons from those characters. If the lesson ends with "Abraham did X, and we should too," the lesson should be reexamined. The point of the passages is to reveal God's character as he keeps his promises and overcomes obstacles. We might appropriately turn the focus by observing something Abraham did that pleased God so we learn what sort of behavior pleases God. We should also resist the temptation to conclude that, since God overcame certain obstacles for the characters in the account, he will do so for us today. God does not work in the same way with everyone. The circumcision rite as a sign of the covenant may not be appropriate to include when telling the story to young children.

10. Abraham and Lot (Genesis 13)

Lesson Focus

The land became too crowded for both Abraham and Lot, so they decided to separate. Lot chose the land near Sodom and settled there. As a result, the remaining land belonged to Abraham.

- God removed an obstacle to Abraham's right to the land.
- God advanced the covenant by giving the land to Abraham.
- God is faithful.

Lesson Application

We can count on God to do what he promises.

- We believe that God is able to remove obstacles that interfere with his plan for our lives (whether or not we recognize them as obstacles).
- We believe that God is faithful to keep his promises.

Biblical Context

The Genesis story is about God's entering into relationship with the people he created in his image. He began by creating us to be in relationship with him. Genesis 1–11 traces the increase of sin alongside the continuing evidence of covenant blessing. In Genesis 12–50 the author turns our attention to the covenant. The blessing in Genesis 1–11 ("be fruitful and multiply") becomes a promise to Abraham ("I will make of you a great nation"). Through the covenant, God reveals himself to and through Abraham and his family. Each narrative shows either how the covenant was progressing (in terms of land, family, or blessing) or how God was in the process of overcoming obstacles to the covenant, whether perceived or real. In this narrative Lot chose to leave the land, thereby removing an obstacle, and God gave the rights to the land to Abraham, an advancement of the covenant promise.

Interpretational Issues in the Story

"Called upon the name of the LORD" (Gen. 13:4). This means to invoke God's presence.

"Jordan Valley" (Gen. 13:10). With a lower elevation, the climate around the valley of the Jordan was more moderate and more temperate.

Background Information

"Negeb . . . Bethel." The Negeb is the arid region between the Judean hill country and the southern highlands. It includes Beersheba and Arad. Bethel is about 50 miles farther north.

Herdsmen and land. Shepherds ranged over a wide area throughout the year so that they would not deplete the grazing land and water supply. Still, even in the wider region there was only sufficient grazing and water for a limited flock.

Sodom and Gomorrah. Sodom and Gomorrah have yet to be identified archaeologically, and their precise locations are unknown. Their location may be either along the northeastern edge of the Dead Sea or the southeastern edge. Some have even postulated that they are submerged beneath the Dead Sea.

Mamre. Mamre is adjacent to Hebron in the Judean hill country, about halfway between Jerusalem and Beersheba. A higher elevation provides more rainfall, and there are springs in the area.

Mistakes to Avoid

First, we cannot conclude that Abraham disobeyed God by bringing Lot with him. Leaving his family meant that he was to give up his place in the family and the status and religious connections inherent in the family. It does not mean that no blood relative was allowed to accompany him. Second, Abraham's offer to let Lot choose first was not just an act of humility or generosity. We don't know what Abraham's motives were, and it is not our place to speculate on them. The detail is important to the story because the result of Lot's choosing is that he, in effect, chooses to leave the land. This meant that the entire land then belonged to Abraham (Gen. 13:14–17). Thus, an obstacle to Abraham's rights to the land was removed, though it was not an obstacle caused by sin any more than was the obstacle of Sarah's barrenness. Covenant progress was made as the entire land came to Abraham. Abraham is offered neither as a bad role model (by taking Lot with him) nor a good one (letting Lot choose first), and the story should not revolve around these behaviors. We also cannot make any judgments about Lot's motives or spirituality because of his choice to move to the valley of the Jordan. The author's intent is not that we should reflect on the different choices Abraham and Lot made.

11. The Birth of Isaac (Genesis 15:1–6; 18:1–15; 21:1–6)

Lesson Focus

God promised that Abraham's descendants would be as numerous as the stars of the heavens, but Sarah was unable to have children. At long last, in her old age, God fulfilled his promise as she gave birth to Isaac.

- God keeps his promises.

- God is able to overcome any obstacle.
- God works in his own time.

Lesson Application

No obstacle in our lives is too big for God to overcome.

- We believe that God can overcome obstacles.
- We recognize that God does not act on our time schedule.
- We believe that God is faithful to his Word.

Biblical Context

The Genesis story is about God's entering into relationship with the people he created in his image. He began by creating us to be in relationship with him. Genesis 1–11 traces the increase of sin alongside the continuing evidence of covenant blessing. In Genesis 12–50 the author turns our attention to the covenant. The blessing in Genesis 1–11 ("be fruitful and multiply") becomes a promise to Abraham ("I will make of you a great nation"). Through the covenant, God reveals himself to and through Abraham and his family. Each narrative shows either how the covenant was progressing (in terms of land, family, or blessing) or how God was in the process of overcoming obstacles to the covenant, whether perceived or real. In these narratives we find God overcoming what has been a major obstacle: Abraham's having a multitude of descendants when his wife could not bear children. When Sarah gave birth, the obstacle was overcome and the covenant moved forward.

Interpretational Issues in the Story

"He counted it to him as righteousness" (Gen. 15:6). Though Paul uses this line in his discussion of faith and works, in the present context this is not a statement concerning Abraham's salvation from sins. Abraham's attitude of faith concerning God's word is the righteous act. Such faith on our part remains a righteous act today.

The Lord appeared to Abraham (Gen. 18:1). God made his appearance through the messengers that came to Abraham and spoke to him through them. The messengers carried the authority of God, so when we read, "the LORD said," it is most likely that God was speaking by means of the messengers, as he did in many other passages.

Sarah's laughter (Gen. 18:12–15). Some have wondered why Abraham laughed (17:17) and was not rebuked, yet here Sarah laughed and was rebuked. Looking closely, however, the Lord's comment in 18:13 was not strictly a rebuke. Alternatively, we could view his comment as taking the opportunity to make the point of 18:14—nothing is beyond God's ability. We might paraphrase, "Sarah is laughing; does she think that this is something that I cannot do? Nothing is impossible for me. Take my word for it—by this time next year she will have a child." Sarah's denial is more of a problem, but even in response to that the Lord merely stated that she *did* laugh. The repeated emphasis on laughter serves a literary purpose, since that is the word that serves as the root for the name *Isaac*.

Background Information

Hospitality. There were few facilities for travelers in the ancient world, so people were dependent on the hospitality of others along their way. Hospitality was considered an obligation that was taken very seriously. It included refuge, amenities (such as foot washing), food, drink, and lodging. Travelers in turn provided news of the outside world. Abraham's preparations for the messengers were extreme, but that was not unusual for hospitality, which was often excessive by design.

Mistakes to Avoid

It would be a mistake to focus attention on Sarah in a critical way. It is certainly not the intention of the text to set her forth as an example of faithlessness or unbelief. She had every reason to be incredulous, and we must remember that nothing has happened up to this point to suggest that their guests were anything more than human travelers. The focus needs to remain on God's overcoming obstacles and keeping his covenant promises. This lesson cannot be extrapolated to the general comment that God takes care of families. This was a very special family in a very special situation, so we must not apply the lesson universally.

12. Hagar and Ishmael (Genesis 16; 21:8–21)

Lesson Focus

Hagar bore a son for Abraham with the expectation that Ishmael would be the promised son of the covenant. But God's plan gradually unfolded, that Sarah would bear the covenant son, and Hagar and Ishmael would become another obstacle that God would overcome.

- God does not always make the details of his plan clear.
- It is not always clear when to patiently wait and when to step out in faith.
- God cares even for those who are not in the direct covenant line.

Lesson Application

Don't be surprised when God's plans take unexpected turns.

- We should not be hesitant to step out in faith but should realize that our assessment of a situation may not always be the right one.
- God is able to overcome obstacles created by our steps of faith as easily as he is able to overcome obstacles brought about when we patiently wait.
- We believe that God will be faithful to his Word and that his plan will be carried out.

Biblical Context

The Genesis story is about God's entering into relationship with the people he created in his image. He began by creating us to be in relationship with him. Genesis 1–11 traces the increase of sin alongside the continuing evidence of blessing. In Genesis 12–50 the author turns our attention to the covenant. The blessing in Genesis 1–11 ("be fruitful and multiply") becomes a promise to Abraham ("I will make of you a great nation"). Through the covenant, God revealed himself to and through Abraham and his family. Each narrative shows either how the covenant was progressing (in terms of land, family, or blessing) or how God was in the process of overcoming obstacles to the covenant, whether perceived or real. In this narrative God overcame the obstacle of a son who had claims within Abraham's family and clarified that Sarah's son would be the son of promise.

Interpretational Issues in the Story

The angel of the Lord (Gen. 16:7). The angel of the Lord is a messenger who brings God's word to people. In the ancient world, direct communication between important parties was a rarity. Diplomatic exchange normally required the use of an intermediary. Messengers were like ambassadors and were vested with the authority to speak for the party they represented and were expected to be treated as if they were the dignitary in person. This is why in some contexts, as here, it is hard to distinguish whether God or the messenger is speaking. The messenger may speak in the first-person as God.

"Return to your mistress and submit to her" (Gen. 16:9). It is interesting

that Hagar was sent back into slavery and abuse and told to have a better attitude about it. We often note in the Bible that God does not overturn social and political institutions, because there are no perfect institutions—they are all subject to our human fallenness.

Background Information

Marriage contracts. In the ancient world marriages represented alliances between clans. They were arranged by parents and were intended to propagate the race and the family. Bearing children was an essential part of the equation. If a woman proved unable to bear children, she could be dismissed with no questions asked. Her status in the family was dependent on bearing children. Marriage contracts therefore sought to protect a wife who could not bear children, and one way to do that was to stipulate the identification of a surrogate. This is exactly what Sarah was doing when she identified Hagar as someone who could bear a child in her stead. This was culturally acceptable and sometimes mandated by contract.

Hagar's status. As long as Sarah had no son of her own, Hagar had a protected status in the family, although, as Genesis 16:4–6 shows, relationships could become difficult. Once Sarah had a child, however, the situation changed and it became desirable for Hagar and her son to leave (21:8–14). In the process she gained the advantage of her freedom.

Mistakes to Avoid

It would be easy to be critical of Abraham and Sarah, since in our culture their decision would be unacceptable, if not repulsive. Abraham's decision strikes the contemporary mind as being motivated by lack of faith at best and lust at worst. These are unfair assessments. As noted above, their society provided this recourse as the most legitimate one when the wife was unable to have children. As for lack of faith, God had not at this point told Abraham who would be the mother of his child but only that he would have a large family. Abraham could easily have concluded that obtaining a child through Hagar was the means that God had chosen. God never rebuked him for this decision, and Abraham did not learn that Ishmael was *not* the covenant son for thirteen more years. Abraham probably viewed using Hagar as a step of faith rather than as a lack of faith. Consequently this story should not be told as a condemnation of Abraham's lack of faith. Ishmael came on the scene for good or ill and became an obstacle. Obstacles can be caused by sin, but not necessarily. God did not remove the obstacle by having Abraham recognize and confess his sin, which we could reasonably expect if a sin were involved. So the story is not about sin or lack of faith; it is about God, who continued to overcome obstacles to establish the covenant according to his plan.

13. Sodom and Gomorrah (Genesis 18:16–19:29)

Lesson Focus

God destroyed the cities of Sodom and Gomorrah for their wickedness but delivered Lot and his family for the sake of Abraham.

- God takes wickedness seriously, and there are consequences for it.
- God is willing to show grace in response to the wishes of his people.

Lesson Application

Wickedness will not be tolerated by God.

- We recognize our wickedness and turn from it.
- We take God seriously.
- We are grateful for the grace of God.

Biblical Context

The Genesis story is about God's entering into relationship with the people he created in his image. He began by creating us to be in relationship with him. Genesis 1–11 traces the increase of sin alongside the continuing evidence of covenant blessing. In Genesis 12–50 the author turns our attention to the covenant. The blessing in Genesis 1–11 ("be fruitful and multiply") becomes a promise to Abraham ("I will make of you a great nation"). Through the covenant, God revealed himself to and through Abraham and his family. Each narrative shows either how the covenant was progressing (in terms of land, family, or blessing) or how God was in the process of overcoming obstacles to the covenant, whether perceived or real. In this narrative the destruction of Sodom and the other cities is set in the context of God's conversation with Abraham (18:16–33) concerning justice. The obedience of Abraham and his descendants is set in contrast to the wickedness of Sodom.

Interpretational Issues in the Story

The sin of Sodom (Gen. 19:5). The story portrays the city of Sodom as rampant with violent people engaged in sexual promiscuity and perversion. Though the text contrasts the hospitality of Abraham in Genesis 18 with the inhospitable reception the angels receive in Sodom (see also Ezek. 16:49), it quickly becomes clear that the problem is much more serious (Ezekiel 16 also couples the injustice with lewd and detestable behavior). Of course, most of this will not come into the discussion with elementary-school-aged children.

Lot's role in the city (Gen. 19:1, 9). It is unclear whether Lot was sitting in the gateway as an elder, as a guard, or as someone trying to identify opportunities to deliver strangers from a horrible fate at the hands of the men of the city. In Genesis 19:9 the citizens accused him of trying to act as their judge, indicating that they still viewed him as an outsider. Even his sons-in-law, who would have been expected to at least patronize him, did not take him seriously.

"Pillar of salt" (Gen. 19:26). We need not think of this as an instantaneous transformation the moment she turned her head. The cities were destroyed by God's raining down sulfur. Mineral salts could have been ignited by explosions and fallen onto the inhabitants. In this scenario, all of the inhabitants would have turned to salt (that is, covered with it). Since the destruction does not begin until Lot and his daughters reach Zoar (19:23–24), it is likely that Lot's wife did not simply look back but that she returned to the city and was swept up in its destruction (cf. Luke 17:28–32).

Background Information

Location. The specific location of these cities is unknown. Hypotheses suggest the northeast side of the Dead Sea, the southeast side, or even submerged under the Dead Sea.

Mistakes to Avoid

Though Lot might be construed as righteous compared to the other inhabitants of Sodom and disgusted by their ways (cf. 2 Pet. 2:7–8), that is not necessarily saying much. In the end, Lot was spared because of Abraham, not because of his personal merit (cf. Gen. 19:29). Lot is not the story. Likewise, the nature of Sodom's sin is not the story but only the magnitude of it.

14. The Sacrifice of Isaac (Genesis 22)

Lesson Focus

God asked Abraham to sacrifice the covenant son, Isaac, and Abraham showed himself willing to obey even when the cost was so high and he had nothing to gain.

- God sometimes asks us to do difficult things.
- God wants people to serve him for who he is, not just for the benefits he has to offer.
- God delights in obedient people.

Lesson Application

We should love God simply for who he is, not because of the benefits he provides.

- We must be prepared to obey whatever God asks of us.
- We trust God through difficult times.
- Our relationship with God is to be based on who he is, not what we get out of it.

Biblical Context

The Genesis story is about God's entering into relationship with the people he created in his image. He began by creating us to be in relationship with him. Genesis 1–11 traces the increase of sin alongside the continuing evidence of covenant blessing. In Genesis 12–50 the author turns our attention to the covenant. The blessing in Genesis 1–11 ("be fruitful and multiply") becomes a promise to Abraham ("I will make of you a great nation"). Through the covenant, God revealed himself to and through Abraham and his family. Each narrative shows either how the covenant was progressing (in terms of land, family, or blessing) or how God was in the process of overcoming obstacles to the covenant, whether perceived or real. In this narrative the obstacle was set up by God himself—the potential loss of the promised son. In the end God reiterated the covenant promises (22:17–18).

Interpretational Issues in the Story

"God tested" (Gen. 22:1). Testing is not the same as tempting. The verb used here is used elsewhere to indicate something that God does (e.g., Deut.

8:2; Judg. 3:4). A test focuses on some value, attribute, or quality in a person, and the test entails stretching something to its limits. When God tests people, it usually involves their faith or faithfulness and calls on them to obey something that is difficult (as here).

"I and the boy will . . . come again to you" (Gen. 22:5). While this could simply be an evasive answer, interpreters have preferred to see it as an expression of Abraham's faith (see Heb. 11:19).

The angel of the Lord (Gen. 22:15). The angel of the Lord is a messenger who brings God's word to people. In the ancient world, direct communication between important parties was a rarity. Diplomatic exchange normally required the use of an intermediary. Messengers were like ambassadors and were vested with the authority to speak for the party they represented and were expected to be treated as if they were the dignitary in person. This is why in some contexts it is hard to distinguish whether God or the messenger is speaking. The messenger may speak in the first person as God.

"Now I know" (Gen. 22:12). We should not conclude from this wording that God had gained cognitive knowledge that he previously lacked; rather, his "knowing" is the result of Abraham's demonstration that he took God seriously ("feared God"). All of Abraham's previous acts of faith included some benefit for him to gain. Consequently, it was difficult to discern whether Abraham's relationship with God was based on expected benefits or was simply a reflection of his esteem for God. In the ancient religious system from which Abraham had been called, relationship with the gods was a mutual benefit arrangement. People took care of the gods, and the gods took care of the people. God had promised to take care of Abraham, but he wanted more from Abraham than participation in a mutual benefit system. God has no needs and hoped for a relationship that was not based on expectation of benefit. In this account Abraham demonstrated that his obedience and faith were not dependent on anticipated gain—he had nothing to gain and everything to lose. God knew what Abraham would do, but God always knows what we will do, yet he still takes delight in our expressions of love, faith, worship, and honor.

Background Information

Region of Moriah. The only other reference in the Bible to Moriah is found in 2 Chronicles 3:1, which identifies it as the site of the temple. If Moriah is Jerusalem, it is strange that it is not referred to as Salem, as in

Genesis 14:18. Also, Jerusalem was a city at this time, and Abraham seems to have been going to a more isolated locale. Having said all that, if Moriah is not Jerusalem, we have no idea where it is.

Sacrifices prior to the law. The instructions for sacrifice come in Leviticus when Israel was in the wilderness. All the religions of the ancient Near East had a sacrificial system, so Abraham would have offered sacrifices in Ur even before the Lord called him. The sacrifices offered by Abraham would have been what Leviticus later calls burnt offerings, and they would have invoked God's presence for making petitions.

Human sacrifice. Archaeological evidence for human sacrifice in the ancient world is sketchy, and there is also very little literary evidence. It is therefore difficult to determine how widespread the practice was. Yet there is sufficient evidence to indicate that it was at least an occasional practice and therefore one with which Abraham would have been familiar.

Mistakes to Avoid

This is never identified in Old or New Testaments as a story that foreshadows the sacrifice of Jesus. The differences are clear. Jesus actually *was* sacrificed, and his sacrifice was certainly not meant to be a test of God the Father's faith. The similarity of a father asked to sacrifice a son is obvious, but the comparison stops there. We should not treat this as a story meant to indicate to Abraham that he was not to carry out human sacrifice, as all the other nations did. The text indicates a different purpose; furthermore, if God had been teaching such a lesson, this would have been a cruel way to do it. He could have just told Abraham that child sacrifice was not necessary.

This is also not a story meant to suggest ways that we can be people of faith like Abraham. Rather, it tells us what kind of faith God wants his people to have (one not interested in benefits). Neither is it meant to tell us not to love our family more than we love God. There is no indication that Abraham's love for Isaac was a problem, and the lesson cited in the text (22:12) says nothing about that love of family. This is also not a story about whether Abraham loved Isaac more than he loved God, or more generally about whether we love anything more than we love God. Instead it is about why we love God. What are our motives? Do we love him only for the benefits we receive (covenant blessings, including, for Abraham, the covenant son)? Finally, this is not a story to tell to young children.

15. Isaac and Rebekah (Genesis 24)

Lesson Focus

God promised Abraham that he would have many offspring and that they would possess the land of Canaan. Abraham knew that Isaac should have a wife from his own people and should remain in the land God had promised them. Abraham and his servant trusted God for his promise, and God in his providence provided a wife who met the need.

- God can work through unusual ways to fulfill his promises.
- God answers prayer.

Lesson Application

God is at work every day to bring about his plans for us and our world.

- We trust God to fulfill his promises.
- We rely on God to direct our ways (for us, through prayer).

Biblical Context

The Genesis story is about God's entering into relationship with the people he created in his image. He began by creating us to be in relationship with him. Genesis 1–11 traces the increase of sin alongside the continuing evidence of blessing. In Genesis 12–50 the author turns our attention to the covenant. The blessing in Genesis 1–11 ("be fruitful and multiply") becomes a promise to Abraham ("I will make of you a great nation"). Through the covenant, God revealed himself to and through Abraham and his family. Each narrative shows either how the covenant was progressing (in terms of land, family, or blessing) or how God was in the process of overcoming obstacles to the covenant, whether perceived or real. This family story shows how God provided the next step in making Abraham into a large family.

Interpretational Issues in the Story

Wife from Abraham's family (Gen. 24:4). Abraham made this requirement for ethnic reasons, not for spiritual reasons. His family had been polytheistic. No one else in the world at this time worshiped Abraham's God. Abraham made this requirement because his family was supposed to be distinct from the peoples around him; intermarriage with them would have resulted in assimilation.

Background Information

Traveling. The distance from Abraham's location near Hebron to his relatives' town of Nahor is about 500 miles. Walking that distance would have taken about a month. Riding the camels would perhaps have cut the time in half.

Servant's method. The servant used an oracle method to choose Isaac's wife: he posed a "yes or no" question, "Is the girl I approach a suitable wife for Isaac?" and identified a mechanism for confirmation (a suitable wife will offer to water the camels). The usual behavior—not making such an offer—would serve as a no answer, while the highly unlikely response from the girl of making the offer would constitute a yes.

Marriages. Marriages in the ancient world represented clan associations and were arranged by the family; they did not function as loving relationships. The family asked Rebekah's opinion only when the servant requested that they leave immediately (vv. 57–58). Often a newly married woman continued to live in her father's house until she conceived a child, for, until then, her status in her husband's household was not secure. Marriages were arranged and involved an exchange of wealth. The groom's family provided a bride price (note the gifts that Abraham's servant presented) while the bride's family provided a dowry. Both the bride price and dowry provided security for a woman who might be deserted or widowed.

Mistakes to Avoid

We should not employ the oracular method used by the servant to discover the will of God. As in the case of Gideon's fleece, God responded here to this method, but his response was an act of grace. This method is problematic because it tries to back God into a corner, dictating how and when he is to communicate his will. We should be reluctant to make such demands of God. This story is not a lesson about discovering the will of God.

Even more importantly, this passage tells us nothing about marriage or how marriage should be pursued. Marriage was a very different institution in the ancient world, and this passage is not meant to teach us about God's heart for marriage. The biblical text does not often offer role models for us to follow. Consequently, we can conclude that this passage is not here to suggest good characteristics in a spouse, such as Rebekah's kindness.

Finally, this passage does not concern the importance of marrying within the faith. Rebekah was not within the faith—she was within the family. In the ancient world, wives (except for royal wives) automatically adopted the gods

(God) of the husband. We have no basis for thinking that Abraham's relatives shared the faith or the God of Abraham. Abraham was called out of his pagan context. There were no worshipers of Yahweh in the world of that time.

16. Jacob and Esau (Genesis 25; 27–28)

Lesson Focus

God gave Isaac and Rebekah two sons and told them the younger son, Jacob, would become the head of the family. Jacob took matters into his own hands and tricked Esau, the older son, and then Isaac into giving him the rights of the older son. Because God had chosen Jacob to inherit the promise, God came to him in a dream and renewed with Jacob the covenant of Abraham.

- God fulfills his promises, even over apparently overwhelming obstacles.
- God works even through flawed people.
- God has a plan for his people.

Lesson Application

We should trust God because he is at work to carry out his plans for us and our world.

- Our choices may have consequences but cannot thwart God's plans for us.
- We believe that God will be faithful to his word.
- We believe that God will carry out his plan despite situations that give no reason for hope.

Biblical Context

The Genesis story is about God's entering into relationship with the people he created in his image. He began by creating us to be in relationship with him. Genesis 1–11 traces the increase of sin alongside the continuing evidence of covenant blessing. In Genesis 12–50 the author turns our attention to the covenant. The blessing in Genesis 1–11 ("be fruitful and multiply") becomes a promise to Abraham ("I will make of you a great nation"). Through the covenant, God revealed himself to and through Abraham and his family. Each narrative shows either how the covenant was progressing (in terms of land, family, or blessing) or how God was in the process of overcoming obstacles to the covenant, whether perceived or real. The Jacob and Esau stories show

God extending Abraham's family into the next generation. These stories also show how the obstacles of favoritism and flawed character threatened the existence of the covenant family.

Interpretational Issues in the Story

Message to Rebekah (Gen. 25:23). This message concerns the futures of the peoples that would come from Rebekah's two sons, not the futures of the two sons themselves. It offers no reason for her to favor Jacob over Esau.

"Esau despised his birthright" (Gen. 25:34). This statement reflects the fact that Esau sold his birthright cheaply, which was obviously poor judgment on Esau's part and had consequences. This account shows the character flaws in both Jacob and Esau.

Angels (Gen. 28:12). The description of the angels' behavior does not suggest that this was a procession in which the angels were simply marching up and down the stairway in ranks. Rather, Jacob saw that the messengers of God used the stairway to go and return from assignments. As he watched, he saw some go up to heaven to report, while others came down to carry out their duty. The ladder was a passageway between heaven and earth.

Covenant blessing (Gen. 28:13–15). This blessing, alluded to also by Isaac as he sent Jacob off, was unconnected to the inheritance rights (Gen. 25:31–34) or the patriarchal blessing (Genesis 27). The inheritance rights gained by Jacob in Genesis 25 concerned material possessions and standing in the family. The patriarchal blessing in Genesis 27 concerned the destiny of the sons and was taken seriously as actually affecting their future. Isaac's blessing was not needed for the Lord to give the blessing in Genesis 28, which served to pass the covenant promises on to Jacob.

Bethel (Gen. 28:19). Bethel means "House of God," a term that was often used to describe a temple. Obviously there was no temple structure in Bethel; Jacob identified the place as a temple because of the stairway and God's presence. A temple was most importantly the sacred space of God's presence, sometimes marked by a building.

Background Information

Birthright. The birthright concerned the material inheritance. The older son would typically get a double share because he had more responsibilities to carry out. Jacob acquired this extra share from Esau, giving him the position of responsibility in the family upon the death of their father.

Blessing. The father bestowed the blessing on his children, making observations about their destinies and so dealing with the future. This was not prophecy, which we know because it is not framed, "Thus says the LORD." Instead, Isaac claimed that the blessing is something he has given, not something that God has said (27:37). God was not obligated to fulfill such pronouncements, but they were taken very seriously. They could not be taken back, because people believed there was power in the spoken word. The words could not be unsaid.

Stairway. It is immaterial whether we describe this as a ladder or a stairway. Most importantly, it served as a portal between heaven and earth, much the same as the ziggurat tower in Genesis 11. Jacob identified the stairway as the gate of heaven, which would have been located at the house of God (28:17), for the ancients believed that temples connected heaven and earth.

Mistakes to Avoid

Rebekah and Isaac may well be criticized for their favoritism, but neither one is more justified than the other. God was in charge of Jacob's destiny—he did not need the parents, or Jacob himself, to ensure that the prophecy was fulfilled. This story is not given to provide advice or warnings about parenting. It does not tell us how to be good parents but shows how God can overcome the obstacles posed by flawed parents.

Likewise, this is not a story to warn us of the consequences of underhanded behavior (like Jacob exhibited) or of having wrong priorities (like Esau did), or about finding ways to get along with others. Nor is it a lesson about each having an appropriate role (e.g., the description of Esau as a hunter). Such conclusions are distractions from the point of the lesson in the text. The characters, Isaac and Rebekah, and Jacob and Esau, are window dressing for narratives that reveal God. The plot turns around these major characters, but the focus of the narratives concerns God's character and actions. If the bottom line of the lesson is encouragement to be or not to be like any of the characters, the lesson has gotten derailed.

17. Jacob and Laban (Genesis 29–32)

Lesson Focus

Jacob ran away to live with his uncle, Laban. Just as Jacob cheated Esau, Laban tricked and cheated Jacob, but God kept his promises to prosper Jacob and bring him back to the Promised Land. Before meeting Esau on his return, Jacob realized his need for God; he struggled with God and received God's blessing.

- God works through difficult situations to mold us into the people he wants us to be.
- God fulfills his promises.
- God can help us rise above our situations.
- God can resolve family conflicts.
- God at times confronts us about our shortcomings.

Lesson Application

We can't do anything without God's help.

- We cannot rely on our own abilities to achieve God's ends.
- We look for the hand of God, even when things don't go according to our plans.

Biblical Context

The Genesis story is about God's entering into relationship with the people he created in his image. He began by creating us to be in relationship with him. Genesis 1–11 traces the increase of sin alongside the continuing evidence of covenant blessing. In Genesis 12–50 the author turns our attention to the covenant. The blessing in Genesis 1–11 ("be fruitful and multiply") becomes a promise to Abraham ("I will make of you a great nation"). Through the covenant, God revealed himself to and through Abraham and his family. Each narrative shows either how the covenant was progressing (in terms of land, family, or blessing) or how God was in the process of overcoming obstacles to the covenant, whether perceived or real. The Jacob and Laban stories show God's promises unfolding as Jacob marries, has children, and returns to the land. God blessed Laban through Jacob, and God overcame the obstacle of Jacob's flawed character.

Interpretational Issues in the Story

Barrenness (Gen. 29:31). The author points to God as the source of blessing through the recurring theme of barren patriarchal wives. God provided children to women who otherwise could not conceive. This shows that God was responsible for the growth of Abraham's family.

Laban's trickery and Jacob's wealth (Genesis 29–32). It is difficult to reconstruct the strategies that each employed against the other, but it is clear that both were trying to get the advantage. The point of the text is that regardless of these strategies, God brought blessing to Jacob.

"The LORD *watch between you and me" (Gen. 31:49).* This "Mizpah benediction" is not a friendly, caring statement. Because these men did not trust one another, they called on deity to hold the other accountable for whatever mischief might be done.

Wrestling (Gen. 32:24). The one wrestling with Jacob is elsewhere identified as an angel (Hos. 12:4). Jacob was not stronger than the angel. The point of the wrestling was not to determine who could physically best the other. Instead, Jacob struggled to gain a blessing, and the angel withheld it until he could bring about submission from Jacob. The angel was unable to prevail until Jacob agreed to terms (Gen. 32:26). When Jacob saw the face of God, he recognized God for who he is and realized his comparative weaknesses.

Background Information

Marriage. These chapters show us many aspects of marriage in the ancient world. Marriages were arranged and involved an exchange of wealth. The groom's family provided a bride price (Jacob did this through his labor) whereas the bride's family provided a dowry. Both the pride price and dowry provided security for a woman who might be deserted or widowed.

Maidservants as surrogates. It was culturally acceptable for a barren wife to designate a surrogate to bear children in her place. Children were highly desired and conferred status upon the wife and insured the family line.

Gods. The *teraphim* in Genesis 31:30–31 are not images of gods, per se, but the current consensus is that they are images of the ancestors. Some groups in the ancient world thought that ancestors were able to bring good or ill to the family; the images provided a medium for the family to honor their ancestors.

Mistakes to Avoid

It is obvious that the characters throughout these chapters continually behave badly, so we should have no inclination to pattern our lives after them. In describing their behavior, the biblical text demonstrates how God works his will despite and sometimes even through the bad behavior of his people. We can derive nothing about family or relationships from these stories. Though we can certainly see some behavior that we would not want to imitate or observe ways in which God brings about healed relationships, these factors are merely described as obstacles that God overcame. The point is that God overcomes obstacles. Even Jacob's prayer (32:9–12) is suspect; we could interpret his actions as a case of throwing God's promises in his face in order to achieve security in a troubled situation. Jacob should not be elevated or always seen positively just because he is counted among the patriarchs whom God used to establish his chosen people.

18. Joseph Becomes a Slave (Genesis 37; 39:1–6)

Lesson Focus

Joseph earned the enmity of his brothers by his dreams and his father's favoritism. They responded by selling him into slavery and then hid their actions by pretending that a wild animal had killed him. God remained with Joseph, however, and made him successful, using these events as part of his plan to preserve his people.

- God works through the trials of life to accomplish his plan.
- God can use even wicked behavior to bring about his plan.

Lesson Application

God will be with those who trust him and cause good to come from the bad times in their lives.

- No matter what goes wrong, we trust that God will help us know how to honor him.
- When we honor God, he can honor us, even in difficult situations.

Biblical Context

The Genesis story is about God's entering into relationship with the people he created in his image. He began by creating us to be in relationship with him. Genesis 1–11 traces the increase of sin alongside the continuing evidence of covenant blessing. In Genesis 12–50 the author turns our attention to the covenant. The blessing in Genesis 1–11 ("be fruitful and multiply") becomes a promise to Abraham ("I will make of you a great nation"). Through the covenant, God revealed himself to and through Abraham and his family. Each narrative shows either how the covenant was progressing (in terms of land, family, or blessing) or how God was in the process of overcoming obstacles to the covenant, whether perceived or real. By the time we reach the Joseph stories, the covenant is progressing nicely. Abraham's descendants have been established in the land and have become a large family through Jacob's twelve sons. These stories turn our attention to God's blessing as he places Joseph somewhere that Joseph can bring blessing to the world as a representative of Abraham's family. Yet we continue to see the obstacles of favoritism and flawed character.

Interpretational Issues in the Story

Joseph's coat (Gen. 37:3). Joseph's coat clearly marks him as his father's favorite; such a coat was not the garb of a common laborer, but we do not know the specific features of the coat (e.g., many colors, long sleeves, or ankle-length). We would therefore do best to simply view it as a special coat.

Joseph's demeanor (Gen. 37:2, 5, 9). It is tempting to psychoanalyze Joseph: Was he conceited? Was he boastful? Did he flaunt his dreams and favored status before his brothers? The text does not give us sufficient information to answer these questions, and they are not important to our interpretation.

Background Information

Dreams. The ancients believed that dreams were one of the ways that deity communicated and were therefore taken very seriously. Though some dreams were obscure and needed interpretation (such as those of Pharaoh and his administrators), Joseph's dreams were fairly transparent.

Geography. Shechem is approximately 50 miles north of the Valley of Hebron, and Dothan is another 14 miles north of Shechem. People in the ancient world traveling by foot could cover 15 to 20 miles per day.

Cistern. Cisterns were for the collection of water (as opposed to wells, which were dug down to a source of water). Typically they were hollowed out of limestone and lined with plaster to prevent seepage. They were periodically dry depending on the season, though even then they could hold remaining stagnant water.

Mistakes to Avoid

This story might tempt us to read between the lines, inserting plot details or expanding on the personalities of the characters. We must resist this inclination, however, because our focus needs to be the authoritative message of the text. We cannot read between the lines and then use our interpretive readings as if they carry the authoritative teaching of the text. If the author is brief on plot details and character development, it is advisable to assume that he omits these so we can concentrate on other more important elements. The author is not trying to warn us against family jealousies or to teach us humility. These may be good and useful lessons, but the text gives no indication that we should focus on these or that it offers authoritative teaching on these issues. We cannot use this story to talk about being helpers (Joseph with his father or with Potiphar), nor can we use this portion of the Joseph story to talk about trusting God when life goes wrong. We are not told whether Joseph was trusting God or not, though he resisted temptation and interpreted dreams, both in God's name. The text tells us the Lord was with him, but it does not say Joseph knew or trusted that the Lord was with him.

19. Joseph in Prison (Genesis 39:7–41:57)

Lesson Focus

Joseph was unjustly put in prison, but God was with him to bless him and give him success. God revealed the interpretation of Pharaoh's dream to Joseph so that Pharaoh made him his second-in-command; thus, Joseph was able to store up grain for the coming famine.

- God brought honor to Joseph because Joseph honored God in his choices.
- God remained with Joseph through all of his trials.
- God was fulfilling his promise to bring blessing to the world through Abraham's family.

Lesson Application

God will be with those who trust in him, and is able to cause even bad things to work for their good.

- Though we cannot expect that God will always bring favorable circumstances from bad ones, we know that he can work through any situation.
- God is carrying out a plan for our lives, even when things are going badly.

Biblical Context

The Genesis story is about God's entering into relationship with the people he created in his image. He began by creating us to be in relationship with him. Genesis 1–11 traces the increase of sin alongside the continuing evidence of covenant blessing. In Genesis 12–50 the author turns our attention to the covenant. The blessing in Genesis 1–11 ("be fruitful and multiply") becomes a promise to Abraham ("I will make of you a great nation"). Through the covenant, God revealed himself to and through Abraham and his family. Each narrative shows either how the covenant was progressing (in terms of land, family, or blessing) or how God was in the process of overcoming obstacles to the covenant, whether perceived or real. By the time we reach the Joseph stories, the covenant is progressing nicely. Abraham's descendants have been established in the land and have become a large family through Jacob's twelve sons. These stories turn our attention to God's blessing as he places Joseph somewhere that Joseph can bring blessing to the world as a representative of Abraham's family. Yet we continue to see the obstacles of favoritism and flawed character.

Interpretational Issues in the Story

Joseph in prison (Gen. 39:20). If Potiphar truly believed his wife, Joseph likely would have been executed. Details in the story suggest that Potiphar was in charge of the prison; therefore, it seems possible that Joseph was simply transferred to another area of Potiphar's responsibility.

Joseph's food program (Gen. 41:33–36). Joseph's food program is not meant to provide a biblical model for economic policies. The Bible is showing God's sustenance of many nations through Joseph's program, not prescribing this sort of policy for all people at all times. The focus is God's provision, not Joseph's policy.

Background Information

Prison. Prisons in the ancient world were used mostly for political prisoners and debtors, not criminals. At times they also perhaps incarcerated those awaiting trial.

Dreams. The dream motif continues, first through Pharaoh's officials, then through Pharaoh himself. Neither set of dreams was transparent, so the dreams required interpretation. Egyptians usually interpreted dreams using dream books, which provided specialists with a key for interpreting symbols. Joseph's interpretations were distinctive because they were not based on training and research but given by revelation from God.

Joseph's position. Some have concluded that Joseph was Pharaoh's vizier, based on his designation as second in command (41:43). Such a conclusion is not impossible, but neither is it necessary. In modern companies, a vice president is often second in command to the president, but there may be numerous such vice presidents in a particular division of the company. This might also have been the case with Joseph. He was responsible for food accumulation and distribution, a position known in Egypt as the overseer of the granaries of Upper and Lower Egypt.

Time period. Because Joseph became a major official in Egypt, we might expect to find mention of him in ancient documents. Unfortunately, we find nothing. In fact, we don't even know where to look, because the pharaoh in the story is not named. We can only guess at what specific time period this was. There is no record of the Israelites, Joseph, or Moses in Egyptian documents of the period.

Mistakes to Avoid

This is one passage from which we might contend that the text does indeed want the readers to "be like Joseph." His resistance to temptation is highly commendable, and the author develops the situation to reveal his reasoning, not just his action (39:8–9). Having said this, however, God's work through Joseph is more important in the text than the character of Joseph. We do well to imitate Joseph in this regard, but the narrator is not holding up the character of Joseph as a model. We also must not generalize from Joseph's experience to everyone else's. God worked a certain way in Joseph's experience, but he may not work in everyone's experiences as visibly. The story helps us to understand that God cares for his people and that he is able to do all things. Our responsibility is to be faithful in hard times, whether or not God delivers us from them. It is best to treat the attempted seduction of Joseph by Potiphar's wife with discretion with the younger ages.

20. Joseph's Family Saved (Genesis 42–50)

Lesson Focus

Because of widespread famine, Joseph's family came to Egypt to buy food. Joseph used a ruse to get them to return, then revealed that, in spite of their intention to harm him, God had sent Joseph ahead to preserve Jacob's family as part of his plan to make them a great nation.

- God plans for the future.
- God takes care of his people.

- Sin has a way of coming back to haunt us.
- God fulfills his covenant promises.

Lesson Application

We should trust God because he is at work to accomplish his plan, even when it seems things are going wrong.

- We realize that God is always in control of what happens in our lives.
- We look beyond offenses done to us to find God's bigger plan.

Biblical Context

The Genesis story is about God's entering into relationship with the people he created in his image. He began by creating us to be in relationship with him. Genesis 1–11 traces the increase of sin alongside the continuing evidence of covenant blessing. In Genesis 12–50 the author turns our attention to the covenant. The blessing in Genesis 1–11 ("be fruitful and multiply") becomes a promise to Abraham ("I will make of you a great nation"). Through the covenant, God revealed himself to and through Abraham and his family. Each narrative shows either how the covenant was progressing (in terms of land, family, or blessing) or how God was in the process of overcoming obstacles to the covenant, whether perceived or real. By the time we reach the Joseph stories, the covenant is progressing nicely. Abraham's descendants have been established in the land and have become a large family through Jacob's twelve sons. These stories turn our attention to God's blessing as he places Joseph somewhere that Joseph can bring blessing to the world as a representative of Abraham's family. Yet we continue to see the obstacles of favoritism and flawed character.

Interpretational Issues in the Story

Joseph and his brothers (Genesis 42–50). Joseph's strategy was designed to determine whether his brothers had changed in the twenty years that he had been in Egypt. He gave them the chance to abandon Simeon (42:33–34) and Benjamin (44:16–17) as they had abandoned him. Once he determined that they had indeed changed, he revealed himself to them.

Moving to Egypt (Gen. 46:1–7). The move to Egypt is a significant step in the flow of the narrative. God leads Jacob's family to the land of Canaan, which he had promised to Abraham. Yet God already anticipated their absence from the land in Genesis 15:13–16. God makes it clear to Jacob that this temporary migration is according to his plan (46:3–4).

Background Information

Cup for divination. Though we cannot be certain that Joseph did not practice divination, an alternative is that the servant was simply using the cup because it was a common piece of equipment for someone in Joseph's role as an Egyptian official. To divine something using a cup generally involved filling the cup with water, pouring oil onto the top, and reading signs from the resulting shapes and appearance.

Mistakes to Avoid

Even though Joseph was the instrument of God who brought deliverance from the famine, we need not think that God approved of everything that Joseph did or that we should imitate him as a biblical model. His policies for Egypt did not focus on sharing; they focused on redistribution. They certainly should not be considered a biblical model for economic policies today. One might also question Joseph's strategy as he interacted with his brothers. He was not showing love to them; he was testing them. The text does not seek to approve or condemn—it simply reports. We cannot derive authoritative guidance from the text about how families are supposed to interact or how past wrongs should be confronted. God's actions through Joseph are much more important than Joseph's actions themselves. Joseph's willingness to forgive his brothers is commendable; he looked beyond their treacherous act and saw the bigger picture of God's plan. The text is calling us not so much to be forgiving as to look beyond our suffering to see God's plan, which is far bigger than our hurts.

21. Baby Moses (Exodus 1:1–2:10)

Lesson Focus

All things that God had told Abraham were coming true. His people greatly increased in number, they lived in a strange land not their own, and they became slaves oppressed by their masters. As the time approached for God to fulfill his promise to bring his people out of Egypt to the Promised Land, Pharaoh contrived to kill all the Hebrew baby boys. When Moses was born, his parents hid him. God protected Moses because he had chosen him to lead the people out of Egypt.

- God is aware of the trials of his people.

- God works behind the scenes through common folks to carry out his plan.
- God raises up leaders to play special roles.

Lesson Application

God always guides and cares for his people in order to accomplish his plans.

- We must trust that God is with us and working out his plan, even when our circumstances are hard.
- When God's plan involves people, he is able to raise them up as his instruments.

Biblical Context

The book of Exodus focuses on God's presence as he delivers his people from slavery in Egypt. Though at the beginning the covenant appears to be in shambles, with no sign of God's presence among his people, the book ends with the building of the tabernacle and God entering the Most Holy Place to dwell in the midst of his freed people. The story of baby Moses begins this process as God arranges for the survival and upbringing of the future deliverer of Israel.

Interpretational Issues in the Story

Time in Egypt (Ex. 12:40). Though the Israelites were in Egypt for over four hundred years, they were not enslaved for most of that time. In the middle of the sixteenth century BC, when the Israelites had already been there for several centuries, a group of Semitic peoples who had ruled for some time in Egypt were driven out, opening up a revival of Egyptian nationalism. This would have been a logical time for the tide to turn against the Israelites.

Background Information

Identity of Pharaoh. The Bible never names the pharaoh who interacted with Moses, and there is insufficient information to determine his identity. Major candidates include Ramesses II in the thirteenth century and Thutmose III in the fifteenth century, but the issue is complex, and in the end we just have to say that we do not know. Likewise, then, we do not know the identity of Pharaoh's daughter.

Israel in Egypt. Unfortunately, there is no evidence from ancient Egypt concerning the events of these chapters. No records from the period hint at the enslavement, the slaughter of the children, the plagues, or the exodus. No reference is found to Moses, though his name is a common element in the names of Egyptian pharaohs (Ramesses, Thutmose). This absence of information is no surprise, however, since the Egyptians did not often preserve a record of negative events.

Mistakes to Avoid

This is not a story about Moses' mother or his sister Miriam, though they play important roles. We may be able to see some important values in their lives or some positive family virtues, but the text passes these by in silence, offering no assessment. It does not portray them as having faith or depending on God to help them. If we get distracted by these incidentals, we risk losing sight of what the text *is* doing.

This is not a story about the families God gives to help and care for us. While it is true that we can observe those things about Moses' family, when we allow them to become the emphasis of the story we lose the big picture about God's beginning to act on behalf of his people. Sometimes the lesson is set forth that just as God cared for Moses, he cares for us. It is true that God cares for us, but we must remember that many babies died at the hand of Pharaoh's policy, and many children today do not experience God's care in tangible ways.

Note that the Israelites were *not* building the pyramids, which were completed at least 1,500 years earlier, but rather store cities. Also, even though Moses grew up in the household of Pharaoh, he was not necessarily an important person with a future in the halls of power. Pharaohs had enormous numbers of children (Ramesses II had ninety sons) and may not even have known all of them by sight. Do not make Moses' role in Pharaoh's household too big a part of this story.

22. Moses and Jethro (Exodus 2:15–22; 18)

Lesson Focus

Moses flees Egypt and encounters a Midianite tribe led by Jethro and marries Jethro's daughter Zipporah. Later, as the Israelites are camped around Mount Sinai, Jethro visits him and observes how much time it is taking Moses to fulfill his leadership role, settling disputes that are brought before him. Jethro advises Moses to appoint judges to deal with most of the cases so that only the most difficult and significant ones will come to Moses. That way Moses can devote his time to getting revelation from God and teaching the people about God and his law.

- God provides leadership for his people by training Moses.
- God cares about providing justice for his people.

Lesson Application

We should trust God to provide the leadership and the understanding that his people need.

- Believe that God will make use of the experiences we have in life to shape us into the people he intends for us to be.

Biblical Context

The book of Exodus focuses on God's presence as he delivers his people from slavery in Egypt. Though at the beginning, the covenant appears to be in shambles, with no sign of God's presence among his people, the book ends with the building of the tabernacle and God entering the Most Holy Place to dwell in the midst of his freed people. This story shows how God prepared Moses in the wilderness for the job of leading his people out of Egypt into the Promised Land. The second part of the story tells of the first step in providing for justice to be carried out for this new nation, the main part of which will come in the Law that is about to be revealed on Mount Sinai. The system of judges provides the administrative structure that will be in place for the application of the Law.

Interpretational Issues in the Story

Priest of Midian (Ex. 2:16; 18:1). As a Midianite priest, Jethro served the Midianite gods. Unfortunately, we do not know who they were, though it is possible that Yahweh was among them, since Midian was a descendant of Abraham (Gen. 25:2).

"The LORD is greater than all gods" (Ex. 18:11). This comment is striking but does not go so far as to say that Jethro discarded idols and from that point on worshiped only Yahweh. The polytheism of the ancient world had ample room for gods to be added when they showed themselves powerful. Jethro was impressed—he had never heard of anything like the working of Yahweh—but the text does not detail Jethro's beliefs.

"You shall represent the people before God" (Ex. 18:19). Moses was

set up to be the final court of appeal instead of having to hear every case at every level. This top position was soon to be that of the high priest, who would wield the Urim and Thummim (see Ex. 28:30). Moses served this role because he could ask God for a judgment in difficult cases. Not all cases required consulting deity, but for the ones that did, Moses' role as prophet was important and necessary. For simple disputes, lower judges trained in judicial wisdom and known for their discernment could suffice.

Background Information

Midian. The major area of Midian was in northwest Arabia just east of the Red Sea, but with flocks and herds the Midianites would have roamed considerable distances. It would not have been unusual for Moses to encounter them in the Sinai Peninsula.

Moses' father-in-law. In Exodus 2:18 reference is made to Reuel, in Exodus 3:1 to Jethro, and in Numbers 10:29 to Hobab. Part of this difficulty is the terminology in Hebrew for in-laws and ancestors. The most likely solution is that Reuel was the head of the clan, Zipporah's grandfather, Jethro was her father, and Hobab was her brother.

Mistakes to Avoid

Teachers must resist reading details into the story that the Bible does not give. Jethro was a priest (Ex. 3:1) and later acknowledged Yahweh's unmatched power, affirming Moses' report of how Yahweh had helped Israel (18:10–11). The text, however, is silent concerning whether Jethro transferred all his loyalties to Yahweh. There is no evidence that Moses learned about Yahweh from him or that Zipporah was a believer. In the ancient world the wife adopted the gods of her husband. The system of justice that Jethro advised Moses to set up is not offered as a biblical model for societies of all times and places. This is not instruction given by God or even explicitly approved by God, so it cannot be taken as the authoritative message of God's Word that we are obliged to obey or are wise to follow. This is not a story about how we can help one another (Moses at the well, Jethro giving hospitality or advice). These are trivial details in the story about God and his people. We need to realize that some of the stories in the Bible are not intended to stand by themselves with a useful independent message. This story is a prelude to the giving of the law and really has little to offer as an independent story for elementary students.

23. The Burning Bush (Exodus 2:11–4:17)

Lesson Focus

God revealed himself to Moses in the burning bush, showing Moses who he is and what he is like. He called Moses to lead the people of Israel out of Egypt and to help them know God's character and power. God promised to be with Moses as he did so.

- God wants to be known by his people.
- God graciously reveals himself to his people.
- God's presence must be treated as holy.
- God equips his chosen leaders to succeed.
- God is aware of the problems his people face.

Lesson Application

God made himself known to Moses through the burning bush. He makes himself known to us through Scripture and his powerful acts.

- We recognize what a privilege it is that God has revealed himself to us.
- We respect the name and presence of God.
- We take advantage of God's revelation by reading the Bible regularly.
- We trust that God knows and cares about our problems.
- We trust God to equip us for the tasks he calls us to.

Biblical Context

The book of Exodus focuses on God's presence as he delivers his people from slavery in Egypt. Though at the beginning the covenant appears to be in shambles, with no sign of God's presence among his people, the book ends with the building of the tabernacle and God entering the Most Holy Place to dwell in the midst of his freed people. The story of the burning bush marks the first appearance of God's presence in the book, not just in the fire but in the name that he gave to Moses.

Interpretational Issues in the Story

"God remembered his covenant" (Ex. 2:24). This wording does not suggest that God had been forgetful. It was used when God was about to act in a situation.

Angel of the Lord (Ex. 3:2). The angel of the Lord is a messenger who brings God's word to people. In the ancient world direct communication between important parties was a rarity. Diplomatic exchange normally required the use of an intermediary. Messengers were like ambassadors and were vested with the authority to speak for the party they represented and were expected to be treated as if they were the dignitary in person. This is why in some contexts, as here, it is hard to distinguish whether God or the messenger is speaking. The messenger may speak in the first person as God.

Holy ground (Ex. 3:5). All manifestations of God's presence become holy ground, sacred space. Those who approach sacred space must meet certain requirements in order to show that they properly recognize God's holiness.

Land of milk and honey (Ex. 3:8, 17). Milk and honey as used here are not the products of agriculture. Milk suggests the land was suitable for herding; honey refers to the sugar of the date palms and indicates that this was a place where the people could cultivate groves of trees.

The name of God (Ex. 3:13–15). The name that God revealed to Moses is built from the verb *to be* and is probably pronounced Yahweh (not Jehovah, a name that resulted from a misunderstanding of the Hebrew). The nuance may simply indicate that God is the "existent one," but the form of the verb suggests rather that he is "the one who causes to be." The name may be indicative of his relationship to the covenant, since through the covenant he caused Israel to be his chosen people.

"Three day's journey into the wilderness, that we may sacrifice" (Ex. 3:18). This is not intended as a deception; it is a reasonable request, and Pharaoh's refusal demonstrates his obstinacy.

Background Information

Midian. The major area of Midian was in northwest Arabia just east of the Red Sea, but with flocks and herds the Midianites would have roamed considerable distances. It would not have been unusual for Moses to encounter them in the Sinai Peninsula.

Sinai or Horeb. The traditional location of Mount Sinai is in the southern Sinai Peninsula, Jebel Musa. Though the traditions for this location go back at least to the fourth century AD, there are reasons to question it (especially the area's lack of water). Given current information, we cannot be certain of the location.

Divine names. In the ancient world, the name of God had power and authority, and, as such, it was used and even abused. A good analogy today is the power and authority that comes with someone's credit card number. As with the giving of a credit card today, back then giving one's name to someone else was an act of trust.

Mistakes to Avoid

Be careful about what you suggest Moses knew or felt as an adult in Pharaoh's house. We do not know that he felt grief for the Israelites. We are not even told whether he knew that they were his people. As always, it is important not to focus too much attention on the human characters in the story. As the story proceeds, Moses' reluctance to go back to Egypt may or may not show a character flaw, but surely the author intends to show that God can overcome any real or imagined obstacles in order to use the person of his choice. We cannot use this lesson to talk about how people make excuses to avoid the call of God or how brothers help one another. Such uses illustrate the error of choosing something trivial in the story and elevating it to the main teaching point. Our goal is to focus the lesson on what comes with authority, which is generally found in God's revelation of himself and his plan.

24. Moses and the Plagues (Exodus 6–12)

Lesson Focus

God kept his promise to give the Israelites the land of Canaan. He had the power to deliver them from the Egyptians through his great and mighty acts.

- God revealed his power to both the Israelites and the Egyptians.
- God showed his superiority over the gods of Egypt.
- God is able to deliver his people.

Lesson Application

God is so strong that nothing can stop him from keeping his promises. Through acts of power he reveals himself to the world.

- We trust that God is able to overcome any obstacle.
- We patiently wait for God's deliverance, which comes in his time.
- We acknowledge that the Lord is God.

Biblical Context

The book of Exodus focuses on God's presence as he delivers his people from slavery in Egypt. Though at the beginning the covenant appears to be in shambles, with no sign of God's presence among his people, the book ends with the building of the tabernacle and God's entering the Most Holy Place to dwell in the midst of his freed people. In the plagues, God shows a new level of his presence with his people as he acts on their behalf.

Interpretational Issues in the Story

The hardening of Pharaoh's heart (Ex. 7:3, 13–14, 22; 8:15, 19, 32; 9:7, 12, 34–35; 10:1, 20, 27; 11:10). Because Pharaoh stubbornly resisted God's requests, God acted to make his punishment clear and proportional to Pharaoh's crime. This has nothing to do with one's ability to repent in response to God.

The destroyer (Ex. 12:23). The Lord traveled through the land using an instrument of destruction. The word translated "Passover" has more to do with standing guard than with passing by (cf. Isa. 31:5, where it is parallel to "shielding"). So, the Lord stands guard at the doorway to keep the destroyer from entering. Blood is smeared over the doorposts to prepare the house for contact with the presence of God.

Background Information

Brick making. Bricks were made with mud, but straw was mixed in so that the bricks would hold together. In the process, straw had to be fetched and broken up while water and dirt were fetched to mix with the straw, and then the mixture was packed into brick molds. After they dried in the sun, they had to be loaded and transported to the building site.

The staff into a serpent. The serpent was a symbol of wisdom and power in ancient Egypt; Moses' ability to control it would have had much meaning to Pharaoh.

Plagues. Some have tried to explain the plagues as a series of natural events that logically led from one to the other. It may be easy to see how frogs would leave a spoiled river; however, it is more difficult to see hail, locusts, or darkness as part of a sequence. Nevertheless, natural explanations need not be problematic. God's work is no less his work just because we find possible explanations. Ancient peoples considered nothing "natural," because deity was involved in everything. The text refers to God's works as "signs and wonders," that is, evidences of God's involvement. This is even true in Exodus 7:9, where many translations have "miracle." Unfortunately, that word assumes our modern distinction between natural and supernatural, a distinction nonexistent in the ancient world. Some also try to align each plague with a particular god of Egypt. This one-to-one correspondence is unnecessary, though undoubtedly the plagues were evidence of Yahweh's superior power.

The Nile to blood. We need not think that the Nile River actually became blood. In Joel 2:31 we read that the moon will be turned to blood, and we understand that as a metaphor. It is just as likely that the Nile became blood-like in color, perhaps due to red algae.

Locusts. Locust plagues in the ancient world were devastating. A large locust swarm could cover as many as 400 square miles, and one square mile could teem with over 100,000,000 insects, each of which could devour its own weight in food each day. Furthermore, if the locusts laid eggs, the problem would recur the next year.

Mistakes to Avoid

It is easy to focus on Pharaoh or Moses for lessons about how we should or should not act, but God is the central figure here. This is not about how Moses conducted himself or the qualities that he might have displayed (patience, perseverance). We also must resist being selective and choosing only portions of the story that reinforce lessons about God that feel comfortable to us. God's revelation of himself is a complete package, and we must accept all or nothing. Some might wonder about the goodness of God, since he hardened Pharaoh's heart and slayed the firstborn throughout Egypt, but we are not in a position to pick and choose those things that we like about God. The Bible's authority is most strongly invested in its depiction of God. We should attribute our discomfort with anything that God does to our lack of understanding, not to God's supposed shortcomings. We dare not think that we could be more just or compassionate than God. He is wise, and we trust that in his wisdom he knows what needs to be done and does it the best way. Be careful about teaching the tenth plague, the death of the firstborn, as this could be disturbing to young children.

25. Crossing the Red Sea (Exodus 13:17–15:21)

Lesson Focus

God, by his great power, is able to save the Israelites from the Egyptians when it seems humanly impossible.

- God protects and delivers his people.

- God punishes those who try to harm his people.
- God has control over nature.
- God overcomes obstacles by his power.

Lesson Application

We can trust God because nothing is too hard for him.

- We must not despair when it seems that there is no way out, though God works differently in each situation.
- We are to have faith in God's wisdom and power.

Biblical Context

The book of Exodus focuses on God's presence as he delivers his people from slavery in Egypt. Though at the beginning the covenant appears to be in shambles, with no sign of God's presence among his people, the book ends with the building of the tabernacle and God's entering the Most Holy Place to dwell in the midst of his freed people. God shows his presence in new ways as he leads Israel out of Egypt by means of the pillar of cloud and fire. He also uses the pillar to protect them from the Egyptians. The parting of the Red Sea stands as an act of his deliverance of his people.

Interpretational Issues in the Story

"The LORD will fight for you" (Ex. 14:14). In the ancient world, battles were fought by the gods, and the nation with the stronger god won the battle. This became a major point in Israelite theology. The battle belonged to the Lord; if he did not fight, the Israelites could not win. God led the armies into battle, and God brought the victories. The path through the sea was not just a matter of God's delivering his people; he was making war on his enemies and fighting against them. Israel had only to watch.

"The LORD will reign forever" (Ex. 15:18). The result of God's victory is his kingship. In these events we see a transition from God as the clan deity of Abraham, Isaac, and Jacob to the national deity of his people Israel. Through the covenant God established his kingship over his people and delivered them from their enemies.

Background Information

Location of the Red Sea. The body of water that we refer to as the Red Sea is not likely to be the body of water featured in this story. If the Israelites were heading to Sinai, they would have had no reason to go south along the west side of the Red Sea. Furthermore, the locations mentioned in the text indicate that they were far north of the Red Sea (14:2, 9). Note also that the Hebrew text refers to the Reed Sea rather than to the Red Sea. The text provides us with enough geographical information to suggest that the Israelites crossed Lake Balah.

Parting of the sea. As with the plagues, it would not be a problem were we to discover a scientific explanation for the parting of the sea. God is at work through what we designate "natural events," such as the development of a child as it is knit together in its mother's womb. The timing of the parting of the sea is alone sufficient to demonstrate this as a work of God by which he brought deliverance to his people. Having said that, a persuasive scientific explanation has yet to be proposed.

Mistakes to Avoid

Certainly God is capable of overcoming any obstacle and delivering from any trouble, but he does not always choose to do so at the time or in the way that we would like. The confidence of the three facing the fiery furnace ought to represent the direction and nature of our faith: "The God we serve is able to save us. . . . But even if he does not . . . we will not serve your gods" (Dan. 3:17–18 NIV). God reveals himself as one who saves, and we experience this attribute of God as he saves us from our sin. Saving from enemies and saving from sin are very different accomplishments, and we should not classify them together. In other words, we should not make this into a lesson about how Jesus saves us from our sin. Though the Israelites celebrated this triumph of the Lord, and rightly so, this is not a lesson instructing God's people to celebrate. It is important to distinguish between that which is *described* in the text and that which is *prescribed* as the mandate of God's Word—the lessons it teaches with authority. The practices described are often good to imitate, but when we teach the Bible we want to focus on its authoritative message. Use caution when considering teaching tools that treat something descriptive in the text as if it were what God's Word is teaching.

26. God Provides Manna and Quail (Exodus 16)

Lesson Focus

God provides food in the wilderness and makes it a test to see whether the people will follow his instructions.

- God is able to provide for the needs of his people.
- God is not limited to the usual means of provision.
- God wants his people to trust him to provide.
- God graciously responds to the pleas, complaints, and grumblings of his people.

Lesson Application

Trust God and obey his Word.

- Our sustenance comes from God, no matter how he provides it; therefore, we should acknowledge him as the source of our food.
- Obedience is important to God, and he rightfully expects it from us.
- We obey God because of who he is and what he has done.

Biblical Context

The book of Exodus focuses on God's presence as he delivers his people from slavery in Egypt. Though at the beginning the covenant appears to be in shambles, with no sign of God's presence among his people, the book ends with the building of the tabernacle and God's entering the Most Holy Place to dwell in the midst of his freed people. God continues to show his presence as he leads Israel by means of the pillar of cloud and fire. He follows up his acts of deliverance by acts of provision.

Interpretational Issues in the Story

Grumbling (Ex. 16:2, 7–9, 12). The grumbling motif plays a significant role throughout Exodus and Numbers; Moses also frequently recalls it in Deuteronomy. This motif is important because it reveals God's longsuffering compassion for his people but also demonstrates how they deserved the very harsh punishment of not being allowed to enter the Promised Land.

Background Information

Elim. Some identify Elim with the Wadi Gharandal, about 60 miles south along the east side of the Gulf of Suez. More likely it is the site known as Ayun Musa, just a few miles south of the tip of the Gulf of Suez.

Wilderness of Sin. The wilderness of Sin is the area in the west-central region of the Sinai Peninsula.

Manna. Several scientific explanations have been offered for the daily provision of manna (secretion of aphids feeding on the sap of tamarisk trees; liquid of the Hammada plant), but none are persuasive.

Quail. Quail fly in large flocks low to the ground, especially when they are getting tired in their migration.

Mistakes to Avoid

Take care not to suggest that God will always provide for our needs. Many believers throughout history have starved to death and many go to bed hungry each night. God specially provides for his people in the wilderness to establish himself as Israel's national God.

27. Water from the Rock (Exodus 17:1–7; Numbers 20:2–13)

Lesson Focus

The Israelites put God to the test, doubting his presence and ability to provide. In spite of their unbelief, God provided water from a rock.

- Whatever we have, God has provided it—God and no one else.
- God's grace is more than his people deserve.

Lesson Application

Trust God to keep his promises.

- It is better to trust God than to doubt that his ways are best and that he can provide.
- God can provide in unexpected ways.

Biblical Context

The book of Exodus focuses on God's presence as he delivers his people from slavery in Egypt. Though at the beginning the covenant appears to be in shambles, with no sign of God's presence among his people, the book ends with the building of the tabernacle and God entering the Most Holy Place to dwell in the midst of his freed people. God continues to show his presence as he leads the Israelites with the pillar of cloud and fire. He follows up his acts of deliverance by acts of provision: manna, quail, and water.

Interpretational Issues in the Story

Putting the Lord to the test (Ex. 17:2, 7). When the Bible speaks of people testing God, this is often a reference to testing value, quality, or attribute, usually God's patience or faithfulness. Here the people tested his patience with their discontent and his faithfulness to provide for them.

Rock at Horeb (Ex. 17:6). This is an important detail. Horeb is another name for Mount Sinai, the place where Moses encountered God in a burning bush (Ex. 3:1; Deut 4:15). This was a place of God's presence. The ancients commonly believed that the sources that watered the earth originated in God's presence (Gen. 2:10; Ezek. 47:1–2). As a result, this was not just a place where God provided water for drinking, but it denotes the fertile and life-sustaining waters that flow from God's presence.

Background Information

Water from rock. Water that collects just beneath the surface of sedimentary rock is called an aquifer. Some of the water might escape if one was to break through the rock surface, but it would have to be an unusually large aquifer to provide the amount of water suggested in the text.

Rephidim. The location of this camp is uncertain. There is a modern wadi called Wadi Refayid, but it is difficult to associate it with Horeb.

Mistakes to Avoid

In Numbers 20 we read an account of another time when God provided water from a rock; these are two distinct incidents with different details. In Exodus 17 Moses was told to strike the rock; in Numbers 20 God instructed him simply to speak to the rock. Because Moses struck the rock contrary to God's instruction, God did not allow him to enter the Promised Land. Numbers 20 involves a much more important issue: Moses commited offense the moment he usurped God's authority. Moses said, "Hear now, you rebels: shall we bring water for you out of this rock?" (Num. 20:10). By this speech, Moses included himself in the act of power—something that God could not tolerate, especially from the leader. The conquest of the land would require a clear distinction between God, who gave them the land, and the human leader. Moses' action blurred this distinction.

28. God Gives the Law (Exodus 19–20)

Lesson Focus

God gives the Israelites the law so they will know what God was like and how the people of God should act toward God and toward each other.

- God gives the law so that people will know how to be holy as he is holy.
- God reveals himself through the law.
- God expects people to be like him by observing his instructions.

Lesson Application

God's law can help us know what God is like and how we should live.

- We seek to be holy as God is holy.
- Even though we do not have to live by Israelite law, these laws reveal how God thinks about holiness; these laws should shape our view of holiness.
- As believers, God is present within us; we should respect this presence.

Biblical Context

The book of Exodus focuses on God's presence as he delivers his people from slavery in Egypt. Though at the beginning the covenant appears to be in shambles, with no sign of God's presence among his people, the book ends with the building of the tabernacle and God's entering the Most Holy Place to dwell in the midst of his freed people. God continues to show his presence as he comes down on the mountain to give the people his law. The law shows the Israelites how they are to treat God's presence and how they need to live so that God's presence can remain in their midst.

Interpretational Issues in the Story

Holiness (Ex. 19:6). God's holiness is the combination of all his attributes. All these attributes combined together distinguish him from us, his creation; nevertheless, our ability to imitate God's attributes distinguishes us from the people among whom we live, thus making us holy relative to our fallen world.

Obedience (Ex. 19:8). The biblical text asks us to listen carefully to the law, to observe the law, and to reflect it in our lives; this is a bit different from obedience. Because some of the laws no longer apply to our way of life, we don't obey them, but we continue to learn from them. All of the law is significant because it reveals God's holiness.

Law and salvation (Exodus 19–20). God never intended the law to bring salvation; rather, it is a revelation of God's holiness and shows what that holiness should look like in the lives of God's people. The law more specifically helped the Israelites to know how they could preserve God's presence and honor his holiness. Salvation is not the issue. In New Testament times, some

Jews understood the law as an essential part of salvation, a view that Paul had to argue against. The Israelites in the Old Testament loved the law and rejoiced in it because it revealed God to them. Imagine if your employer held you responsible for certain behavior but never made his expectations clear. The Israelites recognized that God had graciously revealed his expectations in the law.

"You shall have no other gods before me" (Ex. 20:3). Technically, the Hebrew phraseology indicates that there are no other gods in God's presence. Yahweh does not work in a committee of gods (the pantheon); he alone holds and executes divine authority.

"I the LORD your God am a jealous God" (Ex. 20:5). We usually view jealousy as a negative trait. God's jealousy means that he tolerates no rival. Jealousy arises when illegitimate attention is paid to a third party that violates a bond of faithfulness and loyalty between two parties. It is often a negative trait in humans, as it can expose paranoia or illegitimate expectations and demands or lead to sinful responses. In contrast, God has every right to the loyalty and faithfulness of his people, and any acknowledgment of other gods is a breach of their covenant bond.

Sabbath (Ex. 20:8). When Genesis records that God rested (2:2), it means that all his work of ordering the universe was complete and everything was ready to operate as it was designed to do. Both in the Bible and in the ancient world, deity rested in a temple from where order in the world was maintained. God's resting means that he is in charge and everything is under his control. When God promises rest to his people, it means that he will bring relief from their enemies so their lives can proceed normally. When people rest on the Sabbath, they are enjoying whatever order God has given them in their lives and recognizing his control of the world. He is in charge, and we recognize that by relinquishing our attempts to be in command of our lives. One of the major ways we do that is by not doing our daily chores (our employment) on the Lord's Day.

Honor father and mother (Ex. 20:12). The result of honoring parents is living long in the land (a covenant benefit). This is similar to the New Testament injunction for children to obey their parents "in the Lord" (Eph. 6:1). The wording of both passages demonstrates that the honor due to parents is related to the instruction they provide for living a life pleasing to the Lord.

Murder (Ex. 20:13). The word translated as "murder" here is not the general word for killing but a technical legal term for murder, perhaps more like homicide. Consequently it does not address situations such as capital punishment or warfare.

Covet (Ex. 20:17). To envy someone means to want something similar to what he has; to covet means we want what is theirs. Coveting is often the attitude behind the violation of commandments six through nine.

Background Information

No idols. Ancient peoples believed that the images of the gods were endowed with the divine essence and that certain rituals needed to be performed for the idols to achieve this state. The images mediated divine presence, divine revelation, and worship of the divine as people sought to meet the needs of the gods. Yahweh indicates that no man-made image can serve as his mediator, nor does he have needs.

Name of God. People in the ancient world believed that the name of God had power and authority. We see this idea extend into the New Testament in the Lord's Prayer, which opens with "hallowed be your name" (Matt. 6:9), indicating that we should pray in the powerful name of Jesus. The power and authority of the name of God can be abused and misused, just as someone with your credit card number can misuse your economic authority. The third commandment indicates that we must not abuse God's name for our own ends. Its focus is not against those who treat God's name as having no importance, but against those who well know its power and seek to exploit it. We violate the third commandment when we claim authority for a certain teaching that does not carry biblical authority; that is, using God's authority to validate something we want to teach.

Mistakes to Avoid

Lessons concerning God's law are too often built around the word *rules*, which is misleading. Words that cover the subject more accurately are "God's ways." God's ways include what to think and how to act and live and are to be followed and observed. God's law also communicates an understanding of God's ways in that it reveals who he is and what he is like. Certainly God is interested in obedience, but God's expectations are more complex. Students need to know that their faith is not a matter of keeping a list of rules—faith is a relationship with God. Our behavior is important because our lives reflect our relationship with God when we imitate God's attributes (compare the fruits of the Spirit). The law points us in this direction. No list of rules can cover everything; rules can only give us direction. The spirit of the law is more important and is addressed in the points below.

The First Commandment

- ***Point:*** All divine authority is God's.
- ***Application:*** Not "What have you made a god in your life?" but "Don't think that you control your own life." We are not inclined to delegate authority to other gods but to take it for ourselves.

The Second Commandment

- ***Point:*** No objects can mediate God's presence, revelation, or worship. In the ancient world, worship entailed meeting the needs of the gods (described in Background Information above).
- ***Application:*** Not "What are the idols in your life?" but "God has no needs, people are his only images, his presence is in us as believers, and Jesus is the only mediator."

The Third Commandment

- ***Point:*** There is power in the name of God.
- ***Application:*** Beyond "Don't swear or make false oaths" to "Don't abuse God's name for your own benefit." We violate this commandment when we pray in Jesus' name for our personal gain or when we present our thoughts as the Word of God.

The Fourth Commandment

- ***Point:*** God is in control of your world and your life; therefore, yield the mechanisms by which you try to control them.
- ***Application:*** Beyond "Here is the list of things you shouldn't do" to "How can I be involved in kingdom work instead of my own today and honor God as the one truly in control?"

The Fifth Commandment

- ***Point:*** Receive instruction in godly living from your parents and adopt its values as your own.
- ***Application:*** Not "You are obliged to do everything your parents tell you, even if it is sinful" but "Adopt without rebellion the godly values your parents teach."

The Sixth Commandment

- ***Point:*** Respect the lives of others.
- ***Application:*** Not "As long as you don't murder, you are okay," but "You should rid yourself of any hatred lest your emotions lead you to violence against someone" (see Matt. 5:21–22).

The Seventh Commandment

- ***Point:*** Respect family rights and identity.
- ***Application:*** Not "As long as you don't get involved sexually, you are okay," but "You should combat any lustful urgings and inclinations lest they lead you to disrupt the boundaries of family identity and commitment" (see Matt. 5:27–30).

The Eighth Commandment

- ***Point:*** Respect what belongs to others.
- ***Application:*** Beyond "Don't steal objects that do not belong to you" to "Be careful to respect the property, rights, and freedom of others."

The Ninth Commandment

- ***Point:*** Respect the name and reputation of others.
- ***Application:*** Beyond "Don't lie against someone else in court," to "Don't falsely accuse, slander, or defame others in any way."

The Tenth Commandment

- ***Point:*** Respect the rights and property of others.
- ***Application:*** Beyond "Don't desire what belongs to others," to "Be content with what you have."

29. The Tabernacle (Exodus 25–31; 35–40)

Lesson Focus

God instructed the people to build the tabernacle to serve as his house. After the tabernacle was completed, God came down to place his holy presence there.

- God wants to live in the midst of his people.
- God provided instructions for a suitable place for him to dwell with his people.
- God is worthy of our very best.

Lesson Application

Having God's presence among us is a privilege that should fill us with awe and appreciation of his grace.

- Instead of having God's presence in a building, we can invite the Holy Spirit to dwell within us.
- We recognize what a privilege it is to enjoy God's presence.
- We cannot lose God's presence, but we should still honor it in every way and not take it for granted.
- If important people are honored in certain ways, God ought to receive more honor in those same ways.

Biblical Context

The book of Exodus focuses on God's presence as he delivers his people from slavery in Egypt. Though at the beginning the covenant appears to be in shambles, with no sign of God's presence among his people, the book ends with the building of the tabernacle and God entering the Most Holy Place to dwell in the midst of his freed people. God continues to show his presence as he comes down on the mountain to give the people his law. The book climaxes here as the Lord provides instructions for the building of the tabernacle, then comes down to dwell in the midst of his people.

Interpretational Issues in the Story

Size of the tabernacle (Ex. 27:9–15). We should observe that the courtyard was not big enough for large numbers of people to gather; this structure was not intended as a place for corporate worship. We can use the analogy of a bank: people go there to conduct their business, not to gather. The bank specialists help them conduct their business, and barriers keep them out of certain areas.

Precious materials (Ex. 25:1–7). We may wonder why God required such expensive materials. The idea is that God ought to be given the very best. If human rulers are honored by the use of such materials, God should be more honored.

Ark of the covenant (Ex. 25:10–16). The ark was the most important sacred relic in Israel. It was the footstool of the invisible throne of the invisible God and sat alone in the throne room (Most Holy Place) of the Lord. It was not to be profaned by being handled or even viewed except in particular circumstances. We do not know what became of it.

Background Information

Tabernacle design. The design, dimensions, and materials of the tabernacle follow known conventions from the ancient world. Furthermore, portable shrines are known from the ancient world. God was using familiar ideas to establish his unique presence among his people.

Cherubim. Unlike the chubby, winged infants of medieval art, the cherubim are mighty, fearsome, composite creatures. They are often depicted with the wings of an eagle, the body of a lion, and the feet of an ox, though there are many different combinations. We should not liken cherubim to angels (who ultimately are messengers); rather, we should recognize them as guardians of divine or royal presence. This is their function as they flank the throne of God.

Altar for sacrifices. This altar was in the courtyard where people could approach it with their sacrifices. Sacrifices were of various sorts. Some served as gifts of thanks and included a communal meal, while others served to maintain the sanctity of the tabernacle and provide forgiveness of sin.

Incense altar. The incense altar was much smaller than the altar for sacrifices and was located in the outer chamber just in front of the veil that covered the Most Holy Place. Incense was burnt to provide a pleasant aroma and to provide smoke to mask the divine presence.

Bread of the Presence. The bread was kept in the outer chamber of the tabernacle as a symbol of God's provision for his people (as opposed to what was common in the rest of the ancient world, where people provided food for their god).

Mistakes to Avoid

The tabernacle, and later the temple, was very different from today's churches. A church is a building in which people gather regularly for worship (though of course, technically, the church is people, not a building). The tabernacle and temple both provided a dwelling for God. Today God does not live in a structure; he lives in his people. Therefore, there is no longer a structure that we can compare to the tabernacle or temple. These differences should be made clear to students. It would be entirely misleading and inappropriate to substitute "church" for "tabernacle." Sometimes the detail of the tabernacle is explained in symbolic terms foreshadowing Christ. Though there are occasional references connecting the tabernacle and Christ (see Hebrews 9), there is nothing that is all-encompassing, nor is there a point-by-point comparison. Therefore, any connections are mere speculations. If we seek to convey the authority of God's Word, we should focus on what it does say, not on foreshadowings we devise. Finally, though skilled artisans were used in the building of the tabernacle, and God's spirit strengthened them for the task, this is not a story to encourage us to use our gifts for God. Of course, we *should*, and it is worthwhile mentioning in passing that these artisans *did*, but that should not be the focus of the lesson.

30. The Golden Calf (Exodus 32)

Lesson Focus

The people made a calf of gold and used it for worship. God punished the people but, because of Moses' intercession, did not destroy them.

- God is concerned about how his people worship.
- God takes offense very seriously.
- God listens to the prayers of his people.
- God is willing to give second chances.

Lesson Application

God is willing to give us a second chance when we disobey.

- When we become aware of sin, we should be willing to repent and change.
- We should not be surprised if God punishes us for sin even though he forgives it.
- We should not doubt God and turn to other options.

Biblical Context

The book of Exodus focuses on God's presence as he delivers his people from slavery in Egypt. Though at the beginning the covenant appears to be in shambles, with no sign of God's presence among his people, the book ends with the building of the tabernacle and God entering the Most Holy Place to dwell in the midst of his freed people. The narrative of the golden calf divides the two sets of chapters that present the construction of the tabernacle. Its primary focus is how the people wrongly represent God's presence while Moses is absent.

Interpretational Issues in the Story

"A feast to the LORD" (Ex. 32:5). Aaron declares a feast to Yahweh, thus indicating that he did not view the calf as a different deity.

The role the image was expected to fill (Ex. 32:4). Moses' extended absence stimulated the people to construct the calf. This fact, combined with

Aaron's declaration of a feast to Yahweh, suggests that the calf was designed to replace Moses, not Yahweh. Thus, we should view the calf as a mediator like Moses, not as a god. The people's declaration, "These are your gods, O Israel, who brought you up out of the land of Egypt!" (v. 4) indicates that the calf was the new representative of Yahweh (who brought them out of Egypt). This is a violation of the second commandment, which concerns how Yahweh is worshiped, more than a violation of the first, which concerns worship of another god. But even on that point we should note that the calf is not an image of Yahweh (see comments in Background Information).

God wanting to blot out Israel and relenting (Ex. 32:10–14). Israel's repeated demonstration of faithlessness deserved judgment, so God expressed his intention to wipe them out and start again with Moses. Moses interceded and God relented, but that does not mean that Moses was more gracious than God. The question concerns where the line was to be drawn between mercy and justice. God's justice would have been an appropriate and well-deserved justice. Moses' appeal for mercy was a weak appeal that subverted justice, but God granted his request as an act of grace toward Moses. God sometimes gives us what we ask for, even if it is not best for us. For all we know, Moses' intercession might have resulted in a less satisfactory solution, but we will never know what the results would have been had Moses not interceded. But did God change his mind? Usually when someone changes his mind, we think he is fickle or has found a better way to think. Neither of these can be true of God, nor could Moses remind God of something he had forgotten. Israel's sin created an imbalance. Balance can be brought about either by punishment or compassionate grace—either one might be appropriate. At Moses' initiative, God restores balance through a combination: punishment of the worst offenders but grace that stopped short of entirely annihilating the people.

Background Information

Calf images. Calf images in the ancient world were usually associated with a god but were not regarded as deity. Archaeologists have found a number of calf images, but they are usually quite small (4 to 6 inches long). Reliefs often portray the gods standing on the back of a bull; in this way, the animal served as a pedestal (similar to the function of the ark of the covenant, which served as a footstool). More importantly, the gods in the ancient world were often associated with animals that shared attributes with the deity. This is the most likely understanding of the calf: an emblem animal associated with Yahweh that could mediate Yahweh's presence, as Moses had done.

Making of images in the ancient world. The ancients considered the construction of images a divine activity in which humans played an insignificant role. When the craftsmen finished their work, they would ceremonially throw their tools into the river and declare ritually that they had had nothing to do with the manufacture of the image: the image was crafted by the gods. This may explain Aaron's insistence that he had little to do with the fashioning of the calf (v. 24).

Worship practices. In the ancient world worship involved performing rituals designed to meet the needs of deity so that he would be favorably disposed toward the people. These needs were often met through the mediation of the image of the deity, which was presented with food and clothed and housed in splendor. Israel's rituals and worship were not focused on the needs of their God, for their God has no needs. Images of any sort could only corrupt Israel's worship and her idea of the nature of God and how he works in the world.

Mistakes to Avoid

Do not suggest that Israel was worshiping another god; such an interpretation is too simplistic. This lesson is also not about making something else more important than God. That is not the issue of the golden calf. People who use icons or amulets today as an aid to make God's presence more real are doing something similar to what Israel was doing with the calf. Nothing of this sort can give an adequate sense of God and too easily leads to distorted ideas of him. Even a Bible can be misused in this way. There are no lessons about Aaron or Moses here but only about God. For example, Moses is not providing a mandate or model for intercessory prayer. That does not mean that we should not pray as Moses did, but the text is not offering instruction in that direction or approval of his action.

31. Sukkot/Thanksgiving (Leviticus 23:33–43; Numbers 29:12–34)

Lesson Focus

God commanded the Israelites to celebrate Sukkot, the Feast of Booths, to remember their deliverance from Egypt. The Israelites also used this time to thank God for their harvest.

- God provides food from the harvest.
- God provides ways for us to remember what he has done on our behalf.
- God brought Israel out of Egypt and sustained them in the wilderness.

Lesson Application

It is important that God's people set aside time to thank him.

- We honor God by taking time to acknowledge him as the source of our food.
- We set aside time to remember and to thank God for what he has done for us.
- We remember and thank God for delivering us out of the slavery of sin.

Biblical Context

Leviticus is a treatise on how to honor that which is sacred, beginning with the tabernacle. The book also addresses the need for purity and holiness of the people who enter sacred space and the animals that were used for sacrifices. This section of the book addresses the observance of sacred times, such as the Sabbath and annual festivals, for God commanded his people to set aside certain times to honor him.

Interpretational Issues in the Story

Seven (Lev. 23:34, 36, 39–42; Num. 29:12, 32). The number seven had great significance in the ancient world, though most people groups had not yet adopted a seven-day week, as Israel had. The seven-day structure is obvious in the creation account of Genesis 1 and is also significant for temple inauguration activities. The Sabbath marked off every seventh day.

Rest (Lev. 23:39). Whether rest is connected to the Sabbath or to one of the festivals, God commanded his people to set aside their normal work to acknowledge him as their true provider; any measure of stability or security they enjoyed came about because of God's activity on their behalf.

Sacrifices (Num. 29:12–34). The number of animals sacrificed during this weeklong festival, the Feast of Booths, is staggering (seventy bulls, fourteen rams, ninety-eight lambs, seven goats) but was intended as a recognition of the Lord's bounty on his people. These sacrifices were not offered for a family but for the entire people of Israel. At Thanksgiving, our country slaughters a staggering number of turkeys for our celebrations of thanks. In the Old Testament the sacrifices of the animals served as worship to the Lord.

Background Information

Israelite calendar. The people of ancient Israel had both a sacred and a civil calendar. The sacred calendar began in the spring with the month of Nisan, equivalent to our March/April; Passover was celebrated in the middle of this month. The civil calendar started in the month of Tishri, called the "seventh month," equivalent to our September/October. We know that the civil calendar was separate from the sacred because, even though it is called the "seventh month," Rosh Hashana (New Year's Day) was celebrated at the beginning of this month. The ancient Israelite calendar was a lunar calendar; that is, each month began with the first sighting of the new moon. Every few years the calendar was adjusted to harmonize with the solar year.

Agricultural society. Israel was largely an agricultural society in which each person grew his own food rather than purchase it at a market. As time progressed, developments in the administrative, military, merchant, and guild sectors caused the society to shift, but the early dependence on individual agriculture established the cycle of festivals that marked the various stages of the agricultural process.

Mistakes to Avoid

Many times, lessons on thankfulness focus on things we have rather than on what God has done. While it is true that God is the ultimate source of all we have, we should try to expand students' vision beyond the items themselves to God's role as provider. So, for example, if you have asked, "What are you thankful for?" and someone replies, "Food," attention can be focused on thanking God that he provides us with the food we enjoy eating. Notice that in the Lord's Prayer Jesus urges us to pray, "Give us this day our daily bread" (what God does), instead of "Thank you for our bread" (what we receive).

32. Twelve Scouts (Numbers 13–14; Deuteronomy 1:19–40)

Lesson Focus

God brought the Israelites to the border of the Promised Land and told them to go in to possess it. Moses sent twelve scouts to explore the land. When the scouts returned, they reported that the land was very productive but that the people living there were very powerful and had large fortified cities. Two of the scouts, Joshua and Caleb, encouraged the people to trust God to give them the land, but the other ten discouraged the people with a bad report. The people listened to the report of the ten scouts and rebelled against God. In his mercy and because of Moses' intercession, God did not destroy them; rather, God punished their unbelief by not allowing them to enter the land. Only their children would enjoy the land God had promised.

- God expects his people to trust him.
- God loves his people, but he will not necessarily tolerate every level of insubordination.
- God is longsuffering, but his patience does have limits.
- God still gives the land to his people in fulfillment of his promise, but the unfaithful do not share in the privilege.

Lesson Application

Just as God graciously remained faithful to the Israelites in spite of their unbelief, he keeps his promises to us even when we disobey.

- We must not stretch God's patience with our distrust.
- We take God at his word, even when the obstacles seem insurmountable.

Biblical Context

The book of Numbers recounts how the grumbling discontent of the Israelites and their lack of faith resulted in the wilderness wandering while the first generation died (as they had indicated that they wished [14:2]). Thus, the book transitions from the first generation, which had left Egypt, to the second generation, which entered the land. The story of the scouts is the hinge of the book, since the people's refusal to enter the land in faith causes their doom.

Interpretational Issues in the Story

Milk and honey (Num. 13:27; 14:8). These were not the products of agriculture. Milk suggests that the land was suitable for herding; honey refers to the sugar of the date palms and indicates that this was a place where the people could cultivate groves of trees.

"Like grasshoppers" (Num. 13:33). The common belief that some of the inhabitants of the land were giants is difficult to substantiate. The descendants of Anak (Num. 13:22, 28; Deut. 2:10) are described in general terms as large and tall. This is similar to a modern description of "gigantic" or "huge," so it falls short of "giants." The grasshopper comparison is intended as exaggeration. The size of the Nephilim (giants) is not given; they are

simply listed as also present. Though the narrator gives no measure of their height, the main point—that the peoples are intimidating warriors—is clear (note Deut. 1:28 NIV: "The people are stronger and taller than we are"). We should observe, however, that an Egyptian papyrus from this period (Papyrus Anastasi I) indicates the presence of fierce warriors in Canaan that were seven to nine feet tall.

Moses' intercession (Num. 14:13–19). We should not conclude from this passage that Moses was more gracious than God and that God must be prompted to adopt a more merciful course of action. No human can ever outdo God in his attributes. God sometimes gives us what we ask for, even if it is not best for us; God indicates that the people he would raise up from Moses would be greater and stronger than the Israelites (Num. 14:12). For all we know, Moses' intercession might have resulted in a less satisfactory solution, but we will never know what the results would have been had Moses not interceded.

Background Information

Forty days. Context indicates that we should interpret the forty days as a long period of time rather than as an exact quantity. The text says that the Israelites started in the wilderness of Paran and went as far north as Rehob toward Lebo-Hamath; even if they went by the fastest route straight from Paran to Rehob and back, the journey of 500 to 600 miles would have taken more than forty days. The time would actually have been much longer, for the text reports that the people traversed all over the land. This simply shows the flexible use of the term *forty* in the biblical world.

Fortifications. Numbers 13:28 is a problematic verse. Archaeological evidence from the Late Bronze period has not yet identified cities with free-standing walls, though there were large walled cities in the previous Middle Bronze period. The Middle Bronze period is generally considered too early for the exodus and wandering, but some have wondered whether some of these Middle Bronze walls might still have been in use. The word translated "fortifications" is quite general and simply identifies the city as impregnable. Fortifications of the Late Bronze period featured houses in a perimeter around the city whose back walls were joined to form a barrier. Gates blocked the few openings, which was sufficient to make a city inaccessible and defensible. Deuteronomy uses the expression that the fortifications were "up to the sky" (1:28; 9:1 NIV), which could refer to the gate area. In one other place (Deut. 3:5), however, it indicates specifically that the walls were high. That word for *walls* generally refers to an independent city wall but can be used broadly for a barrier that prevented entry to a city (note Nah. 3:8). Archaeology has yet to clarify this issue.

Mistakes to Avoid

This is not a story about the character qualities of Joshua and Caleb. It is true that they courageously resisted peer pressure, but this is a story of trust in God and obedience to his instructions. The main point is the fact that God was ready to deliver on his covenant promise, but the people failed to have sufficient faith. We also must take extreme care not to present God as mean or harsh. Too many have ideas that the God of the Old Testament was strict, violent, and judgmental and that the God of the New Testament is loving, tender, and patient. This dichotomy is theologically inaccurate and unacceptable. God's grace throughout history exceeds all expectation. His justice is not somehow a lesser attribute. Those who live under persecution would wonder how a God who does not judge the wicked could be a loving God. Grace and justice must work together for either to have meaning. Carefully consider how many details of God's punishment of his people you want to reveal to the youngest children.

33. Korah's Revolt (Numbers 16)

Lesson Focus

Korah and his coconspirators, Dathan and Abiram, were jealous of the leadership role of Moses and Aaron. They complained against them and challenged their position and were supported by 250 other leaders of the people. Moses rebuked them and set up a test, whereby God indicated that the rebels were wrong. The rebels were punished with total destruction.

- God holds leaders accountable for their behavior.
- God takes sin and rebellion seriously.

Lesson Application

God holds leaders to a higher standard of accountability; God's people should not tolerate jealousy or political maneuvering for power among their leaders.

- We must be careful not to take God's holiness lightly.
- We should not think that we can second-guess God's procedures and policies.

Biblical Context

The book of Numbers recounts how the grumbling discontent of the Israelites and their lack of faith resulted in the wilderness wandering while the first generation died (as they had indicated that they wished [14:2]). Thus, the book transitions from the first generation, which left Egypt, to the second generation, which entered the land. The story of Korah's revolt shows that the rebellion against Moses and Aaron, and therefore God's leadership, extended even to the spiritual leaders of the people.

Interpretational Issues in the Story

"All in the congregation are holy" (Num. 16:3). The rebels devised their own theology about holiness and access to the presence of God. Moses insisted that he was following God's instructions, not making up his own guidelines. This has some similarity today to those who claim that Christianity is exclusivistic and that all ways lead to God. Our response is that Christians did not make up the rules or devise the system; rather, it has been given by God in his revelation of himself (16:28).

"Glory of the Lord" (Num. 16:19). The "glory of the Lord" came down on Mount Sinai (Ex. 24:16), filled the tabernacle (Ex. 40:34) and the temple (1 Kings 8:11), appeared to Ezekiel in a vision (Ezek. 1:28), and was seen by the shepherds outside of Bethlehem (Luke 2:9). It was a manifestation that accompanied the presence of God and was perceived as a bright light.

Destruction of families and possessions (Num. 16:32). The families of the rebels were also punished. People in the ancient world and in Israel found their identity in family units rather than in the individual. Decisions were clan decisions; offense was clan offense. Korah was his family, and his family was Korah.

Background Information

Incense censers. Incense was used in the Bible and in the rest of the ancient world as a buffer, obscuring God's presence from prying eyes and providing a pleasant aroma for deity. If the offerer or the procedures did not meet the standards of ritual acceptability, the incense would defile rather than please.

Sheol. The word, translated "grave" in the NIV, is used for the netherworld, a place that was usually entered through the grave. This was neither heaven nor hell; it was simply the place where all the dead go. Israelites as yet had no hope of heaven, nor were they threatened with eternal punishment.

Mistakes to Avoid

This is not a story about Moses' humility. In Numbers the emphasis is on rebellion at every level and why this generation deserved to be prohibited from entering the land. It was important for the next generation to learn the serious lessons about the potential potency of God's holiness and the dangers of political ambition. Keep the focus on God rather than on Moses, Aaron, Korah, or his cohorts. Telling this story to young children would be inappropriate.

34. The Bronze Serpent (Numbers 21:4–9)

Lesson Focus

The people grew impatient and rebelled against God. God punished them with poisonous snakes but made a way for bringing the people back when they repented; they had only to look at the bronze serpent.

- God is both just when people rebel and merciful when they repent.
- God uses a variety of means to inflict punishment, and his relief often comes in ways his people will easily recognize.

Lesson Application

God provides a way to bring people back to him when they rebel: Christ's death on the cross. When we find we have sinned, we repent (turn away from sin).

- Knowing that God will not tolerate rebellion should encourage us to faithfulness.
- We take advantage of the means God has provided for us to repent and be restored.

Biblical Context

The book of Numbers recounts how the grumbling discontent of the Israelites and their lack of faith resulted in the wilderness wandering while the first generation died (as they had indicated that they wished [14:2]). Thus, the book transitions from the first generation, which left Egypt, to the second generation, which entered the land. The story of the bronze serpent offers a final evidence of the failure of the generation that died in the wilderness, failure that included both the people and their leaders.

Interpretational Issues in the Story

Bronze serpent in later history (Num. 21:9). When God ordained the use of the bronze serpent, he used a means that would have been familiar to the Israelites (see Background Information below). This familiarity, however, also created a situation ripe for abuse. We find that such abuse did develop when the people kept the serpent and eventually came to worship it (2 Kings 18:4). Jesus also used the incident with the serpent as an effective analogy for his own death (John 3:14).

Making images (Num. 21:9). It might seem as if God's instructions were a violation of the second commandment against making images. God prohibited the kind of images that people believed bore his essence and served as mediators of worship and revelation. However, the serpent on the pole had no such role; if it mediated anything, it mediated grace—not worship or revelation, as did cult statues.

Background Information

Bronze serpent. Excavations have unearthed an Egyptian temple to Hathor in this region (Timna) that was erected during this time period. The temple was adopted by the Midianites during the Judges period. One of the artifacts discovered in the excavations was a five-inch-long copper image of a snake.

Apotropaic devices. In the ancient world it was believed that the image of something could protect against the thing itself. Thus, there are many apotropaic (protective) amulets of serpents found from the ancient world. It is interesting that God chose to use something that had such magical connections to which it could be identified.

Mistakes to Avoid

The teacher should resist turning this into a story about Jesus and the cross. It is true that this analogy is made by Jesus himself, and so it is valid to make that point in the course of the lesson. But in Numbers it is not a story about Jesus. It has its own purpose and message independent of that connection.

35. Balaam (Numbers 22–24)

Lesson Focus

God blessed Israel through the then internationally known prophet Balaam. In the process, God made it plain that Balaam's reputation meant nothing—

that, in fact, God can speak through a simple donkey should he choose to do so. The blessings pronounced by Balaam reiterated the covenant promises of God to Abraham's family and indicated how God would give them victory over their enemies.

- God can speak through any instrument, no matter how small or great.
- God continued to fulfill the promises he had made to Abraham and to the nation of Israel, even though he was in process of punishing the rebellious generation.
- God controls the destiny of peoples and nations.
- God is able to overcome any obstacle.
- God humbles the proud and defeats the strategies of his enemies.

Lesson Application

We should trust God to fulfill his plans concerning us.

- We trust that God has the future under his sovereign control.
- We try to learn humility rather than indulging in feelings of self-importance.
- We must not be surprised when the plans of the wicked are turned against them.

Biblical Context

The book of Numbers recounts how the grumbling discontent of the Israelites and their lack of faith resulted in the wilderness wandering while the first generation died (as they had indicated that they wished [14:2]). Thus, the book transitions from the first generation, which left Egypt, to the second generation, which entered the land. Through Balaam, God conferred a blessing on the second generation.

Interpretational Issues in the Story

God tells Balaam to go, then blocks his way (Num. 22:20–22). Several Old Testament stories feature a similar occurrence, including Jacob's return to Canaan (Genesis 31–32) and Moses' return to Egypt (Exodus 4). In all these cases, we see that while God directed the men to return, he still had important lessons to teach them before they arrived at their final destination.

Angel of the L*ORD (Num. 22:22–35).* The angel of the Lord is a messenger who brings God's word to people. In the ancient world direct communication between important parties was a rarity. Diplomatic exchange normally required the use of an intermediary. Messengers were like ambassadors and were vested with the authority to speak for the party they represented and were expected to be treated as if they were the dignitary in person. This is why in some contexts it is hard to distinguish whether God or the messenger is speaking. The messenger may speak in the first person as God.

"Balaam the son of Beor" (Num. 22:5). We should probably view Balaam as a freelance prophet rather than exclusively as a prophet of Yahweh; he sought messages from whatever god his clients indicated. Balak did not ask Balaam to speak in the name of the Lord, but that was Balaam's intention (22:8). In 22:18, Balaam referred to "the LORD my God," but until the donkey incident, the narrator speaks of God (generic) interacting with Balaam, rather than the Lord, Yahweh. Whether or not Balaam really considered Yahweh as his God, the text makes it clear that Yahweh was speaking though Balaam (e.g., 23:5, 12, 16).

Background Information

Balaam outside the Bible. A discovery at the site of Deir Allah in the 1960s demonstrates how famous Balaam was; the discovery was a plaster inscription from the ninth century BC that references a vision given to Balaam. The inscription does not refer to the same event known from the book of Numbers but shows that Balaam was a well-known prophet even centuries after his death.

Foreign prophets. The Old Testament text repeatedly shows that other nations and gods had their prophets (see the prophets of Baal and Asherah that served Ahab and Jezebel). Prophets often advised kings, who counted on them to relay information from the deity.

Mistakes to Avoid

The message of the text is about God, not Balaam. We should not focus on what Balaam's good or bad example teaches but on what his oracles tell us about God. Likewise, we should not overemphasize the speaking donkey; the donkey is important only insofar as he indicates that even a dumb beast has more insight than this self-important, internationally recognized authority.

36. Rahab and the Spies (Joshua 2)

Lesson Focus

When Joshua's spies scouted out the city of Jericho, they encountered a Canaanite woman, Rahab, who not only helped them escape (in exchange for her life) but also explained how all her countrymen knew and feared the power of the Lord.

- God demonstrates his power for all to see.
- God uses unlikely people to participate in his work.
- God prepares the way for his people and his work.
- God works behind the scenes in countless ways as he fulfills his promises and carries out his plan.

Lesson Application

We can trust God to prepare the way for us as we do his work.

- We should expect God to be working behind the scenes.
- We should understand how important it is for us to recognize the work of God and respond to it with our lives.

Biblical Context

The purpose of the book of Joshua is summarized in 21:43–45: "Thus the LORD gave to Israel all the land. . . . And they took possession of it, and they settled there. And the LORD gave them rest on every side. . . . The LORD had given all their enemies into their hands. Not one word of all the good promises that the LORD had made to the house of Israel had failed; all came to pass." The book shows how God keeps his covenant promise to give the land to Israel. He prepared them to enter Canaan, sent his commander to lead them (5:13–15), provided aid in battles, distributed the land, and renewed the covenant. The story of Rahab demonstrates how God prepared the way for the Israelites by striking fear into the hearts of the Canaanites.

Interpretational Issues in the Story

Rahab's confession (Josh. 2:8–11). While we often are inclined to focus on plot, the biblical narratives often focus on dialogue, as is the case here: Rahab's confession is the centerpiece of the story. While what she actually said is most important, what she did not say is also notable. Rahab neither denounced her gods nor discarded her idols. Polytheism (worship of many gods) in the ancient world was not just a matter of numbers; it was an open-ended system that could accommodate many deities. While one nation might claim that its gods were stronger, polytheism did not deny the existence of other gods.

God in the heavens above and on the earth beneath (Josh. 2:11). In the polytheism of the ancient world, different gods had different areas of jurisdiction. The Canaanites were impressed that Yahweh had demonstrated his power both as a cosmic deity and as a divine warrior.

Background Information

Polytheistic belief. The people in the ancient world believed in the existence of countless gods, and the relationship between people and the gods was based on mutual need. The gods created people so their own needs would be provided (food, clothing, and shelter); in return, the gods protected and provided for the people. People therefore tended to worship family gods or city gods located in their immediate vicinity so as to provide for their gods through rituals. In Joshua, a new and powerful God was entering their region, and Rahab recognized the need to acknowledge this God, even if she did not yet understand how different Yahweh is from the other gods.

House built into the city wall. Self-standing walls from this period have not yet been excavated at Jericho. An alternative to self-standing walls is that townspeople of this time often built houses around the perimeter of the city, the back walls of which connected to form a wall. This would explain why there was a window from Rahab's house to let the spies down outside the wall.

Mistakes to Avoid

We cannot portray Rahab as a converted monotheist. She does not say that she had turned away from her Canaanite gods or discarded her idols—only that she (and her people) had recognized the power of Yahweh. Rahab's statements about God are more important than what she says about her life and decisions. Through her speech, Rahab represented all the Canaanites, as she acknowledges the power of Yahweh. The story should not emphasize the change in Rahab's life or belief; in fact, her confession does not offer enough information to conclude that her life or beliefs had changed. Those who worshiped many gods were always willing to add another if a deity demonstrated power and became involved in their lives. Teachers should focus on what God was doing through Rahab and how her speech demonstrates that the Canaanites could be held responsible for their refusal to respond to this God whose power was so evident.

Likewise, there is no need to draw attention to her lie, which led the soldiers to look elsewhere. The account is not about solving ethical tensions (i.e., saving life or telling the truth) and offers no guide for doing so. The text simply reports what she did without approving or disapproving of her actions. The early church sometimes interpreted the scarlet cord that Rahab hung as a symbol of the blood of Christ, but since the Bible offers no such interpretation, it should not come into the lesson. Some discretion may be needed with young children regarding the description of Rahab's profession, but the story itself can be used for all age groups to teach the greatness of God.

37. Crossing the Jordan (Joshua 3–4)

Lesson Focus

Just as God demonstrated that he was bringing Israel out of Egypt by parting the Red Sea, he demonstrated that he was bringing them into Canaan by parting the Jordan River. In the process he confirmed that Joshua was to be his instrument, just as Moses had been.

- God provided signs of his role in bringing the Israelites into the land.
- God has power over creation.
- God can overcome any obstacles.

Lesson Application

We can trust God to overcome obstacles that seem to interfere with his promises or plan.

- We should note God's mighty acts in our lives, and it is appropriate to establish ways that we will remember them.
- We should not be surprised when God removes obstacles to his work in our lives.

Biblical Context

The purpose of the book of Joshua is summarized in 21:43–45: "Thus the Lord gave to Israel all the land. . . . And they took possession of it, and they settled there. And the Lord gave them rest on every side. . . . The Lord had given all their enemies into their hands. Not one word of all the good promises that the Lord had made to the house of Israel had failed; all came to pass." The book shows how God keeps his covenant promise to give the land to Israel. He prepared them to enter Canaan, sent his commander to lead them (5:13–15), provided aid in battles, distributed the land, and renewed the covenant. God's provision of a way to cross the Jordan is one of the ways that he brought them into the land. In the process, he showed his support of Joshua's leadership and displayed his power to this second generation of Israel.

Interpretational Issues in the Story

Ark of the covenant (Josh. 3:13). Here the ark serves to demonstrate that God was the one leading the procession, parting the waters, taking them into the covenant land, and leading in battle against enemies. The throne and presence of God went before the Israelites.

Piles of stones (Josh. 4:9). Some translations of the verse give the impression that there was a second pile of twelve stones set up in the middle of the Jordan River. Others translate it as a summary sentence indicating that this was the only pile of stones in the first place they camped. The latter makes more sense from several perspectives, but a confident conclusion is not possible.

Background Information

Location of Gilgal. Unfortunately, we do not know the location of Gilgal, Israel's first camp in Canaan.

Location of Adam. Adam near Zarethan is just south of where the Jabbok River joins the Jordan, about eighteen miles north of the fords of Jordan where Israel crossed. The heavy runoff from the mountains in spring produces floodwaters (note 3:15), and the erosion this causes as the two rivers come together can create bank collapses that have been known to block the Jordan at this location. Despite such an explanation, God's timing is impeccable, as the waters stop just as the priests enter them. Unlike the crossing of the Red Sea (where they walked between the walls of water), here the water is blocked up beyond their sight.

Mistakes to Avoid

Sometimes the lesson is built on the fear of the people, but the text says nothing about the people being fearful. It is ill-advised to build a lesson on a detail the text does not even mention. This story demonstrates that God was the one bringing Israel into the land and that Joshua was his chosen leader. Though God instructed the Israelites to build a memorial, the message of the story is *not* that we need to build memorials. When God performs mighty acts on our behalf, we should certainly make a point to remember them, but the text is more interested in the mighty acts than it is in ensuring a memorial. Care ought to be taken not to suggest that God always removes obstacles. Just because God removed this obstacle for Israel at this point in history does not suggest that he will remove all obstacles in every situation. But it does give us an idea of how no obstacle is too large for him to remove.

38. Joshua and Jericho (Joshua 1:1–11; 5:13–6:27)

Lesson Focus

The victory at Jericho was the first installment of God's promise to give the land of Canaan to the Israelites.

- God is just and brings punishment on those who deserve it.
- God fulfills his promises to his people regardless of the obstacles.
- God leads his people and brings victory.
- God's love and grace do not always take precedence over his justice; otherwise there could never be punishment. Rather, his attributes all work together in perfect balance regulated by his wisdom.

Lesson Application

We can believe what God says. God always keeps his promises.

- We can trust God to fulfill his promises.
- We should not question God's wisdom when he acts in judgment rather than in mercy.

Biblical Context

The purpose of the book of Joshua is summarized in 21:43–45: "Thus the LORD gave to Israel all the land. . . . And they took possession of it, and they settled there. And the LORD gave them rest on every side. . . . The LORD had given all their enemies into their hands. Not one word of all the good promises that the LORD had made to the house of Israel had failed; all came to pass." The book shows how God kept his covenant promise to give the land to Israel. He prepared them to enter Canaan, sent his commander to lead them (5:13–15), provided aid in battles, distributed the land, and renewed the covenant. The story of the fall of Jericho shows that it was Yahweh conquering the land, not Joshua or the Israelites themselves.

Interpretational Issues in the Story

God's commander (Josh. 5:13–15). Regardless of what further description we might offer for this commander, what is important in the story is his role—he was coming to lead the conquest for the armies of God. Joshua was not relieved of duty but subordinated under the rule of this commander. The point is that God was the one who would be fighting these battles and gaining the land for Israel, lest anyone think that this was just a marauding band of displaced peoples looking to justify a land grab.

Destroying the Canaanites (Josh. 6:21). Further evidence that the Lord was the one bringing the victory is the command that the Israelites were not to take the plunder for themselves (6:19). Armies often fought for the plunder to be gained. Before we start talking about genocide and raising questions about Israel or God, we need to note a couple of important facts. (1) God's attribute of love or mercy does not trump all other attributes. Here God was acting appropriately as a God of justice, bringing punishment at the right time on those who deserved it (cf. Gen. 15:16). It doesn't matter a lot whether he used brimstone and fire, as at Sodom, or the armies of his people, as here. (2) All in Jericho were punished because all were part of the Canaanite culture, which was guilty and dangerous to Israel. (3) As Rahab demonstrates, escape was possible for those who responded to God's obvious power and expressed loyalty to him. (4) In the most widespread campaigns (southern, Joshua 10; northern, Joshua 11) the Canaanites were the aggressors. (5) In a fallen world it is unfortunately commonplace that those who might be judged innocent become victims of their leaders (e.g., when terrorists hide away in hospitals or schools). (6) Wording in conquest narratives in the ancient world commonly used wide-ranging universalistic language. What was actually carried out might have fallen far short of the universalistic expressions.

Background Information

Jericho. Jericho was about a twelve-acre site, little more than a garrison, but it protected entry into the land from the east at one of the few places where the Jordan could be forded. The archaeology of Jericho is very complicated and controversial because there has been much erosion on the site. We can have no confidence that the walls have been found, though some still try to make that claim. It was a defensible and strategic location and would have been intimidating. Based on the size of the site today, it seems that it might have taken Joshua's army less than half an hour to march around the city walls.

Role of the ark and priests. In the ancient world every war was holy war because people believed that their gods called them to war, led them in battle, and fought on their behalf. Other nations may have been inclined to put the image of their deity in the vanguard or to carry standards representing deities. For this assault it was the ark and the priests that gave indication of God's presence with the Israelites and made it plain that the battle belonged to the Lord.

Trumpets. The instrument used here is the ram's horn (*shofar*). It cannot play a tune but was used for signaling in both military and worship contexts.

Mistakes to Avoid

When God told Joshua to be strong and courageous and that he would be with him, he was working within the very specific context of the covenant promise to give the land to his people Israel. God was encouraging and equipping Joshua for the task at hand. Joshua could bravely carry out God's work because he was confident that God was with him. The point of the story is not that God will help us each to be strong and courageous in whatever struggles we face. However, if God gives us a job to do, and we are confident that he is with us, we can also be strong and courageous.

The text is not highlighting Joshua as a heroic figure; it is highlighting God as one who uses obedient, everyday people to accomplish his plan. Certainly we have reason to be courageous in living for God, but that is not strictly comparable to Joshua's situation. God is faithful to obedient people. The story is not telling us to be like Joshua; it is showing us that God helps in a variety of ways those who are faithful.

Debating whether God's instructions sounded unusual to the Israelites but they followed them anyway is beside the point. The instructions would not have been as strange to them as they sound to us.

It is not productive to urge students to think about the Jericho walls in their lives that God can bring tumbling down. The text is not trying to teach by means of analogy here. Instead, we can ask students, "Who is God to you?" and "Are you living in his strength and trusting him to work through you?" Be careful how you handle the destruction of Jericho and its inhabitants when telling this story to small children.

39. Achan (Joshua 7)

Lesson Focus

Achan kept some of the plunder of Jericho for himself rather than obeying the instructions to dedicate the spoils to God. In so doing he identified with the Canaanites and was therefore treated accordingly. The first consequence was the loss at the battle of Ai. The second was the destruction of Achan and his family.

- God does not tolerate disobedience.

- God holds accountable even those around the offender, so our sin can affect those near to us.
- God's promises to the people were dependent on their obedience.

Lesson Application

We should take God's commandments seriously and obey them diligently.

- We must be aware of the potential impact of sin on ourselves and on those around us.
- We must obey God.

Biblical Context

The purpose of the book of Joshua is summarized in 21:43–45: "Thus the LORD gave to Israel all the land. . . . And they took possession of it, and they settled there. And the LORD gave them rest on every side. . . . The LORD had given all their enemies into their hands. Not one word of all the good promises that the LORD had made to the house of Israel had failed; all came to pass." The book shows how God kept his covenant promise to give the land to Israel. He prepared them to enter Canaan, sent his commander to lead them (5:13–15), provided aid in battles, distributed the land, and renewed the covenant. The story of Achan shows how seriously God treats disobedience.

Interpretational Issues in the Story

"Tribe that the LORD takes" (Josh. 7:14). This was determined by the casting of lots.

Achan's crime (Josh. 7:1). When Achan took goods as plunder, it was like making a claim that the Israelites had won the battle rather than the Lord. Achan also, in effect, placed himself among the Canaanites (by possessing their goods) and therefore made himself and his family members of the Canaanites. They were therefore treated as if they were Canaanites. This is the reverse of Rahab and her family, who took the part of the Israelites and were treated as if they were Israelites.

Achan's punishment (Josh 7:25). Achan's entire family was punished. This stands in contrast to Rahab's family, which was spared even though they did not necessarily share her convictions. The reason is the same in both cases—identity was found in the family, not in the individual. Achan's and Rahab's choices were family choices, not just individual ones. Therefore, the family was bound up in the consequences.

Background Information

Tearing of clothes, dust on the head. These were typical acts of one in mourning. One explanation for these practices was that they mimicked the appearance of a dead person in the grave, with deterioriated clothes and covered in dust.

Casting lots. The use of lots provided a way for God's direction to be given. Usually the casting of lots involved putting markers into a container and shaking the container until one of the markers bounced out. Because no hand was put into the container to withdraw the lot, no human had a role in the outcome.

Ai. There is still some dispute about the location of Ai but the current consensus identifies it with et-Tell, about nine miles west-northwest of Jericho. Even though the site is more than twice as large as Jericho, it was apparently sparsely populated (7:3) and perhaps not heavily fortified. The problem with the site is that it shows no evidence of having been occupied during the Late Bronze era (the period of Joshua).

Mistakes to Avoid

Of course, one could easily use Achan as a negative role model to warn students not to be disobedient or to steal. With a very slight reorientation—focusing the story on God rather than on Achan—we can note that God intends his commandments to be taken seriously and that disobedience can have significant consequences. One of our goals of teaching is to help students understand that right behavior is based on an understanding of God, not just on imitating or not imitating others. So while it is true that we should not steal or disobey like Achan, the point is that the reason for not stealing or disobeying is that we understand how important obedience is to God. It is true that Achan gives in to temptation, and we should strive to resist temptation. At the same time, this is not a story about resisting temptation. Likewise, this is not just a case of simple theft; it is theft of something that technically belongs to God. It is a covenant violation that impacted God's covenant people and covenant promises—this is the point. This would not be an appropriate story for the youngest children

40. Joshua and the Gibeonites (Joshua 9–10)

Lesson Focus

Joshua was tricked into making a treaty with the Gibeonites. The other cities in the south were distressed by the Gibeonite desertion and laid siege to their city. Joshua responded to the Gibeonite request for help, and God gave the Israelites victory over their enemy.

- God is willing to fight for his people.
- God is responsive to the prayers of his people.

Lesson Application

God is willing to hear our prayers and able to do great things.

- We should make our prayers known to God.
- We should believe that God is able to overcome the difficulties of our circumstances.

Biblical Context

The purpose of the book of Joshua is summarized in 21:43–45: "Thus the LORD gave to Israel all the land. . . . And they took possession of it, and they settled there. And the LORD gave them rest on every side. . . . The LORD had given all their enemies into their hands. Not one word of all the good promises that the LORD had made to the house of Israel had failed; all came to pass." The book shows how God kept his covenant promise to give the land to Israel. He prepared them to enter Canaan, sent his commander to lead them (5:13–15), provided aid in battles, distributed the land, and renewed the covenant. The story of the Gibeonites shows God continuing to take an active role in the victories over the Canaanites. Joshua 9 sets up the situation in order to explain why the southern cities attacked Gibeon and how Joshua and the Israelites got involved. Joshua 10 shows the Lord's role in the battle, which is always the core interest of the narrator.

Interpretational Issues in the Story

"Did not ask counsel from the LORD" (Josh. 9:14). The narrator might have included this statement as a rebuke of Joshua and the elders, but it is also an important detail that explains how this unlikely alliance was formed. More significant is that this serves as another example in which those who intentionally aligned themselves with Israel and Yahweh (like Rahab) found mercy. In contrast, the other cities adopt an aggressive rather than submissive posture and were destroyed. Yahweh did not give approval for this alliance, but he honored it along with Israel.

Swore to them (Josh. 9:15). The covenant was ratified by statements sworn to by oath in the name of deity. Oaths were used for testimony given in court or for agreements made between parties, as here. Oaths called down the severest judgment on any party that would violate the agreement, and they were taken with utmost seriousness. Even though the Gibeonites had lied, the oath was binding.

Joshua's request that the sun stand still (Josh. 10:12–13). Too often we approach this passage with physics rather than with the thinking of the ancient world in mind. The ancients believed that the sun moved around the earth, and that belief is reflected in the request that the sun stop. But in the ancient world, the celestial realm was the place of signs and wonders, not physics and laws of motion. It is important to notice that as Joshua addressed the sun and moon, the sun was over Gibeon and the moon over Aijalon. That means that it was morning, because Aijalon was in the west. Consequently, the scenario is not that dusk was approaching and Joshua needed more time to procure the victory. Rather, it was morning, and Joshua was looking for an edge in the attack after the tiring forced march that had taken all the previous night. When we think of the situation in terms of signs and wonders, we must take note of what we know of celestial divination in the ancient world. It is likely that Joshua was not requesting this sign because he took divination seriously but because he knew that his enemy did (see Background Information below for more details).

"The LORD heeded the voice of a man" (Josh. 10:14). Verse 14 indicates that the day was unique not because of the celestial phenomena that occurred but because God listened to Joshua's prayer. God's listening to prayer and answering it is unique because, in this prayer, Joshua was suggesting to God what sort of divine role God should play. That is usually God's choice and not subject to human input.

Background Information

Gibeon. Gibeon (el-Jib) is located about fifteen miles west of Jericho. Not much has been found at the site from this time period, but serious excavation has not taken place there for half a century, and even then it was not extensive work.

Southern coalition. The southern coalition was led by Jerusalem and includes southern hill country cities such as Hebron and many in the Shephelah, the rolling hills descending to the coast, such as Lachish. The land at this time was not a nation but was populated by scattered city-states, each with its own rulers. Only in times of threat were they likely to band together.

Celestial divination. In the ancient world everyone used a lunar calendar. The month began with the first appearance of the new moon, and the full moon always came in the middle of the month. The months were of variable length depending on when the next new moon finally made its appearance. The length of the month was considered a matter of good or ill omen and was determined by which day the full moon appeared. The first day of full moon is indicated when, in the morning, the moon sits fully visible just above the western horizon, and the sun sits fully visible just above the eastern horizon (at daybreak). In the ancient world, for this to happen on the fourteenth of the month was a good omen—both the month and the days were the right length. If the full moon happened on the fifteenth or the thirteenth, this was a bad omen. According to ancient Assyrian texts, it could mean the destruction of cities or that the land might be overrun by enemies. In the divination texts from Mesopotamia, the observations about these movements of the sun and moon often used language about the sun and moon "stopping" and "waiting" when discussing whether the full moon conjunction will occur. If the month was the "right" length, they would speak of it containing full-length days. Here in Joshua we see the same language of stopping and waiting and the observation that when Joshua's request happened, it was not as on a full-length day. Joshua was asking for the sun and moon to be in the position that the diviners in the enemy camp would interpret as a bad omen for battle so that the Israelites will have the psychological advantage.

Mistakes to Avoid

While it may be true that there is mild rebuke to Joshua for not inquiring of the Lord, this is not supposed to be a lesson about neglecting God in one's decision-making process. Therefore, that should not take central place in the lesson. Nor is it intended to serve as a model for showing mercy when someone lies to us or as a lesson about how God will bring victory to our lives when we acknowledge sinful behavior. These are minor issues in the text and do not carry the teaching of the text. Teachers should also avoid assuming that there was a massive halting of the movement of heavenly bodies. It is not that God could not do such things, but the text does not demand this interpretation. Young children will have difficulty with the whole idea of celestial divination, and in such cases vague wording could be used along this line: "Joshua asked God to give a special sign using the sun and the moon and God listened to his prayer."

41. Joshua Divides the Land (Joshua 13–21)

Lesson Focus

God gave Israel the land he had promised in the covenant with Abraham.

- God is faithful to keep the promises of his covenant.
- God is powerful to overcome obstacles.

Lesson Application

We should trust God to keep his promises and recognize his extraordinary acts on our behalf.

- We believe that God is able to keep his promises.
- We respond gratefully to God when he provides for us.

Biblical Context

The purpose of the book of Joshua is summarized in 21:43–45: "Thus the LORD gave to Israel all the land. . . . And they took possession of it, and they settled there. And the LORD gave them rest on every side. . . . The LORD had given all their enemies into their hands. Not one word of all the good promises that the LORD had made to the house of Israel had failed; all came to pass." The book shows how God kept his covenant promise to give the land to Israel. He prepared them to enter Canaan, sent his commander to lead them (5:13–15), provided aid in battles, distributed the land, and renewed the covenant. The division of the land, though not much of a story, is an incredible climax of the process that had brought the Israelites from their slavery in Egypt to the land that God had promised to Abraham through the covenant made over four centuries earlier. This is fulfillment of covenant promise on a grand scale.

Interpretational Issues in the Story

Land apportionment (Josh. 13:6). Note that some tribes got more land, some got land with more resources, some got land that was more fruitful, and some got land that was more strategically located. Each portion of land became that tribe's "slice of the covenant," yet it was still considered to be God's land that the tribes held in trust.

Levitical cities (Joshua 21). The Levites were the priestly tribe and were not assigned a single territory because they needed to serve throughout the land. Consequently, forty-eight towns scattered throughout the territory were allotted to the Levites. From there they instructed the people and probably collected tithes. Six of these cities were also designated cities of refuge, where someone accused of murder could flee until the case was adjudicated.

Background Information

Tribal territories. These assigned territories became the foundation for the tribal holdings throughout the centuries of the monarchy, though Solomon attempted redistricting for administrative purposes. Tribal lands were further distributed to the clans of the tribe and then to families in the clan. As generation followed generation, sons continued to subdivide the family holdings among them. In theory the lands could never be removed from one clan or tribe to another.

Mistakes to Avoid

We should avoid the "lesson by analogy" approach; that is, we should not challenge students to consider, "What is the land that the Lord has given to you?" The lesson is not carried on the vehicle of the land but is focused on the character of the God who was able to deliver the land. We should not even ask, "What has God promised to you that you can believe he will deliver on?" The problem with doing so is that we often end up identifying "promises" that are not really promises and as a result focus too much on the benefits we stand to receive. It is true that God makes benefits available to us, but our attitude should be like the psalmist's: "There is nothing on earth that I desire besides you" (Ps. 73:25).

42. The Pattern of the Judges and Ehud (Judges 2–3)

Lesson Focus

After Joshua and the generation that saw God's deliverance from Egypt had died, the Israelites stopped following God. Each time a generation fell into apostasy, God allowed Israel to be oppressed by enemies. In their distress, the Israelites cried out to God for help; each time he raised up a leader to deliver the people from the oppressors. When the Israelites cried out for relief from the oppression of the king of Moab, God raised up Ehud to deliver them.

- God takes seriously the sin of his people and brings punishment.

- God is able to bring relief when his people cry out to him for help.
- God controls the nations, even those who know nothing of him.

Lesson Application

The Lord is our God. We will worship him alone and obey him.

- We must not expect that God will just ignore our sin and not bring consequences.
- When troubles come, we must seek God.
- We are to be faithful to God.

Biblical Context

The book of Judges shows the failure of the Israelites to keep their part of the covenant. The cycles (repeating periods of disobedience, punishment, cry for help, deliverance) show how God demonstrated his power and mercy by delivering his people time after time after his justice had demanded that he bring punishment. The book shows that neither the leadership of the judges nor the tribal leadership succeeded in helping the people remain faithful. Instead, the leaders were as bad as the people.

Interpretational Issues in the Story

Cycles (Judg. 2:11–19). The cycle introduced in Judges 2 (disobedience, punishment, cry for help, deliverance) is central to the book. It is the key to God's revelation of himself in the book as one who executes justice, shows sovereignty, and offers mercy. The entire judges period is seen in light of this pattern.

Cried out to the Lord (Judg. 3:9, 15). In most cases through the book of Judges it does not say that the people cried out in repentance (10:15 is an exception) but only that they cried out in distress for help.

Judges (Judg. 2:16). The judges in this book were deliverers. They were called "judges" because they brought justice. They did not bring it through enforcement of the law in the courtroom as in our day; rather, they brought it through battling those who were oppressing the people. In the case of the major judges (the ones connected to cycles) their role was military, not civil.

Left-handed (Judg. 3:15). The Hebrew text indicates that Ehud was "bound with regard to his right hand," which is likely a reference to a type of military training where the natural right arm was immobilized in order to force the soldier to learn skill with both hands. It is the same in sports today in which right-side dominant players are taught to use their left hand or left foot to become more effective. Whole squads of infantry were trained this way (20:16). Consequently, if Ehud had to be trained this way, he was not naturally left-handed.

Background Information

Judges period. The judges period lasted several centuries. The starting date is dependent on what date is assigned to the exodus (still an open question), but the period of the judges came to a close in about 1050 BC.

Baal and Asherah. Baal was the storm god of the Canaanites and was considered responsible for the fertility of the earth. Asherah was associated with the fertility of people. They were two of the principal gods of the Canaanites, which shows that the Israelites were indeed influenced by those who remained in the land. While adopting the worship of Baal and Asherah the people had not necessarily given up the worship of Yahweh. They had simply adopted other gods alongside Yahweh, as polytheists tended to do (cf. 6:13 and 6:25).

Mistakes to Avoid

It is important to make the distinction that the judges were not necessarily heroes; they were people used by God, sometimes despite themselves. The fact that the Spirit of God sometimes came upon them does not mean that they were spiritual people. In fact, the evidence usually points in the other direction. It is God who was delivering Israel through the judge. The focus should not be on the role model provided by the judges (either good or bad) but on what God was doing through them. It is true that children need heroes, but more importantly they need to know God and learn how to interpret the Bible correctly. The fact that Hebrews 11 singles out several judges for their faith does not negate the many bad decisions they made. Avoid putting the judges up on pedestals; the text does not do so. For younger children the teacher may want to use only the part about the cycles, given the graphic violence in the story of Ehud.

43. Deborah and Barak (Judges 4–5)

Lesson Focus

When the Israelites cried out for relief from the oppression of the Canaanites, God raised up Deborah to deliver them. It is clear that the defeat of Sisera's superior army and the death of Sisera were from the hand of God.

- God provided direction for battle and provided victory.
- God can use unlikely people to accomplish his plan.

Lesson Application

The Lord is our God. We will worship and obey him.

- When we are faithful, God is able to do great things through us.
- We should believe that God is able to overcome the most difficult disadvantages.

Biblical Context

The book of Judges shows the failure of the Israelites to keep their part of the covenant. The cycles (repeating periods of disobedience, punishment, cry for help, deliverance) show how God demonstrated his power and mercy by delivering his people time after time after his justice had demanded that he bring punishment. The book shows that neither the leadership of the judges nor the tribal leadership succeeded in helping the people remain faithful. Instead, the leaders were often as bad as the people. Deborah was certainly an exception to this, as she was a faithful prophetess and brought deliverance in association with the commander Barak.

Interpretational Issues in the Story

Deborah's role and Barak's reluctance (Judg. 4:8). Deborah was first and foremost a prophetess, one who brought God's word to the people. People came to her for decisions (4:5) because she would inquire of God for them. It is likely that in this particular instance they came to ask God what they should do about the Canaanite armies. She responded by sending for Barak and giving him God's orders. Barak was not acting cowardly when he insisted that Deborah accompany him. She was the connection to the Lord, and it was the Lord's battle. It shows faith, because he did not want to go in his own strength. The apparent rebuke (4:9) indicates an unexpected result. Most would expect that the glory of the victory would fall to the commander, but Deborah indicates that the glory of the victory would belong to a woman. The text stops short of saying that Barak himself believed that he would gain glory through this. His insistence that Deborah join him already indicates that he did not intend to rely on his own strength.

Background Information

Location of the battle. The Israelite troops mustered on the top of Mount Tabor, where they would not be attacked but could be surrounded. The mountain is isolated in the middle of the Valley of Jezreel, which was a flat area about twenty miles square, and was a regular battlefield because the major international roads in the land passed through it. The Kishon River did not run with water year-long but only during the times when there was runoff from the Carmel mountain range. Therefore, Sisera would not have hesitated to bring his chariots there, but a flash flood could have spelled disaster.

Iron chariots. These chariots were not made entirely from iron. In this period iron was a precious metal and used for decoration. Its strengthening properties also made it useful for reinforcing joints and sheathing the wheels.

Mistakes to Avoid

The story features a number of characters who perform heroically, but, as always, we must keep in mind that the hero is the Lord—he is the one who brings victory and deliverance. Students should not be encouraged to try to be like Deborah—she was a prophetess, and such a role is no longer in existence. God used people of all sorts here, but it is God's work that needs to be the focus. Sometimes points are made about Deborah being obedient or Barak being fearful or even cowardly, but those points do not come from the text and therefore should not be set forth as the lesson from the Bible. It is important that we not impose any limitations as to what God is able to do, but teachers should avoid suggesting that God will overcome every obstacle or disadvantage that the students might have. He is able to, but God works in his own ways. The graphic violence in the act of Jael may make this story inappropriate for younger children

44. Gideon (Judges 6–8)

Lesson Focus

In spite of his weak character, Gideon acted in faith, and God was with Gideon and Israel to defeat the Midianites.

- God can work through anyone to accomplish his plans.
- God at times indulges our weak faith to encourage us.
- God is able to work through few just as effectively as through many.

- God is the one who brings the victory.

Lesson Application

God is with those who trust in him.

- We believe that God can use us for his work regardless of our social status or personal skills or how few our numbers.
- When we are faithful and responsible in small things, God may call us to bigger things.
- We must expect that when God uses us in his work, he may ask us to step out of our comfort zone.

Biblical Context

The book of Judges shows the failure of the Israelites to keep their part of the covenant. The cycles (repeating periods of disobedience, punishment, cry for help, deliverance) show how God demonstrated his power and mercy by delivering them time after time after his justice had demanded that he bring punishment. The book shows that neither the leadership of the judges nor the tribal leadership succeeded in helping the people remain faithful. Instead, the leaders were often as bad as the people. Though God brings victory through Gideon, his weaknesses are evident throughout the narrative.

Interpretational Issues in the Story

Angel of the Lord (Judg. 6:11–12, 20–22). The angel of the Lord is a messenger who brings God's word to people. In the ancient world direct communication between important parties was a rarity. Diplomatic exchange normally required the use of an intermediary. Messengers were like ambassadors and were vested with the authority to speak for the party they represented and were expected to be treated as if they were the dignitary in person. This is why in some contexts it is hard to distinguish whether God or the messenger is speaking. The messenger may speak in the first person as God.

"The Spirit of the LORD clothed Gideon" (Judg. 6:34). In the Old Testament, the Spirit of the Lord was usually seen in empowering people to a task. Today we talk of the Spirit's indwelling people when they become Christians. These are very different things, and therefore this incident in Judges should not be viewed as the beginning of Gideon's spiritual relationship with God. The endowment of the Spirit here has to do with his role as general.

Gideon's fleece (Judg. 6:36–40). This most well-known part of the story is also the most misunderstood. Gideon lays out the fleece not in a grassy field but on the threshing floor, which was usually made of rock. Consequently, it is to be expected that the soft, absorbent fleece would be damp with dew while the rock of the threshing floor remained dry. Gideon is using the dew and the fleece for an oracle. In an oracle, a yes-or-no question was posed to deity, and some mechanism was designated for deity to answer. When something from the world around served as that mechanism, the procedure was to designate normal expected results as one answer and highly unusual, extraordinary results as the other. That is what Gideon was doing here. Since God had already sent an angel to tell him that he was supposed to lead the armies into battle, Gideon wanted to check to see if those orders were still in place. He designed this oracle to give the Lord a chance to communicate a change in orders. Gideon said, "If there is dew on the fleece alone, and it is dry on all the ground, then I shall know that you will save Israel by my hand, as you have said" (v. 37). If the answer was yes (orders unchanged), Gideon asked for the normal occurrence to take place: fleece wet with dew, threshing floor dry. After that happened, however, Gideon found himself still plagued with doubt—what if the Lord was simply ignoring him? So with great apology (appropriate, since God had already given instruction), he then asked for the indicator to be switched; having the fleece dry and the threshing floor wet. This does indeed show a lack of faith on his part.

Water test for warriors (Judg. 7:5–7). Many interpreters have seen in this test an indication of which soldiers were savvy and alert. Unfortunately, interpreters cannot agree on whether the savvy ones were the three hundred who were kept or the rest who were sent home. Others conclude that the test is arbitrary and has nothing to do with military skills. Since the text does not sufficiently clarify the situation, it would be best not to build a particular theory into the lesson.

Ephod (Judg. 8:27). The ephod was originally a piece of clothing (e.g., that worn by the priest, Ex. 28:6–14). In the ancient world around Israel, just as the gods were fed (sacrifices) and housed (temples) they were also clothed (that is, the images were). It is possible that Gideon's ephod represented the clothing of Yahweh (not actually on an image) just as the ark was the footstool of Yahweh's throne. As such it could be used as an oracular device. Since Gideon had been "successful" in gaining an oracle from God by means of the fleece, it would seem that he decided to exploit this success as he set up this oracular device so that he could serve as a mediator of God's communication to the people. If the fleece showed a weakness, as we have suggested, the ephod institutionalizes that weakness.

Background Information

Midianites. The Midianites were semi-nomadic people whose ancestry goes back to Abraham (Gen. 25:2). These were the people that Moses spent his time with during his exile and from whom he acquired his wife (Ex. 2:15–21).

Threshing wheat in a winepress. Threshing is the process by which the grain is separated from the stalk. It was usually done in a large open area of rock or hard pounded dirt (the threshing floor) because the next step was winnowing, which involved throwing the product high in the air so that the wind would blow away the waste and the seed would fall to the ground. The winnowing process could be observed from quite a distance, and, in this case, could draw the invaders who would then confiscate the harvest. The winepress was generally more compact and not necessarily out in the open. By using it, Gideon could not process nearly the volume of grain, but at least the Midianites would not be alerted to the activity. This was not the behavior of a coward but of a careful person trying to provide for his family.

Baal and Asherah. Baal was the storm god of the Canaanites and considered responsible for the fertility of the earth. Asherah was associated with the fertility of people. They were two of the principal gods of the Canaanites, the worship of which influenced those who remained in the land. We should not think that in adopting the worship of Baal and Asherah that the people had given up the worship of Yahweh. They had simply adopted other gods alongside Yahweh, as polytheists tended to do (cf. Judg. 6:13, 25).

Trumpets and torches. Trumpets (here the ram's horn, *shofar*) were used for giving signals for the army, and torches were used to light up the battle arena and form a perimeter for night operations. Usually only a few soldiers were assigned to each task because most were engaged in the fighting. When the Midianites awoke to see three hundred torches and heard hundreds of trumpets sound, they must have immediately concluded that there was an enormous fighting force, since this many could be spared for the noncombat functions.

Mistakes to Avoid

Using a fleece-like test is not an appropriate way to discover God's will. God indulged Gideon's weakness, but that does not mean that he approved of Gideon's procedure. The problem with Gideon's procedure is that it, in effect, pushed God into a corner. No matter what happened, Gideon was going to take the result as God's communication, thus demanding that God communicate in Gideon's way and in Gideon's time. This is not how God ought to be treated. He communicates in his own time in his own way. God is not obligated to respond to such contrived methods. Younger children would certainly have difficulty understanding the premise underlying oracles, which play a visible role in this story. It is interesting that sometimes Gideon is portrayed as a coward in the opening scene, where he was just trying to be cautious and responsible, but as a person of spiritual discernment in the fleece incident, when he was manipulating God. This shows how mistaken we can be when we try to turn the biblical characters into role models. As always, this is not about the hero Gideon; it is about the sovereign God.

45. Jephthah (Judges 10:6–11:40)

Lesson Focus

When the Ammonites oppressed Israel, God brought deliverance through an unlikely leader, Jephthah, despite Jephthah's misguided attempt to assure God's favor. Even though the Israelites were delivered, Jephthah suffered the consequences of his poor understanding of God.

- God may choose unlikely people through whom to work.
- God cannot be bought.
- God at times lets us suffer the awful consequences of our decisions, which sometimes affect others as well.
- God can bring victory despite the weaknesses of his people.

Lesson Application

We should not think that God cannot use us for his work because of our history or status.

- We should seek to honor God as we serve him, lest we suffer the consequences of our foolishness.
- Even though we make mistakes, we should recognize that God can use us anyway.
- Even if we are not rich or important, we may be confident that God can use us.

Biblical Context

The book of Judges shows the failure of the Israelites to keep their part of the covenant. The cycles (repeating periods of disobedience, punishment, cry for help, deliverance) show how God demonstrated his power and mercy by delivering them time after time after his justice had demanded that he bring punishment. The book shows that neither the leadership of the judges nor the tribal leadership succeeded in helping the people remain faithful. Instead, the leaders were often as bad as the people. Jephthah contributes to the author's purpose as a tragic example of how little the people understood of God and his ways and how they tried to manipulate him.

Interpretational Issues in the Story

Mighty warrior (Judg. 11:1). The text identifies Jephthah as a skilled warrior. He may at times have served as a mercenary, other times as an outlaw. His skills gave him something to offer the tribal leaders when they became desperate enough.

"Then the Spirit of the LORD *was upon Jephthah" (Judg. 11:29).* In the Old Testament, the Spirit of the Lord was usually seen in empowering people to a task. Today we talk of the Spirit's indwelling people when they become Christians. These are very different things, and therefore this incident in Judges should not be viewed as the beginning of Jephthah's spiritual relationship with God. The endowment of the Spirit here has to do with his role as general.

Unbreakable vow (Judg. 11:35). Jephthah's vow, like all vows in the ancient world, was made in the name of the deity. It was the promise to give something (usually a sacrifice) in return for some favor or benefit asked for from the deity. People believed that deity would hold people to their vow and that the consequences for breaking it would involve a far greater cost than anything that had been pledged. Jephthah's commitment to carry out the vow is commendable and is all the more tragic in light of his ignorance in making such a vow with the assumption that it would please God.

Sacrifice or dedication (Judg. 11:39). Since the narrative concludes with the statement that Jephthah's daughter was a virgin (11:39), some have tried to make the case that she was dedicated to lifelong service at the sanctuary rather than to slaughter as a human sacrifice. While this option is much more comfortable for us, the text makes it unlikely. First, Jephthah was expecting a human being to meet him (11:31)—no animals would come out of the house to greet him. Second, he specified that a burnt offering would result, a word that always entails the slaughter of the sacrifice. Third, there is no history of women serving the Israelite sanctuary in perpetual virginity. Finally, the emphasis on his daughter's virginity indicates the long-term effect of Jephthah's vow—he had no heir. This is far more significant in the ancient world than it would be in ours.

Support for a human sacrifice (Judg. 11:39). Would any priest do such a thing? Would the people not intervene and prevent it? We must remember that this is the judges period, which was characterized by Israel's participation in all sorts of pagan activity. One of the points of Judges is that God called out flawed leaders from a very disobedient people. Even Israel's priests had adopted the polytheistic thinking and pagan practices of the cultures around them (see Judges 17–21, esp. 18:30).

Background Information

Tribal groups. During the judges period, Israel was governed by tribal leaders in their tribal territories. There was no central civil authority (such as a king), because central authority belonged only to the Lord. When a person from one tribe successfully summoned those from another tribe, it was viewed as the work of the Spirit of the Lord because no one had authority over another tribe. We can see in this passage that there were disputes within and between tribes.

Baal and Asherah. Baal was the storm god of the Canaanites and considered responsible for the fertility of the earth. Asherah was associated with the fertility of people. They were two of the principal gods of the Canaanites, showing how the Israelites were indeed influenced by those who remained in the land. We should not think that in adopting the worship of Baal and Asherah that the people had given up the worship of Yahweh. They had simply adopted other gods alongside Yahweh, as polytheists tended to do (cf. Judg. 6:13, 25).

Chemosh. Chemosh was the national god of the Moabites. Jephthah did not try to mount an argument that Chemosh does not exist (such would have been beyond his theology anyway), but rather that the Moabites should have been satisfied with what they believed Chemosh had given them as their core land holdings.

Mistakes to Avoid

This story is inappropriate for young children. Downplaying Jephthah's error would be a mistake, as would justifying his vow or softening his execution of the vow. The biblical text need not be protected through such strategies. Jephthah is presented with all his problems and weaknesses as the instrument used by God. No one is a perfect instrument. We do not have to salvage Jephthah's character or spirituality just because he was a judge or because the

Spirit of the Lord came upon him. The Spirit did not transform him but gave him authority to raise armies that he had no right to command.

46. Samson and the Philistines (Judges 13–15)

Lesson Focus

God promised Manoah and his wife a son who would deliver Israel from the Philistines. Samson was set apart to God from birth and empowered to fight against the oppressing Philistines.

- God raises up people to serve him in dire circumstances.
- God sometimes uses people even when they are unaware that he is using them.
- God can use even people's mistakes to carry out his plan.

Lesson Application

The Lord is our God. We will worship and obey him.

- Even though God can use us despite our mistakes, we ought to be good stewards of the gifts and roles that he has given us.
- Even though political leaders may at times be unethical, corrupt, and in pursuit of selfish ends, we should recognize that God can use them to accomplish his purposes.

Biblical Context

The book of Judges shows the failure of the Israelites to keep their part of the covenant. The cycles (repeating periods of disobedience, punishment, cry for help, deliverance) show how God demonstrated his power and mercy by delivering them time after time after his justice had demanded that he bring punishment. The book shows that neither the leadership of the judges nor the tribal leadership succeeded in helping the people remain faithful. Instead, the leaders were often as bad as the people. Samson was worse than all the other judges as he pursued his own lust and personal agendas, yet God still used him to deliver the Israelites.

Interpretational Issues in the Story

Angel of the Lord (Judges 13). The angel of the Lord occurs here as well as in the story of Gideon (Judges 6). Some have concluded that the angel is deity because, in his speech and actions, he often merges with the Lord (6:11–14; 13:18–20). Throughout history some have made the more specific claim that he is preincarnate Christ. It must be noted, however, that the angel also distinguishes between himself and God (13:16). In light of the fact that in the ancient world messengers often spoke as if they actually were the one they represented, it is preferable to understand the angel of the Lord as a messenger rather than as actual deity; but a variety of opinions exists.

"A Nazarite to God from the womb" (Judg. 13:5, 7). By design the Nazirite vow was supposed to endure for a designated, limited time of heightened dedication. We do not have enough knowledge of it to know why it included the elements that it did (e.g., prohibition of cutting hair and eating or drinking anything connected to grapes). Only in Samson and Samuel do we see the extension of the vow to someone's entire life.

"The LORD . . . was seeking an opportunity against the Philistines" (Judg. 14:4). This is a rare comment from the narrator identifying God's motivation for what he was doing. God was going to use Samson, whether he would make good choices or bad ones. It does not suggest that Samson had no choices but that God was going to accomplish his plan through Samson, even when he was not honoring the Lord.

The Spirit of the Lord began to stir him (Judg. 13:25). In the Old Testament, the Spirit of the Lord was usually seen in empowering people to a task. Today we talk of the Spirit's indwelling people when they become Christians. These are very different things, and therefore this incident in Judges should not be viewed as the beginning of Samson's spiritual relationship with God. The endowment of the Spirit here had to do with his role as general.

Foxes (Judg. 15:4). The Hebrew word can refer to either foxes or jackals, and the latter is more likely in this context.

Background Information

Location of events. The central area of Samson's early adventures is the Sorek Valley. This is one of the important passes between the coastal plain (Philistine territory) and the central hill country (Israelite territory). Zorah and Timnah are at opposite ends of this valley. Samson eventually ranged throughout Philistine territory and its five major cities: Ekron, Gath, Ashdod, Ashkelon, and Gath.

Killing the lion. In ancient literature, kings and heroes were sometimes portrayed as killing a lion. While this episode fits a standard heroic feat, it also demonstrates Samson's disregard for his vow, as he did not hesitate to scoop honey from the corpse of the lion. This incident also provides a literary function—it gives the basis for the riddle at the wedding.

Samson's wife. Marriages were arranged in the ancient world and represented alliances between peoples. This is why it is so distressing that Samson, supposedly raised to be a deliverer of Israel, wanted to marry a Philistine (oppressors of Israel). Weddings did not feature a sacred ceremony but involved the exchange of wealth (bride price and dowry) and then a feast marking a formal recognition of the marriage. Even then, there was a sense in which the marriage was not finalized until the woman conceived, because the husband could discard her if she was unable to bear children. In some cases she continued to live in her father's house after the feast, and her husband would visit until she conceived a child. Samson assumes this situation and visited one whom he believed was his wife, whereas her father had given her to another.

Mistakes to Avoid

Samson should not be made a model of either heroic deeds or sinful actions, though he is shown doing both. We can neither excuse nor explain his behavior, nor should we lead children to idolize him. Discussion of superheroes should not be the direction of the lesson, nor should anger management or choosing a spouse. Samson is driven by his selfish agendas and is as weak in spirit as he is strong in body. But neither weakness nor strength is the point. He was God's instrument. His strength was given by God and used by God. The weakness was Samson's responsibility, and he suffered the consequences of it. This cannot be turned into a lesson about being kind to animals or about how important it is to obey one's parents because they know best. For younger audiences the treatment of the animals would be inappropriate to include.

47. Samson and Delilah (Judges 16)

Lesson Focus

Samson became infatuated with Delilah, who had conspired for vast sums of money to deliver him to the Philistines. Samson confided to her about his strength and was taken prisoner. Later, when he was brought before the Philistines for ridicule, he pulled down their temple, and Samson as well as many of the Philistines were killed as God's punishment.

- God accomplishes his plans despite the failures of those through whom he is working.
- God allows us to suffer the consequences of our bad choices.
- God is concerned about his people.

Lesson Application

We should believe that God can always find a way to carry out his plan.

- Even when we are misguided, willful, and distant from God, he can use us to carry out his plan, but there may be consequences for our sin.
- We should recognize how God is able to work through events to arrange situations for his plan to be carried out.

Biblical Context

The book of Judges shows the failure of the Israelites to keep their part of the covenant. The cycles (repeating periods of disobedience, punishment, cry for help, deliverance) show how God demonstrated his power and mercy by delivering them time after time after his justice had demanded that he bring punishment. The book shows that neither the leadership of the judges nor the tribal leadership succeeded in helping the people remain faithful. Instead, the leaders were often as bad as the people. Samson continues his wayward behavior in this account, and the Lord shows that he can bring punishment to the Philistines even through Samson's failures. Even in the end, as he is given the Lord's strength to bring down the Philistine temple, Samson can think only of taking revenge.

Interpretational Issues in the Story

Delilah (Judg. 16:4). The text never identifies Delilah as a Philistine. She does not live in a Philistine town. She may have been a Philistine, but we should not assume so. Even an Israelite woman might have been willing to betray her people for the enormous sum offered (5,500 shekels of silver). A normal wage at this period would have been ten to twelve shekels per year.

Samson's hair and strength (Judg. 16:17). Samson's hair was not really the source of his strength. God was the source of his strength, but his uncut hair represented his most minimal commitment to God. With his hair gone, all connection to his commitment was severed. The Philistines believed that Samson's strength was magical, which is why the first explanations Samson gave Delilah were magical in nature.

"The Philistines are upon you" (Judg. 16:9, 12, 14, 20). If Samson saw

that Delilah repeatedly brought the Philistines in once she had bound him, why did Samson keep giving her information? In fact, though it is clear the Philistines were on the premises, the text does not say that the Philistines showed themselves each time; she only wakes him with that cry to see if he can overcome what has been done to him. Only the last time indicates that the Philistines actually attempted to subdue him.

"The L*ORD had left him" (Judg. 16:20).* God had been the source of Samson's strength, not his size, physique, or conditioning, and certainly not his hair, which was merely the sign of his vow to God (regardless of how often he broke it). When God abandoned him to the choices he had made, he had no power to resist.

"He entertained them" (Judg. 16:25). The Philistines brought out Samson to make a mockery of him. Cruel tricks on a blind person would suit the language used here, but the text is not specific.

Background Information

Looms. Looms stretched the warp threads between poles and then passed the shuttle with the thread of the woof between them. In this scenario, Samson's hair substituted for the threads of the woof and was basically sewn into the fabric.

Philistine temples. Evidence from archaeology (such as from the Philistine temple of this period excavated at Tel Qasile) shows that there were a series of paired pillars stretching across the courtyard. They held up the weight of the roof. It is difficult to tell whether the pillars were made of wood resting on stone bases or of stone cylinders positioned on top of one another. In either case, Samson would have twisted the pillars off their bases to bring the roof down.

Mistakes to Avoid

Samson is a tragic figure despite his feats of strength. Teachers should avoid turning him into a hero. Students should not even be led to think that he redeemed himself at the end, for in the end he can think only of revenge.

48. Ruth (Ruth)

Lesson Focus

The book of Ruth portrays a pocket of faithfulness to God in Israel during the period of the judges. The loyalty of Ruth to Naomi and the righteousness of

Boaz form the backdrop to God's gracious provision of offspring to Naomi, through whom will come King David and ultimately Jesus.

- God is faithful to his people.
- God's faithfulness finds root in even the simplest faithfulness of people toward one another.
- God provides for the vulnerable.
- God can use common folk (Ruth) as the foundation for major stages in his plan (David).
- God recognizes and values faithfulness in his people.

Lesson Application

The Lord is our God. We will worship and obey him.

- We must believe that God can preserve his people.
- We should cultivate faithfulness to one another.

Biblical Context

The book of Ruth shows that when people are faithful, God is faithful. It provides a contrast to the book of Judges, showing that even during those centuries of apostasy, faithfulness survived in Israel among some of the common folk. God preserved such families of faithfulness, and that is the very background from which David came.

Interpretational Issues in the Story

Leaving the land (Ruth 1:1). Whenever people were forced to leave the covenant Promised Land, it can be construed as either punishment or neglect of God. Since this story is in the judges period when the people were constantly unfaithful, we can infer that the famine was part of God's judgment. Drought and famine were included in the curses for violating the covenant (Deut. 28:23–24).

Ruth's confession (Ruth 1:16–17). In some senses this is the foundation of the book, but we must observe carefully what it says and what it does not say. Ruth's expression of faithfulness was focused on Naomi, not on Yahweh. Her commitment was to Naomi's God because he was Naomi's God, not because she had been convinced of the theological supremacy of Yahweh and the worthlessness of idols. Her statement was about family—she was going to remain a part of Naomi's family with all that entailed rather than returning to her own family (land, gods, burial). She understood that Yahweh was part of the package deal, but her commitment was to Naomi. Boaz confirmed this

(2:11), and this minimal understanding is important to the book. Her faithfulness put every aspect of her life at risk. This is the kind of faithfulness that God notices and responds to.

Role of the kinsman-redeemer (go'el) (Ruth 2:20). Much of the justice in the ancient world was provided through the family. If property was lost through debt, a *go'el* would seek to recover it. If a family member was killed, a *go'el* would hunt down the killer. If losses from a civil suit were threatening, a *go'el* would seek to assist. A *go'el* protected the tribe's interests and well-being. This included involvement with the remarriage of those who had been widowed and were without descendants, because descendants provided for each family in the tribe from generation to generation. This is also how land was passed and held in the family. It was the role of kinsman-redeemer that Boaz was playing for Naomi and Ruth. The role of *go'el* fell to a member of the tribe through a variety of circumstances. It is logical to infer that the head of the clan was responsible for ensuring that the *go'el* role was carried out.

David (Ruth 4:22). The fact that the book ends with a genealogy leading to David is significant. Having read the book of Judges and being overwhelmed with the centuries of unfaithfulness, we might wonder how there could have been someone like David who was still faithful to the Lord. This book shows us that David came from faithful stock. It also shows us how fragile the thread that led to David. Without Ruth's faithfulness to Naomi, the line would have died and there would have been no David.

Background Information

Moab. Moab is located on the east side of the Jordan River and the Dead Sea across from southern Israel. The Moabites were descended from Lot and therefore related to Israel. In contrast to many places in Israel, the table land of Moab is fertile and suitable to agriculture.

Marriage and religion. In the ancient world, especially in clan-based societies such as Israel, marriage often occurred within the same clan. It was common for a woman to become a member of the man's family. Often, extended families shared homesteads in a family compound. When the wife was from a different tribe, she adopted the tribal identity of her husband. In polytheistic contexts, the wife adopted the gods of her husband's family. This was not a theological decision. Gods were associated with the family, with the town, with the nation, and with the ancestors. Thus, when Ruth married Naomi's son, she would have adopted the God of the family simply as a matter of course. When she decides to stay with Naomi rather than return to her family, she has automatically made the choice to remain aligned with Naomi's God rather than return to the protection of her family's gods. It may be that Ruth had a well-informed commitment to Yahweh, but nothing in her statements to Naomi indicates that.

"Where you die I will die." In the ancient world, everyone believed that the dead continued to exist. Though Egypt had a different understanding of the afterlife, the rest of the ancient world believed that the netherworld was a place neither of reward nor punishment. People thought in terms of joining the community of the ancestors who had died previously. Likewise, the living sought to preserve the memory of the dead as part of their ongoing community. It was often believed that the dead needed nourishment and that the living could supply that. One of the worst things that could happen to people in the ancient world was to die alone with no one to give them proper burial, to remember them, and to provide for their needs (however those needs might be understood). When Ruth committed to dying where Naomi dies (1:17), she indicates that Naomi would not be left alone in death. More significantly, by making this remarkable commitment to Naomi, she jeopardized her own situation, for it would make it likely that she would die alone.

Gleaning. The regulation of leaving for the poor what was missed by the harvesters in the field is not evidenced in other legal collections from the ancient world, though there was widespread concern for caring for the needy. The advantages of the system were twofold: (1) in this way all shared responsibility for the poor; and (2) it involved the poor working for the benefit that they gained. With the system came the inherent dangers of the poor suffering abuse (verbal or physical) at the hands of the workers.

Activities at the threshing floor. After grain was cut down in the fields, it was brought to the threshing floor, an area in the open made of rock or hard pounded dirt. The harvest was spread over the threshing floor where a threshing sledge was pulled over it to separate the grain from the stalk. Then came the winnowing process in which the contents of the threshing floor were thrown high into the air. The grain would fall straight down while the lighter chaff was blown away, which is why the threshing floor had to be in the open. Then the grain was gathered up into piles from where it would be sieved and carried away for storage.

Justice at the city gate or legal transactions at the city gate. The city gate was the main public area of town. Benches typically lined the gate area, and it was there that scribes or witnesses could be found for legal transactions. Elders would at times sit in the gate area to judge cases that were brought for a decision.

Mistakes to Avoid

This short book is filled with impressive characters. Both Ruth and Boaz were remarkable people, and we can learn much from them. The values of friendship, caring for one another, and loving family come through clearly, but what is more important to the book is what God did because of and through the character of Ruth and Boaz. In Judges we found that God can work even through scoundrels. How much more he can do through faithful people! Yes, we would do well to be like Ruth and Boaz in many ways, but the text is meant to point us to God's faithfulness. It would also be a mistake to overplay Ruth's theology. God's faithfulness (eventually realized in David) is seen in all its glory in these circumstances as it dangles by the fragile thread of this young Moabite woman.

49. Eli and Hannah (1 Samuel 1:1–2:11)

Lesson Focus

Hannah is distressed with her inability to have children and goes to God's house offering a vow: if God provides her a son, she will dedicate the son to God for life. God honors her request, and Samuel is born and raised by Eli the priest. These circumstances show God's role in raising up Samuel for the significant role that he will play in bringing God-ordained kingship to Israel.

- God is responsive to the prayer and devotion of his people.
- God sometimes initiates important parts of his plan through common folks who are committed to him.
- God sees people's needs and cares about them.

Lesson Application

We should believe that God is at work carrying out his plan.

- We can pray about our concerns—God hears and cares.
- We should believe that God has a plan and is carrying it out.

Biblical Context

The books of Samuel are about how God established his king, David, on the throne, as a way to show what his own kingship is like. An important part of the book, therefore, is showing that David truly was God's choice for king. David was not an ambitious upstart who overthrew the prior regime and then claimed God had done it—something that happened all the time in the ancient world. The prophet Samuel is the most important piece to this puzzle, because he is the kingmaker. Therefore, the book begins by establishing Samuel's credential as a special instrument of God. He filled three offices: prophet, priest, and judge. This story recounts the unusual circumstances of his birth to a barren woman who then committed him to God for service.

Interpretational Issues in the Story

Yearly worship and sacrifice (1 Sam. 1:3). We are not told whether Elkanah's yearly pilgrimage was connected with one of the three standard feasts. If it was connected, we still do not know which one it was.

Vow (1 Sam. 1:11). Vows in the Bible are generally the promise to give something to God. Many times it was a sacrificial gift. Here it is a son. A vow was not usually a promise to do or become something.

"Ministered to the LORD" (1 Sam. 2:11). From the comment that Elkanah is an Ephraimite (1 Sam. 1:1) we could logically draw the conclusion that he was from the tribe of Ephraim. In contrast, 1 Chronicles 6:26 places him and Samuel in the tribe of Levi, which is more suitable for Samuel's eventual role as priest. We therefore conclude that Samuel's father was a Levite serving in the hill country of Ephraim, where several of the Levitical cities were located. We should also note that in Hebrew Elkanah is identified as an *ephrati* (translated Ephraimite), which is the same word used to describe David's father, Jesse, in 1 Samuel 17:12, who was from the tribe of Judah (note also Mic. 5:2).

"He will give strength to his king" (1 Sam. 2:10). This seems an unusual thing for Hannah to be praying, since Israel has had no kings. Nevertheless, it is evidence that even in these early chapters the scene is being set for kingship to develop.

Background Information

Time period. Precise chronology is not known, but we can place these events with confidence in the middle of the eleventh century BC. This was an interesting time in the ancient world. Major changes had been sweeping the landscape of international politics as the principle powers of the Late Bronze Age (Egypt, Hittites, Assyrians) had for various reasons faded and diminished. A group known as the Sea Peoples had entered the region, and some of them, known to us as the Philistines, had settled along the southern coast of Palestine. The year 1200 BC marks the beginning of what archaeologists designate as the Iron Age, and for the next several centuries the ancient Near East was characterized by a political vacuum with no major powers. It is in this context that David's kingdom was established.

Shiloh. Shiloh was located about halfway between Bethel and Shechem. It was a small site in a strategic location. Soon after this time it was destroyed by the Philistines (see Ps. 78:60 and Jer. 7:12–14), perhaps in the very battle mentioned in 1 Samuel 4. Judges 18:31 reports that it was where the central sanctuary (the tabenacle) was located for a while during the judges period.

Temple. As the story unfolds at the "house of the LORD" (1:7), reference is also made to the temple (1:9), which is not terminology used for the tabernacle. Solomon had not yet built the temple. We might infer that the Israelites had taken over a Canaanite temple and were using it for worship of Yahweh, but the text does not clarify.

Weaned. Weaning generally took place between the ages of two and three.

Mistakes to Avoid

This lesson does not teach that all our requests will be answered in the way that we want them to be. God is carrying out his plan, and he does so through the answer to Hannah's prayer. It is this unfolding plan that should be the focus of the story, not Hannah's circumstances and reactions.

This is not a story about praying when life is getting you down. We should not teach the story by extrapolating Hannah's situation, actions, and character, but by understanding the plan of God unfolding. Peninnah's actions drive Hannah to the sanctuary and to prayer, but she does not pray for grace in dealing with Peninnah. Rather, she has taken Peninnah's scorn to heart and prays that God would resolve her barrenness. The story offers no biblical model on how we should respond to mockers; it only describes what happened on this occasion. For that reason we cannot look to this story to gain pointers about effective prayer. Hannah's prayer was answered because God was ready to provide the king-maker of Israel through her, not because she finally did something right in her prayers.

The story is also not about perseverance in prayer; many barren women have prayed fervently for children yet have not been so blessed. We do well to avoid lessons that take a trivial point described in the story and elevate it to the main point and the authoritative message of the text.

It is common when these early stories about Samuel are told for teachers to conclude that children will not understand the word *temple*, so they substitute the word *church*, which is a serious misidentification. The temple in the ancient world was far different from the church building today. The building that we call "church" is simply the assembly of God's people. It is only a place designated for corporate worship. Even though we sometimes call it "God's house," in reality God is housed within his people, not in a building. In Israel, God chose to live in the temple, and though people gathered in Jerusalem on sacred occasions, the courtyard was not designed for corporate worship and could not accommodate very many. People came to the temple to watch public rituals and to offer sacrifices for themselves or their families. The priests were there to officiate over the rituals and advise about procedures. They also made sure that only those who qualified could enter.

50. Eli and Samuel (1 Samuel 2–3)

Lesson Focus

The account of Samuel in the temple is included by the author because it shows that Samuel was selected by God to the role of prophet, one who speaks God's word. Samuel was thereby unquestionably a man of God and was chosen to initiate kingship in Israel.

- God was taking steps to prepare his people to receive a king.
- God initiated steps to carry out his plan.
- God used Samuel because he listened to and obeyed God.
- God was caring for his people by providing a king.
- God was revealing his kingship to the world.

Lesson Application

Even in dark times God prepares people to be his instruments and carries out his plan through them.

- When we show ourselves to be people who listen and obey, God is pleased to use us in his work, whether the job is big or small.
- We trust that God will prepare us for the jobs he has for us.
- We believe that God will not tolerate sin in those who serve him in high positions.

Biblical Context

The books of Samuel are about how God established his king, David, on the throne, as a way to show what his own kingship is like. An important part of the book, therefore, is showing that David truly was God's choice for king. David was not an ambitious upstart who overthrew the prior regime and then claimed God had done it—something that happened all the time in the ancient world. The prophet Samuel is the most important piece to this puzzle, because he was the kingmaker. Therefore, the book begins by establishing Samuel's credentials as a special instrument of God. He filled three offices: prophet, priest, and judge. This story recounts the unusual beginning of his prophetic ministry; he is one to whom the Lord spoke, and it began at an early age.

Interpretational Issues in the Story

"Ministering before the LORD" (1 Sam. 2:18). The word translated "ministering" is one used for carrying out priestly duties (1 Kings 8:11), but it can also express the idea of attending to someone (as in Gen. 39:4; 1 Kings 19:21). Generally, however, when it is modified by the phrase "before the LORD," as here, it refers to duties in ritual performance and fits with the statement that Samuel was wearing a linen ephod (a priestly apron, cf. 2:28). This suggests that Samuel was not just sweeping up or running errands; however, there were menial tasks carried out by the Levites. These included preparing animals for sacrifice and taking care of what was left after the sacrifice. There was also wood and water to be hauled.

"A little robe" (1 Sam. 2:19). The word translated "robe" refers not to everyday clothing but to a priestly garment (Ex. 28:31–34; 1 Chron. 15:27). The garment described by this word was worn by others besides priests but was typically worn by someone with a particular status or authority.

Setting (1 Sam. 3:3). The comment that the lamp of God had not gone out is likely not referring to some duty of Samuel's, either waiting for it to go out or making sure it did not. The lights on the lampstand in the temple were never to be put out (Ex. 27:21; Lev. 24:1–4). The alternative is to understand this statement as saying that there was still hope—God had not given up on them yet (see it used this way in 2 Sam. 21:17; 1 Kings 11:36; 2 Kings 8:19). The text mentions that Samuel is in close proximity to the ark to hint at what is going to take place. The presence of God is near.

Samuel mistaking the voice (1 Sam. 3:5–6). The importance of Samuel's repeated mistake in thinking that the voice he heard was Eli calling is that it shows that he had no pretensions to the office of prophet. Samuel did not expect to hear the voice of God, had not sought it, and did not recognize it when it came. It is the very opposite of the boy who cries, "Wolf!"

God's message to Samuel (1 Sam. 3:11). It is worth noting that the message Samuel received reinforces what another prophet said to Eli (2:27, 36).

Samuel may not have been aware of the earlier message since it had been delivered personally to Eli. But Eli received confirmation of the message by its repetition, and he would have had instant evidence that Samuel had truly received a prophetic message.

Guilt of Eli's family never atoned for (1 Sam. 3:14). In the Old Testament there is no offering to provide for defiant, continued sin. No ritual remedy is available to avoid judgment. This punishment against Eli's family was not unique but called for by the law (Num. 15:27–31).

Background Information

Temple. It is strange to read of a temple here since the temple was not built until the time of Solomon. The word might be used here for the sanctuary, but perhaps more likely a Canaanite Temple in Shiloh had been taken over for use as a temple of Yahweh.

Dreams. Dreams in the ancient world were considered a means that deities used for revealing information about their will. The dream here in Samuel is more like a vision in that there was conversation between Samuel and God, not just symbolic actions taking place. Visions of this sort are more significant because they don't have to be interpreted.

Mistakes to Avoid

Samuel was receiving a prophetic message spoken audibly in a vision. Be careful not to give the impression that his experience is one that anyone might have. The very point is that this was unusual, if not unique (1 Sam. 3:1). The point of the story is not primarily about obedience to God. It is more important that God spoke to Samuel than that Samuel listened to God. Though many translations refer to Samuel as a "boy" (1 Sam. 3:1), there is no reason to think of him as a very young boy. This same term is used for people in their thirties! It is more likely that he was a teenager. The lesson ought not to stop at the point at which Samuel discovers that it is the Lord and listens carefully. Samuel was given a prophetic message, and it was a message of judgment against Eli, his surrogate father, and Eli's family. Repeating this to Eli would not have been a pleasant task, but it is all to demonstrate that God spoke through Samuel.

The main point is in verses 19–21—the story cannot be told without it. Yet it would also be inappropriate for younger children to be taught the details about the total destruction of Eli's family. That can be handled in vague terms for those age groups, saying, for example, "The Lord told Samuel that he was going to punish Eli's family because they did not honor the Lord," or, "They had disobeyed his law." Younger children will also not be able to understand the role of the prophet, so the point will have to be made about God's speaking often to Samuel and that Samuel's leadership was recognized because of that.

It is common, when these early stories about Samuel are told, for teachers to conclude that children will not understand the word *temple*, and so they substitute the word *church*—this is a serious misidentification. The temple in the ancient world was far different from the church building today. The building that we call church is simply the assembly of God's people. It is a place designated for corporate worship. Even though we sometimes call it "God's house," in reality God is housed within his people, not in a building. In Israel, God chose to live in the temple, and though people gathered in the temple at Jerusalem on sacred occasions, the courtyard was not designed for corporate worship and could not accommodate very many. People came to the temple to watch public rituals and to offer sacrifices for themselves or their families. The priests (Eli should not be designated as a pastor) were there to officiate over the rituals and advise about procedures. They also made sure that only those who qualified could enter.

51. Travels of the Ark (1 Samuel 4–6)

Lesson Focus

The ark was captured when Eli's sons took it into battle thinking that it would gain them victory. In the ancient world the defeat of the Israelite army and the capture of the ark would have suggested to both sides that the Philistine god Dagon was stronger than Yahweh, but the succeeding events proved otherwise, leading to the ark's return to Israel.

- God abandoned his people as punishment for their sin.
- Yahweh alone is God; all others are as nothing.
- God does not choose to give victory in every battle—his purposes are his own.
- God is in sovereign control of everything.

Lesson Application

We believe that the Lord is all-powerful; there is no other God.

- Even when it seems that the Lord is not acting, we believe that his plan is being carried out.

- We should never think that some other god or anything else is stronger than the Lord.

Biblical Context

The books of Samuel are about how God established his king, David, on the throne, as a way to show what his own kingship is like. An important part of the book, therefore, is showing that David truly was God's choice for king. David was not an ambitious upstart who overthrew the prior regime and then claimed God had done it—something that happened all the time in the ancient world. After Samuel's credentials as prophet, priest, and judge had been established, he became the logical kingmaker. The story of the ark brings an end to the judges period of history, as God's ultimate judgment on the people was to abandon them to their oppressors. He did this by leaving the land and bringing judgment on the Philistines without raising up a judge.

Interpretational Issues in the Story

Taking the ark into battle (1 Sam. 4:1–10). The ark was taken into battle to try to bring assurance that God was with them. Many other nations took their images or standards representing their gods into battle for the same reason. They were treating the ark as a religious relic through which God could be manipulated, and therefore it is not the same as when God instructed Joshua to use it at Jericho. Their actions therefore had the exact opposite effect from what they had intended.

Return of the ark (1 Sam. 6:1–19). The Philistines were in a very awkward position. If they were to send the ark back to Israel, they would be admitting that their enemy's God is stronger. They used an oracular method (compare the story of Gideon's fleece) to determine whether the God of Israel was responsible for their difficulties. In an oracle, a yes-or-no question was posed to deity, and some mechanism was designated for deity to answer. When something from the world around served as that mechanism, the procedure was to designate normal expected results as one answer and highly unusual, extraordinary results as the other. Here, if the answer was no—that is, the God of Israel was not responsible for the Philistines' problems—the cows would act as cows always act—they would go to feed their calves, or at least wander off into the fields. If the answer was yes, they would act as no cow would normally act—ignore their calves and turn completely around and head off on their own down the road to Israel.

Plagues and death (1 Sam. 6:5, 19). Both the Philistines, who arrogantly thought Israel's God had been overcome by Dagon (indicated by the placement of the ark in their temple), and the Israelites, who carelessly treated the ark as a curiosity, discovered the cost of neglecting the holiness of God. When the people of Beth Shemesh looked into the ark, they demonstrated insufficient respect for the Lord (just as Eli's sons had done).

Background Information

Dagon. Many reference works claim that Dagon is a fish god, but this is no longer believed to be the case by scholars. A more recent idea is that he was a grain god, but even that view has some uncertainties. He was adopted as the national god of the Philistines, and that is the best way to identify him. The Philistines had settled on the coast of Canaan less than a century earlier than the time of this story and had adopted a god already known in the ancient Near East. In other words, they did not bring Dagon with them.

Ark placed in temple of Dagon. In the ancient world victors in battle often did not destroy the images of the gods of their conquered foes, but brought them to the temple of their own god to sit in captivity and submission. The Israelites had no image of their God, Yahweh, but the ark of the covenant was their most sacred relic, so it was brought to the temple of Dagon in captivity.

Head and hands broken off. When Dagon fell over the first time, it was an indication that he was bowing down before Yahweh. When he fell over the second time, the breaking off of his head and hands indicated that he had been slain in battle. In the ancient world enemy casualities were sometimes counted by making a pile of the heads or hands of the slain. The destruction of Dagon was a very visible way for Yahweh to show the Philistines that he had not been defeated.

Mistakes to Avoid

It is difficult to miss the point of this story, and since there are no Israelite characters to speak of, attention is not drawn to people rather than to God. The common mistakes in telling this story are usually based on a misunderstanding of the ark and Dagon.

52. Saul Becomes King (1 Samuel 8–12)

Lesson Focus

The Israelites demanded a king so that they could be like the other nations. God gave them the king they wanted, even though their ideas of kingship were misguided. Samuel warned them of the dangers in what they were doing but anointed Saul as their king.

- God sometimes gives us what we ask for even though it is not what he would want for us.
- God gave Saul the chance to succeed or fail.
- God is the true king.

Lesson Application

Problems we face are ultimately spiritual problems, and acknowledging God's rule is the solution.

- Before we conclude that our problems are political, we ought to consider the possibility that they are spiritual so we seek out the appropriate type of solution.
- We acknowledge God's kingship above all human authority.
- We should be careful what we ask for, because it may not be what we should be asking for.

Biblical Context

The books of Samuel are about how God established his king, David, on the throne, as a way to show what his own kingship is like. An important part of the book, therefore, is showing that David truly was God's choice for king. David was not an ambitious upstart who overthrew the prior regime and then claimed God had done it—something that happened all the time in the ancient world. After Samuel's credentials as prophet, priest, and judge had been established, he became the logical kingmaker. When the people requested a king, however, their ideas were misguided, so kingship got off to an uncertain start in Saul.

Interpretational Issues in the Story

Samuel's sons as judges (1 Sam. 8:2). Those designated as judges during this period of Israelite history were usually engaged in bringing justice for the people against their enemies (e.g., Midianites, Philistines). But judges were also involved in hearing and deciding disputes, as Samuel's sons were doing here.

Request for a king (1 Sam. 8:6, 19–20). Even from the time of Abraham, God had indicated that Israel would have kings (Gen. 17:6). It is not the idea of kingship that is illegitimate; the problem is the reason the people gave for wanting a king. They had come to believe that their problem was a political one, so they were seeking a political solution. In reality their problem was a spiritual one that required a spiritual solution.

Fighting our battles (1 Sam. 8:7, 20). In the ancient world it was universally believed that gods went out alongside the king and led in battles. But here, when the people ask for a king to lead them in battle, God says that the people have rejected him as king. The people weren't thinking in terms of either God or a king; it wasn't an either-or situation. No one wanted a king who did not enjoy the support of the gods in warfare. God's comment is not a critique of the institution of kingship, but divine insight into the underlying motivation: the people simply did not trust God. It seems that the people were not thinking logically; there was a disconnect. They thought that God could lead their armies more successfully with a different kind of leadership.

Samuel and sacrifice at the high place (1 Sam. 9:12). High place (*bamah*) is the name for a ritual site. Sometimes such sites were on elevated areas, either natural or artificial, but were also located at city gates. Some high places were used to worship Yahweh (as here and in 1 Kings 3:4), but, if not connected to a sanctuary, could be used for whatever god the person performing the ritual wished to acknowledge. Eventually, however, all high places were outlawed and the temple was supposed to be the place where rituals were performed.

Anointing. Anointing was a common practice in the ancient world and was often associated with the enthronement of a king. Of further significance might be that the act designated the king as vassal to God, since in some cultures kings anointed their vassals. Typically olive oil was used.

Saul and Samuel (1 Sam. 9:6). From the start it is evident that Saul is largely unaware or naïve regarding spiritual things. Samuel's circle of activity is focused on the territory that Saul lived in, but Saul seems largely ignorant of the renowned prophet (the servant, not Saul, brings up Samuel, and he is a nameless "man of God").

The Spirit of God rushed upon Saul (1 Sam. 10:6, 10; 11:6). In the Old Testament, the Spirit of the Lord was usually seen in empowering people to a task. Today we talk of the Spirit's indwelling people when they become Christians. These are very different things. This incident should not be viewed as the beginning of Saul's spiritual relationship with God. The endowment of the Spirit here has to do with his role as general. This has nothing to do with gaining or losing salvation. The point of the reference is how God changed Saul's heart (10:9). With this empowering he was more confident about the events that had transpired and his commissioning. From the latter part of the chapter, however, it would seem that the confidence did not last.

Background Information

Royal prerogatives. Throughout the judges period, Israel had no central government administration. There were no taxes for a centralized government, no forced labor for government projects, no standing army, and no governmental overhead. Kingship, therefore, was to bring many changes to the economy. Such administrative costs can be documented thoroughly through records from the ancient Near East.

Procession of prophets. Prophets were common in the ancient world. They served in administrative posts as royal advisors as well as in more informal contexts. They served as spokespersons for a variety of gods. One could be trained to be a prophet as one could be trained to be a scribe or a smith. The prophets seem to have used music to help them enter a state of receptivity to the divine voice. Sometimes trances were part of the process. The verb form used in 10:10–13 suggests that Saul was in a trance.

Mistakes to Avoid

The main mistake to avoid is suggesting that there was something inherently wrong with kingship. Some students may also need help with the idea that God chose Saul as king, when God knew that Saul would fail. It is important to recognize that God chose the best king *in light of the job description that the people presented*; that is, the people asked for the wrong kind of king, so when God gave them the kind of king they asked for, it is no surprise that the king failed. As always, the main focus should be on what God was doing in Israel. The focus should not be on Samuel's possible failure as a parent (8:3) or on Saul's strengths or weaknesses. We should not seek for authoritative lessons from Saul's shortcomings. The narrative is working toward David's kingship and is already making clear that Saul's failure had nothing to do with David, Samuel, or God. When God's criteria for kingship came into play, it was a man like David, not Saul, who filled those criteria.

53. Saul Disobeys (1 Samuel 13; 15)

Lesson Focus

God rejects Saul as king because he disobeys.

- God has higher requirements from those who are in positions of leadership.
- God takes obedience very seriously.

- Even though God can use anyone to accomplish his plan, he has certain criteria that he favors and that lead him eventually to discard or punish.

Lesson Application

God uses those who obey him.

- We seek to obey God rather than rationalize what we think he may want.
- We realize that we can disqualify ourselves from God's use in certain situations by our disobedience.
- We believe that God can use us if we obey and that he may reject us for his work if we don't.

Biblical Context

The books of Samuel are about how God established his king, David, on the throne, as a way to show what his own kingship is like. An important part of the book, therefore, is showing that David truly was God's choice for king. David was not an ambitious upstart who overthrew the prior regime and then claimed God had done it—something that happened all the time in the ancient world. After Samuel's credentials as prophet, priest, and judge had been established, he became the logical kingmaker. Saul's presumption and disobedience led to his rejection by the Lord and set the scene for another king to be chosen using God's criteria.

Interpretational Issues in the Story

Saul's conundrum (1 Sam. 13:8). Saul was in a difficult position. Samuel had not arrived on schedule, and the army was beginning to lose its edge and even to abandon the camp. If Saul had continued to wait for Samuel, he might have lost his army and, for all he knew, Samuel might never come. Saul might have wondered whether Samuel had been killed or captured or was ignoring Saul's request. The alternatives were either to go into battle without sacrifice being offered (and risking God's disfavor) or offering the sacrifice himself (technically against the conditions of his office). He lacked the insight to see the situation and his course of action clearly.

Man after God's own heart (1 Sam. 13:14). It is common to think that the designation of David as a man after the Lord's own heart means that David was a pious and spiritually mature man. Some see David's spiritual nature revealed in the Psalms but then wonder about so many despicable acts that the narratives contain. The seeming contradiction is solved in a deeper investigation into what the phrase in 1 Samuel 13:14 refers to. From the use of the phrase in Psalm 20:4 and Jeremiah 3:15 it can be seen that it does not refer to David's pursuit of the Lord, but to God's choosing of David for his own reasons and according to his own will. The phrase is also used in Babylonian texts to refer to a king putting another king of his own choosing on the throne of a subjugated people. The point here is that while Saul met the criteria given by the people (their job description), David met the criteria that were important to the Lord (God's job description). Minimally, David met the criterion of understanding that God was the one who brought victory (see 1 Samuel 17).

"The LORD regretted that he had made Saul king" (1 Sam. 15:35). Even though the Lord knew what would happen, the whole sequence of events brought him grief. Even human leaders grieve when they have to make hard decisions that will have well-recognized collateral damage; for example, a president might grieve that he has to send soldiers into battle when he knows that some will be killed. The sense of grief does not mean that God wished he had done something differently.

Background Information

Philistine threat. It is clear that the Philistines had made significant inroads into the midsection of the hill country controlled by the Israelites, since the military actions are all in the vicinity of Saul's capital at Gibeah.

Obedience and sacrifice. Saul again showed his spiritual naïveté by thinking that his sacrifices would please the Lord. His actions suggest that he thought sacrifice is more important to God than obedience. In the ancient world there was little to obey—the gods were honored by rituals that gave them food and met other needs. It was therefore through ritual that the god was appeased, and that was all they required. This is why Samuel spoke of divination and idolatry (1 Sam. 15:23). Other nations interacted with their gods through divination and idolatry, believing that gods could be managed or even manipulated. Yahweh was not one of the pagan gods—he expected to be obeyed.

Mistakes to Avoid

Rather than emphasize David's spiritual qualities (though he undoubtedly had many), the emphasis should be on what God values in a king. Among the qualities that are in evidence in these chapters is that God values a king who properly recognizes his own role as well as God's role, and a king who obeys. The idea is not to elevate David, but to understand God. Saul's failures were inevitable. Neither Saul nor David is the focus here. Instead it is important to get a sense of how God is directing history and bringing about kingship among his people.

54. Samuel Anoints David (1 Samuel 16)

Lesson Focus

Having rejected Saul, God directed Samuel to Bethlehem to anoint his chosen king. There, Samuel learned that what impresses people does not count. God has his own criteria and is able to look at a person's heart.

- God looks at people's hearts and assesses them on that basis.
- God empowers people to do the job that he has for them.

Lesson Application

We believe that God is working out his plan and that he can observe the hearts of those he chooses as his instruments.

- We should be concerned about what God sees in our hearts rather than with the superficial things that matter to people.
- We should not think that God is limited by our skills or by how people view us. He sees what we are really like and empowers us to do what he has called us to do.

Biblical Context

The books of Samuel are about how God established his king, David, on the throne, as a way to show what his own kingship is like. An important part of the book, therefore, is showing that David truly was God's choice for king. David was not an ambitious upstart who overthrew the prior regime and then claimed God had done it—something that happened all the time in the ancient world. After Samuel's credentials as prophet, priest, and judge had been established, he became the logical kingmaker. Saul's presumption and disobedience led to his rejection by the Lord and set the scene for another to be chosen using God's criteria. In this story Samuel is directed by the Lord to David and anoints him as the eventual successor to Saul.

Interpretational Issues in the Story

God tells Samuel to lie? (1 Sam. 16:2–3). Samuel was concerned about his life, and God understood Samuel's concern. The sacrifice that God instructed Samuel to use for a cover story is not meaningless—that *is* what Samuel was going to do. But he was also going to anoint the next king, Saul's replacement. This incident is descriptive of Samuel's fears.

Samuel and sacrifices (1 Sam. 16:5). During this period, when a permanent central sanctuary had not yet been firmly established, sacrifices were offered at local high places. It is possible that there was a high place in Bethlehem that served as the site of Samuel's sacrifice. High place (*bamah*) is the name for a ritual site. Some high places were on elevated areas, either natural or artificial, but were also located at city gates. Some high places were used to worship Yahweh (1 Sam. 9:12; 1 Kings 3:4) but when not connected to a sanctuary they were used for rituals designed to acknowledge one's god of choice. Eventually, however, all high places were outlawed, and the temple became the place where rituals were performed.

Spirit of the Lord (1 Sam. 16:13–14). In the Old Testament, the Spirit of the Lord was usually seen in empowering people to a task. Today we talk of the Spirit's indwelling people when they become Christians. These are very different things. This should not be viewed as the beginning of David's spiritual relationship with God. The endowment of the Spirit here has to do with David's role as king. That is why, when the Spirit came on David (v. 13), he left Saul (v. 14). This has nothing to do with gaining or losing salvation. God's Spirit did not authorize two opponents to be king at the same time; rather, the Spirit left one and came on another.

Harmful spirit from the Lord (1 Sam. 16:14–16, 23). We should not think of this as a demon sent by God. The Hebrew word translated "evil" here has a much broader range than our English word and can be used to refer to anything negative. Since God is in control of all, the biblical text would certainly not treat this as an invasion of some spirit that was a counterpart or opponent of God. This could be viewed as punishment from God, but it should not be viewed as God's forcing Saul to be wicked.

David enters Saul's service as harpist and armor bearer (1 Sam. 16:18–21). David's musical skills brought him into employment in Saul's personal staff. It was not unusual for kings to have personal attendants carrying out a variety of tasks. "Armor bearer" was more likely a rank than a specific job. If so, David would not necessarily have been expected to accompany Saul to the battlefield (note his absence in 1 Samuel 17).

Background Information

Anointing. Anointing kings was common in the ancient Near East. In some cultures it was believed to protect from evil influences. In others it was understood as an endowment of life. When done at a coronation it often represented the subordination of the newly anointed king to the deity. In Israel it symbolized the person's elect status as chosen by God to service.

Seeing the heart. The heart (along with other parts such as liver and kidney) was believed in the ancient world to be the seat of emotion and intellect. For the deity to look on someone's heart meant that his character and motivations were being investigated. This was common in the ancient world, as gods were believed to look into a person's entrails to discern his character. Accordingly, this was not a quality unique to Israel's God.

Mistakes to Avoid

This incident is descriptive of Samuel's fears, not an attempt to offer guidelines for truth-telling or to instruct on how to get through sticky ethical dilemmas. Nor should we try to probe into David's family dynamics, seeking to explain why David is out with the sheep and what feelings David's brothers might have had for him, or vice versa. Rather than attempt to psychoanalyze the characters, we are to seek to understand the author's use of the narrative. Whatever the family dynamics may have been, or whatever they would become after David's anointing, we can only guess, which is unproductive because there is no authority behind our guesses. There is no reason to focus the lesson on the human tendency to judge others by outward appearance. The text is more interested in establishing that God does not act like humans do. He is able to look at a person inwardly and gives higher value to that assessment. This comment also reflects on the reasons that people used to choose Saul (1 Sam. 10:23–24).

55. David and Goliath (1 Samuel 17)

Lesson Focus

David trusted God to deliver him from the mighty Philistine, and God was with him.

- God is able to overcome any obstacle.
- God is the one who fights on behalf of his people, and he is the victor.
- God is the hero, the ultimate, divine warrior.
- God is able to accomplish great things through a faithful (even if overmatched) instrument.

Lesson Application

God is with those who trust in him.

- We must be willing to defend the name and reputation of God.
- We believe that God is able to use us in his plan whatever the odds against us might be.
- We are to trust God.

Biblical Context

The books of Samuel are about how God established his king, David, on the throne, as a way to show what his own kingship is like. An important part of the book, therefore, is showing that David truly was God's choice for king. David was not an ambitious upstart who overthrew the prior regime and then claimed God had done it—something that happened all the time in the ancient world. After Samuel's credentials as prophet, priest, and judge had been established, he became the logical kingmaker. Saul's presumption and disobedience led to his rejection by the Lord and set the scene for another to be chosen using God's criteria. Samuel had been directed to anoint David, and in this story we find out what in God's view was so attractive about David.

Interpretational Issues in the Story

Saul's role (1 Sam. 17:25). Saul, Israel's champion, had been chosen because of his warrior potential to fight Israel's battles for them. Nevertheless, Saul went out looking for volunteers and offering lavish incentives. Not only had Saul failed God's criteria, but he had failed with regard to the people's criteria.

Saul's armor (1 Sam. 17:38–39). We should not think of David as a little child on whom the armor was too big, though Saul was undoubtedly bigger than David, so fit would have been a problem. The text indicates that David had not had the experience necessary to use the armor to advantage (17:39). As such it would disadvantage him. He chose mobility over defense.

Saul's failure to recognize David (1 Sam. 17:25, 55, 58). We know from 1 Samuel 16 that David and Saul had already been in contact. So here, when asking whose son David is, Saul might have been wondering whether David's family was already allied with him in some way. Additionally, Saul had made promises to the household of the one who could defeat Goliath, so it was important that Saul learn of the household to which David belonged. Finally, though David has been in Saul's service, there may have been dozens of young men in Saul's service, and Saul might not have paid much attention—they were simply servants. But now David has gotten his attention.

Background Information

Champion warfare and the divine role. In the ancient world people believed that the gods fought in conjunction with the human armies they supported and that the armies with the stronger god would prevail. Certainly it was believed that the gods could work more effectively through large, well-equipped armies and mighty warriors, but a strong god could overcome those factors. As Goliath defied Israel's armies, he was also defying their God—the two cannot be separated. David became indignant for the Lord's reputation, which is a demonstration that he had the quality that God was looking for in a king. He counted on God to win the battle and defend his reputation. Champion warfare could give an initial indicator of which deity was stronger. Just as the stronger god could succeed with his army, he could show his strength through his champion. Here, when the agreement was made to use champions (17:9), the point is not that the side that loses the contest will simply lay down its arms and agree to subjugation but, rather, that both sides would have received a strong indication of which god was stronger, and therefore which side would eventually prevail. If Goliath had won, no one would have been surprised, but for David to defeat this seasoned and formidable warrior gave strong indication of the power of Israel's God.

The giant Goliath. Goliath is never called a giant in Scripture, but his size was communicated to show what an intimidating warrior he was. Textual traditions vary with regard to whether he was 9 feet and 9 inches tall, or 6 feet and 9 inches tall. It doesn't matter much in the end. His size was intimidating, as was his experience, his armor and weapons, and his confidence.

Slings and sling stones. When Goliath mocks David's equipment, he was engaged in the practice well known in modern sports as "trash-talking." Despite his bravado, he was well aware that David carried a dangerous weapon. Slings were among the weapons used by trained divisions in the armies of the ancient world. A leather pouch held the stone, and it was swung by thongs around the head horizontally to gain momentum until one thong was released to project the stone. By this method stones could achieve speeds as high as 125 miles per hour and could be thrown with accuracy for a hundred yards. Sling stones aimed at an object on a horizontal plain were roughly the size of a golf ball or perhaps as large as a squash ball. When slings were used in the siege of a city, the sling was swung vertically and lofted in an underhand motion, and larger stones were used, perhaps as large as a baseball. David would have chosen five stones that were smooth (better aerodynamics) and probably of varying sizes so as to be equipped for a variety of situations.

Mistakes to Avoid

David is not the hero—God is. To paint David as the hero runs exactly opposite to David's own perspective and what the narrator wanted to emphasize. Furthermore, just because God brought down David's enemy does not mean that he will give us victory over all our enemies. We cannot extrapolate this work of God to everyone's situation at any given time. Resist using the method of "lesson by metaphor." We should not be asking, "What giant in your life does God need to overcome?" or "What are the five stones that you have in your bag?" These do not get to the authority of the teaching of the text, clever as they may be. While we might be inclined to say, "Like David, we should trust God," it is more appropriate to say, "Through the story of David we learn that God is trustworthy, so we should trust him." The line between the two is thin, and the result of trusting God is the same; the difference is in the motivating factor. We want students to learn to trust God because of who God is, not because of what someone else did or believed. The narratives put God before our eyes using the story of David. They are not intended to simply put David before our eyes. Imitating David is a poor substitute for basing our behavior on the revealed character of God.

56. David and Jonathan (1 Samuel 18:1–4; 19:1–7; 20:1–42)

Lesson Focus

Though Jonathan was the crowned prince set to succeed his father to the throne, he did not view David jealously, as a competitor, but developed an allegiance to him. In this the narrator demonstrates that David was not set against the house of Saul but received support from all except Saul himself.

- God provides the encouragement and support for his chosen servant as he prepares him for service.

Lesson Application

We should recognize God's hand as he provides support for those whom he has chosen to serve him.

- If God has called us to a task or role, we should believe that he will provide the support needed to proceed.

Biblical Context

The books of Samuel are about how God established his king, David, on the throne, as a way to show what his own kingship is like. An important part of the book, therefore, is showing that David truly was God's choice for king. David was not an ambitious upstart who overthrew the prior regime and then claimed God had done it—something that happened all the time in the ancient world. After Samuel's credentials as prophet, priest, and judge had been established, he became the logical kingmaker. Saul's presumption and disobedience led to his rejection by the Lord and set the scene for another to be chosen using God's criteria. Once David had been anointed and had shown his mettle, the next several chapters of the text develop how David gradually gained the support of every group, beginning with the crown prince, Jonathan.

Interpretational Issues in the Story

Friendship (1 Sam. 18:1–4). In political documents from the ancient world, the term *love* was used by national entities, represented by their leaders, to express a formal bond of allegiance. In this sense there was no personal warmth involved, only a formal commitment. Nevertheless, the word *love* could also be used to express a personal bond. In the case of David and Jonathan, there is every indication that both formal (notice esp. 18:3) and personal levels were involved. Nevertheless, it is the political allegiance that is more important to the narrative than the personal bond, because over the whole second half of the book the narrator is trying to show the support that grew for David from every quarter. Even Jonathan recognized that David was God's chosen man, the one whom he favored.

Jonathan made a covenant with David (1 Sam. 18:3). This was a covenant of loyalty between the two to the effect that they would support each other. For Jonathan this meant that he would support David's accession to the throne (indicated by the things he gave to David). For David, this meant that he would not do violence against Jonathan or his family.

Background Information

Jonathan's tunic. Most of the clothing and equipment mentioned here designated Jonathan's role, status, and office. The word describing Jonathan's tunic often describes a king's robe of office. Therefore, his giving of them to David was not just as gifts of their friendship; it was an acknowledgment of David's new status. It is difficult to determine whether Jonathan was renouncing his role and transferring it to David, but he was certainly showing his personal support for David.

Mistakes to Avoid

This story is not about making friends, having friends, or how to be a friend. We could not say from this story that the Bible teaches us about friendship. Since there is no authoritative teaching about friendship in this passage, to use it that way would be to depart from what the text is doing. The point of the passage is not that we are to imitate either David or Jonathan, though Jonathan's character is undeniably commendable. We must rigorously distinguish between good things we can observe in the text and that which the text is seeking to accomplish. If we focus only on being good friends, we will not gain the truth that the author was laying out—that God was preparing the way to David's kingship by garnering support for him from even the most unlikely people.

57. David and Saul (1 Samuel 24; 26)

Lesson Focus

God protected David as Saul sought his life.

- God works out his plan in his own time.
- God providentially brings about situations that help his people to clarify his will.

Lesson Application

We have to wait on God as he unfolds his plan.

- We have to be very careful as we discern when to step out in faith and when to patiently wait for God.
- We must recognize that God will not always use the most direct or convenient route in carrying out his plan.

Biblical Context

The books of Samuel are about how God established his king, David, on the throne, as a way to show what his own kingship is like. An important part of the book, therefore, is showing that David truly was God's choice for king. David was not an ambitious upstart who overthrew the prior regime and then claimed God had done it—something that happened all the time in the ancient world. After Samuel's credentials as prophet, priest, and judge had been established, he became the logical kingmaker. Saul's presumption and disobedience led to his rejection by the Lord and set the scene for another to be chosen using God's criteria. Once David had been anointed and had shown his mettle, the text develops over many chapters how David gradually gained expressions of support. It is important for the narrator to show that David did not seek Saul's life or his throne—it was Saul who sought David's life. That is why the two instances when David could have taken Saul's life but did not (1 Samuel 24 and 26) are important. Also, notably, in both cases Saul himself confirmed David's destiny and admitted that he was the one at fault.

Interpretational Issues in the Story

Dialogue (1 Sam. 24:8–21). As elsewhere, the importance of this account is found in the dialogue, here between David and Saul. David's claim of innocence is important by itself but is made stronger by Saul's confession. He acknowledged David as more righteous, admitted that David had not acted against him, and confirmed that David would be king. This was important for the author, who wanted to make clear that David was not a usurper. (See a similar dialogue in 1 Sam. 26:15–25.)

"Deep sleep from the LORD" (1 Sam. 26:12). In the biblical and ancient world people believed that the gods were involved with everything that happened, yet, as here, when something struck them as out of the ordinary, they sometimes specified it as having come from the Lord. This is different from "supernatural" because everything is supernatural. This sleep is considered extraordinary because, under normal circumstances, there was no way that David and his men could have penetrated so deeply into the royal camp and found everyone asleep. This was evidence to the narrator that God was supporting David in many ways.

Background Information

Saul's hem. The hem of Saul's robe would have distinguished him as king. For David to cut that off could have been seen as symbolic of David's seizing kingship or removing Saul from office, similar to stealing his crown. This explains why David's conscience was pricked.

Serving other gods. When David declared there are men who might tell him, "Go, serve other gods" (26:19), his point was that by preventing him access to the sanctuary of Yahweh, Saul had forced him to look to other gods for support. Gods were generally associated with their sanctuaries and territories. As David had been forced into other territories, he had also been pushed toward other gods.

Mistakes to Avoid

This is not a lesson about being kind to our enemies. It is true that David refused to kill Saul, but in the first incident he symbolically stripped him of his kingship, and in the second he was asking for trouble. Neither incident is designed to offer a biblical guide to interacting with those who oppress us. What is most important is that David was not seizing kingship opportunistically but was trusting God with the details. Saul was the cause of the friction, not David. As 1 Samuel 25 illustrates, God would judge David's enemies; David had no need to take things into his own hands.

58. David and Abigail (1 Samuel 25)

Lesson Focus

David's men protected the flocks of a local sheep owner, Nabal, who insulted them and refused to give them their due. David was on his way to punish the man's stinginess when he was met by the man's wife, Abigail, who was humble, apologetic, gracious, and generous and affirmed David's destiny. After God punished her husband, she married David.

- God protected David from rash vengeance.
- God's destiny for David was recognized by the common people of the land.
- God is the one who brings vengeance.

Lesson Application

Vengeance is in the hands of the Lord.

- We leave vengeance to God.
- We are thankful that God is able to protect us from rash acts.
- We recognize that God's plan is secure as he works out the details in sometimes mysterious ways.

Biblical Context

The books of Samuel are about how God established his king, David, on the throne, as a way to show what his own kingship is like. An important part of the book, therefore, is showing that David truly was God's choice for king. David was not an ambitious upstart who overthrew the prior regime and then claimed God had done it—something that happened all the time in the ancient world. After Samuel's credentials as prophet, priest, and judge had been established, he became the logical kingmaker. Saul's presumption and disobedience led to his rejection by the Lord and set the scene for another to be chosen using God's criteria. Once David had been anointed and had shown his mettle, the text develops over many chapters how David gradually gained expressions of support. It is important for the narrator to show that David did not seek Saul's life or his throne—it was Saul who sought David's life. This narrative is flanked by two instances when David could have taken Saul's life but did not (1 Samuel 24 and 26). Here, Abigail affirmed that God would deal with David's enemies. Also important is her affirmation that David would be king.

Interpretational Issues in the Story

David's desert occupation (1 Sam. 25:4–8, 15–16). Outcasts forced to live as David and his men were living had few options. They could become bandits and survive by victimizing others. They could become mercenaries and sell their military skills in return for the plunder they would gain. They could seek to hire themselves out in honest employment by providing security and protection for wealthy citizens. Here he was doing the latter, but by 1 Samuel 27 they had been forced into serving as mercenaries because of Saul's persistent pursuit. In all this, it is important to remember that the author was not trying to whitewash David. David's mercenary activity was disgraceful and villainous, and it is possible that even here his offer of protection had an edge of extortion connected to it.

"A sure house" (1 Sam. 25:28). This is an expression of what is going to become the Davidic covenant (2 Samuel 7) and, as in all these narratives, it is leading up to that momentous pivot point in the theological history of Israel.

"Bundle of the living" (1 Sam. 25:29). This expression most likely refers to the same thing as the "book of life," which, in the ancient world, was a reference to the idea that deity kept accounts of those who were to live and die.

Background Information

Desert of Maon/Carmel. This is not Mount Carmel but an area about eight miles southeast of Hebron.

Sheep shearing. Wool was one of the staple economies in the ancient world. Sheep-shearing time was one of feasting and generosity. Three thousand sheep produced some three tons of wool.

Marriage. David was already married, but he was also in the process of building alliances. Marriage by kings in the ancient world was used to seal a treaty. Here, David's marriage to Abigail was an important tie to one of the wealthier families of the region. Polygamy was allowed in the ancient world but was usually only practiced by kings or by men whose first wife was barren.

Mistakes to Avoid

Nabal, the fool, was ungrateful and insulting; Abigail displayed many fine qualities; David was angry and rash but then humble and forgiving. Despite these observations, the story is not attempting to instruct in character traits, whether worthy or unworthy. The fact is we could find many ambiguous aspects (David's possible involvement in extortion, Abigail's actions as self-preservation rather than graciousness) that demonstrate the problem with such an approach. The issue at hand is revealed in Abigail's speech as she joined the line of witnesses testifying to God's destiny for David.

59. David at Ziklag (1 Samuel 30)

Lesson Focus

David and his men returned to Ziklag to find the city sacked and their loved ones taken. David pursued them and recovered what had been taken.

- The battle belongs to the Lord.
- God graciously allows the recovery of goods lost through foolishness (David should never have tried to go to battle alongside the Philistines).
- In the bigger picture of God's plan for David to become king, these events remove David from any thought that he was involved in Saul's death.

Lesson Application

A universal teaching is difficult to discern, as it is setting up another point about how David was far away when Saul got killed.

- We can have confidence in God's control when he allows us to see his plan unfolding.

Biblical Context

The books of Samuel are about how God established his king, David, on the throne, as a way to show what his own kingship is like. An important part of the book, therefore, is showing that David truly was God's choice for king. David was not an ambitious upstart who overthrew the prior regime and then claimed God had done it—something that happened all the time in the ancient world. After Samuel's credentials as prophet, priest, and judge had been established, he became the logical kingmaker. Saul's presumption and disobedience led to his rejection by the Lord and set the scene for another to be chosen using God's criteria. Once David had been anointed and had shown his mettle, the text develops over many chapters how David gradually gained expressions of support. It is important for the narrator to show that David did not seek Saul's life or his throne—it was Saul who sought David's life. This account shows that although David initially joined the Philistine muster, he did not go to battle but was far away chasing the Amalekites. Thus, he could not have been responsible for the death of Saul.

Interpretational Issues in the Story

Ephod (1 Sam. 30:7). This was the garment of the priest that held the Urim and Thummim, the instruments used to make inquiries of God and to receive oracular responses. Asking oracles was not the same thing as prayer in that it was not conversation with God but a process to get answers from God on specific questions.

Sharing of plunder (1 Sam. 30:23–25). David's policy was founded on a theological principle—the plunder came by the Lord's hand and therefore none can claim it as a result of their military prowess. Consequently the plunder did not belong only to those who fought (as if it was their victory), but to David's entire band, who had suffered losses and served in various ways.

Background Information

Amalekites. We know of these descendants of Abraham's (Genesis 25) only from the biblical text. In stories spread through the early texts from Exodus through Samuel, they posed a constant problem to Israel and were found over a wide area, leading to the conclusion that they were nomadic or semi-nomadic.

Ziklag. The location of Ziklag is unknown, though it can be confidently located in the region west and a bit north of Beersheba.

Brook Besor. Located twelve to fifteen miles south of Ziklag (depending on the location of the city).

Mistakes to Avoid

This is an odd story to tell to children, but it appears often enough in curriculum. The lesson usually presented is either about praying (from 30:7) or sharing (from 30:23–25). Neither is appropriate. David was not praying; he was asking an oracle so that he would have guidance for a course of action. This procedure has no validity today. Nor was David sharing out of generosity; he was making a statement of theological significance about the nature of the battle that was fought.

60. David's Kingship (2 Samuel 5–7)

Lesson Focus

God kept his promise to make David king of Israel, gave him success, and made a covenant with him.

- God is faithful to keep his promises.
- God is able to overcome any obstacle.
- God reveals what we need to know about his plan.
- God delights in bringing success to those who serve him.

Lesson Application

We can believe what God says. God always keeps his promises.

- We trust God to keep his promises and depend on him to carry out his plan.
- We recognize that God should receive credit for our successes.

Biblical Context

The books of Samuel are about how God established his king, David, on the throne, as a way to show what his own kingship is like. An important part of the book, therefore, is showing that David truly was God's choice for king. David was not an ambitious upstart who overthrew the prior regime and then claimed God had done it—something that happened all the time in the ancient world. After Samuel's credentials as prophet, priest, and judge had been established, he became the logical kingmaker. Saul's presumption and disobedience led to his rejection by the Lord and set the scene for another to be chosen using God's criteria. Once David had been anointed and had shown his mettle, the text develops over many chapters how David gradually gained expressions of support. In these chapters David was finally brought to the throne and established an empire, and God blessed him with a covenant. These chapters are the centerpiece of the books of 1 and 2 Samuel.

Interpretational Issues in the Story

David and the ark (2 Sam. 6:2). It is not coincidental that the ark was returned to a central positioning in 2 Samuel 6 and that the covenant was made with David in 2 Samuel 7. The former shows David's intentions to honor the Lord; the latter shows the Lord's intentions to honor David. The return of the ark ended the long period that began with the ark being captured by the Philistines (1 Samuel 4). Though the ark had long since returned to Israel, it was off to the side. The significance of the ark's capture was that God was leaving the land of his unfaithful people (Ps. 78:60–61). Here the Lord was officially and publicly returning to the land, and his blessing and protection would be restored.

Uzzah (2 Sam. 6:6). Uzzah was supposed to follow instructions by using poles to carry the ark so a cart could not flip it out. Instead, he chose to transport the ark the way that the Philistines had done. Once that mistake was made, there were no longer any right choices. For those who might think this was harsh on God's part, we must remember first that God has higher expectations of those who serve in spiritual leadership (Uzzah was of the priestly family). We must also keep in mind that God's holiness is not superseded by his love or mercy. It is easy for us to say "God is love" and conclude that his love will negate his justice. If that were the case, he would never punish and his justice would not be evident. God's attributes are expressed in perfect balance.

Linen ephod and sacrifices (2 Sam. 6:14, 18). The Hebrew word for David's offering sacrifices is sometimes used to describe the priest's performing the actual ritual but is also used to describe the person who brought the offering (e.g., Judg. 6:26; 1 Sam. 1:21). The linen ephod was typically a priestly garment, but here David clothed himself in it because he was involved in a sacred procession and wanted to posture himself among the priests.

Background Information

Jerusalem. Jerusalem's king had been defeated at the time of Joshua (Josh. 10:22–23; 12:10) but the city is not listed as conquered in the battle itinerary of Joshua 10. The city is identified as conquered by the tribe of Judah in Judges 1, but apparently the city was not resettled. Consequently, it continued to be inhabited by the Jebusites throughout the centuries of the judges until the time of David. In this time period only the southern ridge of the city was occupied, extending south of the modern wall of the Old City. Archaeologists have identified some fortifications believed to belong to the Jebusite period and have uncovered a large monumental structure that the excavator believes to be David's palace. The southern ridge covers about ten to twelve acres.

David and the temple. It was common in the ancient world for kings to construct (or restore) a temple to the chief deity of the city. All in the ancient world believed a king must have the sponsorship of a god, and this relationship was often expressed in temple building. Therefore, it was not unusual that David desired to build a temple to the Lord. God's response, however, was that he was going to establish a house (dynasty) for David. God's response would not have seemed unusual in the ancient world, as gods expressed their support of a king through oracles. By separating the temple building from the covenant, it is made clear that David did not gain God's favor for his dynasty by building the temple. This is not the Great Symbiosis of the ancient world in which kings met the need of gods for opulent housing, and deity promises success and security for the king.

Mistakes to Avoid

Be cautious regarding how the Davidic covenant is attached to Jesus. It is true that Jesus fulfilled the Davidic covenant and that he is the rightful heir to the eternal throne of David, but the wording of 2 Samuel 7 is not anticipating Jesus, as is clear from the condition about what God would do when David's successor(s) sin (7:14). The trajectory of the covenant would eventually lead to Jesus, but that unfolded over time. The section of the story in 2 Samuel 6 involving Uzzah should not be used with younger children.

61. David and Mephibosheth (2 Samuel 9)

Lesson Focus

David sought out Jonathan's son Mephibosheth and brought him under his care and protection, demonstrating that he was not carrying out a vendetta against the house of Saul. God, not David's political ambition, had brought David to the throne.

Lesson Application

We should believe that God established David's throne.

Biblical Context

The books of Samuel are about how God established his king, David, on the throne, as a way to show what his own kingship is like. An important part of the book, therefore, is showing that David truly was God's choice for king. David was not an ambitious upstart who overthrew the prior regime and then claimed God had done it—something that happened all the time in the ancient world. After Samuel's credentials as prophet, priest, and judge had been established, he became the logical kingmaker. Saul's presumption and disobedience led to his rejection by the Lord and set the scene for another to be chosen using God's criteria. Once David had been anointed and had shown his mettle, the text develops over many chapters how David gradually gained expressions of support. It is important for the narrator to show that David did not seek Saul's life or his throne—it was Saul who sought David's life. The narrator continues this theme upon David's becoming king by showing that David did not exterminate Saul's line, as was commonly done by newly installed kings to eliminate competing claims to the throne. David cared for Saul's family, fulfilling his promises to both Jonathan and Saul (1 Sam. 20:15; 24:21).

Interpretational Issues in the Story

Kindness (2 Sam. 9:1–7). The word translated "kindness" most often has to do with loyalty or faithfulness to a covenant agreement. David had sworn to Saul and Jonathan that their descendants would be treated well, and David was honoring that oath. David might also have been exhibiting a graciousness of personality, but that is not the nuance of this word.

Background Information

Eating at the king's table. This was a way of indicating that someone was under royal protection and care. Whether that person actually ate at the same table or not, provisions or rations were supplied from the king's house. Key advisors were provisioned in this way, but so were politically dangerous people being detained and carefully supervised. Verses 11 and 13 indicate that Mephibosheth lived in Jerusalem and was treated as one of the king's sons, which suggests that he actually did eat with the king daily. Even though food was grown for him on his ancestral land holdings (v. 10), those holdings had been granted to him by the king's largesse (v. 7), and therefore the king was providing for him.

Mistakes to Avoid

The story should not be used as offering biblical instruction on being sensitive to disabled people. What is remarkable about David's act is not that Mephibosheth was lame, but that he was of the line of Saul and therefore posed a potential threat to David's claims to the throne. Even David's act of kindness is remarkable, but not because the recipient was lame; after all, it could easily be argued that by this course of action David was able to keep a close eye on a potential troublemaker. The Bible makes clear that David was innocent of acting against Saul. God was the one who brought David to the throne because of Saul's failures. Conversely, some claim that David was an astute politician who used intrigue and negative propaganda in his coup against Saul. David's kindness was unusual, but for political reasons, not sociological ones. Even so, David is not presented here as a model of kindness toward one's enemies. The text is establishing David as God's chosen king, so it is important to eliminate other political explanations of David's presence on the throne.

62. David and Bathsheba (2 Samuel 11:1–12:14)

Lesson Focus

David failed by abusing his power and taking another man's wife (Bathsheba), getting her pregnant, then arranging for her husband (Uriah), who had been his friend and compatriot for many years, to be killed in battle. God pronounces judgment through the prophet Nathan.

- God does not abuse his power and is not pleased when power he has granted is abused by those who represent him.
- God expects his people to respect marriage and life.
- Even those selected by God for special tasks sometimes fail, and God holds them accountable.

Lesson Application

We are accountable to God for representing him appropriately in the roles he has given us.

- We believe that God will hold us accountable and act accordingly.
- We respect life and marriage.

- We hold lightly whatever power we have over others.
- Any power or authority we have is granted by God, and we should use it wisely. (When teaching this to elementary children, abuse of power might be defined as bullying, when someone who has status by popularity or skill uses that position to put down or belittle others.)

Biblical Context

The books of Samuel are about how God established his king, David, on the throne, as a way to show what his own kingship is like. An important part of the book, therefore, is showing that David truly was God's choice for king. David was not an ambitious upstart who overthrew the prior regime and then claimed God had done it—something that happened all the time in the ancient world. After Samuel's credentials as prophet, priest, and judge had been established, he became the logical kingmaker. Saul's presumption and disobedience led to his rejection by the Lord and set the scene for another to be chosen using God's criteria. Once David had been anointed and had shown his mettle, the text develops over many chapters how David gradually gained expressions of support. God gave him great success and established his covenant with David, but David could not resist using his power to achieve his own sinful ends. The second half of 2 Samuel shows how David reaped the consequences of his faults and sins.

Interpretational Issues in the Story

"When kings go out to battle" (2 Sam. 11:1). Some interpreters have considered this at least a tacit accusation against David—why was he staying at home? But there were often good reasons for a king to stay at home while his army was in the field. Sometimes it had to do with domestic or succession issues. Other times it reflected that a battle was relatively insignificant or would involve a prolonged siege. Perhaps David was returning an insult to the young rebel king, in effect saying, "You are not even worth my personal attention." There is plenty of guilt for David in this passage; we need not invent additional claims against him.

Parable of the merciless sheep owner (2 Sam. 12:1–4). Some might wonder why this was the story Nathan chose to tell when the offenses of David were adultery and murder. The fact is, however, that adultery and murder were only the blossoms of a more deep-seated problem—abuse of power. So Nathan told a story about abuse of power.

Background Information

Besieging Rabbah of the Ammonites. The Ammonites had broken treaty with David and insulted his emissaries (2 Samuel 10), so David sent his army to lay siege to their capital city and remove their offensive young ruler. Rabbah is the name of the city, which is located about forty-five miles east of Jerusalem.

Bathsheba's identity. Eliam and Uriah, Bathsheba's husband, had been important officers of David's since the wilderness days (note 2 Sam. 23:34, 39). He knew them well and probably had known Bathsheba since she was a little girl. Furthermore, her grandfather was one of David's primary advisors, Ahithophel. It may be this betrayal by David that made Ahithophel willing to support Absalom's revolt against David (2 Sam. 16:15).

Bathing on the roof. Only the king's palace roof would have afforded a glimpse of her rooftop, and it was likely sufficiently distant that he could see only that someone was bathing, but without a clear view. Nevertheless, the idea of a woman bathing was provocative enough, especially since he undoubtedly knew whose house it was. David's Jerusalem was a small place, and he would have known who lived in each of the several dozen houses that he could view from his rooftop. In 11:3 the NIV provides the subject of the second sentence ("the man") but the Hebrew indicates no change of subject—David inquired about Bathsheba, noting to himself that she was beautiful and that her husband was not at home. So he sent messengers to proposition her.

Restore fourfold. Fourfold restitution is what the law called for when something was stolen (see Ex. 22:1). Perhaps it is no surprise that, from this point forward, four crowned-prince sons of David died, most by execution (Bathsheba's son, Amnon, Absalom, and Adonijah).

Mistakes to Avoid

Bathsheba's reputation should not be impugned here. She was not being seductive or improper by bathing on the roof, and she had no choice once David had sent for her. Whatever guilt she may or may not have had, the text does not indicate it, and that is God's business. David is treated as the guilty party. Uriah's behavior was above reproach and Joab's actions reflected his loyalty to David. Like Bathsheba, both were pawns of the king's machinations. The focus of the narrative should not be on the behavior of Bathsheba or Joab, or even for that matter on David's. The text tells us that his behavior displeased the Lord (11:27) but that is no surprise. The account is not to tell us to act like Uriah or not to act like David. It is telling us the circumstances by which David's kingship derailed. We are not looking for moralistic lessons but for an understanding of God's plan and the part David played in it. Some become distressed over how so godly a man (as evidenced in the Psalms) could be guilty of such heinous crimes. It is important to recognize that we are all fallen humans and that even the best of us succumb to human failings. We need to resist putting heroes on pedestals and instead pay attention to the God who works through our flaws and accomplishes his plan despite us.

This lesson is sometimes used to teach concepts such as "Be sure your sins will find you out," or "You can hide your sins from man, but not from God," or moral lessons such as "Guard your eyes from sin." These are all true biblical teachings, and their connections with the story are transparent. If we need to be reminded of these lessons, by all means we should use this opportunity to do so. Nevertheless, we still have to ask the important question, To what purpose is the author using this story? To the extent that we can answer that, we will discover the authoritative teaching of the text. One might ask, can't the text do all this at once? It can, but it doesn't. While there are always truths we can learn, the ones the text is teaching have priority. Here chapter 12 tells us precisely what those are.

63. David and Absalom (2 Samuel 15–18)

Lesson Focus

Absalom, David's son, had himself crowned king and drove David from the throne. A civil war was fought, and when Absalom was killed, David was restored to kingship. This is an example of how God brought judgment against David for his sins against Bathsheba and Uriah.

- Even when God forgives, he does not necessarily shield from all consequences of sin, and those consequences can be severe and heartbreaking.
- God holds his chosen leaders to high levels of accountability.
- Even though Absalom's coup was part of David's punishment, God still held Absalom responsible for his rebellion, and he suffered the consequences of his choices.

Lesson Application

When we choose to sin, we should recognize that God holds us responsible for our actions.

- We should be faithful to God because he takes sin seriously.
- We must recognize that sin has consequences.

Biblical Context

The books of Samuel are about how God established his king, David, on the throne, as a way to show what his own kingship is like. An important part of the book, therefore, is showing that David truly was God's choice for king. David was not an ambitious upstart who overthrew the prior regime and then claimed God had done it—something that happened all the time in the ancient world. Once God had established David on the throne and made a covenant with him, David's kingdom grew and he was successful. Unfortunately, however, David's character flaws and weaknesses caught up with him, and in the latter part of the book the narrator traces some of the consequences that resulted for David's family.

Interpretational Issues in the Story

"No man designated by the king to hear you" (2 Sam. 15:3). It is difficult to determine whether Absalom was criticizing the king for not having enough representatives or for not spending enough time himself in audience, but he certainly was criticizing the king. Every claim of injustice in the land would have been at least tacitly a criticism of the king.

"Let him curse, for the LORD has told him to" (2 Sam. 16:11). David was not claiming to have inside information; he was drawing deductions from the events that had occurred. David was being driven from his throne in his capital city by his own son. Many Israelites would have seen this as a clear indication that David was out of favor with God and receiving punishment at his hand. The Lord had "told" Shimei to curse because of the circumstances; that is, it appears obvious that God had cursed David, which would have invited others to join in that chorus, for which Shimei had good cause, being, as he was, of the house of Saul. This is important to the Absalom stories, for it shows that David was well aware that the events unfolding represented the judgment of God.

Absalom's advisors (2 Sam. 17:1–14). Ahithophel's advice was for Absalom to act quickly, thereby resulting in minimal death within the army (support Absalom would need to succeed). Ahithophel realized that if David was out of the way, the opposition to Absalom would be minimal. Hushai's advice played to Absalom's vanity, which had always been his weakness.

Background Information

King judging by the gate. In the ancient world the king was also the supreme court—difficult cases came to him. Major cities had a king's seat by the gate where he would hold audience at regular intervals to hear cases.

Location of the battle. David left Jerusalem because he did not want to bring civil war to the capital. He fled into Transjordan, which moved the war out of the central core of the country. Mahanaim was an important (and presumably defensible) administrative center about thirty-five miles from the fords of the Jordan.

Mistakes to Avoid

Though David had his strengths and weaknesses as a father, the narrator was not seeking to instruct the reader in principles of parenting. Neither David nor Absalom was used by the narrator to indicate how God's people should or should not act. Generally, the selection of what to include in the book was driven by a desire to show God's plan unfolding and the nature of God as he deals with his people. The behavior of people is described, but the text consistently avoids offering principles for living from that behavior. That David may have been merciful to Shimei (16:11) or Absalom (18:5) is simply narrative fact, not moral lesson. Perhaps David was wrong to be inclined toward mercy on Absalom. God did not offer approval or disapproval of David's actions, and without understanding David's motives, neither can we. We cannot claim that mercy is always right regardless of the circumstances; i.e., sometimes it is necessary to hold people accountable for their actions. This story should not be part of the curriculum for younger children.

64. Solomon Asks for Wisdom (1 Kings 3:1–15)

Lesson Focus

God promised David that one of his sons or heirs would succeed him as king of Israel. Solomon was one fulfillment of this promise. Solomon, like all Old Testament kings, was to show what God was like as a king in the way he ruled the people and served God. The Israelites were to see God as king through the actions of Solomon. Solomon's request for wisdom pleased God, because Solomon's use of wisdom would help the Israelites to see how wise God is.

- God is wise and he desires rulers to be wise.
- God is able to provide wisdom to those who seek it.

Lesson Application

We can act in such a way that our friends can see God in what we say and do.

- We must seek to be wise so that people will see God's wisdom in us.
- We should ask God for wisdom because he delights in giving wisdom.

Biblical Context

First and 2 Kings are about the failures of kingship. The books of Samuel relate how God set up kingship in such a way that kings were supposed to be extensions of his kingship and would thus reveal what God's kingship was like. With only a few exceptions, however, the kings of Israel and Judah failed to approach this ideal. The books of 1 and 2 Kings portray this road of failure in the stories of one king after another. Here we see that Solomon began well and had the right idea of what was necessary for successful kingship.

Interpretational Issues in the Story

Dream at the high place (1 Kings 3:5). Since the temple had not yet been built, worship had not yet been consolidated at one place. Eventually high places were eliminated, but here at the high place at Gibeon Solomon offered sacrifices to honor the Lord. In the ancient world when kings slept at a sacred site, it was sometimes with the hope that they would have a dream in which they would gain revelation from God. Whether or not Solomon had that end in mind, God did indeed appear to him. God questioned Solomon about his desires in relation to his role as king.

Limits to Solomon's wisdom (1 Kings 3:7–9). The wisest king eventually made some of the most foolish decisions. Solomon asked for wisdom to make his ruling decisions well. Kings had to pass judgment in cases that were brought before them and had to make both domestic and international policy decisions. Solomon recognized his lack of experience in these areas and felt his inadequacy. The wisdom to rule was asked for and granted. But we know that those who may be capable of wise leadership do not always make wise personal choices, as Solomon illustrates.

Background Information

High places. High place (*bamah*) is the name for a ritual site. Sometimes such sites were on elevated areas, either natural or artificial, but were also located at city gates. Some high places were used to worship Yahweh (as here and in 1 Kings 3:4) but, if not connected to a sanctuary, could be used for whatever god the person performing the ritual wished to acknowledge. Eventually, however, all high places were outlawed, and the temple was supposed to be the place where rituals were performed.

Solomon's wives. The Bible does not condemn Solomon for his wives but for the worship of their gods (11:4). In the ancient world marriages were arranged, and for a king marriages represented political alliances. Having many wives was then an indication of the power and influence of a ruler. We should not think that Solomon was a slave of his lust and just wanted to marry every woman that he saw. The wives represented royal marriages between major political powers, while the concubines represented alliances with smaller tribes in which the woman brought no dowry to the marriage.

Gods of his wives. Usually wives adopted the gods of their husband because their marriage represented a transition into another clan or tribe. But royal wives were different because they served as emissaries of their people in the court of the king they married. Therefore, just as ambassadors today are granted sovereign territory inside the nation where they are living, it would have been expected that a place to worship their gods would be provided to the wives who came from other countries.

Mistakes to Avoid

It is true that God is wise and that he wants all his people to be wise. It is also true that God encourages his people to ask for wisdom (James 1:5). These are both part of the lesson application mentioned above. But we must exercise some care in how we associate those ideas with this story. In other words, we cannot put ourselves in the shoes of Solomon—we are not kings and God is not making that same offer to each of us. From this story we understand that God is the source of wisdom and that he values wisdom. It is on the basis of this understanding of God that we gain confidence to seek wisdom.

65. Building the Temple (1 Kings 6–8)

Lesson Focus

Solomon built a temple so that God could live in the midst of his people in Jerusalem. The temple was completed and dedicated to serve as God's dwelling place.

- God desires to live in the midst of his people.
- God's relationship with his people involves his presence being with them.
- God deserves all the highest quality of materials and workmanship.
- God reigns from his temple.

Lesson Application

We can enjoy the presence of God.

- We are God's people today, and God's presence is in us. We are the temple (1 Cor. 3:16; 6:19).
- We should do all that we can to ensure that the holiness of God's presence is maintained.
- We should treat God's presence with higher honor than we give to anything else.

Biblical Context

First and 2 Kings are about the failures of kingship. The books of Samuel relate how God set up kingship in such a way that kings were supposed to be extensions of his kingship and would thus reveal what God's kingship was like. With only a few exceptions, however, the kings of Israel and Judah failed to approach this ideal. The books of 1 and 2 Kings portray this road of failure in the stories of one king after another. Solomon began well and had the right idea of what was necessary for successful kingship, but he also had areas of failure. His crowning achievement, and the high point of 1 and 2 Kings, was the construction of the temple in Jerusalem, which was the place of God's throne and from where God exercised his kingship.

Interpretational Issues in the Story

Temple and church (1 Kings 6:1). The temple in the ancient world was far different from the church building today. The building that we call "church" is simply a place for the assembly of God's people for corporate worship. Even though we sometimes call it "God's house," in reality God is housed within his people, not in a building. In Israel, God chose to live in the temple, and though people gathered in Jerusalem on sacred occasions, the courtyard was not designed for corporate worship and could not accommodate very many. People came to the temple to watch public rituals and to offer sacrifices for themselves or their families. The priests were there to officiate over the rituals and advise about procedures. They also made sure that only those who qualified could enter.

Background Information

Jerusalem at the time of Solomon. The temple was built on the property purchased by David just north of the city as it stood in David's day. This area is at a higher elevation than the rest of the city, which was appropriate for the temple site. This extended the city walls by a couple of acres.

Temple design. The temple built by Solomon followed a design well-known in the ancient Near East (see illustration p. 446). It had a portico and two chambers arranged along a straight-line axis. Proportions and dimensions also show some similarity. In the text, the execution of the details is attributed to Solomon (e.g., 6:2–6, 14–36) rather than to God's instructions. God's speeches focus on how the temple will function (6:11–13). In the ancient world deity was sometimes cited as the source of the architectural design. That is not the case here, leaving us to infer that Solomon simply followed current practices and made use of portions of the pattern in the tabernacle.

Temple building in the ancient world. In the ancient world temples were often built by a king to gain the favor of a deity and to solidify the sponsorship of the god. The temple supposedly provided the god a place to dwell in the midst of the land where he or she could receive the offerings and gifts of the people. The deity would in turn provide blessing and protection. Elsewhere in the ancient world, gods were perceived as having needs such as food and shelter that could be met through the temple and its rituals. In contrast, the God of Israel had no needs and the temple was to provide for relationship.

Sacred space. Sacred space was established on land that was believed to be inhabited by the presence of a deity. On such sacred spaces temples were built and rituals performed. Priests performed the rituals and provided instruction about the deity and how he was to be worshiped. Rules for purity and access to the sacred space were established, and these had to be carefully observed. Sacred space contained graded areas of increasing holiness as one approached the center, where the deity dwelt, with each successive area characterized by stricter regulations and more limited access. The book of Leviticus describes how sacred space was to be maintained.

Mistakes to Avoid

The temple and the church are totally different, so the terms should not be used interchangeably. The temple was a building; the church is a group of people. The temple was a place for God's presence where rituals were performed. The church building is a place where God's people gather on a regular basis to engage in corporate worship. Temples had limited access; churches have open access. There can be many church buildings; there was only supposed to be one temple (for one God). It would create significant misunderstandings for the students to try to merge these two together.

In response to Solomon's prayer of dedication of the temple, God says, "If my people who are called by my name humble themselves, and pray and seek my face and turn from their wicked ways, then I will hear from heaven and will forgive their sin and heal their land" (2 Chron. 7:14). The promise of living in a covenant land was given to Israel. The promise was put into effect through the temple and the covenant. We do not live in a covenant land nor do we have a temple functioning in geographical sacred space. Though the promise is not to us, it still reveals important things about God that we should take to heart. God does want his people to seek him and to turn from wickedness. God does desire us to be in relationship with him, and he is ready to pour out his blessings. This verse, then, is not a promise for us to claim, but it helps us to know God better and to understand what he wants from us. Sometimes lessons on the temple building focus on Solomon's following all the Lord's specifications. That is a key element in the construction of the tabernacle in Exodus, but it is difficult to find building instructions by God in Kings and Chronicles. Therefore, this should not be the focus.

66. Queen of Sheba (1 Kings 10:1–13; 2 Chronicles 9:1–12)

Lesson Focus

The queen of Sheba visited from far away because she had heard of Solomon's wisdom. What God had given Solomon had caused his reputation to spread to the far reaches, and the queen came, observed, and confirmed.

- God was the source of Solomon's great wisdom.
- God had made himself known beyond Israel through Solomon's success as king.
- God is a great king and can make great those who are faithful to him.
- God delights in bringing honor to those who honor him.
- God is a wise and just king.

Lesson Application

We should recognize that wisdom and greatness have their source in God.

- We should desire that whatever gifts God has given us would result in glory given to him.
- We recognize God's kingship.

Biblical Context

First and 2 Kings are about the failures of kingship. The books of Samuel relate how God set up kingship in such a way that kings were designed to be extensions of his kingship and would thus reveal what his kingship was like. With few exceptions, however, the kings of Israel and Judah failed to approach this ideal. The books of 1 and 2 Kings portray this road of failure in the stories of one king after another. Solomon began well and had the right idea of what was necessary for successful kingship, but he also had areas of failure. Just as the books of Samuel accumulate testimony concerning God's choice of David, so this section of Kings accumulates testimony that God provided Solomon with unparalleled wisdom.

Interpretational Issues in the Story

The queen's visit (1 Kings 10:1). This ruler traveled far for a visit. Aside from the spoken reason of curiosity concerning Solomon's reputation, state business was likely also involved. Formalizing trade agreements and protecting trade interests was important. It is also possible that some of the gifts she brought could be understood as tribute that acknowledged Solomon's suzerainty. But the text is less interested in political and economical rationale than it is in the queen's assessment of Solomon.

The queen's confession (1 Kings 10:6–9). The queen's speech is the heart of the story. In it she confirmed that Solomon's reputation had spread far and wide and that what she observed exceeded all expectations. She indicated how Solomon's wisdom should result in happy and successful people. Most importantly, she praised Yahweh as the source of Solomon's success and concluded with a reference to the covenant and to the result of justice and righteousness. This is testimony to what God's kingship is all about.

Background Information

Sheba. Sheba was located in the southwestern corner of the Arabian Peninsula, perhaps in modern Yemen, a strategic location that connected to land trade routes from Mesopotamia, and it benefited from the sea trade up and down the Red Sea.

Qualities of kings. Throughout the ancient world the ideal king was understood as someone wise and just. Both gods and peoples were interested in kings' displaying these important qualities. It is no surprise then that these are the criteria by which Solomon was evaluated.

120 talents of gold. The extravagance of the queen's gift, equivalent to about four tons of gold, is indication of the honor that she gave to Solomon.

Mistakes to Avoid

While Solomon's magnificence is detailed in the text, it is clear that ultimately this was not to elevate Solomon, who was given wisdom and everything else, but to elevate the God who gave such wisdom and was the source of it. If students come out of the lesson being in awe of Solomon rather than of God, we have failed. As always, there are many trivial things in the story that must not be made the focus of teaching. No biblical model for hospitality is given here, nor can we infer that God is honored by the accumulation of wealth. The trivial details must be left in the background and not turned into the lesson of the text.

67. Solomon: Failure and Disobedience (1 Kings 11)

Lesson Focus

Solomon disobeyed God by marrying wives from countries in which God had forbidden such alliances, by worshiping idols, and by failing to worship and love only the one true God. As a result, God caused enemies of Solomon to take most of the kingdom from Solomon.

- God is a jealous God and does not tolerate the unfaithfulness of his people, particularly kings.
- God holds leaders of his people accountable for their disobedience.
- God wants to be the sole object of worship.

Lesson Application

God wants us to obey him and to worship him. In this way we show others that we love God, and others can see God in what we do.

- We are to worship God alone.
- We believe that God will hold his people accountable.

Biblical Context

First and 2 Kings are about the failures of kingship. The books of Samuel relate how God set up kingship in such a way that kings were supposed to be extensions of his kingship and would thus reveal what his kingship was like. With few exceptions, however, the kings of Israel and Judah failed to approach this ideal. The book portrays this road of failure in the stories of one king after another. Solomon began well and had the right idea of what was necessary for successful kingship, but he also had areas of failure.

Interpretational Issues in the Story

Solomon's evil (1 Kings 11:6). Solomon's most significant fault was worshiping the gods of his wives (11:4). In Deuteronomy, when Moses addressed some of the inherent problems with authority figures, he warned that the king "shall not acquire many wives for himself, lest his heart turn away" (Deut. 17:17; cf. 7:3). It does *not* say, "He must not take many wives because God's design is one woman for one man." The problem was not seen as polygamy but as false worship.

In love (1 Kings 11:2). In these contexts love does not refer to personal emotional sentiments but to loyal attachment. (It is the same Hebrew word used in 1 Kings 5:1; NIV: "been on friendly terms.")

Background Information

Royal marriages. We should not imagine that Solomon's wives and concubines were women with whom he was interested in having a relationship. Whenever a king made an alliance, whether with a nation, a city, a clan, or an important family, the alliance was sealed with a marriage to a significant member of that group. Thus, Solomon's wives were a reflection of his political success and the extent of his influence. Normally a wife adopted the religion of her husband, but in political marriages such as Solomon's, the wives' own form of worship was typically accommodated.

Ashtoreth, Molech, Chemosh. Ashtoreth (Astarte) was consort of the Canaanite god Baal; Molech was the national god of the Ammonites; and Chemosh was the national god of the Moabites.

High places. High place (*bamah*) is the name for a ritual site. Sometimes such sites were on elevated areas, either natural or artificial, but were also located at city gates. Some high places were used to worship Yahweh (as here and in 1 Kings 3:4), but, if not connected to a sanctuary, they could be used for whatever god the person performing the ritual wished to acknowledge.

Eventually, however, all high places were outlawed and the temple was supposed to be the place to perform rituals.

Mistakes to Avoid

The text does not tell us that Solomon fell in love with women from other countries (despite common translations of 1 Kings 11:1). Marriage was a political matter used to make alliances between nations and powerful families. Love had little to do with it in most cases. Having many wives served as an indication of political power. The trouble came when Solomon began worshiping with them. Since the ancient institution of marriage was so different from ours, and royal marriages were so different from the experience of common folks, we can conclude that the lesson here cannot be focused on choosing spouses wisely. Most people in the ancient world did not choose their spouses, and Solomon's choices were politically determined.

68. Jeroboam Disobeys God (1 Kings 12:25–33; 13:1–5; 14:7–11)

Lesson Focus

Jeroboam caused the people of Israel to worship in improper ways. Because of this disobedience God did not bless Jeroboam and took the throne from him.

- God cannot be worshiped in just any way.
- God expects to be obeyed.
- God is who he is and must not be misrepresented.

Lesson Application

When we develop wrong ways to think about God, it makes God unhappy. When we obey God and worship him properly, others can know God better by watching us.

- Our worship of God needs to be appropriate.
- We need to be careful not to represent the Lord improperly.
- We should read the Bible to get an accurate picture of what God is like and should be careful not to distort that picture to accommodate what we think God should be like or what will meet our needs.

Biblical Context

First and 2 Kings are about the failures of kingship. The books of Samuel related how God set up kingship in such a way that kings were designed as extensions of his kingship and would thus reveal what his kingship was like. With few exceptions, however, the kings of Israel and Judah failed to approach this ideal. The books of 1 and 2 Kings portray this road of failure in the stories of one king after another. Solomon had demonstrated wisdom and justice as God had blessed him, but his failures led to the split of the kingdom. At this point the book begins the litany of failures, particularly evident in the Northern Kingdom (Israel) begun by Jeroboam.

Interpretational Issues in the Story

Rehoboam, Jerusalem, and Yahweh (1 Kings 12:26–27). Through the decades of the kingship of David and Solomon in Jerusalem, a strong bond had been formed between the political position of the Davidic kings, the capital city of Jerusalem, and the worship of Yahweh in the temple. Then Rehoboam, Solomon's son, ruled as king of Judah in Jerusalem. Jeroboam, king of Israel, to the north, was reluctant to allow his subjects to travel to Jerusalem to worship at the temple because it might have weakened his grasp politically. He set about providing an alternative.

Golden calves (1 Kings 12:28). The biblical text never suggests that these calves are other gods. Some kings are condemned for worship at the high places and for honoring Baal or Asherah (Canaanite gods) but there is no suggestion that the calves represent these gods. It is most likely that Jeroboam was promoting the calves as a way to worship Yahweh. Consequently this should be considered more a violation of the second commandment than the first (though the calves were not truly intended to be an image of the deity either).

High places (1 Kings 12:31). "High place" (*bamah*) is the name for a ritual site. Sometimes such sites were on elevated areas, either natural or artificial, but were also located at city gates. Some high places were used to worship Yahweh (as here and in 1 Kings 3:4), but, if not connected to a sanctuary, they could be used for whatever god the person performing the ritual wished to acknowledge. Eventually, however, all high places were outlawed and the temple was supposed to be the place where rituals were performed.

Misrepresenting God (1 Kings 12:28). Just as Jeroboam fashioned the calves to suit his political needs, we often read the Bible and draw selectively from it to formulate an understanding of God that is convenient and comfortable. This is a distortion that must be avoided.

Background Information

Dan and Bethel. At the time of the narrative, these two towns already had an ancient heritage in Israel. They were conveniently located at the northern and southern borders of the land that had become the Northern Kingdom of Israel. Bethel has not been extensively excavated, but at Dan the cultic area that had the calf has been unearthed.

Calf images. In this time and region gods were frequently portrayed standing on the back of a bull. But Jeroboam has no god standing on the backs of the calves, which might indicate that Yahweh was still understood as the invisible God. If the calf was a pedestal, it served a function similar to the ark of the covenant, which was viewed as a footstool. But it is likely that there is more going on here. The pedestal animals set up to the gods often served as emblems. An emblem animal was one that shared and represented some of the principal attributes of the deity. Images of emblem animals were viewed as containing the divine essence and as being able to receive the worship given to the god. In this sense, technically, the calf was not the deity but stood in for the deity in important ways.

Mistakes to Avoid

We should not develop the teaching of this lesson through metaphor, for example, asking, "What are the idols in your life?" That would take us in the wrong direction, since these images were actually being used to worship Yahweh. Younger children will not be able to grasp the nuances of the nature of the calves very easily.

69. Elijah and the Ravens (1 Kings 16:29–17:6)

Lesson Focus

In response to Ahab and Jezebel's support of Baal, God announced a drought through Elijah and then showed that he could take care of his prophet even as he punished the people.

- God controls the weather and is the one who sends rain and provides food.
- God will not tolerate competition.
- God is sovereign; other gods are useless.

Lesson Application

We should believe that God is the source of our sustenance and acknowledge our dependence on him.

- We worship God alone.
- We recognize God as our provider.

Biblical Context

First and 2 Kings are about the failures of kingship. The books of Samuel relate how God set up kingship in such a way that kings were designed to be extensions of his kingship and would thus reveal what his kingship was like. With few exceptions, however, the kings of Israel and Judah failed to approach this ideal. The books of 1 and 2 Kings portray this road of failure in the stories of one king after another. Solomon had demonstrated wisdom and justice as God had blessed him, but his failures led to the split of the kingdom. The books then begin the litany of failures, particularly evident in the Northern Kingdom, Israel, and primarily shown by the golden calves. In Ahab and Jezebel an even greater threat arose as they attempted to set up Baal as the national god in place of Yahweh.

Interpretational Issues in the Story

Agenda of Ahab and Jezebel (1 Kings 16:31–33). As early as the Judges period the Israelites continually turned to Baal worship, but in doing so they did not necessarily reject worship of Yahweh. They probably continued to think of Yahweh as their national God and simply added Baal, Asherah, and others as gods and worshiped them in various ways (cf. Judg. 6:13, where Gideon clearly worships Yahweh, and 6:25, where other gods are prominently worshiped). But Ahab had something different in mind. Apparently, through the influence of Jezebel, Baal was being put in the place of Yahweh as the national god. Supporters of Yahweh were being executed because it had become a political issue.

Ahab (1 Kings 16:29). Ahab reigned from 874–853 BC. His father had founded a new dynasty and had succeeded in making peace with both northern neighbors (Phoenicia and Aram) and southern ones (especially Judah). Relationship to the northern neighbors was the impetus for adopting some of their gods and religious ideas and practices.

Jezebel (1 Kings 16:31). Jezebel was a Phoenician princess who married Ahab in a political arrangement between Israel and Phoenicia. As an international political wife, she was not expected to leave her gods behind (she was like an ambassador in Ahab's court). In these stories, however, we find that she was an aggressive evangelist for her gods, as she sought to elevate them above Yahweh. Elijah was an obstacle to her political and religious ambitions, so she sought to execute him.

Elijah the prophet (1 Kings 17:1–6). The prophets during this period tended to serve as advisors to the king. Sometimes this was a formal role (Nathan serving David) but in times when the king was being warned of unacceptable behavior, the prophet was not officially recognized by the king. Unlike later prophets such as Jeremiah, these early prophets tended mostly to address the king rather than speak directly to the people.

Background Information

Baal and fertility. "Baal" is a title ("lord") and was used for a variety of gods (even Yahweh; see Hos. 2:16). In Canaanite regions the title was usually applied to Hadad, the storm god. In Phoenicia, where Jezebel was from, the name Baal might have applied to a different deity, with Baal Melqart being the usual suggestion. Not much is known about Melqart, though he appears to have been a warrior god and a dying-rising god associated with the cycles of nature.

Religious persecution. Usually in polytheistic systems there was no religious repression because all gods were recognized as legitimate (though some were stronger than others). People were welcome to worship whatever god they chose. In situations like the one we find in these chapters, an attempt was being made to elevate one god over another, thus creating political conflict. The resulting persecution was over political and economic power, not theological doctrines.

The Brook Cherith. The location of this place is still unknown. Part of the problem is that the Hebrew of 17:3 could be translated "on the way to the Jordan" rather than "east of the Jordan." Those who look for it west of the Jordan associate it with one of the wadis that runs to the Jordan, such as Wadi Kelt near Jericho, Wadi Swenit a little farther north, or Wadi Faria that meets the Jordan at the ford of Adam. For those who consider it to be east of Jordan, the Wadi Arnon on the east side of the Dead Sea has been a favorite choice. Ravens frequent such areas and often hide food to retrieve later.

Mistakes to Avoid

This story should not be used to teach that God will provide food for his starving people, because that is not always true. Unfortunately, many Christians have starved to death over the centuries. Even a general lesson about God providing our needs is not to the point. In this story God is showing his power over Baal, who was being promoted as the provider of water and food. The point here is that Yahweh is the supplier; he is more powerful than Baal.

70. Elijah and the Widow's Oil (1 Kings 17:7–24)

Lesson Focus

Elijah was directed to the region of Zarephath near Jezebel's hometown, where a poor widow would provide food for him. In this way God again showed that he is the one who provides food, even in Baal's territory. When her son died, Elijah was able to bring him back to life through God's power.

- God is the provider of food.
- God wants us to trust him for provision.
- God is the giver of life.

Lesson Application

We should believe that God is the one who provides life and sustenance for life.

- We trust God for provision.
- We understand that life is in God's hands.

Biblical Context

First and 2 Kings are about the failures of kingship. The books of Samuel related how God set up kingship in such a way that kings were designed to be extensions of his kingship and would thus reveal what his kingship was like. With few exceptions, however, the kings of Israel and Judah failed to approach this ideal. The books of 1 and 2 Kings portray this road of failure in the stories of one king after another. Solomon had demonstrated wisdom and justice as God had blessed him, but his failures led to the split of the kingdom. Then the books begin the litany of failures, particularly evident in the Northern Kingdom, Israel, and primarily shown by the golden calves. In Ahab and Jezebel an even greater threat arose as they attempted to set up Baal as the national god in place of Yahweh. In this account the Lord not only continues to provide for Elijah but shows that he can provide for people who live in Baal's home region.

Interpretational Issues in the Story

"I have commanded" (1 Kings 17:9). It is interesting that the woman had no knowledge of such a command. We can see then that it is not that God had spoken to the woman somehow, but that he had arranged for such an outcome.

"The LORD your God" (1 Kings 17:12). The woman had apparently recognized Elijah as an Israelite, perhaps by his accent or clothing, so she offers her oath in that name. This is not, however, an indication that she shared his belief.

"Stretched himself upon the child" (1 Kings 17:21). Just as we might use CPR, artificial respiration, or the Heimlich maneuver, Elijah was using a technique known and practiced in the ancient world. Regardless of the thinking behind the technique or how it was supposedly effective, God responds with the restoration of life.

The widow's declaration (1 Kings 17:24). Although she was impressed with Elijah's demonstration of power and thereby saw him as a true servant of deity, and although he was a true prophet, a mouthpiece for Yahweh, we still know nothing of her personal convictions. Polytheistic people in the ancient world believed that all gods are powerful, though some more than others. There is no evidence for thinking that she had converted to a faithful worship of the one God, Yahweh.

Background Information

Zarephath. Now known as Sarafand, this town was located along the Mediterranean coast between the towns of Tyre and Sidon (in modern Lebanon) and was therefore outside the land of Israel and in the heart of Jezebel's home territory—a stronghold for Baal worship.

Baal. "Baal" is a title ("lord") and was used for a variety of gods (even for Yahweh; see Hos. 2:16). In Canaanite regions it usually was applied to Hadad, the storm god. In Phoenicia, where Jezebel was from, it might have been a different deity, Baal Melqart being the usual suggestion. Not much is known about Melqart, though he apparently was a warrior god and a dying-rising god associated with the cycles of nature.

Flour and oil. Grain and oil were major exported goods from this harbor town and, as staple products, are indicative of the fertility of the land. Again Yahweh is showing that he can provide sustenance for the needy, even in Baal's home territory. Theoretically Baal, as a fertility god, should have been able to provide these basics.

Mistakes to Avoid

While God provided for the widow, her son, and Elijah, we must be careful not to suggest that he will always do so for any of us in every circumstance. It is more important for us to recognize God as the source of whatever provision we have and the giver of life. He is able to do all things, but here the Bible is not teaching what he will do for all, but only what he did for some on this occasion and, therefore, what he is capable of doing at any time. It would be inappropriate to formulate this lesson into a promise that students can claim. Narratives do not provide us with general promises.

71. Elijah and the Contest (1 Kings 18:16–46)

Lesson Focus

The Lord demonstrated that he alone is God by withholding then sending rain and by sending fire from heaven.

- God controls the weather and brings fertility to the land and food to the people.
- Yahweh alone is God.

Lesson Application

We should believe that the Lord alone is God and live in accordance with that belief.

- We trust God to provide.
- We acknowledge God as the source of our food.

Biblical Context

First and 2 Kings are about the failures of kingship. The books of Samuel relate how God set up kingship in such a way that kings were designed to be extensions of his kingship and would thus reveal what his kingship was like. With few exceptions, however, the kings of Israel and Judah failed to approach this ideal. The books of 1 and 2 Kings portray this road of failure in the stories of one king after another. Solomon had demonstrated wisdom and justice as God had blessed him, but his failures led to the split of the kingdom. The books then begin the litany of failures, particularly evident in the Northern Kingdom, Israel, primarily shown by the golden calves. In Ahab and Jezebel an even greater threat arose as they attempted to set up Baal as the national god in place of Yahweh. In this account the Lord brings an end to the drought in the context of a direct confrontation between his prophet Elijah and the prophets of Baal.

Interpretational Issues in the Story

Function of the contest (1 Kings 18:23–24). The end result of the day's activities is that the drought came to an end. Both Baal and Yahweh were petitioned for rain, with the objective being that the more powerful god would provide it. The burnt offering was made because this particular offering was designed to accompany petitions. The god who responded to the petition for rain would answer by igniting the sacrifice, indicating that he had accepted the offering. Then, when the rain came, it would be clear which god had sent it. In this sense, the contest was more about sending rain than about igniting a sacrifice. Elijah serves as the champion of Yahweh's kingship and sovereignty.

Elijah's speech (1 Kings 18:21). Later prophets called on the Israelites to repent and return to the Lord, but here Elijah just chided them for their ambivalence. They refused to take a position and undoubtedly, like their forefathers, were trying somehow to live in both worlds, holding on to both Baal and Yahweh. Elijah called on them to make a decision.

"Ran before Ahab" (1 Kings 18:46). This final verse is a transition to the next chapter and need not be included in this story. But if it is mentioned, note should be made that Elijah's running ahead of the king does not suggest a race but an entourage of allies (notice 2 Sam. 15:1 for the same phrase). In this case, it suggests that Ahab was convinced and had aligned himself with Elijah, who officially accompanied him back to Jezreel.

Background Information

Baal. "Baal" is a title ("lord") and was used for a variety of gods (even Yahweh, see Hos. 2:16). In Canaanite regions it usually was applied to Hadad, the storm god. In Phoenicia, where Jezebel was from, it might have been a different deity, Baal Melqart being the usual suggestion. Not much is known about Melqart, though he appears to have been a warrior god and a dying-rising god associated with the cycles of nature.

Mount Carmel. The Carmel range (not really a single peak) cuts off the international trade route known as the Coastal Highway and forms a natural boundary between the coastal regions. Though Israelite tribes had been granted territory all the way to Tyre, the Carmel range may have been serving in this period as the border between Israel and Phoenicia.

Calling down fire. The fire served as a way to determine which God would send the rain. The fire had other aspects to it, such as the fact that Baal was reputed to be a storm god and was often portrayed with lightning bolts in his upraised fist. So, again, Yahweh was challenging Baal at his own game.

Elijah's taunts. To those familiar with God as he is presented in the Bible, the content of the taunts in 18:27 sound like ridiculous suggestions. Literature concerning Baal and other gods in the ancient world, however, indicates that these are some of the activities that engaged (and distracted) deity. The gods were envisioned as living much like humans do: they traveled and slept and were in other ways indisposed or unavailable. The suggestion that Baal was sleeping is particularly relevant because he was often considered to be a dying-rising fertility god; that is, he was believed to go down to the realm of death during the winter and return from his sleep in the netherworld when the rains came for the new agricultural season. Various rituals were designed to awaken him from the netherworld and return fertility to the land so that crops would grow.

Mistakes to Avoid

We trivialize the lesson if we suggest that the story teaches us to stand up for our faith and defend God's reputation to those who don't believe. Of course, those are good things and we should do them, but that is not the lesson of this passage. The point is Yahweh's supremacy, not Elijah's boldness. Certainly the latter may be noticed and commended, but the focus of the lesson needs to be on God. The students should respond to God, not to Elijah.

72. Elijah at Mount Sinai (1 Kings 19:1–18)

Lesson Focus

The success on Mount Carmel impressed Ahab, but not Jezebel, who then threatened Elijah's life. Elijah fled to Mount Sinai where God appeared to him. The prophet resigned his office, and God instructed him to appoint successors, indicating that the situation was not as hopeless as it appeared.

- God's work will always have resistance.
- God has more alternatives than we know.
- God works in many different ways.
- God strengthens and encourages those who are faithful to him.

Lesson Application

We should have confidence that God's plans cannot be thwarted.

- We recognize that none of us is indispensable.
- We trust that God has strategies we cannot see or anticipate.
- We expect resistance when we are doing God's work.
- We must not expect to do God's work in our own strength.

Biblical Context

First and 2 Kings are about the failures of kingship. The books of Samuel relate how God set up kingship in such a way that kings were designed to be extensions of his kingship and would thus reveal what God's kingship was like. With only a few exceptions, however, the kings of Israel and Judah failed to approach this ideal. The books of 1 and 2 Kings portray this road of failure in the stories of one king after another. Solomon had demonstrated wisdom and justice as God had blessed him, but his failures led to the split of the kingdom. The books then begin the litany of failures, particularly evident in the Northern Kingdom, Israel, primarily shown by the golden calves. In Ahab and Jezebel an even greater threat arose as they attempted to set up Baal as the national god in place of Yahweh. In this account a depressed and weary Elijah is commissioned to appoint some political and prophetic successors as God's plan continues to unfold.

Interpretational Issues in the Story

Elijah flees (1 Kings 19:3). We cannot say whether Elijah was justified in his fear. Moses also fled from a ruler who tried to kill him (one of the many connections between Elijah and Moses). In any case, God was providing for Elijah and strengthening him for the trip.

"Angel of the LORD" (1 Kings 19:7). The angel of the Lord is a messenger who brings God's word to people. In the ancient world direct communication between important parties was a rarity. Diplomatic exchange normally required the use of an intermediary. Messengers were like ambassadors and were vested with the authority to speak for the party they represented and were expected to be treated as if they were the dignitary in person. This is why in some contexts, as here, it is hard to distinguish whether God or the messenger is speaking. The messenger may speak in the first person as God.

Wind, earthquake, fire (1 Kings 19:11–12). These effects sometimes accompanied the appearances of God (see esp. Ex. 19:16–19 when he appeared on Mount Sinai to the Israelites in the wilderness). Elijah was in that same place, and after God's presence came down, he would speak with Elijah as he had spoken with Moses.

Low whisper (1 Kings 19:12). The translation of verses 11–12 has some complexities. Though it is usually translated so that Yahweh is speaking in a "low whisper," an alternative is that the text refers only to the echoing stillness that followed all the destructive forces that had passed. In that case, it is only in the silence that Yahweh's voice can be heard. Consequently, it should not be intimated that Yahweh speaks with a "still small voice." How we translate the verses is not significant to the point that God is speaking. Elijah's experience is comparable to what Moses experienced in the same place when he asked to see God's glory (Ex. 33:18–23).

Anointing Hazael, Jehu, Elisha (1 Kings 19:15–17). Elijah was to arrange for the succession to the thrones of Aram and Israel. God was about to reorder the politics of the region, thus demonstrating that he was the one in control. Ahab's line will be brought to an end. God also accepted Elijah's resignation (19:4, 14) and had Elijah anoint his successor, Elisha, and begin to train him.

Background Information

Jezebel. Jezebel was a Phoenician princess who married Ahab in a political arrangement between Israel and Phoenicia. As an international political wife, she was not expected to leave her gods behind (she was like an ambassador in Ahab's court). In these stories, however, we find that she was an aggressive evangelist for her gods, as she sought to elevate them above Yahweh. Elijah was an obstacle to her political and religious ambitions, so she sought to execute him.

Horeb. This is an alternate name for Mount Sinai. Throughout Elijah's career we see echoes of Moses, and this is one of the more significant instances, as he goes to the renowned mountain apparently hoping to have a conversation with God, though there was no reason to think that God's special presence was available on the mountain in any continuing fashion.

Hazael. As the most successful of the kings of Aram, Hazael (c. 842–800 BC) greatly increased the pressure on Israel. During his reign he conquered large tracts of the northern kingdom, Israel. Here his rule was appropriately announced as bringing judgment on Israel for the false worship instituted by Ahab and Jezebel and too easily adopted by the people. When Elisha actually anointed Hazael (2 Kings 8:8), such an act from this widely known prophet was taken as giving justification for assassinating the king and taking his place, and Hazael did so. This was the power of the prophetic word.

Jehu. Jehu (841–814 BC) put an end to the house of Ahab and had Jezebel killed. He was politically conservative. His destruction of Baal worship might have been motivated more by political maneuvering against the house of Ahab than by covenant faithfulness. Jehu continued in the use of the golden calves. He began a new dynasty that lasted almost a century. He is portrayed in 1 Kings 19 as one who brought judgment rather than relief, restoration, or spiritual renewal.

Mistakes to Avoid

The "still small voice," the wording in some translations, has little to do with the lesson other than to illustrate that God's presence is manifest in many different ways. This should not be a lesson about listening to God or about how God speaks. Elijah here is not a role model for good or ill. It is true that he grew depressed about his inability to change circumstances, forgetting that God is the one who will make changes at the right time, and it is true that we can talk to God when we grow discouraged. However, this narrative does not provide a biblical model for such behavior. The lesson is built around what we learn of God, not what we can learn from Elijah.

73. Naboth's Vineyard (1 Kings 21)

Lesson Focus

Ahab coveted Naboth's vineyard, but Naboth refused to sell. Jezebel arranged a false accusation against Naboth that resulted in his execution, whereupon Ahab took the property. God, through Elijah, pronounced judgment on Ahab and Jezebel for their injustice.

- God holds rulers accountable for their actions.
- God punished Ahab and Jezebel for their sins of injustice and abuse of power.
- Coveting leads to other sins.

Lesson Application

Leaders are accountable for injustice and abuse of power.

- We should recognize that coveting can easily lead to other sins.
- When we hold positions of leadership, we are responsible for using power appropriately and being just in all our ways.
- We should trust that God will judge sin.

Biblical Context

First and 2 Kings are about the failures of kingship. The books of Samuel relate how God set up kingship in such a way that kings were designed to be extensions of his kingship and would thus reveal what God's kingship was like. With only a few exceptions, however, the kings of Israel and Judah failed to approach this ideal. The books of 1 and 2 Kings portray this road of failure in the stories of one king after another. Ahab and Jezebel are the most prominent examples of injustice and worship of other gods. This account gives an illustration of the heinousness of their crimes and results in Elijah pronouncing God's judgment on them.

Interpretational Issues in the Story

Palace of Ahab in Jezreel (1 Kigns 21:1). Jezreel was located about twenty miles northeast of the capital city, Samaria. Jezreel was at the eastern end of the Valley of Jezreel and therefore enjoyed a more moderate climate than Samaria, which was in the hills. Sections of the palace of Ahab have been excavated.

"Inheritance of my fathers" (1 Kings 21:3). The land of the Israelites was their little portion of the covenant, because God had promised the land to Abraham, and it had been distributed by Joshua. As a result, land was not sold. If it temporarily changed families, it had to be restored in the year of Jubilee (Lev. 25:13–17, 23–24). Naboth considered the property a covenant benefit, and Ahab's seizure was a covenant violation.

"Proclaim a fast" (1 Kings 21:9). Fasting was often called for when there was a sense that sin was affecting the community. In this case, on the basis of the false witnesses, Naboth was going to be convicted of the sin and executed.

"You have cursed God and the king" (1 Kings 21:10). Since a fast had been declared, we can infer that some sort of crisis in the community had occurred that was believed to be punishment from God for someone's offense. Naboth was seated in a prominent place, suggesting that he was prominent in the community and therefore could have done something to bring God's judgment. Cursing God and king involved making accusations that maligned or discredited either one. In this situation, the accusation might have been that Naboth claimed that the king was responsible for their crisis or that God was being unfair (cf. Isa. 8:21). That is why two false witnesses were seated by Naboth, so that they could claim they had overheard him cursing God and the king.

Background Information

Vineyard and vegetable garden. It was common in the ancient Near East for kings to have gardens adjoining their palaces. They were like parks and were used for the king's enjoyment and for receiving visitors. In 21:2 Ahab specifies that he wants to use Naboth's vineyard for a garden. The translation "vegetable" garden might be too specific, though certainly the word is used for greens that are eaten rather than for plants for shade or decoration. Another detail that could be noted is that vineyards take some years before they are productive, so it is wasteful to uproot one.

Stoning. Someone who was to be stoned was taken to an isolated place, stripped, and cast down by a witness over a precipice that was at least twice the height of the man (as later regulations dictated). Large stones were thrown down on top of him, with the trial witnesses throwing the first ones. In this mode of punishment all took responsibility, but it was indeterminable which person brought on the death, much like with a firing squad.

Dogs licked up. Dogs ran wild in the streets of most towns. They were scavengers rather than pets. The idea that dogs would devour human bodies is not only repulsive but also highly significant. In the ancient world, including Israel, people believed that the grave was the entryway to the netherworld and a peaceful afterlife. Those who were not buried were doomed to be wandering spirits.

Sackcloth. Sackcloth was rough material worn to indicate mourning. It was designed to be uncomfortable.

Mistakes to Avoid

Lessons on this story typically focus on the dangers of coveting—"Don't be like Ahab"—or on the graciousness of God's forgiveness as seen in 21:28–29. It is true that the story illustrates both. But the indictment and judgment theme is more fitting to the role that the story plays in the book. God's pronouncement of judgment on the house of Ahab should be foremost in the lesson.

74. Elisha Succeeds Elijah (2 Kings 2:1–14)

Lesson Focus

With Elijah's ministry complete, God took Elijah and prophetic leadership passed to Elisha, his apprentice.

- God provides for continuing prophetic guidance to his people.
- God honors his faithful servants.

Lesson Application

We trust God to provide continuing leadership for his people, even in troubled times.

Biblical Context

First and 2 Kings are about the failures of kingship. The books of Samuel relate how God set up kingship in such a way that kings were designed to be extensions of his kingship and would thus reveal what his kingship was like. With few exceptions, however, the kings of Israel and Judah failed to approach this ideal. The books of 1 and 2 Kings portray this road of failure in the stories of one king after another. Solomon had demonstrated wisdom and justice as God had blessed him, but his failures led to the split of the kingdom. The books then begin the litany of failures, particularly evident in the Northern Kingdom, Israel, primarily shown by the golden calves. As kings became worse, God began to display his kingship through the prophets instead of through the kings. This was particularly true in the ministry of Elisha, who begins his prophetic leadership role in this story.

Interpretational Issues in the Story

Double portion (2 Kings 2:9). Here Elisha was not asking to be twice the prophet Elijah was or to have twice the power. In inheritance laws, a double share of the inheritance was given to the firstborn, who then took over the responsibility and leadership of the family. Elisha asked to be designated the heir to the leadership position held by Elijah; however, the inheritance was not in the form of possessions but of the spirit. Elisha was to receive twice that of any other successor.

Chariot, horses, and whirlwind (2 Kings 2:11). Fire and whirlwind were generally associated in the ancient world with a storm god whose chariot is the storm cloud. In 1 Kings 17–18 Elijah contended on Yahweh's behalf against Baal, a storm god. He demonstrated that Yahweh was the Storm God (he sent fire to consume the sacrifice and then sent rain), not Baal. Of course, Yahweh filled every divine function, but Elijah had been most involved with showing Yahweh to be the true Storm God. It is therefore appropriate that fire and whirlwind with chariots and horses was his vehicle.

Taken (2 Kings 2:9–11). The conclusion is often made that here Elijah was taken to heaven to be with God, and the words could be seen to support such a conclusion. But we should not be too hasty. The Israelites had been given no hope of heaven, and the death of Jesus, the mechanism by which we can go to heaven, had not yet been provided. It is clear from the passage that, when it was reported that Elijah had been taken up to heaven, the other prophets were anxious to discover where he was put back down (v. 16). The confusion comes because the Hebrew word for *heaven* can refer either to the sky or to the place of God's dwelling. We can only go so far as to conclude that Elijah was taken up into the sky. We have insufficient evidence to conclude that he was taken to heaven to be with God.

Background Information

Sons of the prophets. From the contexts in which references to the sons of the prophets occur, they appear to be a band of prophets and perhaps prophets-in-training. From scattered information we might conclude that training to be a prophet involved learning techniques that made one receptive to divine messages.

Location. Elijah often replicated acts done by Moses, and so it is not a surprise to see him moving across to the east side of the Jordan near Jericho at the end of his life. The text does not mention Mount Nebo, where Moses died, but it puts Elijah in the same vicinity.

Cloak. Clothing often gave indication of one's office, status, or vocation. In addition, wearing the clothes of another was thought to establish some relationship between the parties. Though not much information exists, Zechariah 13:4 seems to suggest a particular type of clothing that was associated with a prophet, but some three centuries separate Elijah and Zechariah. Regardless, the fact that it was given to Elisha is an indication that God had made him Elijah's successor.

Mistakes to Avoid

It is true that Elijah's being taken up gives him a high status among the characters of the Old Testament. But the narrative is not given so that others might aspire to the same sort of recognition. The narrative does not teach how God honors those who have been faithful to him. Since we cannot be certain that Elijah was taken up to heaven to be with God, we cannot draw a comparison to the way we might go to heaven. The right focus is that God provides for those bereft of a great leader. God provides others to take up their roles. God's provision should be the focus, not the stature of Elijah or Elisha.

75. Elisha and the Widow's Oil (2 Kings 4:1–7)

Lesson Focus

God provided for a widow's needs through Elisha and in doing so used the prophet to reveal his kingship. A good king cares for the needy, and since the kings were not following God, God used the prophet to show this aspect of his kingship.

- God cares about needy people.
- God is able to provide.

Lesson Application

We should believe that God is concerned about people's needs and that he is compassionate.

- We believe that as king, God cares for all his people.
- We trust that God is able to meet needs in unexpected ways.
- We must not be afraid to bring our needs to God for his help.

Biblical Context

First and 2 Kings are about the failures of kingship. The books of Samuel relate how God set up kingship in such a way that kings were designed to be extensions of his kingship and would thus reveal what his kingship was like. With few exceptions, however, the kings of Israel and Judah failed to approach this ideal. The books of 1 and 2 Kings portray this road of failure in the stories of one king after another. Solomon had demonstrated wisdom and justice as God had blessed him, but his failures led to the split of the kingdom. The books then begin the litany of failures, particularly evident in the Northern Kingdom, Israel, primarily shown by the golden calves. As kings became worse, God began to display his kingship through the prophets instead of through the kings. This was particularly true in the ministry of Elisha, who here provided for the needs of the poor and destitute (as the king was supposed to do).

Interpretational Issues in the Story

Sons of the prophets (2 Kings 4:1). From the contexts in which references to the sons of the prophets occur, they appear to have been a band of prophets and perhaps prophets-in-training. From scattered information, we might conclude that training to be a prophet involved learning techniques that made one receptive to divine messages.

"What have you in the house?" (2 Kings 4:2). Elisha worked with what the woman had and with what she could do rather than making a pile of money or supplies appear on her table. Though this story is not a teaching model, we can observe that God sometimes works in ways that involve us.

The multiplied oil (2 Kings 4:5). Numerous parallels exist between the ministries of Elijah and Elisha. This account can be compared to that in 1 Kings 17:7–16. This account also bears some similarity to the multiplied loaves and fishes in the ministry of Jesus (note also 2 Kings 4:42–44). The point is similar in both Testaments: God takes care of the basic needs of his people through the one who represents his just kingship in the world.

Background Information

Widows. Widows in the ancient world were often left without support structures. No pensions or welfare system provided for them, but only living descendants or compassionate family members.

Enslavement by creditors. Debt slavery was common in the ancient world. Most people grew their own food, and a couple of bad harvests back-to-back could bring starvation with insufficient food to eat and no seed to plant the next year. At times the only option was to send family members into a wealthier household to work off debt incurred when buying grain. Debt-slaves were sometimes well-treated and helped back to solvency, while others were treated cruelly in an attempt to extend the period of enslavement.

Mistakes to Avoid

God provided directly for this widow, but that does not mean that all widows can expect this kind of result. Stories such as these are not intended to lead us to certain expectations but to help us to recognize the power of God.

76. Elisha and the Shunammite Woman (2 Kings 4:8–37)

Lesson Focus

God brought blessing to a woman who cared for Elisha by providing a son and then bringing that son back to life when he died unexpectedly.

- God delights in bringing blessing to those who serve him.
- God uses his servants to be the mediator of blessing.

Lesson Application

We should believe that God is reigning as king and that he is concerned about the needs of his people and his servants.

- We trust God to provide as we seek to be faithful to him.
- When we help others, we serve as an extension of God's care for his people.

Biblical Context

First and 2 Kings are about the failures of kingship. The books of Samuel relate how God set up kingship in such a way that kings were designed to be extensions of his kingship and would thus reveal what his kingship was like. With few exceptions, however, the kings of Israel and Judah failed to approach this ideal. These books portray this road of failure in the stories of one king after another. Solomon had demonstrated wisdom and justice as God had blessed him, but his failures led to the split of the kingdom. The book then begins the litany of failures, particularly evident in the Northern Kingdom, Israel, primarily shown by the golden calves. As kings became worse, God began to display his kingship through the prophets instead of through the kings. This was particularly true in the ministry of Elisha, who here provided for the needs of the poor and destitute (as the king was supposed to do).

Interpretational Issues in the Story

"A word spoken on your behalf to the king or to the commander of the army" (2 Kings 4:13). Elisha was likely suggesting that he could use his influence with Israelite leadership to gain the woman some tax relief. Her response, that she has a home among her own people, suggests that she was well cared for.

"Neither new moon nor Sabbath" (2 Kings 4:23). New moon and Sabbath were times when people had the leisure to consult a prophet, since those were days of rest and celebration.

"All is well" (2 Kings 4:26). The woman told Gehazi that all was well (*shalom*) most likely because she wanted to make her case personally to the prophet rather than communicate through the servant.

Background Information

Shunem. This town was at the eastern end of the Jezreel Valley on the southwest slope of the Hill of Moreh.

Shunem to Mount Carmel. The distance between the two sites was about fifteen miles. By riding a donkey at a good pace, the woman could have made the trip in a few hours.

Elisha's procedure. Just as we might use CPR, artificial respiration, or the Heimlich maneuver to respond to someone's condition, Elisha used a technique known and practiced in the ancient world, probably believed to facilitate the transfer of life force. Regardless of the thinking behind the technique or its intended effect, God responds with the restoration of life.

Mistakes to Avoid

Just as this story cannot be used to suggest that God will help women to have children or bring children back to life, the story is not about how God provides housing for his people. Such a suggestion misrepresents God, because many of his people throughout the ages have not had adequate housing. It is true that whatever housing we have, God has provided, but that is not why the narrative is here. These are all examples of inappropriate extrapolation and treat the narrative as offering models for behavior that simply cannot be sustained. In the same way, this cannot be considered as a lesson solely about kindness. God was providing blessings for his people through those who love and serve him.

77. Elisha and Naaman (2 Kings 5)

Lesson Focus

Naaman learned that the Lord is God when no one but God was able to cure his skin disease.

- God chooses particular situations to demonstrate his power.
- God is able to heal.

Lesson Application

The Lord is a powerful God. He can do things no one else can.

- We recognize the power of God.
- We ought to be prepared to be used as God's instruments.

Biblical Context

First and 2 Kings are about the failures of kingship. The books of Samuel related how God set up kingship in such a way that kings were designed to be extensions of his kingship and would thus reveal what his kingship was like. With few exceptions, however, the kings of Israel and Judah failed to approach this ideal. The books of 1 and 2 Kings portray this road of failure in the stories of one king after another. Solomon had demonstrated wisdom and justice as God had blessed him, but his failures led to the split of the kingdom. The books then begin the litany of failures, particularly evident in the Northern Kingdom, Israel, primarily shown by the golden calves. As kings became worse, God began to display his kingship through the prophets instead of through the kings. This was particularly true in the ministry of Elisha, who here became involved in international politics, stepping in to serve when the king was frustrated and defensive.

Interpretational Issues in the Story

"A letter to the king of Israel" (2 Kings 5:5). From the response of Israel's king, it becomes clear that the letter Naaman carried from his king was intended to put some pressure on Israel. The letter perhaps also provided the commander with safe passage and allowed him to gain audience with the king of Israel.

Naaman's confession (2 Kings 5:15–18). Naaman went further in his confession of the true God than we see with Rahab, Ruth, or the Ninevites of Jonah because he proclaimed that there is no God but Yahweh. He further indicated his commitment not to offer sacrifices to any other god. This shows a commitment to monotheism.

Load of earth (2 Kings 5:17). Naaman's request to carry dirt back to his homeland comes after Elisha refused to accept a gift, and there is a relationship between the two. Many times when rituals were performed in the ancient world, they were accompanied by gifts for the deity meant to appease the deity's residual anger. It is possible that this was Naaman's goal in offering a gift to Elisha. Accordingly, the specialist (Elisha) was seen as having a position of power, and if his favor could be gained, he could continue to intercede on behalf of the one offering the gift. When Elisha refused the gift, Naaman chose another option for gaining continuing favor with Yahweh. With the dirt, he could build an altar from Yahweh's land and offer sacrifices for that purpose. Even though Naaman had left behind his other gods, his thinking still, unsurprisingly, shows pagan elements, primarily in the concept that sacrifices met the needs of the gods and gained their favor. It also appears that he felt it was important to use local dirt rather than his native dirt, reflecting a typical non-Israelite territoriality.

Background Information

Arameans (NIV). Some translations use later terminology such as "Syria" and "Syrians." Aram was the area just north of Israel with its capital in Damascus. During this time the Arameans were engaged in military actions against Israel.

Naaman's disease. Today leprosy is called Hansen's disease. The Hebrew word often translated "leprosy" does not refer to one specific disease but to the symptom of scaly skin. Today we call it psoriasis, eczema, seborrheic dermatitis, and other fungal diseases. Hansen's disease was virtually unknown in the ancient world prior to the time of Alexander the Great. From the descriptions of the scaly skin condition in the Bible, it is evident that it did not correspond to Hansen's. It was considered unclean likely because the flaking off of skin was associated with the deterioration of a corpse after death. Things considered unclean were often associated with death even though the conditions were not life-threatening. Other cultures apparently shared these opinions about skin conditions.

Elisha's procedure. The procedure of dipping seven times in a river is known from some Mesopotamian healing rituals. As was often the case, Elisha used procedures that were recognizable and familiar to his clients. What differentiates Elisha's procedure is the lack of any ritual incantations accompanying the ritual act. Verse 11 shows that Naaman expected more involvement from the specialist.

Mistakes to Avoid

Given the tendency to focus on the young characters when teaching children, many focus this story on the Israelite girl who pointed the way to Elisha. This approach should be resisted. The girl played a role, but the story is not about her, and the authoritative teaching of this narrative is not to be found in her behavior. Nor is the lesson found in the deception of Elisha's servant Gehazi. In these narratives we should not focus on how people do commendable or wicked things, but on how God works out his plan. He used the girl's faith, and he punished Gehazi's duplicity. We therefore learn about God and his ways, and that becomes the basis for people to live faithful lives and to resist temptations in whatever situation they find themselves.

In another direction, we cannot claim that this narrative offers a model for ministry. We should not think that because Elisha would not accept a gift that the Bible is teaching that people doing God's work should not receive pay. Naaman's offer was not simple payment for services, and it was not the means by which Elisha made his living.

78. Elisha and the Aramean Army (2 Kings 6:8–23)

Lesson Focus

Elisha and his servant saw the sovereignty and power of God demonstrated in his defeat of the Aramean (Syrian) army.

- God is the one who brings victory.
- God is able to protect his servants.

Lesson Application

God is more powerful than any king or army.

- We believe that God can bring victory, no matter what the obstacles.
- We believe that God can protect us, though in his wisdom he does not always choose to do so.

Biblical Context

First and 2 Kings are about the failures of kingship. The books of Samuel relate how God set up kingship in such a way that kings were designed to be extensions of his kingship and would thus reveal what his kingship was like. With few exceptions, however, the kings of Israel and Judah failed to approach this ideal. The books of 1 and 2 Kings portray this road of failure in the stories of one king after another. Solomon had demonstrated wisdom and justice as God had blessed him, but his failures led to the split of the kingdom. The books then begin the litany of failures, particularly evident in the Northern Kingdom, Israel, primarily shown by the golden calves. As kings became worse, God began to display his kingship through the prophets instead of through the kings. This was particularly true in the ministry of Elisha, who here became involved in international politics as he became the instrument by which Yahweh led the armies of Israel and defeated the enemy.

Interpretational Issues in the Story

Elisha as surrogate king (2 Kings 6:9–10). The king was supposed to be God's representative, as together they led armies into battle. At the beginning of this narrative Elisha was conferring with the king, as prophets did in the ancient world, giving information from the deity. In the main segment of the story Elisha ends up in a more military role as he captures the opposing army and delivers it to the king. In this way God's kingship was revealed through Elisha rather than through the king.

Horses and chariots of fire (2 Kings 6:17). This army should not be considered guardian angels. They represented the Lord's army, which does battle with the enemy. The text has some ambiguities with regard to the stationing of this divine army. Many translations suggest that the hills around the city were filled with the army. The Hebrew text uses the singular, "hill," that is filled as the army surrounds Elisha. An alternative, then, is not that the Lord's chariots and horses surrounded the city in the hills, but that they were serving as bodyguards for Elisha.

Blindness (2 Kings 6:18). This term is used elsewhere only to describe what happened to the men of Sodom who surrounded Lot's house.

Treating the army kindly (2 Kings 6:22–23). A captured army became part of the plunder, as they would have been had they surrendered. Though a king had the option to retain them as slave labor, Elisha fed them and sent them back home. This signified a peace initiative. Elisha's choice is not meant to offer a biblical model for warfare, for, in other circumstances, other options might have been preferred or commanded by the Lord.

Background Information

Prophets in the ancient world. Prophets known from the ancient world generally served as formal or informal advisors to the king. They were regularly asked for advice concerning military actions, because the king wanted assurance that his deity was supporting him. In some cases prophets even accompanied the armies into battle so that the king could get continuing instruction from the deity (see Judges 4 where Barak wanted Deborah to accompany him).

Dothan. Dothan was a twenty-five-acre site along the road between Samaria and the Jezreel Valley situated in a valley and surrounded by choice pasture land. Excavations indicate that it was destroyed in the ninth century, probably by the Arameans.

Dothan to Samaria. The distance between the two was about ten miles.

Mistakes to Avoid

This story should not be used to suggest that angels always surround God's people to protect them. That would be inappropriate extrapolation. Furthermore, the angels in this story are not guardian angels; they are the army of the Lord. This military support for Elisha should not be taken as an indication of how God regularly works. It is simply the procedure that he used on this occasion to demonstrate his kingship. The kindness of Elisha is also not the lesson of the story. A good king knows when to execute judgment and when to be merciful (cf. 1 Sam. 15:33). Elisha was serving in a king's role, and his choice of mercy resulted in the cessation of hostility between Aram and Israel. The new Aramean policy was not necessarily reciprocated kindness. They may simply have become convinced that with Elisha in Israel, continued military activity was futile.

79. Joash (2 Kings 11:1–12:16; 2 Chronicles 24)

Lesson Focus

Joash was saved by people faithful to the Lord. As king, he helped turn the people back to God, guided by the wise Jehoiada. He even restored the temple.

- God preserved a king from David's line in accordance with the covenant he had made with David.
- God worked through a faithful priest to punish the wicked queen and bring restoration.

Lesson Application

No matter how bad things get, God is able to set things right again. He is a God who delights in giving second chances by getting us back on track.

- We should not be surprised when God turns things around and the wicked are judged.
- We should trust God to carry out his plan at the right time.
- We should strive to be the kind of faithful people that God can use.

Biblical Context

First and 2 Kings are about the failures of kingship. The books of Samuel relate how God set up kingship in such a way that kings were designed to be extensions of his kingship and would thus reveal what his kingship was like. With few exceptions, however, the kings of Israel and Judah failed to approach this ideal. The books of 1 and 2 Kings portray this road of failure in the stories of one king after another. Solomon had demonstrated wisdom and justice as God had blessed him, but his failures led to the split of the kingdom. The books then begin the litany of failures, particularly evident in the Northern Kingdom, Israel, primarily shown by the golden calves. When a marriage alliance was made between the north and the south, the influence of Ahab and Jezebel spread to the kingdom of Judah, and their daughter, Athaliah, nearly wiped out the Davidic line. This story tells how the line was preserved in Joash, a Davidic king restored to the throne, and how he restored the temple.

Interpretational Issues in the Story

The testimony (2 Kings 11:12). The king had particular responsibility for the keeping of the testimony, or covenant, because of his leadership role. If the king did not set the example, faithfulness would dwindle among the people. It is difficult to tell whether the testimony refers to something that should be connected with Moses or David, or whether it refers to a document containing the agreement between the king and the people (several are mentioned in 11:17). It is most likely something similar to Deuteronomy, where the terms of the covenant between God and Israel had been established. The agreements in 1 Kings 11:17 are different documents and were more focused on the current situation and administration.

Temple and church (2 Kings 12:4). The temple in the ancient world was far different from the church building today. The building that we call a "church" is simply the place for the assembly of God's people, a place designated for corporate worship. Even though we sometimes call it "God's house," in reality God is housed within his people, not in a building. In Israel, God chose to live in the temple, and though people gathered in Jerusalem on sacred occasions, the courtyard was not designed for corporate worship and could not accommodate very many. People came to the temple to watch public rituals and to offer sacrifices for themselves or their families. The priests were there to officiate the rituals and advise about procedures. They also made sure that only the qualified could enter.

Original funding (2 Kings 12:4–5). Three sources of funding are listed in 12:4 (2 Chron. 24:4 and 9 list only one). Presumably each of those went into different accounts, because each priest was to use the surplus from his account to contribute to the rebuilding effort.

Priestly delay in repair (2 Kings 12:6–7). The funding (12:4–5) does not work because, as often happens, there never seemed to be sufficient surplus. The revised financing arranged for the three sources of funding listed in verse

4 to be deposited in a box for the building fund rather than given to the priests in charge of the accounts. Other funds used for the operation of the temple were still collected by the priests (v. 16). There is no indication of financial irregularity or abuse on the part of the priests.

Donations people brought. (2 Chron. 24:10). The officers and people rejoiced and brought their contributions. The tax that Chronicles refers to was mandated, not given by free will, but 2 Kings 12:4 lists other contributions that were not mandated. The rejoicing of the people indicates that they had caught the vision for the restoration project.

Background Information

Restoring or repairing temples. In the ancient world kings often undertook the task of temple building, repairing, restoring, enlarging, or purifying as an act of piety, seeking to gain the favor of a deity. In this case, some repair was being done, but more important was the purification and restoration from the wickedness and false worship of Athaliah.

Mistakes to Avoid

The significant space dedicated to discussion of the financing of the temple restoration (1 Kings 12:4–16) might lead to the conclusion that the passage is about finances. But there are no biblical models for fundraising campaigns offered here, nor is there any instruction to people about giving. As always, it is unsound to try to develop authoritative teaching around something that is simply described in the text. God is honored in this building program, and the temple work is successfully concluded; however, that does not mean this is the Bible's teaching on how such things ought to be done (not to mention that there is no comparable project that could be undertaken today). Discussion of the financing demonstrates the king's diligence in restoring the temple and the people's willingness to be a part of its restoration through their monetary contributions. Thus, Joash stands as one of the exceptions to the litany of failures carried on through the books of Kings, though Chronicles identifies some of his failures toward the end of his reign. The text describes the rejoicing that surrounded the restoration project, but this should not be taken as a mandate to all God's people to give cheerfully. We should always rejoice when God's work is moving forward and be eager to take part. However, this story does not tell us to have such attitudes but about God's work through Joash to restore the temple.

80. Hezekiah and the Assyrian Army (2 Kings 18–19; 2 Chronicles 32; Isaiah 36–37)

Lesson Focus

When Judah was attacked by the Assyrian army, Hezekiah cried to God for the deliverance of his people and the vindication of God's name. God's sovereignty and power were demonstrated when he put to death the whole Assyrian camp.

- God responded to the kings who were faithful to him.
- God is able to defeat the mightiest armies in the most difficult situations.

Lesson Application

God is more powerful than any king or army. He is Lord over everyone.

- We believe that God is able to overcome any power that stands against him and his people.
- We trust God in our times of trouble.

Biblical Context

First and 2 Kings are about the failures of kingship. The books of Samuel relate how God set up kingship in such a way that kings were designed to be extensions of his kingship and would thus reveal what his kingship was like. With few exceptions, however, the kings of Israel and Judah failed to approach this ideal. These books portray this road of failure in the stories of one king after another. In Hezekiah we find one of the exceptions—a king who got rid of false worship and brought reform to Israel. When the Assyrians attacked, he trusted God, and God brought deliverance.

Interpretational Issues in the Story

Sennacherib's messages (2 Kings 18:19–25, 28–35). The messages of Sennacherib conveyed by his field commander are the centerpiece of the narrative. Like Goliath's speech in 1 Samuel 17, Sennacherib was defying the God of Israel and declaring him powerless. The fact that Assyria had defeated all the other gods they had faced (gods fought for the armies, so to defeat the armies was to defeat the gods) was the basis for the Assyrian claim that no deity could stand before them. Of course, Yahweh rose to the challenge and showed his power, just as he had with David and Goliath. It is in Israel's weakness that God showed himself strong.

Background Information

Sennacherib and his representatives. Sennacherib succeeded his father to the throne of Assyria in 704 BC. He successfully expanded the Assyrian empire. His representatives are identified in the biblical text (2 Kings 18:17) by title rather than by name.

Sennacherib's siege of Jerusalem. Sennacherib's campaign took place in 701 BC. Preserved records of this campaign are included in four clay prisms that he had inscribed and which include reference to Hezekiah and Jerusalem. Though he claims to have had Hezekiah confined as a bird in a cage, he gives no indication of the outcome of the battle. When he had wall-panel reliefs carved of his great victories, he did not portray the siege of Jerusalem but his conquest of Lachish (2 Kings 18:17). Lachish was the Israelite garrison that guarded the way to Jerusalem. This suggests that he had nothing to boast about in Jerusalem.

Role of Isaiah. Isaiah was likely a court prophet whom Hezekiah counted as one of his advisors. Most kings in the ancient world had prophets in their administration to give them messages from the deity.

Mistakes to Avoid

God came to Hezekiah's aid and defeated his enemies, but we cannot conclude that God will always come to our aid and defeat our enemies. To do so is attempting to read something into the text that is not there. He is capable of doing so, and often does, but for various reasons may choose not to do so.

81. Hezekiah's Illness (2 Kings 20:1–11; Isaiah 38)

Lesson Focus

Hezekiah became ill and was told that he will die. God answered his prayer for healing as a response to his faithfulness and gave him fifteen additional years of life.

- God responds to faithfulness.
- God can heal and extend life.
- God listens to prayer.

Lesson Application

We should believe that God is responsive to faithfulness.

- We should be faithful because we know it matters to God.
- We should not expect God always to heal (or fix other problems)—he acts in his wisdom.
- We should not hesitate to pray for healing because we know God hears, whether he heals or not.

Biblical Context

First and 2 Kings are about the failures of kingship. The books of Samuel relate how God set up kingship in such a way that kings were designed to be extensions of his kingship and would thus reveal what his kingship was like. With few exceptions, however, the kings of Israel and Judah failed to approach this ideal. The books of 1 and 2 Kings portray this road of failure in the stories of one king after another. In Hezekiah we find one of the exceptions—a king who got rid of false worship and brought reform to Israel. His faithfulness is the focus of this narrative.

Interpretational Issues in the Story

Sequence (2 Kings 20:6). We can infer that the Assyrian siege reported in 2 Kings 18–19 had not yet occurred. In Isaiah 36–39 the narratives are also in this reversed order. In Isaiah the reversal is logical because the visit of the Babylonian envoys (Isaiah 39) has been placed so as to transition into the passages that deal with the exile (Isaiah 40–55). Apparently, then, 1 and 2 Kings have used Isaiah as a source of information and therefore followed Isaiah's order.

Asking for a sign (2 Kings 20:8). Hezekiah's asking for a sign could indicate lack of trust but not necessarily so. Deuteronomy 18:21–22 indicates that a true prophet was known by his prophecies coming true. One way this was tested was by asking for a sign. Since Isaiah had said that Hezekiah would die, it is not surprising that Hezekiah wants some assurance that he will not die. We should also recall that Isaiah's father, Ahaz, was specifically asked to designate a sign to test the prophecy (Isa. 7:10–14).

Background Information

Prophetic confirmation. In the ancient world prophecy was one form of divination. When a prophet spoke to the king of Assyria, the king routinely sought confirmation about the prophecy from other omens using a variety of divination methods. In Israel, most forms of divination were forbidden, so when there was the need to confirm a prophetic oracle, asking for a sign was one way to proceed.

Stairway of Ahaz. This was some sort of timekeeping device, but the specifics are unknown. Timekeeping in the ancient world was done through the use of shadows on structures or through the dripping of water out of a basin at a regulated rate. No use of shadows on steps has been attested with certainty, though there is one possible example from Egypt.

Mistakes to Avoid

It is important that the students understand that God will not always respond and bring healing, although he certainly is able to. Important also is that God values our faithfulness and hears our prayer. But he does not always heal. Some have argued that Hezekiah's healing was negative in the end—his wretched son Manasseh was twelve when he came to the throne, suggesting that he was born during Hezekiah's fifteen-year extension. This conjecture should not be pursued, however, because it is possible that Manasseh came to the throne as a co-regent before Hezekiah's death. Finally, it should not be suggested to students that God caused the shadow to move backward by reversing the movement of the earth. God, of course, can do whatever he wants, but there are other options besides that of the earth moving backward. For example, either the object that cast the shadow or the stairway on which the shadow was cast could have shifted. We simply do not know, so there is no point in speculating.

82. Josiah and Reform (2 Kings 22:1–23:3; 2 Chronicles 34)

Lesson Focus

Josiah was made king when he was eight years old, and God helped Josiah be a good king. Josiah obeyed God by helping the people to worship only God, so God blessed him. Josiah told the people to obey God's word in the book found in the temple.

- God is pleased by acts of faithfulness.
- God is pleased with those who humble themselves before him and respond to him by repenting of sin.

Lesson Application

God's Word tells us how to obey God. When we obey, others can see God and understand what he is like. When we obey, God is pleased.

- We should be diligent to obey God and be faithful to him.
- We should be conscientious about how God's presence is maintained. (God dwells in us, and we should seek to keep our hearts and minds holy.)
- We should repent of our sin.

Biblical Context

First and 2 Kings are about the failures of kingship, whereas 1 and 2 Chronicles, written a century and a half later, are about how God rewards faithfulness and punishes wickedness. Josiah is offered as an example of a faithful king. Since at the time of the writing of Chronicles (c. 400 BC) there was no king in Israel, the author emphasizes the spiritual nature of the kingdom as it was maintained by the priests and Levites and dominated by the temple.

Interpretational Issues in the Story

Sequence (2 Kings 22:1–23:3). Josiah came to the throne in 640 BC as a child. In his twelfth year, 628, he began to purge Judah of false worship (2 Chron. 34:3–7). In his eighteenth year, 622, he turned his attention to the cleansing of the temple, as he continued to rid the land of false worship (2 Chron. 34:8–10; 2 Kings 22:3–7). The reading of the law spurred him and the people on to continued reform (2 Chron. 34:33; 2 Kings 23:4–20). Chronicles has a more detailed report of the reform than do the books of Kings.

Temple and church (2 Kings 22:5). The temple in the ancient world was far different from the church building today. The building that we call "church" is simply the place for the assembly of God's people, a place designated for corporate worship. Even though we sometimes call it "God's house," in reality God is housed within his people, not in a building. In Israel, God chose to live in the temple, and though people gathered in Jerusalem on sacred occasions, the courtyard was not designed for corporate worship and could not accommodate very many. People came to the temple to watch public rituals and to offer sacrifices for themselves or their families. The priests were there to officiate over the rituals and advise about procedures. They also made sure that only those who qualified could enter.

Temple cleansing (2 Chron. 34:11). Temple restoration was an activity of kings in the ancient world and entailed various activities: actual maintenance if the structure had been neglected; purification if the rituals had been neglected; restoration of focus if other gods had been introduced; or beautification if some of the glory or resources had been depleted. The Chronicler indicates here that actual repair was being carried out, but given the apostasy of Josiah's predecessors, ritual cleansing was also necessary.

Book of the Law (2 Kings 22:8). From the information given about the Book of the Law (the connection to Moses, 2 Chron. 34:14; inclusion of curses, 2 Chron. 34:24) we can infer that it contained at least some version of the book of Deuteronomy, but it is difficult to be more specific than that.

Elders of Judah and Jerusalem (2 Chron. 34:29). The elders represent a carryover from the old tribal system set up from Israel's earliest history. Before there were kings, there were elders. The elders were connected to clans and continued to exercise political influence.

Background Information

Asherah poles. Asherah was a Canaanite deity connected to fertility. The Asherah poles are thought to have been stylized trees (either man-made or old, dead trees on which trunk and limbs remained). Other false worship is referred to in Josiah's reform, including getting rid of the priests who worshiped the heavenly bodies (a common practice in the ancient world).

Foundation deposits. In the ancient world, documents that contained the instructions for the building of the temple and important information about the relationship between the deity and the people were commonly stored in a foundation box built into the temple. The Book of the Covenant is mentioned here and would be a logical document to include in a foundation deposit. The point is that we should not think that Hilkiah found the Book of the Law in something like a broom closet behind the buckets. He most likely would have been looking for the foundation deposit. It is also possible that the document was in the temple archives.

Mistakes to Avoid

Josiah was an eight-year-old child when he came to the throne but the reform did not begin until he was in his mid-twenties (622 BC). As anxious as we are for youth to identify with children in the Bible, Josiah is no longer a child at the time of this narrative. The text is not pushing an identification—"be like Josiah"—but is trying to show how Josiah pleased God, and how God worked through Josiah's faithfulness. It is a small but important difference, but students ought to be led to think of their response to the text as that of growing their knowledge of God rather than that of seeking to emulate Josiah.

83. The People Return and Rebuild the Temple (Ezra 1–6)

Lesson Focus

God brought his people back to the land of Israel from their captivity in Babylon, as he had promised, and they rebuilt the temple. God's presence was reestablished among his people.

- God is able to carry out his plan and fulfill his word through the prophets.
- God is able to overcome opposition against his people.
- God is able to work through unbelieving leaders to further his plan.
- God desires to manifest his presence in the midst of his people.

Lesson Application

We should trust that no obstacle is able to stand between God and the accomplishment of his plan.

- We should believe that God will fulfill his word.
- We should not be surprised when God moves in remarkable ways.

Biblical Context

The purpose of the books of Ezra and Nehemiah is to show the many ways that God was at work to restore the people of Israel to their land. God brought the Israelites favor with the Persian rulers and helped them overcome the obstacles presented by their enemies as they rebuilt the walls of Jerusalem and set up the law as the foundation of society. The books recount the restoration of the temple, the community, Jerusalem, and the covenant. This section of the book of Ezra looks back on the various stages of the rebuilding of the temple.

Interpretational Issues in the Story

Exodus and return from exile (Ezra 1:3). There are many important similarities between the exodus from Egypt and the return from Babylonian exile nearly a thousand years later. Among other things, both involved bringing the Israelites into the covenant land, and both were accompanied by the construction of a sanctuary for the Lord's presence.

Returns from exile (Ezra 2:1). These chapters in Ezra recount the details of the first return from exile in 538 BC. The leaders of this group were Zerubbabel the governor and Jeshua the high priest. The focus was the rebuilding of the temple and reestablishment of the Jews in the land. About fifty thousand returned at this time. The second return, recorded in Ezra 7–10, came in 458 BC and was led by Ezra. Less than two thousand returned this second time. The third return, recorded in Nehemiah, came in 444 BC and focused on the rebuilding of the walls of Jerusalem and the establishment of the law as the foundation of Jewish society. It is unknown how many returned this third time.

Proclamation of Cyrus (Ezra 1:2–4). An ancient document referred to as the Cyrus Cylinder preserves a decree allowing repairs to be made to temples that had been damaged and rebuilding of those that had been destroyed. It included the return of the sacred objects. Cyrus did not make this decree through any particular acknowledgment of the God of Israel. All peoples of the empire were given the same instructions and support.

Background Information

Chronology. Babylon fell to Cyrus and the Persians in 539 BC. Within a few years the people of Israel who had been deported to Babylon were allowed to return and rebuild. The altar was soon rebuilt, but the temple was not completed until 516 BC in the days of Darius the Great. Several obstacles had to be overcome both from the Persian administration and from the neighbors of the Jews.

Cyrus. The policy of the Persian Empire toward their subject peoples was different from that during the Assyrian and Babylonian Empires. By allowing the people to return to their lands and build their temples, Cyrus fostered a sense of comfort with Persian rule and perhaps even complacency. The goal was to enable the people to experience peace and prosperity without any real independence or land ownership. They could live in their homeland and worship their own gods. In this way he sponsored the return of the Jews and the rebuilding of their temple, just as he did for numerous other peoples who had been deported by the Babylonians.

Mistakes to Avoid

It would be a mistake to equate the temple with the church buildings we use today. They have very different functions. The temple is a building; the church is a group of people. The temple was a place of God's presence where rituals were performed. The church building is a place where God's people gather on a regular basis to engage in corporate worship. Temples have limited access; churches have open access. There can be many church buildings; there was only supposed to be one temple for one God. Attempting to merge temple and church when teaching this passage will lead to misunderstanding of the text.

84. Ezra (Ezra 7; 8:15–36; Nehemiah 8–9)

Lesson Focus

Ezra obtained permission from the king to lead another group back to Israel. When he got there, he read the law (the terms of the covenant) to all the people in Jerusalem, and the people repented and renewed the covenant.

- God brought his people back from exile to Jerusalem just as he promised.
- God was able to use the Persian kings to achieve his purposes.
- God wants his people to be faithful to the covenant.

Lesson Application

We should believe that God is faithful to his promises, and we ought to be faithful to him.

- We believe that God can overcome any obstacle to carry out his plan.
- Reading God's revelation of himself will help us know him better and know how we are supposed to live.
- We repent when we become aware of sin in our lives.

Biblical Context

The purpose of the books of Ezra and Nehemiah is to show the many ways that God was at work to restore the people of Israel to their land. God brought the Israelites favor with the Persian rulers and helped them overcome the obstacles presented by their enemies as they rebuilt the walls of Jerusalem and set up the law as the foundation of society. The books recount the restoration of the temple, the community, Jerusalem, and the covenant. Nehemiah 8–9 concerns the return of the people from exile to Jerusalem at the time of Ezra and the reading of the law for the instruction of the people. This is a key section to the book, as the law is here established as the basis for the post-exilic community.

Interpretational Issues in the Story

Ezra's credentials (Ezra 7:11). Ezra was in the high priestly line going back to Aaron (Ezra 7:1–5). He was also trained as a scribe and as a specialist in the Law of Moses. There are many traditions about Ezra that are plausible but difficult to substantiate. He may have played a role in the final editing and collection of the Old Testament canon and in the institution of the synagogue concept.

"Book of the Law of Moses" (Neh. 8:1). This is a scroll that includes either the entire Pentateuch or some part of it. In this time period people, even when literate, tended to receive and absorb information by having it read aloud to them.

"Read from the book . . . clearly" (Neh. 8:8). Here the biblical text was being expounded, i.e., interpreted and applied to their situation.

Background Information

Chronology. Ezra lived during the reign of Persian King Artaxerxes I in the middle of the fifth century. He recorded the rebuilding of the temple even though he personally did not return to Jerusalem until almost sixty years later. When Ezra returned in 458 BC, it would be another thirteen years until Nehemiah came, the wall rebuilt (completed October 27, 445 BC), and the law read (probably in the next month).

Artaxerxes's financial support. The Persians sponsored the temples of peoples in their realm. To them, such financial support constituted worship, since it supposedly helped meet the needs of the god, and the god was to bring blessing to them in return. Polytheists rarely disputed the existence of any of the gods that others worshiped, but they did not feel any faith allegiance to those gods. Artaxerxes's gifts were to ensure the favor of Israel's God for his rule and his continuing success.

Sackcloth. Sackcloth was rough material worn to indicate mourning. It was designed to be uncomfortable.

Mistakes to Avoid

The point of this narrative is not the importance of reading our Bible. It is true that what Ezra read is part of our Bible and that it is important to read God's self-revelation, but there is more going on here. By reading the Law of Moses, Ezra was confronting the people with their violations of the covenant. Now that they had returned to the land, they needed to be more careful about keeping the covenant so that they might remain in the land, a covenant benefit. Consequently, the point of the narrative is recommitting to faithfulness to God.

85. Nehemiah (Nehemiah 2; 4; 6:1–15; 12:27, 43)

Lesson Focus

God kept his promise to return the Israelites to their own land. He has the power to bring them out of exile and help them rebuild the city of Jerusalem, just as he had promised. They responded by committing to obey the law.

- God is committed to his people and is able to carry out his plan for them.
- God responds to the prayers of his people.
- God is able to protect his people from trouble.
- God helps his people to accomplish that which is seemingly impossible.

Lesson Application

We should believe that God is so strong that nothing can stop him from keeping his promises.

- We trust that God can accomplish much through us when we are willing to take risks to do his work.
- We trust God to carry out his plan.
- We should be responsive to God's leading.

Biblical Context

The purpose of the books of Ezra and Nehemiah is to show the many ways that God was at work to restore the people of Israel to their land. God brought the Israelites favor with the Persian rulers and helped them overcome the obstacles presented by their enemies as they rebuilt the walls of Jerusalem and set up the law as the foundation of society. The books recount the restoration of the temple, the community, Jerusalem, and the covenant. These sections of the book of Nehemiah concern the rebuilding of the walls of Jerusalem despite opposition and the reading of the law for the instruction of the people.

Interpretational Issues in the Story

"No longer suffer derision" (Neh. 2:17). The ruined walls were a disgrace because they were testimony to God's punishment for their offenses against him.

Their neighbors oppose the rebuilding (Neh. 4:1–3). Israelite neighbors opposed the rebuilding likely because Nehemiah, as governor, had reduced the territorial control of some of the other provincial rulers, particularly Sanballat, the governor of Samaria. It is also possible that a fortified city would have been viewed as a threat.

Background Information

Chronology. Artaxerxes reigned from 465–424 BC and was the king of Persia who interacted with both Ezra and Nehemiah. It was a turbulent period, as there were rebellions in many parts of the empire.

Cupbearer. The cupbearer in the ancient court was not a menial position. It was a high administrative position that carried the responsibility of protecting the king and his household from any threat.

Wall of Jerusalem. Nehemiah's wall was completed on October 27, 445 BC. A few sections of the wall built at the time of Nehemiah are visible today as a result of ongoing excavations in Jerusalem.

Mistakes to Avoid

Much about Nehemiah is commendable. His leadership was successful, but it does not offer a "biblical" pattern of leadership that should serve as a pattern for all leadership. His prayers were constant, but they do not offer a model for prayers nor is this intended to be a lesson on the necessity of prayer. His risk-taking is admirable, but the point of the narrative is not that we should emulate Nehemiah and take risks for God. It cannot be claimed that failure to use leadership principles from Nehemiah would result in disobeying the Bible. It is the picture of God that we are compelled to embrace. The noteworthy behavior of the characters may prove inspirational to us but does not come to us as authoritative.

86. Esther (Esther)

Lesson Focus

King Xerxes of Persia made Haman his highest ranking official. When Mordecai, a Jew, refused to bow down to Haman, Haman looked for a way to destroy the whole Jewish population of the Persian Empire. But God was at work through Mordecai and Esther to deliver his people.

- God sometimes accomplishes his purposes by working behind the scenes.
- God can use regular folks to do remarkable things for his kingdom.
- God is sovereign over rulers and kingdoms.
- God brings the plots of the wicked against them to their ruin.

Lesson Application

We should believe that God is at work through the everyday circumstances of our lives to accomplish his purposes.

- We must never think that God is absent when we don't see obvious indications of his activity.
- We believe that God can bring down the most powerful of villains.
- We believe that God can turn around kingdoms and national policies.
- We should be willing to act on behalf of God and his people, not because Esther did, but because we realize that God can use his people when they are willing.

Biblical Context

The purpose of the book of Esther is to show that God can accomplish his purposes just as easily through seeming coincidences as he can through grand miracles of deliverance. Though he works behind the curtain, he is just as much in control. Events that others see as chance or fate can be seen by believers as signs of God's sovereignty.

Interpretational Issues in the Story

Mordecai refused to bow to Haman (Est. 3:4). The only explanation provided by the text for why Mordecai refused to bow to Haman is that "he was a Jew." The book never mentions God (which seems intentional), so it does not clarify whether Mordecai's motivation was theological. Bowing to a human ruler was not an act of worship and was not forbidden to even the strictest of Israelites. An explanation is to be found in the ancestry of Mordecai and Haman. Mordecai is identified as from the tribe of Benjamin and a son of Kish (2:5). This links him to Saul (1 Sam. 9:1). Haman is identified as an Agagite (Est. 3:1), which links him to the Amalekite king that Saul fought against (1 Sam. 15:20, 32–33). It may be then that Mordecai's attitude was ethnically motivated. Whether that was the case or not, we cannot assume that his behavior was motivated by faithfulness to the Lord to the extent that we make that the focus of the lesson.

"Deliverance will rise" (Est. 4:14). Mordecai almost bullies Esther into going before the king. What is of interest here, however, is the confidence that deliverance will come. Again, the text avoids making a reference to God, but the implication is clear enough. This confidence testifies to the belief that God defends and protects his people.

Background Information

Chronology. This period of history features the Greek and Persian wars. These include the battles of Marathon (490 BC), Thermopylae and Salamis (480 BC), and Plataea and Mycale (479 BC). The dismissal of Vashti came early in Xerxes' reign, prior to the launching of the Persian campaign against the Greeks in 481 BC. The search for Esther came after he returned in 479 BC. The events reach their conclusion in 473 BC.

Characters in the book. Ahasueras is known in the Greek sources as Xerxes. He ruled from 486 to 465 BC. None of the other characters in the book are known from extrabiblical sources of the time.

Mistakes to Avoid

Though both Esther and Mordecai have admirable traits, the text should not be used to try to encourage students to be like Esther or Mordecai. Esther showed great courage, but the biblical text is not trying to teach readers to be courageous. It is about God and how he works in the world. He uses people's traits and strengthens them for tasks, but the Bible is designed to enable us to know God better, more than to help us be like Esther. We should likewise refrain from leading students to think that God will accomplish this sort of deliverance on their behalf. God is able, but in his wisdom he chooses which course of action to follow case by case.

87. Job (Job)

Lesson Focus

The purpose of the book of Job is to test God's policies concerning justice. The book concludes that we cannot assess God's justice because we can never have enough information to do so; instead, we must infer his justice from his wisdom—and he *is* wise.

- God's attributes are not consistently manifested in nature (nature is not just, and justice is not the foundation of the world's operation).
- God delights in blessing the righteous.
- God is wise.
- God's justice is beyond our ability to assess.

Lesson Application

We can trust God's wisdom even when we cannot make sense of our experiences.

- The fallen world does not operate by justice.
- We should pursue disinterested righteousness, that is, righteousness for the sake of righteousness.
- Because we believe that God is wise, we can trust him to be just.
- When we suffer, we should focus on the future (what ***purpose*** God has) rather than the past (what is the ***cause*** of our suffering).

Biblical Context

The adversary claimed that God's policy of blessing righteous people is flawed because they will then be motivated by prosperity rather than simply by the desire to be righteous. When Job began to suffer, he likewise concluded that God's policies are flawed. Thus, the question is established: How can God run the world with justice and still promote true righteousness? Job's friends thought that Job must have been suffering because he was wicked. Both Job and his friends believed that if God runs the world and is truly just, then the world must operate justly; thus, God's policies were under investigation. The book builds the case that the world actually operates on a foundation of wisdom, not justice. God did not try to defend his justice, because no one is in a position to assess his justice. The conclusion of the matter and the point of the book is that the complexity of the world prevents us from having sufficient information to assess God's justice. However, we do have sufficient information to affirm that he is wise. If we believe he is wise, then we can believe he is just.

Interpretational Issues in the Story

Retribution principle. The retribution principle expressed the belief that the righteous prosper and the wicked suffer. This belief was assumed and expressed by both Job and his friends.

Adversary or challenger (Job 1:6). In the book of Job, the Hebrew word *satan* is a role, not a name, so it is best to translate it as "the challenger." A variety of beings could serve the role of challenger, so it is not certain that this was the same individual who eventually carried the name Satan in the New Testament. Here he can be described as someone who challenges the policies of God, and God takes the challenge seriously.

Background Information

Job's friends. The advice of Job's friends reflects the standard conclusion of the ancient world: deity had been offended by something and had brought punishment. They believed that regardless of whether Job was able to identify what his offense might have been, he should take any action that would appease the anger of deity in order to get his blessings back. If Job were to have done this, it would have proved that the adversary's accusation was right—Job didn't care about righteousness so long as he enjoyed prosperity. But Job refused that path (27:1–6).

Mistakes to Avoid

Caution must be exercised in putting too much emphasis on the challenger (*satan*). The text makes it clear that though the challenger is the instrument, God is the one ultimately responsible for Job's troubles (e.g., 1:21 and 2:3). The lesson from the book is not about Satan. Though Job and his friends believed that Job was being tested, the book makes clear from the beginning—from everyone who counts—that Job was righteous. It is not Job who was being tested, but God's policies. So while Job believed himself to be the defendant of his own righteousness, he was in reality the star witness for the defense of God's policies. We should not teach from this book that Satan might be causing us to suffer or that God tests us by sending suffering. The book does not offer an answer to why righteous people suffer but rather advises us how to think through our suffering, to realize that we live in a fallen world and that God is wise.

Nor should we teach that the point of the book is to emulate Job. The book shows that Job misunderstood many things, though he is commendable for maintaining his integrity. Job's commendable attitude aside, righteousness is more important than prosperity, but that is not because Job had that opinion but because that is what honors God. God restored Job's health and possessions at the end, but this does not guarantee the same results for us if and when we persevere through suffering. The point being made in the book is that God was determined to continue his policy of blessing righteous people, contrary to the challenger's claim that blessing corrupts people's motives.

The book of Job is also not about how we should or should not be a friend to the suffering. No psychological tips or strategies should be put forth from the book, as if God were providing a counseling resource. While children can begin to understand that God is both wise and just, the sophistication of the book's argument will make it difficult to teach to younger ages.

88. Isaiah's Temple Vision (Isaiah 6:1–8)

Lesson Focus

Isaiah was given his prophetic commission by the heavenly assembly. He was purified for the task and told to expect little in the way of response.

- God sends out his people as messengers.
- God purifies us for the task before us.
- God does not always expect us to succeed in the tasks we do for him.

Lesson Application

If God calls us to a task, we should be responsive to the call and go, regardless of what the outcome might be.

- We determine to carry out our tasks for God regardless of whether we meet standards for success that we or others establish.
- We understand that serving should be accompanied by purification.

Biblical Context

This story recounts Isaiah's commissioning as a prophet. He was given his task, which, as can be seen from the latter part of the chapter, was going to be largely unfruitful because the people would not respond to his messages from God. The major theme in Isaiah is found in the repeated call to trust the Lord rather than alliances, strategies, or other gods.

Interpretational Issues in the Story

"Saw the Lord" (Isa. 6:1). Isaiah was in the throne room, the Most Holy Place, and only priests were allowed in there. Isaiah was not a priest, so we deduce that this was a vision. Therefore, there was no danger to Isaiah in "seeing the Lord," as there would have been had God's real presence been manifested.

"Touched my mouth" (Isa. 6:7). Isaiah was not just in the presence of the throne of God, but he was standing before the heavenly assembly ("Who will go for *us*," v. 8). It was believed that by this council, prophets were commissioned and given a message and were to report to it. For this sacred task Isaiah needed to be purified. The cleansing of the lips in Mesopotamia was often symbolic of the cleansing of the whole person.

Background Information

Large size of God. Gods from the ancient world are typically portrayed as having been very large. In a temple from this period at Ain Dara in Syria, huge footprints are carved showing the path of the deity walking into the temple.

Seraphim (Isa. 6:2, 6). These creatures are mentioned as heavenly only here, but elsewhere the word is used to refer to flying serpents (Isa. 14:29; 30:6; see also the serpents in the wilderness in Numbers 21:4–9). Serpents with wings were royal guardians in Egyptian art.

Role of the prophet. A prophet is a messenger or mouthpiece for God given the task of proclaiming God's plan. The plan proclaimed could pertain to the past, present, or future, so it is inaccurate to refer to a prophet as one who simply foretells or predicts the future. The prophets' messages usually fell into one of four categories: indictment (what the people were doing wrong), judgment (what God was going to do about it), instruction (what the people should do to get back on track), and hope (God's plans for restoration after the judgment). The prophet always understood what his message was, though he rarely knew how or when it would be fulfilled. We should not assume that the prophet had inside information about the fulfillment of his message that he was holding back. The most important part of prophecy is to understand the message, which is what we are intended to look for. Fulfillment comes about in the gradual unfolding of events and is God's business.

Mistakes to Avoid

This story is often told in connection with missions. It must be noted, however, that there are significant differences between the commissioning of a prophet and the calling of a missionary. Both go with a message, but the prophet was going to God's people, not to those in need of a message of salvation. Often the prophet focused on messages of offense and coming judgment. The most important and useful common ground is that God calls people to serve him by relaying important messages. This story can be used as an analogy, but we should not go so far as to suggest God is still calling today, "Whom can I send?" Of a more minor nature, students should be cautioned that seraphim are not angels. Angels are messengers; seraphim, from all appearances, are guardians. The same is true of cherubim. Many have inferred that angels have wings because of biblical descriptions of cherubim and seraphim containing wings. But these are not angels, and angels are never described in the Bible as having wings, though occasionally one will fly.

89. Jeremiah's Scroll (Jeremiah 36)

Lesson Focus

Jeremiah wrote a scroll to be read to King Jehoiakim to warn him of the Lord's anger with his people. In this way God showed that he takes sin seriously but often provides warning when his judgment is near. Jehoiakim, however, refused to listen.

- God often gives warning of judgment.
- God may use even wicked nations to bring judgment against his people.
- God is in control of the course of history.

Lesson Application

We should respond to God's warnings with repentance.

- We are to be humble and repentant when God's Word convicts us of sin.
- We must not think that we can escape God's judgment by ignoring it.

Biblical Context

Jeremiah served as prophet in Judah during the transition from the Assyrian Empire to the Babylonian Empire. The book is full of God's warnings concerning the sins of Judah and Jerusalem and what God will do to punish them. But it also contains oracles of hope for restoration after the judgment. This account indicates how deserving the king was of God's judgment as he was antagonistic toward God's messenger and God's word.

Interpretational Issues in the Story

Cutting and burning the scroll (Jer. 36:23). Prophetic words were believed to be powerful. The very speaking of them assured their fulfillment. That is why sometimes the prophets were held guilty simply for speaking the words. The king's cutting and burning of the scroll was a ritual act designed to counteract the efficacy of the words contained on it.

Background Information

Chronology. The scroll was read in the ninth month of the fifth year of Jehoiakim—604 BC. At that time Nebuchadnezzar had already defeated the Egyptians at Carchemish and had taken control of what had previously been the Assyrian Empire, which, at that time, included Judah. In that year he demanded that all the nations of the area come and submit to him and pay tribute. This is a critical period as Jehoiakim had to decide whether to align himself with Egypt or Babylon or try to remain independent.

Scroll. Scrolls of this period were generally made of papyrus, though occasionally animal skins were used. The cutting and burning described in the text suggests that this one was papyrus. An average scroll contained about twenty sheets glued together. It was about fifteen feet long and one foot tall.

Banned. In 36:5 we read that Jeremiah had been banned from the house of the Lord. Jeremiah had probably been banned from the temple precincts because he was viewed as a troublemaker and insurrectionist. The spoken prophetic word was considered powerful—the very speaking of it was effective. Consequently, prophets who spoke negative messages were viewed as traitors.

Reading documents. The ancient world was largely hearing-dominant. People did not own or read books. Information was passed when documents were read aloud. Jeremiah had the scroll written for precisely this purpose—to be read aloud to the people, then to the leaders, and then to the king.

Mistakes to Avoid

Jehoiakim was hard-hearted, and Baruch was courageous and faithful, but these are not the focus of the narrative. Rather than serving as models for our behavior, the narrative focus is on the way God interacted with his people.

90. Jeremiah and the Fall of Jerusalem (Jeremiah 37–39)

Lesson Focus

Jeremiah was imprisoned for his judgment oracles that announced the Lord's punishment of his people—the destruction of the temple and the fall of Jerusalem.

- God is able to deliver his servants even in disastrous times, but there are no guarantees that he will do so.

- God brings judgment on his people when they are stubbornly unrepentant and unfaithful.
- God is sovereign over the nations.

Lesson Application

We should believe that God takes our sin seriously and will judge it.

- We acknowledge that God will not always spare his people from persecution or judgment.
- We must not be surprised when God uses even wicked people to carry out judgment against his people.

Biblical Context

Jeremiah served as prophet in Judah during the transition from the Assyrian Empire to the Babylonian Empire. The book is full of God's warnings concerning the sins of Judah and Jerusalem and what God will do to punish them. But it also contains oracles of hope for restoration after the judgment. This account brings to a climax the judgment of God as Jerusalem, along with the temple, was destroyed by the Babylonians.

Interpretational Issues in the Story

Zedekiah and Jeremiah (Jer. 37:2–7). Although King Zedekiah was not willing to respond to Jeremiah's indictments of him (37:2), he wanted Jeremiah to pray for him (37:3) and asked for prophetic information about what was going to happen (37:7). This is easily explained by stubborn self-reliance and unwillingness to change coupled with an anxious curiosity. He was probably still somehow hoping that the Lord will say everything would be all right.

Imprisoned (Jer. 37:15). Prisons in the biblical world were not like the ones we know today. Punishment for criminals was not usually extended confinement. There were places of confinement in military installations for people awaiting trial or for political prisoners, but these could not accommodate very many, and the institution was not set up for long-term imprisonment (like the jail behind the sheriff's office in cowboy movies with two cells for short-term confinement). Something like a cistern was used for such imprisonment.

Background Information

Chronology. The city of Jerusalem fell to the Babylonian king Nebuchadnezzar in 586 BC after a two-year siege. Zedekiah had been on the throne for about ten years and had finally decided to rebel with promises of military support from Egypt. By this time Jeremiah had been prophesying for over forty years.

Nebuchadnezzar. Nebuchadnezzar was a remarkable king whose reign was filled with military and political success. His building projects were grand and extensive and brought Babylon to the height of its glory. It is hard to imagine a more successful king, so it is noteworthy that God demonstrated his sovereignty over him.

Mistakes to Avoid

We cannot assume that just because God brought about Jeremiah's release from prison that he will do the same sort of thing for others of his people. Many of God's people have spent decades in prison and died there. God is able to do anything, but in his wisdom he decides what to do when and for whom. Another matter is that in biblical times God gave his prophets interpretation of historical events so that certain occurrences would be known as the judgment of God. Today we do not have similar prophetic voices to tell us how to interpret events relative to God's work. We cannot assert with confidence that particular political events show either God's favor or punishment.

91. Daniel and the King's Food (Daniel 1)

Lesson Focus

Daniel and three other young Jewish men were taken from Jerusalem to serve King Nebuchadnezzar in Babylon. Daniel resolved not to defile himself with food from the king's table. God was with these young men and caused things to go well for them.

- God cares for his people.
- God notices the faithfulness of his people.
- God is the source of whatever success we experience.

Lesson Application

God is in control, even in difficult circumstances.

- We can trust that God is with us even in hard times.
- We should be faithful to God in all situations.

Biblical Context

The book of Daniel is about the sovereignty of God expressed at two levels. First, he shows his sovereignty in bringing blessing and protection on individuals who are faithful to him in difficult situations. Second, God is sovereign over the kings, nations, and empires of the world. In this account Daniel and his friends determined to remain faithful to God, and he brought them success.

Interpretational Issues in the Story

King's food (Dan. 1:8). The king's food refers to any food that was provided using the palace budget. This indicates that Daniel and his friends were under royal sponsorship. The Hebrew word translated "royal food" is a Persian loanword and is not fully understood. There is no reason to think of it as a meat dish. Greek sources suggest it was a baked product of barley and grain, but it is not necessarily limited to that. In contrast Daniel asked for a food product that is sometimes translated "vegetables," but the term usually describes seed to be planted or to be used as fodder for animals. One possibility is that it refers to grain rations that required preparation for use by soldiers and others.

Daniel's motives (Dan. 1:8). Daniel and his friends expressed their desire not to "defile" themselves. The difficult question is why the king's rations would defile someone and a soldier's rations, if that is what Daniel requested, would not. The nature of the ingredients is not demonstrably different, so we might consider that it had to do with the way the food was prepared. Whatever the issue, an argument cannot be sustained that Daniel's decision had to do with (1) unclean foods (he also refused the king's wine, which was not unclean); (2) a vegetarian diet (Daniel temporarily abstained from meat [10:3], from which we can infer that he normally ate it); or (3) junk food.

Background Information

Daniel's situation. Though Daniel did not have a choice about going to Babylon, he was not a captive or prisoner. He had been commandeered by the Babylonian court for training. As one of the promising young people of a subject nation, he was going to be prepared for a career in service to the king of Babylon. Some became diplomats; others, advisors to the king. A variety of specialized functions were filled in this way. Above all, the objective in the training was that they would become thoroughly Babylonian in their outlook and loyalty.

Language and literature of Babylon. By this point in history the Babylonians' Aramaic was the widely used language of the empire, but their heritage and traditional literature was largely in Akkadian. Aramaic was a language closely related to Hebrew, and it used an alphabetic script that made it easier to learn and use than Akkadian, which used a cuneiform syllabic script. Daniel was most likely being taught Akkadian and introduced to the vast literature written in that language. Particularly important was the divination literature, which gave guidance to the interpretation of dreams and omens. Daniel eventually showed expertise in these areas, but it is never suggested that he drew on the literature that Babylonian experts used.

Mistakes to Avoid

This story is often misused. It is not about how people should eat—we are not called to imitate Daniel's dietary choices. In fact, we don't even know what those choices were and why he made them. Something that Daniel would have viewed as defiling would not necessarily be defiling today (note Acts 10 where even unclean food is treated differently). This is not about food offered to idols. That is a New Testament issue, not an Old Testament one. There is no reason to think that the food provided to Daniel had been offered to idols. The point is simply that Daniel made a decision about his food that, to him, represented an act of faithfulness to God. Instead of trying to imitate Daniel's act of faithfulness (whatever it entailed), we should strive to be faithful to God in whatever ways we can. Likewise, we cannot use this story as offering guarantees that God will bring prosperity and success if we are faithful. Here he does, and we know that he is able, but that does not constitute a promise that he will always do so.

92. Nebuchadnezzar's Dream Statue (Daniel 2)

Lesson Focus

God gave Nebuchadnezzar a dream that showed his plan for kings and empires. God gave Daniel the interpretation of the dream that spared his life along with the lives of the king's other advisors.

- God has a plan for history and at times reveals that plan.
- God protects his faithful people.

- God can work through dreams, though they are not reliable sources of revelation.
- God controls even the most powerful kings and empires.

Lesson Application

We should believe that God is in control of the kings and kingdoms of the world.

- We are to focus on God's kingdom rather than be distracted by the world's kingdoms.
- We are called to be faithful to God, whatever our circumstances.
- We believe that God can deliver us from trouble, realizing he may not always do so.

Biblical Context

The book of Daniel is about the sovereignty of God expressed at two levels. First, God shows his sovereignty in bringing blessing and protection on individuals who are faithful to him in difficult situations. Second, God is sovereign over the kings, nations, and empires of the world. In this account, as God gave Daniel the interpretation of Nebuchadnezzar's dream, he shows himself powerful to protect Daniel's life and that he is in control of the flow of kings and empires. He also indicates that in his control of history the kingdom of God is coming.

Interpretational Issues in the Story

Four kingdoms (Dan. 2:37–43). It is not necessary that we know the identity of the four kingdoms but there are a couple of important options. One identifies the four kingdoms as Babylonian/Medo-Persian/Greek/ Roman, while another defends the lineup as Babylonian/Median/Persian/ Greek. Since the biblical text never clarifies the fulfillment, we do not know. More important than the identity of the kingdoms is that, whatever they are, God is in control and they were temporary. The kingdom of God will overcome all.

Symbols in dreams and visions (Daniel 2). Prophecy is intended to reveal God and his plan, but symbols may conceal information. Nevertheless, it is tempting to speculate what they stand for. We cannot arrive at anything authoritative through speculation. If the biblical text has not told us what a symbol stands for, we don't need to know. Generally, the message of a dream is made clear, even if the symbols are mystifying. Here, the message is four kingdoms and then the kingdom of God.

Nebuchadnezzar's request (Dan. 2:5–6). One possible reason that Nebuchadnezzar would demand that his wise men tell the dream is that it would be very easy to interpret the dream as portending the overthrow of his throne or kingdom, something a competing faction might make up to use against him. Only deity could provide the interpreter with the dream so as to give confidence that the interpretation was actually the message from the deity and not part of a political conspiracy.

Nebuchadnezzar's declaration (Dan. 2:47). Nebuchadnezzar was obviously very impressed with Daniel's God, but this doesn't necessarily indicate what his true beliefs were. Nebuchadnezzar was prepared neither to discard his other gods nor to proclaim the God of Daniel as the chief God of Babylon. It was not unusual in the ancient world for a worshiper to talk to or about a particular god as if that one was the only god and the wisest or most powerful among gods. Such standard rhetoric can be seen here. The display of wisdom and power that Nebuchadnezzar witnessed demanded recognition, and he was glad to offer it. His respect for Daniel's God was greater, but his belief system remained unchanged (as later texts in Daniel show).

Background Information

Nebuchadnezzar. Nebuchadnezzar was a remarkable king whose reign was filled with military and political success. His building projects were grand and extensive and brought Babylon to the height of its glory. It is hard to imagine a more successful king, so it is noteworthy that God demonstrated his sovereignty over him.

Dream interpretation. In the ancient world, dream interpretation was the province of experts who engaged in research to arrive at their results. They were not expected to divine what the dream actually was. Instead, given the dream as reported, they would go to the dream books, where a variety of elements were listed along with what they portended, and from that research they would compile an interpretation.

Images of mixed elements. Statues of mixed elements were not unusual in the ancient world. Since images of gods were often clothed, only the parts that were seen needed to be of the highest-quality metals, thus the head of gold. Some images were made of bronze and then coated in various parts with gold or silver. Mixed iron and clay might refer to the use of terracotta inlays on the feet.

Mistakes to Avoid

This story has nothing to tell us about God working through dreams except that he can do so. It does not commend to us the idea that we need to look at our dreams as messages from God. In the Old Testament (and perhaps today) God typically uses dreams with those who have little knowledge of him. Second, we must not treat this narrative as if it is all about identifying future kingdoms and therefore requires us to try to identify the kingdoms. Remember that prophecy is more interested in revealing God than in revealing the future. Third, we must be careful to avoid suggesting that God will always bring deliverance from death threats as he did for Daniel and his friends. God is able, but he offers no guarantees.

93. The Fiery Furnace (Daniel 3)

Lesson Focus

Shadrach, Meshach, and Abednego refused to worship a gold image set up by King Nebuchadnezzar. They knew God had the power to save them if he wished, but they determined to remain faithful regardless of the consequences.

- God delights in the faithfulness of his people.
- God is able to deliver but may not always choose to do so.
- God is with us in our most dangerous situations.

Lesson Application

God is in control, even in difficult circumstances.

- We determine to be faithful whatever the cost.
- We trust God to do what he decides is wise to do.

Biblical Context

The book of Daniel is about the sovereignty of God expressed at two levels. First, God shows his sovereignty in bringing blessing and protection on individuals who are faithful to him in difficult situations. Second, God is sovereign over the kings, nations, and empires of the world. In this account God showed himself powerful to protect the lives of Shadrach, Meshach, and Abednego, as they were faithful to him, refusing to bow down to the statue.

Interpretational Issues in the Story

Nature of the statue (Dan. 3:28). The implication is that the statue depicted diety, and that is certainly the most likely explanation, though an image of the king is also possible. The required bowing down indicates the demand for respect that was given to people in authority and does not necessarily suggest ritual action or allegiance to a god. But the friends clearly believed that such action would compromise their faithfulness to Yahweh, so they refused. It is unlikely that a statue of a deity would have been out on a plain rather than in a sacred enclosure with altars and other equipment for rituals to be performed. An alternative is that the image portrays a symbol associated with the deity (e.g., a crown or weapon). If they bowed down to a statue of the king, they were aligning themselves with his god.

Furnace (Dan. 3:6). A plain is not the most likely place for a furnace, so it is probable that the furnace was used to make the statue.

"A son of the gods" (Dan. 3:25). Since "a son of the gods" is an observation by Nebuchadnezzar, it should not be given a great amount of theological credibility. In Nebuchadnezzar's mouth this was simply an expression that identified the fourth individual as godlike. In 3:28 he refers to the being as an angel (messenger). There is no reason to think of this as "Son of God," that is, Christ.

Background Information

Nebuchadnezzar. Nebuchadnezzar was a remarkable king whose reign was filled with military and political success. His building projects were grand and extensive and brought Babylon to the height of its glory. It is hard to imagine a more successful king, so it is noteworthy that God demonstrates his sovereignty over him.

Occasion. It is likely that a group of officials is being asked to take an oath of loyalty at the dedication of the statue.

Dimensions of the statue. The odd dimensions have attracted attention. If it was a human figure, a proportion that is ten times higher than its width would be a caricature. An alternative is that the nine-foot-wide image was sitting atop a pedestal ninety feet high. Another is that the plain abutted a cliff, and the image was set up on the cliff face ninety feet high. We know that kings often tried to set their inscriptions or reliefs in inaccessible places that could be seen from a distance but not reached for defacing.

Mistakes to Avoid

The courage of Shadrach, Meshach, and Abednego is admirable, commendable, and remarkable. Their faithfulness despite the jeopardy to their lives should be something we all aspire to. But the text wants us to focus more on what God did for and through them than on the friends themselves. We might well call them heroes, but we are not called through the story to be heroes. We need instead to focus on the faithfulness and power of God. That is where the text ends up, as Nebuchadnezzar, the most powerful king in the world of that time, acknowledges the superiority of God. All the Babylonians were on the plain to recognize the power and authority of Nebuchadnezzar and his gods, but the story ends with Yahweh, the God of Israel, being the most powerful of all.

94. The Humbled King (Daniel 4)

Lesson Focus

God gave Nebuchadnezzar a dream warning him about his pride, and when Nebuchadnezzar did not change, his authority was taken away, demonstrating that God is the one who gives authority and takes it away.

- God is sovereign over kings and kingdoms.
- God is the one who grants authority and he can take it away.
- God humbles the proud.

Lesson Application

We should recognize that all authority comes from God.

- We trust God and his plan for the world.
- We believe that God will judge those who defy him.
- We understand that no one is above God.
- We understand that God disapproves of human arrogance.

Biblical Context

The book of Daniel is about the sovereignty of God expressed at two levels. First, God shows his sovereignty in bringing blessing on and protection to individuals who are faithful to him in difficult situations. Second, God is sovereign over the kings, nations, and empires of the world. In this account God shows himself as the one who puts kings on their thrones and removes them.

Interpretational Issues in the Story

Watcher (Dan. 4:13). The watchers, or messengers, are known from a number of books written during the period between the Old and New Testaments. In addition, Mesopotamian literature attests to seven sages who were watchers, caretakers, of a sacred tree.

Nebuchadnezzar's condition (Dan. 4:25, 32). The translations of 4:34 ("my sanity was restored," NIV) lead many to think Nebuchadnezzar's malady was madness. In the Aramaic text it says that his knowledge was restored to him. In ancient Mesopotamia it was not unusual to describe uncivilized humans as ignorant and living like animals. The description may then suggest that he lived as an outcast from society and was brought from the pinnacle of sophisticated civilization (king of Babylon) to the very lowest, uncivilized form. It is difficult to tell whether this should be assessed as insanity.

Nebuchadnezzar's praise (Dan. 4:34–35). Nebuchadnezzar is obviously very impressed with Daniel's God, but this doesn't necessarily indicate his true beliefs. Nebuchadnezzar is prepared neither to discard his other gods nor to proclaim the God of Daniel as the chief god of Babylon. It was not unusual in the ancient world for a worshiper to talk to or about a particular god as if that one was the only god and the wisest or most powerful among gods. Such standard rhetoric can be seen here. The display of power that Nebuchadnezzar witnessed is demanding of recognition, and he was glad to offer it, but his belief system likely remained unchanged.

Background Information

Nebuchadnezzar. Nebuchadnezzar was a remarkable king whose reign was filled with military and political success. His building projects were grand and extensive and brought Babylon to the height of its glory. It is hard to imagine a more successful king, so it is noteworthy that God demonstrated his sovereignty over him.

Babylon. Babylon was the center of culture in the ancient world. Nebuchadnezzar was one of its prime architects, and its beauty impressed everyone who saw it. Its Hanging Gardens were declared as one of the seven wonders of the ancient world. The Euphrates River was channeled through the city to create parks and waterways. Temples, palaces, and gates were all beautifully built and decorated. A small part of the grandeur has been unearthed by archaeologists and can be viewed in the museums of the world today.

World tree. In the ancient world people envisioned a huge cosmic tree at the center of the earth that held up the heavens and reached down into the netherworld. As here in 4:10–12, it was seen as sheltering creatures of all sorts. God used a familiar image to communicate to Nebuchadnezzar. It would have been quite devastating to have such a tree cut down. It represented world order, and the king, as a personification of this tree, was seen as the one who established world order.

Mistakes to Avoid

Just as not all faithful people are delivered from danger, not all proud people are brought down in dramatic or noticeable ways. The results we see here are not guarantees or promises. The focus of the lesson is the attributes of God and what pleases him and what brings his anger.

95. Belshazzar's Feast (Daniel 5)

Lesson Focus

God had appointed the time for the overthrow of Babylon in accordance with its offenses. He announced his intentions through Daniel on the night before the fall of the city, showing his control of the flow of kings and kingdoms.

- God gives kings and kingdoms their authority and takes it all away in his time.
- God is sovereign over all.
- God uses means that are familiar to people to communicate to them.
- God will not be mocked or ridiculed.
- God deserves recognition for the role he plays.

Lesson Application

We should recognize that the time of the wicked is measured and that God's judgment will come.

- We must never doubt that God is in control of the flow of political events.
- We are not to discount God.
- We acknowledge God for the blessings and success he brings to us.

Biblical Context

The book of Daniel is about the sovereignty of God expressed at two levels. First, God shows his sovereignty in bringing blessing and protection on individuals who are faithful to him in difficult situations. Second, God is sovereign over the kings, nations, and empires of the world. In this account God shows himself as the one who has put kings on their thrones and can remove them.

Interpretational Issues in the Story

Hand (Dan. 5:5). In the ancient world the right hands of enemy casualties often were cut off and piled up to give graphic evidence of the magnitude of the victory. At an earlier time, when the image of Dagon fell over before the ark of the Lord, its hands were broken off as a signal of defeat (1 Samuel 5). Here, the Babylonians were recalling the victories of their gods before whom Yahweh was just one in a string of casualties among the defeated gods. Their use of the goblets from the temple was supposed to give a reminder of their past victories over various gods. But instead of appearing as a lifeless, detached hand, a disembodied yet very alive hand wrote a message on the wall for the doomed king.

The message (Dan. 5:25). The wise men could not read the message. Onc possible reason is that the message was written in an obscure language. Even had it been written in Aramaic, it could have been written without word divisions, or in columns instead of rows. Alternatively, perhaps the wise men could read the words perfectly well but could offer no interpretation of their meaning.

Background Information

Chronology. The time of the narrative is 539 BC. Cyrus had conquered the Medes over fifteen years earlier and had spent the first twenty years of his reign consolidating and expanding his power. Earlier in the year, he had begun his move against Babylon. His armies had recently taken the strategic cities of Opis and Sippar that protected the way toward Babylon. King Nabonidus, father of Belshazzar, had been with the army at Opis and had fled. Belshazzar knew that the Babylonian armies and stronghold had been decimated and that there was nothing left to prevent the city from being overrun by the Persians. Their only hope was in the gods, so the feast was designed to toast the past victories of the gods (including their victory over Jerusalem) with the hope that the gods would intervene on their behalf.

Belshazzar. Though Belshazzar had not replaced his father, Nabonidus, as king, he had been made official co-regent while his father spent some thirteen years in Teima in Arabia. Therefore, he was rightly referred to as king and appropriately offered the interpreter of the message the third-highest place in the kingdom.

Mistakes to Avoid

This is not a lesson urging readers to imitate Daniel's long life of commitment to God. Daniel is a commendable figure, but the point of the book and this story is trivialized if we look only at the characters. The point is what we learn of the awesome, sovereign God of the universe. We can acknowledge that Belshazzar was a weak king, but his incompetence is no more a lesson to us about leadership than was Nebuchadnezzar's competence. The Bible is not giving authoritative lessons on weak or strong leadership in the stories of these kings.

96. Daniel and the Lions (Daniel 6)

Lesson Focus

Daniel was faithful to God, and the Lord rescued him from the lions.

- God is able to deliver his faithful people from the persecution of even powerful people.
- God's kingdom is greater than any earthly kingdom, and his kingship is greater than that of any human king.

Lesson Application

God is with those who trust in him.

- We trust God to be with us in times of trouble.
- We remain faithful to God even if it gets us in trouble.

Biblical Context

The book of Daniel is about the sovereignty of God expressed at two levels. First, God shows his sovereignty in bringing blessing and protection on individuals who are faithful to him in difficult situations. Second, God is sovereign over the kings, nations, and empires of the world. In this account God shows himself as the one who protects his faithful servant even against the plots of powerful people.

Interpretational Issues in the Story

Darius's first decree (Dan. 6:7). The nature of the decree is a difficult issue. Persian kings were not known for self-deification, nor were they engaged in persecution of those who worshiped other gods. In fact, Cyrus sponsored the rebuilding of temples throughout his realm so that all gods would be honored and worshiped. Furthermore, those who were polytheistic tended to be open-minded about all the gods. One would not want to make any of the gods angry, and in order to avoid that, no god was deprived of worship. Most of the religions of the ancient world featured daily times of prayer, so it is unlikely that the king decreed a universial prohibition against prayer. The prohibition here likely has something to do with the establishment of Zoroastrianism, a Persian religion that gained royal support at this time. Perhaps the decree had something to do with prayers being channeled through the king as high priest, but we really don't know. Therefore the issue should be handled in somewhat general terms, for example, that Daniel's enemies got the king to give a decree about praying that they could use to get Daniel in trouble.

Darius's second decree (Dan. 6:26). Like similar declarations by Nebuchadnezzar (Daniel 2, 3, 4), Darius indicated that everyone should give respect to Daniel's God. He words show that he was impressed, but they fall short of suggesting that he discarded his other gods to proclaim the God of Daniel as the chief God of Babylon or the Persian Empire. It was not unusual in the ancient world for a worshiper to talk to or about one god as if that one were the only god and the most powerful one. Such standard rhetoric is seen here. The display of power that Darius witnessed demanded praise, and he was glad to offer it, but his belief system likely remained unchanged. Furthermore, the declaration calls for "fear and reverence," not for rituals and temples. There is no call for the law to be taught, the covenant to be joined, idols to be abandoned, or monotheism to be adopted.

Background Information

Time period. The event should be placed within the first couple of years after the fall of Babylon, so perhaps 535 BC at the latest. Daniel had been taken to Babylon as a teenager in 605 BC. Therefore, he would have been over eighty years old at this time.

Darius the Mede. There was a Persian king named Darius who began ruling about 520 BC, but that was too late to be Darius the Mede. In Daniel, Darius is specifically called a Mede and placed in the time of Cyrus (6:28). This Darius is seen as the ruler of the city of Babylon after the city fell to Cyrus. He is not known from historical sources outside the Bible. Some would say that Darius is just another name for Cyrus, while others have tried to identify him with Gubaru, who was appointed governor of Babylon by Cyrus. There is insufficient information to make a decision on this difficult question.

Mistakes to Avoid

Teachers should not resort to application by metaphor, such as "What are the lions in your life that you would like God to protect you from?" God does not always deliver his faithful people, though he is able to do so. Neither can we extrapolate the idea of guardian angels watching over us. Furthermore, the story is not calling us to be like Daniel, though we might be glad to have his faithful courage, but to understand the power of God. We should not depict the lions as cute, cuddly friends of Daniel. Their ferocity and threat are important for understanding the full measure of the power of God. If we turn them into "conversation partners," we give a fictional feel to the narrative that undermines its power. Daniel's faith and persistence in prayer are commendable and admirable; the message, however, is not found in the lions or in Daniel, but in the decree of Darius concerning the greatness of Daniel's God. Finally, we cannot teach that Darius and the whole empire became worshipers of Daniel's God. The text simply does not support that claim, and neither does history.

97. Jonah (Jonah)

Lesson Focus

God shows compassion where he wills.

- God is responsive to small steps in the right direction.
- God's compassion is not earned and never deserved.

Lesson Application

God sometimes shows compassion on us by giving us a second chance when we don't deserve it.

- We respond to God's Word by taking steps in the right direction.
- We recognize that God's compassion is great.

Biblical Context

The book of Jonah is about how people respond to the Lord and how the Lord responds to them. Both the sailors and the Ninevites, though pagans, were responsive to what they saw the Lord doing. Jonah, a prophet who should have known better, was the least responsive and had to be taught a lesson about God's compassion.

Interpretational Issues in the Story

Jonah's prophetic mission (Jonah 3:4). Jonah was sent to denounce Nineveh, not to save it. His word to them was a word of judgment. He did not even name Yahweh and he did not confront them with their offenses, instruct them as to what they ought to do, or offer any hope for them to avoid the judgment. If the text does not offer this information, we cannot read those things between the lines and assume that they occurred.

Great fish (Jonah 1:17). Nothing in the text indicates the species of the creature, and while a whale cannot be ruled out (they would not have distinguished sea-dwelling mammals from fish), the text is vague.

Fish as rescue, not punishment (Jonah 2:6, 9). Jonah's prayer demonstrates that he saw the fish as deliverance, not judgment. He was drowning, and the Lord used the fish to save his life.

Jonah's prayer (Jonah 2:4, 7–9). Jonah offered no repentance and did not ask forgiveness when he prayed inside the fish. He assumed that since the Lord had saved him from death, he had been restored to favor. He spoke ill of those who worship idols, which apparently included the sailors (whose response had been far better than his own) as if he was insisting, "At least I'm not a pagan idol-worshiper!" He made no mention of his disobedience and indicated no willingness to go to Nineveh. The vows he referred to (v. 9) would have involved sacrifices of thanksgiving at the temple for his rescue. This prayer was a farce, and Jonah was still unchanged (as the rest of the book demonstrates).

Ninevite response (Jonah 3:5). The Ninevites believed what Jonah said, but that does not mean they converted to his God. He never even told them the identity of his God, and there is no indication that they got rid of their idols or understood the law. They repented, but any Assyrian would have done so under these circumstances. If they had been convinced that some god was angry at them and about to destroy them, they would have sought to appease that god. That is how they took Jonah's warning. In the ancient world people believed that there were all sorts of powerful gods, but they only worshiped the ones they believed had power over their lives. Jonah was informing them that a God they had not recognized had noticed them and was going to act against them, and they were grateful for this information. Likely they checked Jonah's message against their omens and afterward were eager to respond.

Sackcloth (Jonah 3:5). Sackcloth was rough material worn to indicate mourning. It was designed to be uncomfortable.

Jonah's refusal to go (Jonah 1:3; 4:2). As Jonah indicated (chap. 4), he did not want to go because the sequence of events was entirely predictable. He knew that the Assyrians would respond with their appeasement techniques and superficial repentance to his judgment message, but that God would be gracious and relent. He was angry about this easy grace.

Object lesson (Jonah 4:5–8). God put Jonah in Nineveh's shoes. Just as Nineveh faced an impending disaster, Jonah faced an impending weather situation. The Ninevites tried to protect themselves with repentance and Jonah tried to protect himself with his hut. Both were inadequate. God provided extra protection for Jonah through a plant. Then God did to Jonah what Jonah wanted him to do to Nineveh—removed his protection. Jonah was not happy about losing God's gracious compassion when it was he, not the Ninevites, who had received it. This is how God made the point that his compassion is given as an act of grace. Once that is understood, we realize that if we overestimate the Ninevite response, we minimize the element of God's compassion. The whole point is that God responds with compassion to even the smallest steps in the right direction.

Background Information

Nineveh. In the mid-eighth century BC, when Jonah lived (2 Kings 14:25), Nineveh was a major city in the Assyrian province of Nineveh. At this time the kingdom of Assyria was fragmented with provinces acting as almost independent entities. The city was about two and a half miles in circumference, about the same size as Jerusalem. About fifty years later (700 BC), Sennacherib made Nineveh the capital city of the Assyrian Empire, bringing it to prominence in the ancient world.

King of Nineveh. One would generally expect the text to refer to the king of Assyria. We would not expect a king of Nineveh, but we would also not expect the king of Assyria to be in Nineveh, because Assyria was fragmented and Nineveh was a province, not the capital. More likely, the ruler of the province would legitimately have been identified with the Hebrew word translated "king."

Mistakes to Avoid

Many mistakes are made when teaching the story of Jonah. The inclination is to make Jonah a missionary who brought a message of hope that was followed by a great conversion among the people of Nineveh. But a prophet was not a missionary preaching good news of hope. Jonah did not have a missionary calling, message, or attitude. His message was only one of judgment.

The story is also not about salvation or going to heaven. Eternal life in heaven is not set forth in the Old Testament. Therefore, we cannot use the story of Jonah as one to tell our friends about Jesus or about leading people to salvation. When teaching about Jonah's reluctance to go to Nineveh, we ought not to conclude that his reason was political resentment or prejudice. Furthermore, though it is certainly true that if God is intent on a person doing something or going somewhere, his plan will be irresistible, but the point of the story isn't that we cannot run from God. God did not allow Jonah to escape the commission, but that does not mean that God will always act in the same way. Focusing on such things detracts from the very important theological message that the book offers: God responds with compassion to small steps in the right direction. God wants people to be responsive to him.

New Testament

98. The Angel Visits Joseph (Matthew 1:18–24)

Lesson Focus

God told Joseph that Mary will bear God's son, Jesus, who will save people from sin.

- Jesus is God in the flesh and represents God's presence with us.
- Jesus is the Son of God.
- Jesus will bring salvation.

Lesson Application

We thank God that he sent his Son, Jesus, to us to be the Savior.

- We believe that Jesus is the Son of God.
- We acknowledge that Jesus was born with no human father.
- We trust Jesus for salvation.

Biblical Context

This account is found only in Matthew, whose interest was in adjusting expectations people had about Jesus and the kingdom of God. He wanted his readers to understand Jesus' mission and what discipleship involves. The announcement to Joseph follows the genealogy that shows Jesus in the line of kings and indicates how Jesus fulfilled the Immanuel prophecy. The Immanuel prophecy was important to Matthew as a way to heighten the expectations of the people of his day who did not consider incarnation (Immanuel—God with us—in the flesh) and virgin birth as part of the messianic profile.

Interpretational Issues in the Story

Angel of the Lord (Matt. 1:20, 24). Angels are messengers of God. They may or may not look different from regular people, and people can also be designated as God's messengers. Here, unlike in the announcement to Mary, the angel appears in a dream.

Birth announcement (Matt. 1:21). It is common for those who were to have an important role in God's ongoing plan to have their birth announced by God or his messengers (compare Isaac, Samson, and Samuel).

Child from the Holy Spirit and Son of God (Matt. 1:20). There is important theology in the narrative concerning the very nature of Jesus. Without human father, he is both divine and human. We speak of Jesus as being human in that he lived, suffered, and died as we do; we speak of him as divine in that he is fully God who came and lived among us. He is one with the Father. Jewish expectations concerning the Messiah did not include the idea that he would be divine, so this was new revelation to their thinking.

Fulfillment (Matt. 1:22). The Israelites of the Old Testament and the Jews of the New Testament had not expected the Messiah to be born of a virgin. (They read Isa. 7:14 differently.) So this fulfillment would have been astonishing. Another remarkable and unexpected element can be seen in the way this gave new meaning to "Immanuel" (God with us). Instead of God's being with his people by helping them and delivering them from enemies (as in Isaiah), Jesus is God become flesh to live among his people (see John 1:14).

Background Information

Women pledged to be married. Marriages were typically arranged by parents. Agreements between the families of a couple were often made when the children were young. Such agreements were formal contracts. Marriage often took place soon after the young girl became fertile, between twelve and fourteen years of age. Mary was likely quite young.

Divorce. The pledge had been made and the families had sealed the agreement, even though the marriage had not been consummated. Mary's pregnancy, if made public, could feasibly have resulted in her being put to death, but this was not generally practiced.

Messages in dreams. In Luke, an angel of the Lord came to Mary—apparently a bodily appearance (like Abraham's visitors in Genesis 18) rather than a vision or a dream. In contrast, the angel appeared to Joseph in a dream. In the Old Testament God generally communicated in dreams to non-Israelites (e.g., Pharaoh, Nebuchadnezzar) or to people not yet established in their faith (Jacob, Genesis 28; Joseph, Genesis 37; Solomon, 1 Kings 3; note the exception in Dan. 7:1). Dreams with symbolic elements (such as Pharaoh's dreams in Genesis 41) require interpretation, whereas message dreams, like this one, do not.

Mistakes to Avoid

We should be cautious about explaining the virgin birth in terms of physiology. We need not be so particular as to suggest that the Holy Spirit implanted sperm. In the ancient world people were unaware of the reproductive system containing sperm and eggs. They believed that a man delivered the seed and a woman was simply an incubator rather than someone who provided half the genetic components. The theology is not built around a modern understanding of physiology and does not require it. The process of Jesus' birth is a mystery. The issue of the virgin birth ought to be handled carefully with younger children who are unaware of what is involved in conception.

99. The Magi (Matthew 2:1–12)

Lesson Focus

The magi learned of Jesus' coming. These foreigners acknowledged and worshiped him as King of the Jews.

- God was already spreading news of Jesus beyond the borders of Israel.
- God can use unconventional means to communicate in ways that people can understand.

Lesson Application

We worship Jesus because he is Savior and King.

- We recognize Jesus as king and honor him with how we live our lives.

Biblical Context

This account is found only in Matthew's Gospel. Matthew's interest was in adjusting people's expectations about Jesus and the kingdom of God. He wanted his readers to understand Jesus' mission and what discipleship involves. The story of the Magi gives important affirmation to several key points in Matthew, particularly Jesus' kingship and the gospel reaching beyond the borders of Israel.

Interpretational Issues in the Story

Star (Matt. 2:2). The Magi reported that they had seen his star, which, by itself could refer to any astronomical sighting that they considered significant. Many theories have been offered, such as Halley's comet, a conjunction of planets, or a supernova, but all have problems. Other interpreters have considered the possibility that the star was entirely supernatural and therefore not identifiable with any known body or astronomical event. The timing of the Magi's visit relative to the time of Jesus' birth is another uncertainty. Even though it would have taken the Magi a few months to prepare for the journey and to travel to Israel, it is possible that they had observed the star some time before the birth of Christ and understood it as a sign of an event that was about to happen.

Coming to Jerusalem first (Matt. 2:1). Since the Magi went first to Jerusalem, with no indication that they got there by following a star, we can infer that the star's appearance somehow communicated to them that an important new king of the Jews had been born. It would have been logical to find such a king in Jerusalem. The only reference to the star going before them comes as they traveled to Bethlehem from Jerusalem.

Stopped (Matt. 2:9). The text refers to the star going before them and then stopping somewhere, behavior uncommon to stars or other known celestial phenomena. Nevertheless, as the stars or planets shift in their positions night to night (astronomers talk about rising and setting), movement can be traced. Further, celestial omens in the ancient world often referred to stars or planets stopping or standing. When this occurs in a particular portion of the sky, that is, in a constellation or in one of the signs of the zodiac, it could indicate to specialists particular geographical locations. We cannot conclude that the star pointed out a particular house or place. The text does not say that the star stopped over the house or even over the place, but that it stopped where the child was. It remains a mystery how they knew precisely where to look.

Background Information

Magi. The history of the magi goes back to Persia in the sixth century BC where they were known as ritual experts. Among their specialties was the reading of astrological omens. By Roman times they were highly respected experts in using the celestial bodies to interpret what the gods were doing. The text does not indicate specifically where they came from, and there is no reason to think of magi in this period as residing only in Persia.

Gifts. Gold and spices were extravagant luxuries highly valued in the ancient world. No indication is given concerning how much of these were given, but the gift would likely have provided a substantial resource for the upbringing or ministry of Jesus. Some have seen significance that myrrh is a burial spice, but that is not its only use, and there is no reason to think that this was given as preparation for Jesus' death.

Mistakes to Avoid

This is not a lesson urging us to be like the magi, i.e., seeking Jesus, acknowledging Jesus as king, and giving him valuable gifts. Rather than trying to be like the magi, we ought to recognize the worth of Christ and respond to him. It is true that this is what the magi are doing, but we do it because of who Christ is, not because the magi did it. Teachers should not portray the magi as seeing Jesus in the manger. The text makes it clear that Mary and Joseph were in a house by the time the magi came, and it is possible that this was as much as two years later (notice that Herod killed babies two years old or less). On the other hand, since the biblical text never mentions Jesus' being born in a stable (see p. 336 [Birth of Jesus]), the couple may have been given room within a couple of days in the house in the courtyard of which the manger had been located. If so, that would be the house to which the magi came. Nevertheless, since the family left for Egypt after the visit of the magi, it must have been at least two months after the birth of Jesus, since the events of Jesus' circumcision and the visit to the temple for purification (Luke 2) would have meant that Joseph and Mary had stayed in Bethlehem for at least forty days after the birth.

We have no knowledge of the identity or names of the magi, nor do we know anything of their previous or later stories except from much later traditions, which cannot be accepted with confidence. It should also be noted that even though there were three kinds of gifts, the text never tells us how many magi there were. As teachers we want to be careful not to mix tradition with Scripture. Finally, these are not kings and should not be referred to as such. Note that younger children may not be ready to understand Herod's murder of the innocents.

100. The Baptism of Jesus (Matthew 3:13–17; Mark 1:9–11; Luke 3:21–22; John 1:29–34)

Lesson Focus

Jesus was baptized to show his willingness to serve God. When he was baptized, God showed that Jesus is his Son and the Messiah through the signs that John the Baptist saw.

- God proclaimed that Jesus is his Son and that he is pleased with him.
- Jesus is the one who will take away the sins of the world.
- Through John God revealed Jesus to Israel and the world.
- Jesus will baptize with the Holy Spirit.

Lesson Application

Jesus is the Messiah, the promised Son of God, and sins can be forgiven through Jesus Christ.

- We believe that Jesus is the Son of God.
- We believe that Jesus came to take away our sin.

Biblical Context

This account is one of the few that occur in all four Gospels, despite the different purposes of each Gospel writer. It initiates the ministry of Jesus. The account brings John and Jesus together, giving a prophetic affirmation to Jesus' ministry, and it features the affirmation of the Father through the Holy Spirit in the form of the descending dove. This brought Jesus into the public eye, as the people were finally introduced to the one John had been talking about. The Gospel of John offers the most extensive treatment, as he is interested particularly in the signs that build the case that Jesus is the Christ, the Son of God (John 20:31).

Interpretational Issues in the Story

Baptism (Matt. 3:13). John's baptisms in the wilderness were for symbolic purification from sin and represented repentance. Even though he was sinless, Jesus came to be baptized to "fulfill all righteousness" (Matt. 3:15). For him, it represented commitment to do the will of the Father and served as the commissioning and initiation of his ministry. He was pursuing a path of obedience to God and to his calling.

Spirit of God descending (Matt. 3:16). This is more like the role of the Spirit in the Old Testament that gave revelation from God to prophets and empowered people with authority for their ministry. Endowment with the Spirit in this way met the needs of the moment.

Background Information

Area of Jordan for baptisms. The wilderness that John lived in was the Judean wilderness, the desolate region extending southeast from Jerusalem along the shore of the Dead Sea. Heading east from the northern end of the Judean wilderness, one would get to the Jordan River near Jericho. This is where John conducted his baptisms. It is also from there that Jesus went into the wilderness to be tempted. The traditional mount of temptation is just west of Jericho in the vicinity of the Wadi Qelt.

Lamb of God. Since this identification is made in reference to taking away sins, it most likely refers to Jesus as the Passover lamb. The Passover was one of the major rituals of Israel in which a lamb was used.

Voice from heaven. A number of affirmations of Jesus' role are combined here. Jews of the period had come to the conclusion that the Spirit of God was less active in their day, that prophecy had ceased, and that some sort of voice from heaven was the best they could expect. The combination of all three would have given indication that the messianic age was upon them.

Mistakes to Avoid

This should not be made into a lesson on how important it is for people to be baptized. Jesus' submission to baptism is never pointed out as an example for all his followers to imitate (notice there is no reference to his disciples' being baptized).

101. The Temptation of Jesus (Matthew 4:1–11; Mark 1:12–13; Luke 4:1–13)

Lesson Focus

Jesus was tempted in the same ways that we are but he did not give in; he used his knowledge of God's Word to resist. He showed his readiness to carry out his role as the Son of God on earth.

- Jesus resisted temptation and remained faithful to his calling.
- Jesus was strengthened to carry out his role and ministry.
- God does not shield us from all temptation; in fact, his Spirit can at times lead us into places where temptations will present themselves (which is why we pray, "Lead us not into temptation").
- Jesus served God, not Satan.

Lesson Application

Even though Jesus was God, he was tempted to do wrong things. Being committed to our role in God's plan for us can help us resist sin.

- We recognize that we will also undergo temptation as we seek to follow God's calling in our lives.
- We can resist temptation as we focus our attention on God and his Word.
- We understand that God can help us to resist temptation and thereby deliver us from evil.

Biblical Context

A detailed description of the temptation of Jesus is given in both Matthew and Luke after the story of Jesus' baptism. In both cases the account is intended to show further preparation of Jesus for the ministry that he was about to undertake. It is used to demonstrate that Jesus had an appropriate perspective concerning his power and calling. He provided food for the masses but not for himself; he provided protection for his followers but did not engage in foolish behavior; he preached the kingdom of God but did not seek power at any cost. These accounts make clear that Jesus was serving God.

Interpretational Issues in the Story

Led up by the Spirit (Matt. 4:1). This is a very important detail. It shows that the Devil is not simply an opportunist but that it was God's will for Jesus to be tempted. Though not in any sense a "good guy," the Devil is carrying out the role he was supposed to play rather than serving as a powerful enemy of God.

Role of Scripture (Matt. 4:4). Scripture was used by Jesus to repel the suggestions made by the Devil. It is important to note that the temptations included a combination of unobjectionable elements that gave them a persuasiveness that could lead to easy rationalization. Nothing is wrong with having food, God does offer protection to his faithful ones, and the kingdoms of the world do belong to Jesus. The temptation was to gain these ends in the wrong ways. Like Adam and Eve, Jesus was tempted by something that could be understood as good (they were offered the opportunity to be like God), but unlike them, he resisted.

Angels ministering to Jesus (Matt. 4:11). Like the role of the Spirit, the presence of the angels helps the reader to understand that the temptation was part of God's preparation of Jesus for his ministry.

Background Information

Devil or Satan. In the Old Testament, the Hebrew word *satan* is a role, not a name, and a variety of beings could play that role. By the New Testament, the concept focuses more on a chief of demons, the representative of this enemy force who is sometimes referred to as the Devil. Names such as Satan or Beelzebub also occur. Like Jesus' baptism, the temptation was a rite of passage that Jesus had to endure as a human in order to begin his ministry. This was not a case of Satan as God's enemy trying to derail a plan of salvation but a tempter confronting Jesus in his humanity against whom Jesus must succeed where Adam and Israel failed.

Fasting. To fast for forty days and nights is not a unique accomplishment in Scripture (cf. Moses, Ex. 34:28), but it does imply divine sustenance (divinely provided food and drink sustained Elijah for forty days and nights, 1 Kings 19:6–8).

Time in the wilderness. Like Israel, Jesus spent time in the wilderness (forty days, rather than forty years) and faced temptations similar to those faced by Israel, but he overcame them. The traditional place of the temptation is in the Judean wilderness near Jericho.

Pinnacle of the temple. This most likely refers to the southwest corner of the wall around the temple mount that provided a view over the place where the valleys of Kidron and Hinnom came together. The precipitous drop would have been about 450 feet.

With the wild animals in the wilderness. People in both Old and New Testament times associated the wilderness with threatening spirits and often identified these spirits with the animals that lived in these deserted areas. Both aspects were part of Jesus' encounter with the spirit world and its dangers.

Mistakes to Avoid

Do not overplay the role of the Devil in this narrative. The fact that the Spirit drove Jesus into the wilderness is clear indication that God was in control of the process of Jesus' preparation for ministry and that the Devil was serving a designated role. The Devil was no more a threat to Jesus than the storm on the sea, but Jesus had to overcome both to demonstrate who he is. Even though Christ underwent temptation (and it is important that he did so), the main purpose of the Gospel writers in giving us this account is to make clear whom Jesus was serving (he was occasionally accused of serving Satan).

We cannot extrapolate from Jesus' experience a list of the ways in which we might be tempted. There are many ways to be tempted, and we are not being prepared for the same sort of life and ministry that Jesus was. Furthermore, it is fine to resist temptation by calling to mind the statements of Scripture, but the point of the account is not to give us a model for resisting temptation. Likewise the text is not teaching that we ought to memorize Scripture so that we can resist temptation. Scripture memorization has many benefits, but that is not the teaching of the text here.

102. Jesus Calls Disciples (Matthew 4:18–22; 9:9–13; Mark 1:16–20; 2:13–17; 3:13–19; Luke 5:1–11, 27–32; 6:12–16; John 1:40–51)

Lesson Focus

Jesus chose people to help him do his work, and he taught them all about God's kingdom and trained them to proclaim and advance the kingdom.

- Jesus is the Messiah, the Son of God.
- Jesus uses his people to advance the kingdom.
- Jesus came to restore sinners.

Lesson Application

We believe that Jesus is the Messiah God promised to send.

- We recognize that Jesus is the Messiah, the Son of God.
- We do our part to proclaim and advance the kingdom of God.
- Knowing who Jesus is, we choose to follow him.

Biblical Context

Since this account is used by all four Gospel writers, we infer that it is central to what they wanted to convey about the ministry of Jesus, yet we can see different emphases in each. Matthew, Mark, and Luke present the disciples as "fishers of men," gathering people into the kingdom, and report on Jesus' call of Matthew (Levi) from among the tax collectors. Luke has the additional account of the large catch of fish (5:1–11) prior to Peter's call in order to record Peter's observation that he was a sinful man. This fits Luke's emphasis on Jesus' mission to save sinners. Mark includes Jesus' commissioning of the Twelve as they are sent out to preach and to have authority over demons (3:14–15). John's account has a different focus. He shows the response of the disciples in their confessions that Jesus is the Messiah, the one written about by Moses and the prophets, the Son of God, and the King of Israel. These all accord with the purpose of John's Gospel (John 20:31).

Interpretational Issues in the Story

"You shall be called Cephas (which means Peter)" (John 1:42). Cephas is the Aramaic word for "rock," and *Peter* is the Greek word. Changing or giving some-

one a name was often an exercise of authority, though it is possible here that Jesus was simply giving Peter a nickname; Jesus still at times referred to him as Simon.

Written about in Moses and the prophets (John 1:45). Philip was likely referring to the description of the ideal prophet likened to Moses (Deut. 18:18).

Angels ascending and descending on Son of Man (John 1:51). This is a reference to Jacob's dream (Gen. 28:12). The stairway or ladder used by the angels in the dream was the connecting link between heaven and earth that served as the means by which the presence of God came to humanity. Jesus identified himself as that connecting link and the means for God's presence to be established on earth in a new way, which is alluded to in John 1:14.

Background Information

Fishing. Fishing was done from shore or further out in the lake from a boat. A boat from the time of Jesus has been excavated from the shores of the Sea of Galilee. It is about twenty-five feet long and nearly eight feet wide. It carried about a dozen men, and perhaps as many as sixteen. Fishermen used circular nets about twenty feet in diameter with weights along the edge so that they would sink to the bottom and trap the fish.

Followers of great teachers. It was common for disciples to approach a teacher and request the privilege of shadowing him and learning from him.

Tax collectors. These were typically Jews who worked for the Roman government. That alone was enough to make them despicable to their fellow countrymen. In addition, they often became wealthy from the excess taxes they collected to line their own pockets. Taxes were collected from a variety of sources, including fish that were caught, goods that were sold, or goods that were moved from one place to another by travelers, much like customs officials collect taxes today.

Mistakes to Avoid

Andrew and Philip are sometimes featured when teaching the narrative as an example of those who went and told others about Jesus. We do well to tell others, but the story is not told to encourage us to be like Philip or Andrew. The disciples were called to proclaim the kingdom and the gospel, but the story is told to show that, even this early, the disciples recognized Jesus as the Son of God. We should also be careful about making judgments concerning why Jesus chose the disciples he did. Some of them may have had faith, but others may not have—we are not told. Certain character traits or skills might have commended them, but since we can only speculate about such things, we should not present the disciples as the focus of the lesson.

103. The Sermon on the Mount (Matthew 5:1–7:29; Luke 6:20–45)

Lesson Focus

Jesus taught the people how to think about the law and life if they would be his disciples.

- The law is not just a list of rules; it penetrates every aspect of life.
- The spirit of the law affects attitudes and thoughts.
- Prayer focuses on God and his kingdom.
- God wants us to enjoy the blessings of his kingdom.

Lesson Application

We should be kingdom-minded people.

- We love our enemies and are willing to be generous with our time and goods.
- We seek God's kingdom.
- We are meant to have an impact on the world for the kingdom, not just enjoy its benefits.
- We trust God for our needs and make sure that we have our priorities focused on the kingdom of God.

Biblical Context

Matthew starts his Gospel with testimony about who Jesus is (chaps. 1–8). Next he turns to the problems that disciples in the kingdom will face (chaps. 8–10) and then to adjusting expectations people will have of Jesus and the kingdom of God (chaps. 11–13). Though Luke includes parts of the Sermon on the Mount, Matthew contains the most complete and most familiar presentation. It provides a suitable introduction to Matthew's presentation of Christ's teaching about discipleship. Luke mentions that there was a large audience in addition to the disciples. Some feel that Luke's record reflects a different occasion.

Interpretational Issues in the Story

Beatitudes (Matt. 5:3–11). Being blessed refers to enjoying the favor of God. The blessings to enjoy can be found in the second part of each of the verses in the beatitudes (e.g., to be comforted, to be shown mercy, to see God). They describe a blessed condition in the kingdom of God.

Jesus fulfilling not abolishing the law (Matt. 5:17). The law was intended to help Israel understand what it means to be holy as God is holy. Jesus fulfilled the law by giving us the ultimate picture of holiness and an understanding of how to pursue holiness. This aspect of the law would never be abolished.

Spirit of the law (Matt. 5:21–42). In the Old Testament the book of Deuteronomy expressed the spirit of the law through legal sayings that built off the Ten Commandments. In the Sermon on the Mount, Jesus likewise addressed the spirit of the law. Angry words may seem preferable to murder, but from God's perspective, in the kingdom of God, disciples are also held accountable for angry words.

Be perfect (Matt. 5:48). This does not refer to moral flawlessness but to the goal of total commitment.

The Lord's Prayer (Matt. 6:9–13). Notice that Jesus does not draw this model prayer from the Psalms, nor does he focus it on other people's circumstances and needs. The Lord's Prayer focuses on the importance of God's name and kingdom, our reliance on him for provision, and on what kind of people we are. These are important aspects of prayer that often get lost in our practice. It might be interesting to discuss with students what possible answers to this prayer might look like.

Fasting (Matt. 6:16–18). The importance of fasting is not what someone abstains from, but what is done with one's time and goods while fasting. Fasting is not merely a discipline; it has an objective, primarily a focus on one's spiritual condition.

Seek first the kingdom of God (Matt. 6:33). We need to guard against teaching that those who seek God's kingdom are given a blank check from heaven. The point is that we should not worry because God provides for us what he knows we need.

Background Information

Location. The traditional site of the Sermon on the Mount is along the northwest shore of the Sea of Galilee, west of Capernaum, just east of Tabgha (the traditional site of the feeding of the five thousand). It is more likely that Jesus sat at the bottom of the mount (Luke 6:17). Any travel away from the shore of Galilee involves going up into the hills.

Oaths. In Jesus' time, oaths were broken through all kinds of loopholes. Jesus denounced this practice; someone's word is to be binding.

Eye for an eye. The earliest laws from the ancient world, even before

Moses, tried to ensure just punishment of crimes. The Old Testament stipulation of an eye for an eye was meant to limit punishment (i.e., no more than an eye for an eye). In the Sermon on the Mount Jesus was not seeking to establish a civil legal system. His point was that our personal lives need not be run like a judicial system—we should be willing to forgive and be disadvantaged in our personal relationships.

Mistakes to Avoid

Jesus' words include many hard teachings that can be easily misunderstood. Students may well have questions about some of them: "Doesn't 'an eye for an eye' sound harsh?" "Are we supposed to be doormats for any bully who comes along?" "Can I really ask for anything in Jesus' name and get it?" "Why does Jesus say we should be meek?" "What does it mean to love our enemies if our enemies are terrorists?" These can be quite a challenge for teachers because we all struggle with how to appropriate them. In the brief notes we include here, we only scratch the surface, and teachers should try to anticipate some of the questions and prepare to answer them. Check the Further Resources section at the end of this volume for sources that provide a more detailed treatment of the Sermon on the Mount. Some of these teachings will be inappropriate for younger children.

104. Building on the Rock (Matthew 7:24–27; Luke 6:46–49)

Lesson Focus

Jesus encouraged disciples to put his words into practice like a wise man building his house on a foundation of rock.

- Jesus' teaching should be put into practice.
- Wisdom is found in obedience.

Lesson Application

We should modify our lives so that they reflect the values Jesus taught.

- We seek a firm foundation for our lives, and that is to be found in the teachings of Jesus.
- We do not call him "Lord" if we are not doing what he says to do.
- True faith is evidenced in obedience.

Biblical Context

In both Matthew and Luke this parable is linked with discussion of a tree and its fruit. In both cases the issue concerns kingdom living and comes soon after the Sermon on the Mount. Those who seek to be disciples of Christ should practice the teaching of Christ, which involves putting his words into practice.

Interpretational Issues in the Story

Parable focus. Parables are not allegories in which everything in the parable stands for something. Sometimes the people or situations in a parable are intentionally exaggerated to make a point. Many times parables are about the nature of the kingdom of God. This parable's principle is that those who will withstand final judgment are those who have conducted their lives according to the teachings of Christ.

"These words of mine" (Matt. 7:24). Jesus indicates that it is not the Torah or the Law or Moses that should be obeyed, but his words.

Background Information

Built on the rock. In Galilee many houses were built of stone (basalt) and one did not have to dig far to reach the basalt bedrock. It could barely be imagined that someone would have been so lazy and careless as to build on the hard packed sand around the Sea of Galilee. Seasonal flooding would eventually undermine the stability of such a house.

Mistakes to Avoid

Parables sometimes exaggerate to make a point, and this is a good example: no one would build the way that the foolish person builds. Many parables are about the nature of God's kingdom and the character of those who seek it, and that is the case here. The parable is not urging us to think about building or houses, foundations or storms. It is about the responsibility to heed the words of Christ in order to be wise citizens of the kingdom. The classic children's song that says, "Build your life on the Lord Jesus Christ and the blessings will come down," misses the point. Blessings are not mentioned anywhere in the parable, and positing Christ as the rock is pushing the analogy too far. Wise living must be based on something that will endure. When we teach "build your life on Jesus (the Rock)," students can easily conclude that if they have faith in Christ, life will be smooth and prosperous. That is not the point.

105. The Centurion's Servant (Matthew 8:5–13; Luke 7:1–10)

Lesson Focus

Jesus healed a centurion's servant from a distance because of the centurion's faith.

- Jesus has authority.
- Jesus has power to heal.
- Jesus is responsive to the faith of the people that he encountered.

Lesson Application

We should be people of faith who recognize the authority of Jesus.

- We have faith in the authority of Jesus to do what he says he will do.
- We believe that Jesus has the power to heal.

Biblical Context

Matthew starts his book with testimony about Jesus (chaps. 1–8). His interest is in adjusting expectations people have about Jesus and the kingdom of God. He wants his readers to understand Jesus' mission and what discipleship involves. Here, he addresses the eligibility of Gentiles and indicates that those of faith will have a seat at the messianic banquet. Luke's interests are in the saving acts of God and the way that Jesus fulfills the historical kingdom of God begun in the Old Testament. His account of this story says nothing of the messianic banquet, instead emphasizing the faith of the centurion.

Interpretational Issues in the Story

"I am not worthy to have you come under my roof" (Matt. 8:8; Luke 7:6). Many Jews considered it unacceptable to go into a Gentile's home because doing so made them ritually unclean. The centurion showed his understanding of this obstacle and asked only for the command to be given.

Sending Jewish elders (Luke 7:3) versus coming himself (Matt. 8:5). Luke simply gives more detail than Matthew. The centurion said all these words to Jesus through intermediaries.

Amazed by the centurion's faith (Matt. 8:10). Many would have put stock in the actual process of touching the infirmed or in saying words of power over them. The faith of the centurion is expressed in his recognition that Jesus needed no such elements to exercise his authority.

At table (Matt. 8:11). A common theme in Matthew is the messianic banquet, here attended not just by Jews. The messianic banquet was considered one of the important features of the coming kingdom (see Isa. 25:6–9).

Sons of the kingdom thrown out (Matt. 8:12). This does not suggest that people of faith will be cast out but rather those who believed that being Jewish automatically gave them a place at the table.

Background Information

Capernaum. The city was located on the northwestern shore of the Sea of Galilee. Population estimates based on the size of the excavated town suggest that no more than a thousand people lived there. Archaeologists have found evidence of a military garrison.

Centurion. This was an officer in charge of a relatively small number of soldiers (60–80) stationed in Capernaum. He was a Gentile, but as the text indicates, he respected the Jewish population and was respected by them.

Built the synagogue. Centurions were paid well and typically had no family. It was not unusual that a Gentile who respected Israel's God would have made donations, but to provide enough funds for the building of the synagogue would have been extraordinary.

Mistakes to Avoid

Though we do want to encourage students to have faith in the same way that the centurion had faith, it is our goal to respond appropriately to Jesus rather than to be like someone who responded appropriately. The centurion is not a role model, but he is an illustration. The importance of the centurion's faith can get lost if we make this a story about asking Jesus for help.

106. Jesus Stills the Storm (Matthew 8:23–27; Mark 4:35–41; Luke 8:22–25)

Lesson Focus

Jesus showed that he is God by exercising his authority over the elements.

- Jesus has power over nature.
- Jesus is God.

Lesson Application

We know that Jesus is God.

- We believe that Jesus is God.
- We must understand that everything is under the power of Jesus.

Biblical Context

Three of the four Gospels have the sequence of stilling the storm, casting out demons, and raising the girl from the dead (with a couple of intervening stories in Matthew between the second and third). The stories serve as examples of the sorts of signs and wonders that Jesus performed as his ministry got started. The stories raise the issue of faith and generate questions from the disciples about Jesus' identity. These continue as themes throughout the Gospels.

Interpretational Issues in the Story

Rebuking the sea (Matt. 8:26). This motif is known from the Old Testament in famous events such as the parting of the Red Sea. In the ancient world, the sea was sometimes considered a chaos enemy that needed to be defeated, and Jesus' rebuke carried such implications. In the ancient world there was a strong belief in the threats posed against life and order in the world. The most potent threats came from the sea, demons, and death. It is interesting that these three are the targets of the three stories presented together in the Gospels.

Background Information

Storm. Because of the atmospheric conditions that result from the Sea of Galilee being nestled between mountains, wind storms are frequent, come on rapidly, and can be severe. These were not rain storms; notice that the wind and the waves obey him. Based on the disciples' reaction to the storm, it was likely quite severe. Those who were fishermen would have been used to storms and not easily ruffled by a storm of average strength. In modern times, waves as high as ten feet have been recorded on the Sea of Galilee where this occurred.

Boats. The fishing boats used on the Sea of Galilee were not large. They held ten to fifteen people comfortably. Excavators have recovered a boat from this period that gives a good idea of its dimensions (about 25 feet by 7.5 feet) and features (four oars and short decks in front and back).

Mistakes to Avoid

Teachers should avoid allegorizing the story by talking about the storms of life that Jesus can calm with "Peace! Be still!" Jesus chides the disciples for their lack of faith, but the more important point is reflected in their amazement: "Who then is this?"

107. The Madman of Gadarenes (Matthew 8:28–34; Mark 5:1–20; Luke 8:26–39)

Lesson Focus

Jesus confronted powerful demons possessing a man and sent them into a herd of pigs, which then destroyed itself.

- Jesus has power over all spirit beings.
- Jesus is recognized as the Son of God by the spirits.
- Jesus overcomes that which is unclean.

Lesson Application

We should recognize the power of Jesus.

- We believe that Jesus is the Son of God.
- We recognize that Jesus has power over all beings.

Biblical Context

In the three Synoptic Gospels this account comes right after the calming of the storm. There is similarity between the two events because both represent outside powers that threaten humans. Jesus was showing his control over every power in the cosmos. It is appropriate that the wind and sea obey him and become calm and that spirits acknowledge him as "Son of the Most High God" and also are tamed and driven out.

Interpretational Issues in the Story

"Two demon-possessed men" (Matt. 8:28). Matthew, as in a number of other cases, has two where the other Gospel accounts speak of only one (e.g., two blind men, 20:30; two donkeys, 21:2). We could assume either that there were two but Mark and Luke mention only the one, or that there was only one but Matthew was using a Jewish literary technique of doubling for emphasis.

"Among the tombs" (Mark 5:3, 5; Luke 8:27). Tombs were places of death, and the dead were unclean. Demons were sometimes referred to as "unclean spirits" (Luke 8:29).

"No one could bind him" (Mark 5:3). People were inclined to bind those who might harm themselves. Spirit-possessed individuals did not tend to terrorize others. Some translations of Matthew 8:28 indicate that he was violent, but the Greek word refers to something or someone difficult to bear or hard to deal with. Mark and Luke give more details and make it clear that doing violence to passersby was not the issue. He was just very frightening and unnerving to be around.

"Torment us before the time" (Matt. 8:29). Mark and Luke both refer to torment, but only Matthew clarifies that torment before the appointed time was the final judgment.

Abyss (Luke 8:31). This is a technical reference to a place where spirits were held captive until the time of judgment (cf. Rev. 20:1–3). It appears in intertestamental literature, so it was a familiar idea.

Entered pigs (Matt. 8:32). Pigs were raised in Gentile areas such as this. Just like graveyards and spirits, pigs were unclean to Jews.

"Leave their region" (Matt. 8:34). The presence of Jesus had become unnerving to the observers.

Background Information

Gadarenes or Gerasenes. Both Gedara (Matthew and Luke) and Gesara (Mark) were in the region of Decapolis, but neither was very close to the Sea of Galilee. The alternative suggestion is Gergesa, modern Kursi, which is the traditional site of the event.

Decapolis. The region of Decapolis was mostly on the eastern side of the Sea of Galilee and the Jordan River, though it included Scythopolis (ancient Beth Shean). It was called Decapolis because there were ten major cities in the region.

Demons. The speech of the demons and their influence on the pigs demonstrate that demons were considered spirit beings, not just psychological conditions. In the general backdrop the effect of demons was often negative, as here, but they were not always considered intrinsically evil (just like the storm in the previous section, which has negative impact, is powerful and frightening but is not intrinsically evil). The nature of the presence of demons in Jesus' time is highly controversial. Teaching vague ideas about demons rather than attempting to venture something definitive is wise, since we just don't know for sure. At this time period it was believed that demons could die. Though exorcism of demons was common among the Jews of this time, practitioners generally used incantations, spells, or magical objects. Jesus did none of this.

Mistakes to Avoid

Be careful not to overstate the role and power of demons. The demons here are not portrayed as enemies struggling against God, any more than the storm and sea in previous stories were enemies struggling against God. The point is not to try to make us aware of the power of demons, but to make us aware of the power of Christ over the spirit world. It may be preferable to refer to them as "spirits" so that the popular modern images of demons from books, movies, and video games do not cloud the issue. We need not be concerned about the poor animals, the pigs, or about Jesus' role in the loss to the pigs' owners. The pigs were likely raised for sacrifices to pagan gods. Likewise, while Jesus was caring for someone (the madman) who was very different, that is not the main point of the story. This story would be inappropriate for younger children.

108. Jesus Heals a Paralytic (Matthew 9:1–8; Mark 2:1–12)

Lesson Focus

Because of the faith that the paralytic and his friends had, Jesus forgave the paralytic's sins. To demonstrate that his authority came from God, he also healed the man.

- The kingdom of God is characterized by forgiveness and healing.
- Jesus has the power to forgive sins and to heal.

Lesson Application

Because he is the Son of God, Jesus has the power both to forgive sins and to heal.

- We believe that Jesus can forgive our sins.
- We believe that Jesus has the power to heal even though he may choose not to do so in every case.

Biblical Context

Matthew gives examples of various sorts of wonders that Jesus performed that led up to the sending out of the Twelve with authority to preach the kingdom and perform wonders. Mark places special emphasis on the wonders that Jesus performed, and this is one of the accounts introducing tthat theme.

Interpretational Issues in the Story

Sins and health (Matt. 9:5). It was not uncommon in the ancient world for illness to be seen as punishment for sin. Jesus worked within this way of thinking, knowing well the connections that his audience would make. Regardless of popular opinion, however, the sick man, like all of us, needed forgiveness of sins, even if sin was not the cause of his paralysis. Both forgiveness and healing are characteristics of the kingdom of God that Jesus came preaching.

Son of Man (Matt. 9:6). This is a title drawn from Daniel 7, and by New Testament times it had come to be used as a title of the Messiah. Jesus often used it in reference to himself.

Background Information

Opening in the roof. The roof of a typical home in Galilee was constructed with wooden crossbeams covered with reeds and mud. They were temporary constructions that had to be redone annually. It would have been easy for the friends to make a hole through which to lower the sick man. Generally the roof was reached by means of a ladder or stairway on the outside of the house.

Mat. The man's bed was a mat. Some beds from the ancient world, known from archaeological finds, were comprised of light wooden frames with cloth or net webbing.

Mistakes to Avoid

The focus of the story is Jesus, so the friends of the man should not be emphasized. It is true that the friends showed faith by their actions, and they went to great extent to help their sick friend, but it is a mistake to say that the Bible is teaching us that we should be good friends.

109. Jairus's Daughter (Matthew 9:18–26; Mark 5:21–24, 35–43; Luke 8:40–42, 49–56)

Lesson Focus

Jesus raised a girl from death, leading people to conclude he was the Messiah.

- Jesus has the power to raise the dead.

- Jesus is compassionate and responsive to people's expressions of faith.
- Jesus demonstrated that he was the Messiah.

Lesson Application

Jesus is the Messiah, the Savior of the world.

- We believe that Jesus is the Messiah.
- We must have faith in Jesus.

Biblical Context

The story is told in three of the Gospels, the Synoptics. There are different stories surrounding it in each Gospel, but each Gospel contains a sequence of stories that show Jesus doing a variety of wonders and then commissioning the Twelve to replicate his wonders. This serves as an example of what the disciples would be able to do in the name of Jesus.

Interpretational Issues in the Story

"Not dead but sleeping" (Matt. 9:24; Mark 5:39; Luke 8:52). Sleep and death were understandably tied together in the ancient world, since the dead can look like they are asleep. Furthermore, someone in a coma has symptoms of life, such as breathing, and symptoms of death, such as being unresponsive to her surroundings. The line between life and death was not as clear as it is today. Nonetheless, Jesus did not deny that she was dead. His comment indicates that her condition was not permanent; it was more like sleep than death.

"Laughed at him" (Matt. 9:24; Mark 5:40; Luke 8:53). This comment is recorded in all three Gospels and served to prepare the disciples for how they will be received.

"Tell no one" (Luke 8:56). Someone who had raised a little girl from the dead would surely be deluged with requests to repeat the wonder, but Jesus performed his wonders selectively as he gave evidence of who he is. He did not come to spend all his time as a miracle worker. We find that Jesus was more interested in teaching people about the kingdom of God than in proclaiming himself as the Messiah. Since Jews of the day had some mistaken expectations of the Messiah, Jesus preferred to give them an accurate picture of the kingdom so that they would recognize him as King of that kingdom.

Background Information

Ruler of the synagogue. This was a lay person rather than a priest or Levite. He was an administrator, like a chairman of a church board is today. He was an important and influential person among the Jewish residents of the town (possibly Capernaum, see Matt. 9:1, but Mark 6:1 might suggest otherwise).

Mourning rituals. Flutes were the common instruments used in mourning because of their somber, haunting tones. Even the poorest of families hired professional mourning women whose job was to lead in the expression of grief, both audibly and dramatically.

The girl's hand. Touching a dead person made one ritually unclean, so most avoided it whenever possible, yet that is exactly what the ruler asked Jesus to do (Matt. 9:18).

Mistakes to Avoid

For older students, be sure to include the story that interrupts the story of Jairus' daughter about the woman who touched Jesus and was healed. As all three Gospels show, the stories belong together, as each one deals with Jesus bringing resolution to someone unclean.

110. Different Kinds of Soil (Matthew 13:1–23; Mark 4:3–8, 14–20; Luke 8:5–8, 11–15)

Lesson Focus

Jesus talked about seed cast on different types of surfaces and how each one reacts, in order to emphasize the importance of hearing the words of his teaching about the kingdom.

- Jesus preaches the kingdom with the intention that people respond.
- Jesus wants people to obey his teaching and bear fruit.
- Jesus wants his people to take root in the kingdom.

Lesson Application

We should respond to the message of the kingdom.

- We are to hear and obey.
- We root ourselves in the teaching of Jesus.

Biblical Context

In all three Gospels this parable introduces the concept of parables and is the first major parable given. Unlike most of the others, a detailed explanation is offered along with the telling. Matthew gives seven parables of the kingdom, whereas Mark includes two additional agricultural parables, and Luke isolates this one from the rest of the parables he records. They all present this parable as a lesson concerning the need for people to hear the word of the kingdom preached by Jesus.

Interpretational Issues in the Story

Parable focus. Parables are not allegories in which everything in the parable stands for something. Sometimes the people or situations in a parable are intentionally exaggerated to make a point. Many times they are about the nature of the kingdom of God. The principle in this parable is that people respond to the preaching of the kingdom in a variety of ways, but the best approach is to hear and produce fruit.

Secrets (Matt. 13:11). This terminology is used to talk about what had been hidden but was now being revealed.

Seed (Mark 4:14; Luke 8:11). In this parable we are told that the seed refers to the word of God taught by Jesus.

"To them it has not been given" (Matt. 13:11). Even though judgment is imminent, people will not respond (just as warned by the prophets in the Old Testament). The proclamation of the message of the kingdom establishes the guilt of the hard-hearted. The parable form of Jesus' teaching is not an obstacle; the hardness of hearts is. That is why he says, "He who has ears to hear, let him hear" (Luke 8:8; see also Matt. 13:43).

Evil one (Matt. 13:19), Satan (Mark 4:15), Devil (Luke 8:12). The point of the parable is not to offer teaching about the nature and activities of Satan. Evil, in any of its manifestations (including our own fallenness) can be an obstacle to receiving the Word, so Satan cannot be used as an excuse for our hard-heartedness.

Background Information

Hundredfold. An indicator of a very good harvest but not fantastical or unheard of.

Sowing. Usually seeds were cast by hand from a bag, and plowing came as the next stage so that the seeds were covered over. Rocky soil is common throughout the land of Israel, so the scenario painted is a realistic one.

Mistakes to Avoid

Parables are not allegories in which everything in the parable stands for something. With this parable, some make the mistake of attempting to identify the sower, the seed, the soil, or the harvest—something the Gospel writers do not do. The parable is about the nature of the kingdom of God, and, as Jesus' explanation indicates, it focuses on the soil. As such we do not need to speculate on the identity of the sower or the nature of the seed. We are called to do evangelism, but that is not the point to be taken from the parable.

111. Finding Treasure and the Pearl (Matthew 13:44–46)

Lesson Focus

A man bought a field where he knew there was a treasure, while another sought an exquisite pearl to purchase. Both sold all they had to make the purchase of that which was of untold value.

- The kingdom of God is of matchless value and worthy of pursuit.
- Everything else is worthless in comparison to the kingdom of God.

Lesson Application

We should recognize the value of the kingdom of God.

- We believe that the kingdom of God is of supreme value.
- We value the kingdom above all else and seek it out.

Biblical Context

Matthew sought to adjust expectations people have about Jesus and the kingdom of God. He wanted his readers to understand Jesus' mission and what discipleship involves. These two short parables are found only in Matthew and constitute a pair in his sequence of eight parables that describe the nature of the kingdom.

Interpretational Issues in the Story

Parable focus. Parables are not allegories in which everything in the parable stands for something. Sometimes the people or situations in a parable are intentionally exaggerated to make a point. Many parables are about the nature of the kingdom of God. The principle here is that the kingdom of God is a priceless find without parallel and is worth any sacrifice.

"Sells all" (Matt. 13:44). One need not think that in either parable the

purchaser irresponsibly impoverished himself. Parables often rely on hyperbole. The point is that all other possessions are dispensable to gain that which is most valuable.

Background Information

Buried treasure. With no banks and the threat of warfare and robbery, it was not unusual for people to bury caches of coins. Over time, as disasters came and property changed hands, all knowledge of the buried treasure was forgotten.

Pearls. Barely known in the ancient world, by New Testament times pearls had become recognized as having great value.

Mistakes to Avoid

It is useless to discuss the ethics involved in hiding a treasure and buying a field. This was not intended as ethical instruction. Nor were pearls being singled out as something to be desired. These are analogies of the value of the kingdom. In each case, it is the entire process that pertains to the kingdom, though its pricelessness is primary. Parables are neither historical accounts nor allegories in which everything in the parable stands for something. We need not figure out what the field stands for, nor should we think that Jesus is the one "who gives his all." We do not have to figure out what the covering up of the treasure stands for or what significance there might be that the man in the second parable is a merchant. Some have suggested that the parable has to do with the cost of discipleship in which all is given up to follow Jesus. That fits with the value of the kingdom but is not the main focus.

112. John in Prison (Matthew 14:1–12; Mark 6:14–29)

Lesson Focus

Herod wondered whether Jesus was John the Baptist come back to life. Herod had had John beheaded in order to fulfill an oath he had made.

- God does not always protect his servants from disaster.
- Setbacks for God's people do not mean that God is weak or unconcerned.

Lesson Application

God's people must expect opposition and suffering.

- We should not expect that faithfulness to God will protect us from suffering or death.
- We must expect persecution and oppression.

Biblical Context

This account occurs in the same location in Matthew's and Mark's Gospels, between the rejection of Jesus at Nazareth and the feeding of the five thousand. Matthew ties it to the difficulties that disciples will face and Mark ties it to opposition to the gospel and the suffering of those who follow Jesus.

Interpretational Issues in the Story

"Herodias, his brother Philip's wife" (Matt. 14:3; Mark 6:17). History knows of a Philip who was the tetrarch assigned to the territory in the northern section of Israel centered around Panias (Caesarea Philippi) and ruled from 4 BC until AD 33 or 34. Many believe, however, that the Philip in this story was a half-brother of Herod Antipas and a private citizen in Rome. The dancer Salome was the daughter of Herodias and Philip. She later married Philip the tetrarch. Herod Antipas and Herodias had fallen in love on one of Antipas's visits to Rome during which he stayed with his brother. Herodias insisted that he divorce his current wife, who was the daughter of the Nabatean king Aretas IV. In AD 36 Aretas attacked Antipas's armies in retaliation for the humiliating divorce of his daughter. So Salome became the stepdaughter of Herod Antipas after he married Herodias.

Background Information

Herod the tetrarch. This is Herod Antipas, son of Herod the Great. He began ruling a portion of his father's kingdom at the age of seventeen and reigned from 4 BC until AD 39. His territory was in Galilee. This is the same Herod who met with Jesus at the time of his trial. He was eventually deposed and banished to Gaul, along with Herodias, when he demanded, at her insistence, that Emperor Caligula give him the title of king.

Location. Though Herod's capital was at Tiberias on the west coast of the Sea of Galilee, his palace or fortress, which had been built by Herod the Great, was at Machaerus, east of the Dead Sea in the territory of Perea, which he also ruled. According to Josephus this is where John had been imprisoned and where the birthday party was taking place.

Mistakes to Avoid

Though without a doubt Herod committed gross crimes, that is not the point of the story. Nor is John the Baptist's courageous truth telling, even though we admire John for being so outspoken in his ideals. The point in both Gospels concerns the fact that followers of Jesus must be prepared to suffer and even die for the sake of the gospel. This is not an appropriate story for younger children.

113. Jesus Feeds the Five Thousand (Matthew 14:13–21; Mark 6:30–44; Luke 9:10–17; John 6:1–15)

Lesson Focus

This story is all about Jesus and the demonstration that, as God, he is able to provide food for hungry people in exorbitant proportions.

- Jesus showed that he is God by his miraculous provision of food.
- Jesus showed that he is compassionate as he cared for the needs of the people.
- Jesus hinted at his messianic role by providing a feast for the people.

Lesson Application

We should believe that Jesus is God.

- We believe that Jesus can provide our needs.
- We understand that Jesus feels compassion for all people.

Biblical Context

Matthew begins to deal with Jesus' mission in Matthew 14—who Jesus came to and who may come to him. The feeding of the five thousand begins this section and shows that the people came to Jesus with needs, which he met. This contrasts with the end of the section (chapter 19) where the rich young man came with wants and was turned away. Mark's Gospel is designed to demonstrate that the crucifixion was not unexpected. The Gospel begins and ends with declarations that Jesus is the Son of God (1:1; 15:39). Mark features miracle stories that stand in contrast to opposition from authorities and the repeated lack of understanding of the disciples (the reaction of the disciples is strongest in Mark, 6:37; see also 6:52). Luke's interests are in the saving acts of God and the way that Jesus fulfills the historical kingdom of God begun in the Old Testament. Jesus is portrayed as the king who brings salvation (cf. 19:10), so Luke adds the detail that he spoke to them about the kingdom (9:11) and follows up with a discussion of who the crowds and the disciples say that Jesus is. Peter answered that Jesus is God's Messiah. In this connection, the event is reminiscent of the messianic banquet in Isaiah 25:6–8; 65:13–14 (see Interpretational Issues below). John includes the story in the first part of his Gospel, which is sometimes called the "Book of Signs." His signs serve as a major part of John's case that Jesus is the Christ (John 20:31). John notes that this event happened near the time of Passover (6:4) when the coming of the Messiah was most anticipated. John's story differs from the accounts in the other Gospels: the people identified Jesus as "the Prophet," and he withdrew lest they "take him by force to make him king" (6:14–15). This miracle must be understood in connection with the Bread of Life discussion in John 6:25–59.

Interpretational Issues in the Story

"Test him" (John 6:6). When God or Jesus tests people, it is usually to see if they have sufficient faith or to discover what is most important to them. This is a passing detail in the story and does not help us to define the teaching of the passage.

Messianic banquet. Isaiah 25:6–8 provides the foundation for this banquet at which God will provide a rich feast for all peoples and remove the disgrace of his people. It became very popular at the time between the Testaments, and by New Testament times had become a prominent part of people's thinking and expectation concerning the messianic age. A number of Jesus' parables, miracles, and teachings, especially in Matthew, should be understood in that context (e.g., the Parable of the Wedding Banquet [Matt. 22:1–14] and the Parable of the Ten Virgins [Matt. 25:1–13]).

Background Information

Bethsaida. The traditional site of the feeding of the five thousand is Tabgha, about two miles southwest of Capernaum on the shore of the lake. Matthew gives no geographical information. Mark has Jesus send the disciples from the site of the feeding to Bethsaida by boat (6:45), while Luke seems to locate the feeding itself in Bethsaida (9:10). The site of Bethsaida has not been identified with certainty. Extensive excavations of the site et-Tell, about four miles east of Capernaum on the shore of Galilee but on the eastern side of the Jordan, have been happening for many years, but despite the confident identification of the excavators, there are many reasons for skepticism, and many experts remain unconvinced.

Providing food when none is to be had. This is reminiscent of when God provided manna for the people of Israel in the wilderness after they had left Egypt (notice John 6:31: soon after the feeding, Jesus identified himself as the Bread of Life and alluded to the manna in the wilderness). Mark uses the imagery of a shepherd providing for his sheep. Jesus also shows himself in the role of a well-known prophet. Elisha fed one hundred with twenty loaves and some left over (2 Kings 4:42–44).

Bread and fish. Though bread and fish were staples in the diet of that time, in John's account the bread is identified as barley bread (6:9), the food of the poor. Some translations of John identify the fish as "small" (NIV), thus indicating on both counts how meager the fare was.

Size of the crowd. The largest villages in Galilee had a population of three thousand, so five thousand men plus women and children represented a phenomenal crowd.

Mistakes to Avoid

This is not a story about sharing (i.e., the boy who shared his lunch). The boy is mentioned only in John, and even there his willingness is not mentioned. The boy may have been willing, but that should no more be the focus than should sitting in groups of a particular size or helping to clean up after the meal. These are trivial issues. The reference in all four Gospels to the five loaves and two fish emphasizes how little there was to begin with. Other details not to emphasize include the disciples' incredulity at the number fed; or God taking little things and turning them into something great; or Jesus praying before the meal was eaten, or the disciples gathering up the leftover food, which is included to indicate the magnitude of the multiplication, not that they let nothing go to waste. In teaching younger ages, the emphasis should be simply that Jesus is God and that he cares about the people and is taking care of them. Older groups may be able to understand more about the messianic banquet and the connections to Moses, Elijah, and Elisha.

114. Jesus Walks on Water (Matthew 14:22–33; Mark 6:45–52; John 6:16–21)

Lesson Focus

When Jesus demonstrated his power over the water and the storm, his disciples worshiped him as the Son of God.

- Jesus has power over nature.
- Jesus is the Son of God.

Lesson Application

Jesus is the Son of God.

- We believe that Jesus is the Son of God.
- We worship Jesus and have faith in him.

Biblical Context

In all three Gospel accounts this story comes right after the feeding of the five thousand. Although this can be considered as simply the chronological sequence of events, there is also a connection between them as indicated by Mark 6:51–52.

Interpretational Issues in the Story

"To the other side" (Matt. 14:22; Mark 6:45). One has to read several Gospel accounts to get a clear picture of the movement from place to place. In John 6:1 Jesus had gone over to the far side (the east side) of the Sea of Galilee. In Mark, Jesus and his disciples tried to get away from the crowds by getting in a boat and going across the sea toward the west side, but the crowds followed around the shore. This sets the scene for the feeding of the five thousand around the traditional site of Tabgha, southwest of Capernaum. After the feeding, Jesus sent the disciples in a boat over to Bethsaida on the north shore of the Sea of Galilee (Mark 6:45), where they apparently waited for him. When he didn't come, they concluded that he had gone to Capernaum and headed back in that direction (John 6:16), when they were waylaid by the storm. They were driven about by the storm until Jesus met them walking on the water and they finally came to dock in Gennesaret (Mark 6:53), south of Capernaum.

"He meant to pass by them" (Mark 6:48). This wording might evoke

some of the appearances of God to important persons in the Old Testament (Moses [Ex. 33:19]; Elijah [1 Kings 19:11]).

Ghost (Matt. 14:26; Mark 6:49). The disciples were most likely thinking of an evil spirit rather than the ghost of a dead person.

"It is I" (Matt. 14:27; Mark 6:50; John 6:20). This is the same statement used at the burning bush when God told Moses, "I AM WHO I AM" (Ex. 3:14).

"You of little faith" (Matt. 14:31). Though Peter had shown more faith than the others—enough to actually climb out of the boat—it was insufficient.

Son of God (Matt. 14:33). Recognizing Jesus as the Messiah is not as significant as recognizing him as the Son of God. Even though the Israelites were at times referred to as God's sons, and kings were seen to be in father-son relationships with God, the use by the disciples went beyond these. They were designating Jesus as deity.

"They did not understand about the loaves, but their hearts were hardened" (Mark 6:52). When Jesus fed the multitude, it should have been clear that he was the Son of God. But the disciples had not yet acknowledged the obvious. By saying that their hearts were hard Mark is not suggesting that they were unbelieving but that they were too set in their worldview to embrace the truth.

Background Information

Prayer in the mountains. The region around the northern end of the Sea of Galilee contains the mountainous Upper Galilee on the west side of the Jordan River and what today is known as the Golan Heights on the east side of the Jordan. When one is at the Sea of Galilee, mountains are never far away.

Boats. A boat from the time of Jesus has been excavated from the shores of the Sea of Galilee. It is about twenty-five feet long and nearly eight feet wide. It could carry about a dozen men, perhaps as many as sixteen. Such boats were equipped with oars; some had simple masts as well, though a sail was not used in a storm.

Storms on the Sea of Galilee. Because of the atmospheric conditions that result from the Sea of Galilee being nestled between mountains, wind storms are frequent, come on rapidly, and can be severe. It is important to note that these are not rain storms. The lake is about five to six miles across at its widest point.

Fourth watch. This was between 3:00 AM and 6:00 AM.

Gennesaret. A heavily populated fertile plain between Tiberias and Capernaum.

Mistakes to Avoid

While it is always a good thing to draw students into the story, we must do it in ways that won't distract from the point. In a story such as this one, it might be tempting to ask, "How do you think Peter felt as he got out of the boat?" or "Do you think that you would have gotten out of the boat?" But such questions focus too much on Peter's particular experience, when the focus needs to be on Jesus. Attempting to make an analogy between the disciples' boat and the students' various forms of earthly security is also to miss the point. While it is important to encourage students to live a life of faith and take radical steps of faith, the point is recognizing who Jesus is so as to inspire our faith. Consequently, we must also avoid applications such as, "When we take our eyes off Jesus, we sink," or, "Jesus can keep us safe, and when we call on him to save us, he will." We miss the point if we rely on allegory and talk about the waves as our problems and the boat as our security. Finally, though all three Gospel accounts indicate that Jesus went into the hills to be alone, only Matthew mentions that he was praying. Since the others neglect to note that, we must conclude that prayer is not the point of the lesson.

115. Transfiguration (Matthew 17:1–13; Mark 9:2–13; Luke 9:28–36)

Lesson Focus

By appearing in glory with heavenly companions, Jesus showed that he is God. The voice from heaven also identified him as God's Son.

- Jesus is God.
- Jesus knew that he would have to suffer and die.
- Jesus represents continuity between the Old Testament promises and the kingdom of God fulfilled in him.

Lesson Application

We believe that Jesus is God, and we therefore listen to him.

- We acknowledge Jesus as God.
- We listen to what Jesus says, for his words are the very words of God.

Biblical Context

In all three Gospel accounts, the transfiguration is preceded by the confession of Peter and Jesus' prediction of his death. It is followed by the casting out of a spirit from a boy. This account serves as an important part of the announcement of the arrival of the kingdom of God.

Interpretational Issues in the Story

"His face shone like the sun, and his clothes became white as light" (Matt. 17:2). God's presence is sometimes conveyed as a glowing light, as in the pillar of fire in Exodus, and sometimes angels have a shining appearance (e.g., at the tomb [Matt. 28:3]), as did Moses' face after he met with God (Ex. 34:29–30).

Importance of Moses and Elijah (Matt. 17:3). Moses (Exodus 34) and Elijah (1 Kings 19) both had experiences of encountering God on Mount Sinai. Jewish belief at the time of Jesus expected the appearing of a Moses-like figure (from Deut. 18:15, 18) and an Elijah-like figure (from Mal. 4:5). Jesus identifies John the Baptist with Elijah (Matt. 17:11–13), and he himself is the prophet like Moses. This is perhaps indicated by the voice from heaven that says, "Listen to him" (Matt. 17:5; Mark 9:7; Luke 9:35)—the same instruction as given in connection to the prophet to come in Deuteronomy 18:15. The intertestamental book 4 Ezra indicates that a sign of the end of the age is that people will see those who were taken up and did not taste death (6:25–26). In all these ways, the appearance of Moses and Elijah indicated the coming of the kingdom of God.

"Cloud overshadowed them" (Matt. 17:5; Mark 9:7). In the Old Testament, God's glory was masked in a cloud (Ex. 19:18).

"Spoke of his departure" (Luke 9:31); "Tell no one . . . until the Son of Man is raised from the dead" (Matt. 17:9; cf. Mark 9:9). Though in different ways, each of these Gospel writers makes clear what the transfiguration was about. Coming after Peter's confession, there is affirmation from heaven that Peter has identified Jesus correctly ("This is my Son"). Coming after Jesus' prediction of his death, there is indication of the resurrection and ascension. The subject of the discussion is at least as important as the glory of the event.

Son of Man (Matt. 17:9). This is a title drawn from Daniel 7 and, by New Testament times, had come to be used as a title for the Messiah. Jesus often used it in reference to himself.

Background Information

Location. The traditional site, going back to the fourth century, is Mount Tabor in the Jezreel Valley. The text, however, says that they went to the mountain to be alone, an unlikely occurrence on Mount Tabor, since there was a Roman camp stationed there. The other main possibility is Mount Hermon in the north, right by Caesarea Philippi, where they were when Peter made his confession. Mount Hermon is the highest mountain in the region. It is unlikely that they went all the way to the top since it is snow covered most of the year.

Three tents. The Greek word for *tent* is the same word used to describe the tabernacle in the New Testament. It was a place where the glory of God could be sheltered from casual viewers, for whom it was dangerous. This would fit with the comment in Mark that the disciples were frightened.

Mistakes to Avoid

Be sure that the emphasis of the lesson is on Jesus and his role and on the kingdom of God rather than on Moses, Elijah, and the bright lights. It was the expectations connected to Moses and Elijah from the Old Testament and in Jewish tradition that gave significance to their appearance here. There is no reason to speculate that it had to do with their spirituality or faithfulness.

116. Lost Sheep and Lost Coin (Matthew 18:12–14; Luke 15:4–10)

Lesson Focus

Jesus used a story about a lost coin and a lost sheep to show how much he seeks "lost" people, those who need to be sorry for their sin and turn to God.

- God seeks diligently those who are lost or have strayed.
- God's kingdom values those who might seem of little intrinsic value.
- God finds joy when the lost is found.

Lesson Application

Jesus loves us and came to save us, even though we are sinners.

- We should be those who help seek, not those who need to be sought.
- We repent of our sin and become members of the kingdom.

- We join the celebration when the lost have been found.

Biblical Context

Only Luke has the telling of the lost coin, and Matthew and Luke make very different uses of the story of the lost sheep, perhaps suggesting that Jesus used the parable numerous times in varying circumstances. In Matthew Jesus is talking to the disciples about the significance of children, the "greatest" in the kingdom of heaven, who are diligently sought. In Luke the audience is the Pharisees and teachers of the law, and the context concerns Jesus eating with sinners. Matthew emphasizes the diligence of the search, while Luke is more focused on the celebration when the lost is found.

Interpretational Issues in the Story

Parable focus. Parables are not allegories in which everything stands for something. Sometimes the people or situations in a parable are intentionally exaggerated to make a point. Many parables are about the nature of the kingdom of God. Here, the principle is that all are able to be included in the kingdom, even those who stray or who are little valued. God diligently seeks out such as these for his kingdom, and there is joy in the finding.

Shepherd (Matt. 18:12). Though shepherds were sometimes despised, the shepherd was also a picture of leadership and even kingship in the ancient world and the Old Testament. Jesus is to be understood as playing the role of shepherd in the parable, but the parable does not go so far as to identify him as the Shepherd King who leads Israel as the Messiah. He is intent on being a shepherd to all his people (children and sinners included), for all have a part in the kingdom.

"Who need no repentance" (Luke 15:7). Jesus is not implying that some people never need to repent, but that not everyone needs to all the time. A person's repentance is important to God, but the text does not suggest that God is displeased with those who are not currently in need of repentance. Compare the father's statement to the older brother in Luke 15:31–32.

"Joy before the angels of God" (Luke 15:10). Jewish tradition believed that angels were extremely interested in what went on in the human world.

Background Information

One hundred sheep. This is a good-sized flock but not exorbitant. It indicates that the sheep owner was successful, though not necessarily wealthy.

Leaving the ninety-nine. Shepherds often worked in groups, so this shepherd would not have been considered careless or irresponsible for leaving the other sheep. Certainly the ninety-nine were no less valued. Nor is the shepherd's behavior characteristic of an unusually attentive shepherd; the point is that any shepherd would act this way.

Ten silver coins. The silver coin of this day was a drachma, one day's wages for a man. Some suggest that a woman received only half that amount. This is therefore neither a large sum of money nor a pittance. Some suggest that this is part of the woman's dowry, representative of her security. If so, it is a poor dowry, but all the more reason that its loss would be of concern.

Mistakes to Avoid

Since parables are not allegories, God is no more allegorized as a shepherd than he is allegorized as a woman in the lost coin. The analogy concerns the intensity of the search, not the identity of the one who is searching. Sometimes people or situations in a parable are intentionally exaggerated to make a point. In these cases the size of the celebration is exaggerated relative to that which had been lost. The parable does not concern the intrinsic value of that which was lost or, for that matter, what was set aside in order to pursue the search. Many parables are about the nature of the kingdom of God. Both contexts here indicate the worth of searching hard for something that is of value. The intention is not to identify children or sinners as either sheep or coins. The point is not to get people to realize they are lost, but to indicate that Jesus seeks us diligently.

117. The Unmerciful Servant (Matthew 18:21–34)

Lesson Focus

The king forgave a man a great debt, but that same man refused to forgive another a much smaller amount owed to him. As a result, the king severely punished him.

- God forgives even great sins.
- God is compassionate and merciful.
- God expects us to show compassion and mercy.

Lesson Application

We should be willing to forgive the offenses of others against us.

- We must not keep track of how many times we have forgiven someone.
- We should believe that God forgives our sins.
- We are to be compassionate and merciful.

Biblical Context

This parable is found only in Matthew, whose interest is in adjusting expectations people have about Jesus and the kingdom of God. He wanted his readers to understand Jesus' mission and what discipleship involves. In this context the issue for disciples concerned forgiveness and what their stance toward it ought to be. It follows Matthew's account of how people ought to act when someone has something against them.

Interpretational Issues in the Story

Parable focus. Parables are not allegories in which everything stands for something. Sometimes the people or situations in a parable are intentionally exaggerated to make a point. The principle here is that in the kingdom of God, even great debts may be forgiven. We should forgive as God forgives.

"As many as seven times" (Matt. 18:21). Jewish teaching in the Talmud allowed for forgiveness three times. Compared to that, Peter's offer of seven was generous.

"Seventy times seven" (Matt. 18:22). This is not an actual sum but hyperbole to indicate that there are no limits on forgiveness.

"Delivered him to the jailers" (Matt. 18:34). The NIV has "turned him over to the jailers to be tortured," but this does not portray God as a torturer—it is hyperbole. It indicates the way a king presumably acted when meting out a severe punishment. The servant's behavior warrants a sharp contrast between mercy and judgment.

Background Information

Ten thousand talents. This is an exorbitant amount meant to give an exaggerated picture. One talent would have represented income for perhaps twenty years of labor.

Sold to repay debt. Years of debt slavery would not have begun to recover what the man owed, since slaves were sold for anywhere from 500 to 2,000 denarii. Selling his entire family would not have recovered even one talent.

One hundred denarii. This is substantial—about three months' pay—but it pales in comparison to the debt that had already been forgiven the first man.

Mistakes to Avoid

It would be a mistake to teach that the character of God is precisely represented in the king who judges harshly (though v. 35 indicates some level of comparison). Many parables are about the nature of the kingdom of God, and this one is introduced in just that way. It is not meant to determine how often we ought to forgive but to emphasize the importance of forgiveness. The parable turns on a contrast between the forgiveness that the first man received and that which he refused to give.

118. Jesus and Children (Matthew 19:13–15; Mark 10:13–16; Luke 18:15–17)

Lesson Focus

The disciples felt that Jesus was too busy to be bothered with children, but Jesus showed his love for the children by taking them in his arms.

- Jesus welcomes even those with no political or social status.
- The kingdom of God is not gained by one's power or prestige.

Lesson Application

Jesus loves children.

- We will be careful not to view God's kingdom in elitist terms.
- We should not think that we need to earn a place in God's kingdom by earthly means.

Biblical Context

In each of the Gospel accounts, the story emphasizes the simple belief of the children to indicate the essential response to the kingdom of God. In Matthew and Mark the story follows the discussion about divorce, and in so doing contrasts the simple acceptance of the gospel by children to the previous complex and difficult teachings. In Luke the story is preceded by the parable of the Pharisee and the tax collector, which addresses the issue of the importance of humility before God, fittingly illustrated by children. In all three Gospel accounts, it is followed by the rich young ruler's question of what he must do to enter the kingdom, providing a contrast to the children.

Interpretational Issues in the Story

Disciples rebuked the people (Matt. 19:13; Luke 18:15). The story does not explain why the disciples rebuked those who brought children to Jesus. In all likelihood, the disciples thought this mundane practice a distraction from more important things Jesus had to do. Given the crowds that followed Jesus, it is understandable that welcoming children would have been quite time-consuming.

Receiving the kingdom like a little child (Mark 10:15; Luke 18:17). The accounts surrounding this short narrative show people trying to understand and enter the kingdom in different ways. They tried to reason it out (Matt. 19:25); they tried to be impressive (Matt. 19:19–20); and they tried to earn their way (Luke 18:11). A child does not rely on such things.

Background Information

Blessing children. People sought out spiritual leaders or teachers to bless children with the hope that the blessing might protect the children's lives. Child mortality rates were very high.

Mistakes to Avoid

The analogy of coming to Jesus like children should not be misconstrued; in other words, believers are not to be naïve or intentionally keep themselves ignorant.

119. Worker and Wages (Matthew 19:30–20:16)

Lesson Focus

A landowner hires workers at different hours of the day but then pays them all the same wage.

- Life in God's kingdom does not always work according to human expectation.
- God is charitable.
- God's kingdom is open to all.

Lesson Application

Instead of worrying about what others get, we should be concerned about what kind of disciples we are.

- We will not begrudge God's mercy to others.
- We are to be committed disciples.
- We leave the details of God's mercy up to him.

Biblical Context

This parable is found only in Matthew, whose interest was in adjusting expectations people have about Jesus and the kingdom of God. He wanted his readers to understand Jesus' mission and what discipleship involves. This parable is preceded by a proverbial saying, "Many who are first will be last, and the last first" (19:30), and ends with a nearly identical saying, "So the last will be first, and first last" (20:16), giving the impression that the parable is designed to clarify the saying.

Interpretational Issues in the Story

Parable focus. Parables are not allegories in which everything stands for something. Sometimes the people or situations in a parable are intentionally exaggerated to make a point. Many parables are about the nature of the kingdom of God. Here, the parable is introduced with something about the kingdom of heaven: "But many who are first will be last, and the last first" (19:30). Unexpectedly charitable treatment is one of the features of the kingdom. Disciples should be those who act charitably and will be treated charitably. It is easy to think, "What is the least I have to do?" or, "I do a lot more than other people" (19:27), or, "Those others did less than I did—why do they get the same treatment?" Such thinking is unworthy of disciples in the kingdom.

First and last (Matt. 19:30; 20:16). These words are in the plural, indicating they are not an assessment of an individual. "The last" could be the poor, vulnerable, or self-sacrificing, and "the first" those who are wealthy, privileged, or ambitious. Given Matthew's emphasis on discipleship, disciples are the ones who are last but will be first, in contrast to those whose priorities make them uncommitted disciples.

Background Information

Hiring practices. Certain seasons required additional labor forces, and hiring decisions were made on a day-to-day basis.

Denarius. A denarius was the typical wage for a full day of labor, typically twelve hours.

Mistakes to Avoid

We should not think of the landowner as acting the way that God acts or of the payment as a direct correlation of how people are treated in heaven. Those allegorical associations are not the point of the parable, nor is it about people who receive Christ late in life and so get the same benefit of eternal life. The equal payment made to the workers hired later is a deliberate exaggeration. The unrealistic nature of the landowner's behavior would have drawn the attention of listeners, but it was not designed to give instruction about how to handle employees or how wages should be structured. The hired men all worked, so this is not a contrast of grace versus works, nor is it about Jews versus Gentiles. Even focusing the lesson on issues such as fairness or generosity is problematic.

120. Jesus and Bartimaeus (Matthew 20:29–34; Mark 10:46–52; Luke 18:35–42)

Lesson Focus

Jesus showed his messianic identity as well as his love and mercy to a blind man by healing him.

- Jesus is the Messiah.
- Jesus cares for the downtrodden and disadvantaged.
- Jesus has the power to heal.

Lesson Application

We should understand that Jesus is king and his kingdom is concerned about the poor and sick.

- We believe that Jesus cares about each one of us in his kingdom.
- We believe that Jesus is the Messiah.
- We believe that Jesus is powerful enough to heal.

Biblical Context

All three Gospel accounts note that Jesus was addressed as "Son of David," and Luke notes that Bartimaeus followed Jesus praising God. Both these details lead up to the Triumphal Entry, which will occur when he arrives at Jerusalem within a day or two.

Interpretational Issues in the Story

Blind men (Matt. 20:30). Matthew, as in a number of other cases (e.g., two demoniacs [8:28]; two animals [21:2]), has two—here, blind men—where the other Gospel accounts speak of only one. We could assume that although there were two, Mark and Luke mention only the one that was well known, Bartimaeus; or we could assume that there was only one but that Matthew was using a Jewish literary technique of doubling for emphasis.

Son of David (Matt. 20:31). This was not just a genealogical identification of Jesus. The blind men were acknowledging him as Messiah. When Jesus began his ministry, reading from the scroll of Isaiah in Nazareth (see Luke 4:14–21), he read the prophecy indicating that the Messiah would bring sight to the blind. Here, just before he prepares to enter Jerusalem as king, it is appropriate that he should give sight to the blind.

"Be silent" (Matt. 20:31; Mark 10:48; Luke 18:39). It is likely that the crowd was aware that Jesus was going to Jerusalem to present himself as king, and they did not want to be delayed by something as seemingly insignificant as a blind man. But Jesus again indicated by his attention that his kingdom is made up of such people.

"Throwing off his cloak" (Mark 10:50). Very soon, multitudes would be throwing their cloaks before Jesus.

Background Information

Beggars. As is still true today, beggars in Jesus' day tended to situate themselves in well-traveled areas. Back then they congregated by city or temple gateways or along major routes. They preferred locations that were sheltered from the weather, particularly the sun.

Timing. Jesus was on his way to Jerusalem, about fifteen miles away, where he would enter as king. The healing of the blind occurred within two weeks of his crucifixion.

Jericho. The Gospel accounts vary concerning whether Jesus was leaving or entering Jericho. It is therefore important to note that New Testament Jericho was in the vicinity of Herod's palace, about a mile south of Old Testament Jericho, so it is likely he was moving between the two.

Mistakes to Avoid

The account is not just about Jesus caring for the sick; the contrast and the context are important. He takes time for the blind man (or men) even when he is headed toward one of the most important moments in his ministry. Furthermore, his healing of the blind should be seen not just as personal compassion but as an indication of the nature of his kingdom, as it cares for all the needy. When teaching the lesson, the emphasis ought not to be on the persistence of the blind. Their persistence is described but not commended as behavior to imitate.

121. The Triumphal Entry (Matthew 21:1–11; Mark 11:1–10; Luke 19:29–44; John 12:12–19)

Lesson Focus

Jesus showed that he is the Messiah by fulfilling the prophecy of the king coming on a donkey.

- Jesus was proclaimed Messiah by the people.
- Jesus took on the role of Messiah in the things that he did.

Lesson Application

Jesus is God, the Savior.

- We acknowledge Jesus as the king who came to save us.
- We sing our praise to Jesus as the one God promised.

Biblical Context

In Matthew the Triumphal Entry is followed by the cleansing of the temple and healing the blind and the lame. These activities were associated with the Messiah. In all the Gospels this event leads up to the activities of what we call Passion Week. The acclamation of Jesus as king turned quickly to accusations and condemnation as the week progresses.

Interpretational Issues in the Story

Donkey and colt (Matt. 21:2, 7). Matthew, as in a number of other cases, includes two of something (e.g., two demoniacs [8:28]; two blind men [20:30])—in this case animals, a donkey and a colt—where the other Gospel accounts include only one. We can link Matthew's inclusion of two animals with Zechariah 9:9, which could be interpreted either as parallelism or as referring to two animals. The argument for two animals here could also be based on the idea that a younger donkey is more docile if the mother is kept with it.

Colt never ridden (Mark 11:2). A donkey never ridden was suitably pure for royal use.

Cloaks and palm branches spread on road (Matt. 21:8). Palm branches were symbolic of national hope for Jerusalem. The date palm was abundant in Israel and one of the staple products of the economy. Soon after this time, date palms were portrayed on coins stamped by the rebels against Rome. In the early spring in Jerusalem, the branches of palm trees were still small. Cloaks were used to spread in front of a king as early as 2 Kings 9:13.

Hosanna (Matt. 21:9). The combination of "Hosanna," which is the Greek pronunciation of the Hebrew, *Hoshia-na*, "please save us," with the designation "Son of David" shows that Jesus was being hailed as the Messiah, the expected king who would sit on the throne of David and restore the spiritual and political fortunes of the Jews. Luke makes this explicit as the people shout, "Blessed is the king who comes in the name of the Lord!" John also reports the shout, "Blessed is . . . the king of Israel!" See Psalm 118:25–26 for some of this wording.

"The very stones would cry out" (Luke 19:40). Isaiah 55:12 features nature crying out, and in Habakkuk 2:11 the stones in the walls of the city cry out.

"This is the prophet Jesus" (Matt. 21:11). Matthew indicates that the people recognized Jesus as a prophet. Luke does not name him as a prophet but tells Jesus' oracle of judgment against Jerusalem (19:42–44) in prophetic fashion.

Background Information

Bethphage, Mount of Olives. Following the road from Bethany to the west, climbing the eastern side of the Mount of Olives, was the small village of Bethphage, apparently where the donkey was procured. It was only about a mile from the walls of Jerusalem. As Jesus rode down the western flank of the Mount of Olives, he passed through the Kidron Valley on his way up to the city. His entrance may have been through the Golden Gate on the eastern side of the temple mount or through the gate just south of the temple mount with entry into the temple area through the Huldah gates on the south. In the

Kidron Valley he would have encountered thousands camped there for participation in the Jerusalem festivities surrounding the celebration of Passover.

The feast. The feast John mentions was the Passover, one of the three pilgrimage feasts for which crowds made their way to Jerusalem to celebrate. The Psalms contain a series of hymns that were sung by the pilgrims traveling to Jerusalem (Psalms 113–118), and one of those is quoted here by the people. Psalm 118 would have been fresh on their minds. Passover was when the Jews celebrated their deliverance from slavery, so here at that very celebration it is appropriate that the people were crying out for deliverance (Hosanna!).

King riding on donkey. Zechariah 9:9 makes the statement that the king would come riding on a donkey and offering salvation. In Old Testament times the royal mount was typically a mule, but in some contexts the use of a donkey emphasized peaceful intentions.

Mistakes to Avoid

Downplay the element of coming on a donkey as a fulfillment of prophecy. The significance here is that the people have recognized who Jesus is and proclaimed him to be the promised king who will bring deliverance. As Jesus receives the acclaim of the people, he is fulfilling the role of Messiah. If we try to build the lesson around the idea that Jesus is king of our lives, we lose the aspect of the type of kingship that Jesus is associating with in this narrative. The kingship proclaimed here does not pertain to his lordship over the lives of individuals but to his messianic role on the throne of David, his place in God's plan for the kingdom. Likewise, if we make the story just about praising Jesus in general, we dilute the powerful image that is central to the people's praise in this account—they were praising him as a king who had a right to David's throne.

122. Cleansing the Temple (Matthew 21:12–13; Mark 11:15–18; Luke 19:45–46; John 2:12–17)

Lesson Focus

Jesus interferes with the commercial activities that supported the rituals of the temple to make the point that judgment is coming and that neither their rituals nor the temple will spare them from it.

- Going through the motions of ritual is not sufficient to please God.

- God wants us to live lives that honor him, not depend on superficial actions.
- God is not impressed by outward actions that do not reflect the right heart attitude.

Lesson Application

Obedience is better than sacrifice.

- We honor God with our lives every moment, not just with occasional activities.
- We examine our motivations and attitudes to be sure we are pleasing God.

Biblical Context

Matthew, Mark, and Luke recount the temple cleansing after the Triumphal Entry, while John reports it right after the account of changing water to wine. It is possible that Jesus drove out the moneychangers on two (or more) occasions, but an alternative simply understands that John sometimes arranged his material topically rather than chronologically. Most importantly, all four Gospel writers use the story in the context of judgment coming on Israel and the temple.

Interpretational Issues in the Story

Sold and bought (Matt. 21:12). A pillared portico (a stoa) surrounded the outer courts of the temple, but stretching from east to west along the southern side was the royal stoa (see illustration on p. 448). Most people entered the temple courts from the south, so it was here that commercial activities related to the temple took place. Temple currency (Tyrian shekels) was required, so many had to exchange their native money for these shekels. Also, people traveled to the temple from all over the country, making it impractical to bring with them animals for sacrifice. Travelers could purchase sacrificial animals at the temple marketplace. All these services were necessary, but the activities generated profit for the proprietors, so corruption was common.

Drove out (Matt. 21:12; Mark 11:15; Luke 19:45; John 2:15). It is interesting to note that two of the Gospels indicate that Jesus drove out not just the sellers but also the buyers (Matt. 21:12; Mark 11:15). Some interpreters therefore conclude that this incident is not just a condemnation of corruption but an intentional disruption of temple operations to make the point that the temple was to be destroyed and replaced (in John 2:19–21 Jesus identifies himself as the new temple). Others have concluded that the location of the market inside the temple court rather than outside is the problem to which Jesus was reacting. Another theory suggests that Jesus was reacting to the fact that the high priest had recently relocated the stalls for buying animals from the Mount of Olives to the court of the Gentiles to serve the needs of the Passover crowds.

"Den of robbers" (Matt. 21:13; Mark 11:17; Luke 19:46). Jesus was quoting Jeremiah 7:11, the prophet's famous temple sermon. Jeremiah had accused the people of habitually and blatantly violating the covenant and then believing that God would not destroy them in order to preserve his temple, his dwelling place. The reference to robbers is not to invoke a particular crime but stands for all the covenant violations of Israel—the Greek here and the Hebrew in Jeremiah both point to something more general, like "rebels" (see Dan. 11:14, NIV, for the same word). Criminals don't commit criminal activity in their dens; that is where they go to hide after their crimes have been committed. In other words, the temple had become a refuge for rebels against God.The point of the saying in Jeremiah, and likely in the Gospels, is that the temple will not protect them—it too will be destroyed. This fits the context in all four Gospels. It is a condemnation of the belief that ritual activities would cover the crimes of people and spare them from coming judgment.

Background Information

Royal stoa. The royal stoa where the commercial activities took place featured 162 pillars in four rows. There was an apse at the eastern end where the Sanhedrin met.

Money-changers. Jewish law prohibited the coining of money, based on an interpretation of the second commandment about making images. Many of the coins minted at this time contained the image of the emperor or carried symbols of Roman domination of the Jews. Tyrian shekels were required for temple taxes and donations since they were a high grade of silver and did not bear the forbidden images. On the reverse side, however, they did bear the image of the god Melqart (the Roman Heracles).

Temple and church. The temple in the ancient world was far different from the church building today. The building that we call "church" is simply the place for the assembly of God's people for corporate worship. Even though we sometimes call it "God's house," God is housed within his people, not in a building. In Israel, God chose to live in the temple, and though people gathered in Jerusalem on sacred occasions, the courtyard was not designed for corporate worship. People came to the temple to watch public rituals and to offer the sacrifices for themselves or their families.

Mistakes to Avoid

Jesus was not trying to reform the temple; its time was done. He was not condemning the commercial activity in the temple, which was necessary for its operations. The problem was not with what the people were doing in the temple, but what they were *not* doing in the temple or in their lives—honoring God. Since the temple was not used the way our churches are, no lessons should be based on perceived similarities between the two. The point of the story is not that commercial activities in church buildings are wrong but that God was not being honored in the place of his presence.

123. Waiting at the Wedding (Matthew 25:1–13)

Lesson Focus

This parable features ten virgins waiting for the bridegroom to arrive. Five were well prepared, but five were not and ended up missing out.

- God expects us to be prepared for the kingdom.
- Some will not enter the kingdom.

Lesson Application

We should prepare for the kingdom and be ready for it whenever it arrives.

- We are to live in a state of expectation for the kingdom.
- We make sure that we are prepared at all times for the kingdom.

Biblical Context

This account is found only in Matthew, whose interest was in adjusting expectations people have about Jesus and the kingdom of God. He wanted his readers to understand Jesus' mission and what discipleship involves. This parable is part of the game plan presented in the final chapters, as it shows the importance of being ready for the kingdom to unfold. Jesus had just finished talking about the fact that the hour of Christ's coming in power is unknown, and the story following this one gives the parable of the talents and then proceeds to the separation of the sheep and goats.

Interpretational Issues in the Story

Parable focus. Parables are not allegories in which everything in the parable stands for something. Sometimes the people or situations in a parable are intentionally exaggerated to make a point. Many parables are about the nature of the kingdom of God. The principle in the parable of the ten virgins is that the coming of the kingdom will separate those who have been prepared for it and those who have not. The time of the kingdom's coming is not known, so followers need to be wise as they anticipate its arrival.

Refusal to give (Matt. 25:9). The wise virgins refused to give their oil to the foolish. This is not allegory, so every detail need not stand for something. Nevertheless, the story could easily have been told without this detail. It may indicate the fact that those who are prepared are resolute—they will not risk being caught without that which is needed. It is part of the lesson about the necessity of being prepared.

Background Information

Virgins waiting for the bridegroom. Difference of opinion exists as to whether these virgins represent the bride's attendants preparing for procession to the groom's house for the wedding ceremony or members of the groom's family waiting at his home for the bride and groom to arrive. The fact that these ceremonies often took place at night creates the need for lamps and oil.

Oil for the lamps. It is not clear whether the text refers to lamps or torches, but both need oil in order to provide light. The main difference between them is how long they will burn.

Mistakes to Avoid

When teaching the parable, avoid attempting to identify the parties involved. Instead of linking the bridegroom to God or Jesus, it is preferable to portray the arrival of the bridegroom as the arrival of the kingdom of God, for which some will be prepared and others not.

124. Three Stewards (Matthew 25:14–30; Luke 19:12–27)

Lesson Focus

A master entrusted three of his servants with different sums of money and on his return asked for an accounting.

- The kingdom of God is a trust that requires faithfulness.
- God holds people accountable for being faithful servants to the kingdom.

Lesson Application

We should be faithful to the kingdom of God.

- We recognize that the kingdom has been entrusted to us.
- We recognize that God will hold us accountable.

Biblical Context

The parable in each of the two Gospels is similar but also sufficiently different so that each might represent a different telling. In Matthew, the parable appears after the Triumphal Entry, and in Luke it is told preceding it as Jesus is traveling from Jericho to Jerusalem. Both placements indicate the growing attention on the imminent departure of Jesus. In Matthew the parable appears in the section that concerns the game plan for the future. In Luke the protagonist in the parable is a man who goes into a far country to procure a kingdom, and many of the points of the parable are mirrored in Luke's report of the Triumphal Entry.

Interpretational Issues in the Story

Parable focus. Parables are not allegories in which everything in the parable stands for something. Sometimes the people or situations in a parable are intentionally exaggerated to make a point. Many parables are about the nature of the kingdom of God. This parable follows the theme of a master entrusting something to his servants during his absence and determining how they have done upon his return. The principle is that the kingdom has been entrusted to the people of God and they should be faithful stewards who expect to be held accountable.

Audience (Matt. 25:14–30; Luke 19:12–27). Some have seen the parable as addressing an audience who would see themselves at the beginning of the story (the master, Jesus, is ready to leave), while others understand the audience to be those who see themselves at the end of the story (the master, Jesus, is "returning" in the Triumphal Entry and the destruction of Jerusalem is imminent). The issue centers on whether the parable concerns the kingdom of God as it should be managed when Christ departs to heaven or how it has been managed by the Jews throughout history and more recently during the teaching ministry of Christ. It theoretically could be interpreted either way. Most likely, Matthew intended the former and Luke the latter.

The harsh conclusion (Matt. 25:28–30; Luke 19:26–27). Jesus may correspond very generally to the master, but we should not expect alignment of all the specifics (e.g., who is he getting the kingdom from?). The harsh response may well give the general sense that there will be harsh judgment for those who have not acted faithfully, even though it does not detail the nature of the judgment. The details are part of the exaggerated language that is often used to good effect in the parables.

Background Information

Went into a far country to receive a kingdom. Traveling to obtain civil power was well recognized by the Jewish population because Herod, Archelaus, Antipas, and Agrippa all had to go to Rome and petition Caesar for approval to become kings.

Talents and minas. Matthew speaks of talents while Luke refers to minas. This is a great difference, because a talent (about 75 pounds) was equivalent to fifty or sixty minas. Both accounts, however, involve significant sums of money. This might also reflect two different tellings of the parable.

Darkness, weeping, and gnashing of teeth. This language in Matthew 25:30 would have been familiar to a Jewish audience. It was used to describe a place of judgment (hell, Gehenna) in literature that had been written in the centuries between the Old and New Testaments. The third steward was not a true member of the kingdom and would suffer the consequences.

Mistakes to Avoid

Parables are neither historical accounts nor allegories in which everything in the parable stands for something. Accordingly, we ought not to identify this parable as specifically referring to the ascension and eventual return of Christ, for there are too many details that don't fit. Jesus has already received the kingdom. Likewise, God should not be interpreted as the harsh master. "Talents" in the New Testament world referred to a monetary measurement and had nothing to do with skills or abilities, so avoid turning the parable into a lesson on how we should use our abilities in the service of God. Even a general emphasis on stewardship is unlikely, given the context of the Triumphal Entry. The parable is about faithfulness and accountability in general. It is the kingdom that has been entrusted—not gifts or possessions. The fact that the monetary amounts given in Matthew's rendition are exorbitant, with the smallest, one talent, being equivalent to a minimum of twenty years of labor, shows that the parable is intended to be unrealistic in its details.

125. Judas Betrays (Matthew 26:14–16, 23–25, 47–50; 27:3–10; Mark 14:10–11, 43–45; Luke 22:1–6, 47–53; John 13:26–30; 18:1–5; Acts 1:18–19)

Lesson Focus

Judas agreed to turn Jesus over to the authorities, betrayed him with a kiss in the garden, then returned the money out of guilt and killed himself in his remorse.

- God's plan included the betrayal of Jesus by one of his disciples, and Jesus was aware that this would happen.
- Jesus was betrayed by a friend.
- God was in control of events as they brought his plan to completion.
- Even though betrayal was part of God's plan, God did not force an unwilling Judas to betray. Judas was responsible for his crime and suffered death as a result.

Lesson Application

What appear to us to be obstacles can be used as part of God's plan.

- We believe that difficulties we face in life are not obstacles to God.
- We are responsible for our own bad choices even though God can use them for his glory.
- Our choices have consequences, but God's plan is never in jeopardy.

Biblical Context

The final events of Jesus' life are covered by all the Gospels and, as might be expected, follow in chronological order. Each writer offers slightly different wording or chooses to omit or supplement according to his particular interests, and these individual aspects can be studied with benefit.

Interpretational Issues in the Story

Manner of Judas's death (Matt. 27:5; Acts 1:18). Matthew and Acts appear to give differing accounts of the death of Judas, but it is not difficult for the two accounts to be reconciled. Someone who hanged himself in an isolated area was unlikely to be cut down and buried quickly. Either the rotting of the rope or the desiccation of the corpse could have led to the results described in Acts. An alternative is that the branch chosen for the hanging was not thick enough and broke under Judas's weight, causing the results that killed him.

Satan entered Judas (John 13:27). It is difficult to determine what this means. Demon possession is not the answer, because Judas was responsible for what he did. The terminology of Satan entering someone is used in intertestamental literature to describe the prompting of a person to do evil against one of God's agents (e.g., King Manasseh, who took Isaiah's life in *Martyrdom and Ascension of Isaiah).*

"Throwing down the pieces of silver into the temple" (Matt. 27:5). The word used here for *temple* refers elsewhere in Matthew to the actual building, not just to the courts. Only priests were allowed in the temple. At this point, however, in Judas's frame of mind, no taboo or potential condemnation would have deterred him from storming into the actual temple and flinging the money down.

Background Information

Chief priests, Pharisees, elders, officers of the temple. The chief priests were the religious leaders of the temple and in charge of the Sanhedrin. The temple guard, officers of the temple, were the police force (Jews, not Romans). The elders were lay leaders given oversight of the families of Israel. Pharisees were the teachers of the law who had authority in the synagogue.

Thirty pieces of silver. The text does not indicate denomination of the coins. If the coins were denarii or drachmas, they represented a month's wages. If they were staters, as one manuscript variant suggests, the amount was four times more. Thirty pieces of silver brings to mind the thirty shekels mentioned in Zechariah 11:12, a price associated with the life of a slave.

Potter's field. The traditional location of the potter's field is just south of Jerusalem where the Kidron and Hinnom valleys meet. However, that identification is made unlikely by the fact that the tombs found there were for the upper levels of society.

Mistakes to Avoid

The significance of the story is Jesus and the plan of God rather than Judas and his treacherous betrayal. We don't know Judas's motives and cannot reconstruct what was on his mind, so he should not be the focus of the lesson. Likewise, we should not speculate on Satan's thoughts or strategy in the event.

126. The Last Supper (Matthew 26:17–29; Mark 14:12–26; Luke 22:7–20; John 13:1–30)

Lesson Focus

Jesus shared a Passover meal with his disciples just before he was betrayed and gave them instructions for a continual observance to commemorate the events about to unfold.

- Jesus wants us to remember his death for us through a ceremony.
- Jesus died for us.

Lesson Application

By taking Communion, or celebrating the Eucharist, we remember what Jesus has done for us.

- We partake regularly of Communion.
- We meditate regularly on the death of Jesus for our sins.

Biblical Context

The final events of Jesus' life are covered by all the Gospels and, as might be expected, follow in chronological order. Each writer offers slightly different wording and chooses to omit or supplement material according to his particular interests, and these individual aspects can be studied with benefit.

Interpretational Issues in the Story

"A man carrying a jar of water" (Mark 14:13; Luke 22:10). It is likely that the disciples entered the city near the Gihon Spring where most people in the city got their water. Encountering someone carrying a jar of water was not unusual, but a man's carrying it was.

"One who is dipping bread . . . with me" (Mark 14:20). Jesus had just

made clear that one of the Twelve will betray him. Dipping bowls containing oil or paste-based garnishes were scattered around the table so that all could reach them, and guests dipped bread into them as they ate. Also, the bitter herbs served at the Passover were usually dipped into a puree of fruit, nuts, and sour wine (*haroshet*). Jesus' comment does not offer a secret clue as to the identity of the betrayer; he says only that his betrayer is at the table. In the Gospel of John, however, another detail is given that does identify the betrayer, a detail that was provided to John privately at the supper and recorded in his Gospel (John 13:26–27). There was particular treachery in betraying someone after sharing a meal together.

"Son of Man" (Matt. 26:24; Mark 14:21). The title is drawn from Daniel 7, and by New Testament times it had come to be used as a title of the Messiah. Jesus often used it in reference to himself.

"New covenant in my blood" (Luke 22:20). Covenants in the Old Testament world were generally ratified by the shed blood of a sacrificed animal, so this would have been familiar language to the disciples, even though the blood here was represented symbolically. Jesus did not designate himself as the Passover lamb who would be slaughtered to give them life. The new covenant was referred to several times in the Old Testament, most notably in Jeremiah 31:31–33. Covenants in the ancient world were renewed when parties engaged in the covenant changed or the circumstances associated with the covenant changed. From that we can infer that the death of Jesus brought a changed circumstance that brought new terms to the covenant between God and his people.

Background Information

Day of Unleavened Bread. The Passover is the meal that initiates the seven-day feast of Unleavened Bread. It was being celebrated by Jesus and his disciples on Thursday evening, Nisan 15 on the Jewish calendar. Days began at sunset, so the Thursday evening meal was the beginning of this day.

Upper room. There is a building on Mount Zion, just south of the modern-day walls outside the Zion Gate, that is the traditional site of the Last Supper. The current building was built by the Franciscans in the fourteenth century, but the traditional identification is much older and is archaeologically and geographically credible.

Reclined at table. In formal dining settings there were wide, low couches arranged around tables set up in a U formation. Guests reclined propped up on one elbow with their legs stretching away from the table.

The most important person was placed in the center of the short segment of the formation.

Breaking bread. Jewish meals were opened with a standardized prayer of thanksgiving while holding bread high in one's hand, much as we hold up glasses for a toast today. After the blessing, the one who had pronounced the blessing would break the bread to indicate the start of the meal. At the Passover celebration, the bread is held up and identified as the bread of affliction eaten by the Israelites when they came out of Egypt. Jesus gave this common breaking of bread a new significance: it would thereafter represent the affliction of Jesus, not Israel. This is one of many ways throughout Jesus' ministry that he identifies himself as Israel's representative.

Cup. Celebrants drink wine at four points at the Passover meals: (1) at the beginning; (2) just before the meal; (3) after the meal and its concluding prayer; and (4) after the Scripture reading from Psalms 115–118. Scholars are not agreed on which occasion was used by Jesus to make his remarks, but the most common interpretation suggests it was the third.

Mistakes to Avoid

The disciples had little understanding of what was about to unfold. They did not know that Jesus was going be arrested, tried, and executed over the next twenty-four hours. They were aware that events had been moving rapidly since the Triumphal Entry and they knew the danger that was posed by their presence in Jerusalem. The perspective of the Gospel writers sees the event through the eyes of Jesus. Thus, the focus of the story ought to be on what Jesus knows and is doing rather than on what the disciples do not know. Although there is some legitimacy to thinking about Jesus as the Passover lamb (1 Cor. 5:7), we ought not to shape the teaching of the lesson on that theme since Jesus' words take it in a different direction.

127. Peter's Denial (Matthew 26:31–35, 69–75; Mark 14:66–72; Luke 22:54–62; John 18:15–18, 25–27; 21:15–25)

Lesson Focus

Peter denied he was Jesus' friend, but Jesus forgave Peter and made him a leader of God's people.

- Jesus recognizes our human weaknesses and forgives our shortcomings.
- Jesus has jobs even for those who have made mistakes.
- Jesus knew what Peter was going to do.

Lesson Application

Jesus shows his love and forgiveness to his followers.

- We recognize that Jesus is willing to forgive us when we fail.
- We must not be so self-righteous as to think we cannot fail.

Biblical Context

The accounts of Peter denying Jesus are interwoven throughout the Passion narratives in the appropriate chronological place. The restoration of Peter is reported only in John and is placed in the last chapter after what is presented as the purpose of the book (John 20:31). This gives the account the appearance of an appendix, but it provides an important record of Jesus' commissioning, which was the next step in the gospel of Jesus spreading to the world.

Interpretational Issues in the Story

Invoked a curse and swore (Matt. 26:74; Mark 14:71). The text does not specify on whom Peter called down curses, though the ESV and other translations include "on himself," implying that he was calling for curses to come upon him if he was lying. Alternatives are that he was cursing the ones who were accusing him of knowing Christ or that he was actually cursing Christ, amplifying his sense of guilt. Certainty is not possible.

"Do you love me?" (John 21:15–17). Some interpreters have seen a lot of significance in the fact that John used two different words for "love" in the exchange between Jesus and Peter. In the first two questions Jesus uses the word *agape*, and Peter answers with the word *phileo*. In the third, Jesus and Peter both use *phileo*. Some believe this was merely a way for Jesus to test the seriousness of Peter's commitment. Other interpreters simply point out that John often used synonyms stylistically to avoid redundancy. In other contexts in the New Testament, the words are used interchangeably. The threefold repetition need not suggest that Jesus was unconvinced by Peter's affirmation. Alternatively, the threefold repetition might have been used to lend solemnity and confirm that the words were meant sincerely. Peter's threefold denial could be taken the same way, but we need not think that Jesus asked three times *because* Peter denied three times.

Background Information

Rooster crows three times. Jesus was likely not referring to the crowing of a rooster at dawn. Research has confirmed three distinct times of rooster crowing at night in Palestine, about 12:30 AM, 1:30 AM, and 2:30 AM.

The high priest. The Church of Saint Peter Gallicantu in the area between Mount Zion and the City of David is the traditional site of the house of Caiaphas the high priest where Peter sat in the courtyard and denied Jesus, though scholars today are not convinced. They focus instead on an area in the modern Jewish Quarter where palatial mansions from that time have been excavated.

Location of Peter's restoration. The traditional site of the event of Peter's restoration, the Church of the Primacy of Saint Peter, is located along the northwest shore of the Sea of Galilee at Tabgha, adjacent to the site of the feeding of the five thousand. The ruins of a fourth-century church have been found there. Warm springs are said to have flowed into the sea here making a spot where fish would gather.

Mistakes to Avoid

Teachers should be careful not to focus too much on Peter. Neither his failure nor his restoration is the main point. It is true that we should not be ashamed of Christ, but that is not the point of the story. The text does not want us either to look down on him for his weakness or to elevate him because of his commission. The focus is on Jesus, his character and plan.

128. Gethsemane and the Trial before the Sanhedrin (Matthew 26:36–68; Mark 14:32–65; Luke 22:39–53; John 18:1–14, 19–24)

Lesson Focus

Jesus prayed with his disciples in the garden and then was arrested and tried before the Jewish authorities of the Sanhedrin.

- Jesus knew that suffering was coming but prayed that he might do the Father's will.
- Jesus submitted to the Father and to the authorities.
- Jesus acknowledged that he is the Messiah and the Son of God and was accused of blasphemy.

Lesson Application

Those who acknowledge that Jesus is the Son of God should also submit to the Father and be willing to suffer along with Christ.

- We must be willing to suffer as Jesus was willing to suffer.
- We can expect to be persecuted when we acknowledge that Jesus is the Son of God.

Biblical Context

The final events of Jesus' life are covered by all four Gospels and, as might be expected, follow in chronological order. Each writer offered slightly different wording and chose to omit or supplement according to his particular interests, and these individual aspects can be studied with benefit.

Interpretational Issues in the Story

"Pray that you may not enter into temptation" (Matt. 26:41). Since Jesus did not specify the temptation facing the disciples, we can only guess. Many think he was referring to the temptation to desert and deny him.

"I am he" (John 18:5–6, 8). In the Greek translation of the Old Testament, this is the phrase used by God to identify himself to Moses at the burning bush, "I AM" (Ex. 3:14). This connection would not have been lost on the Jews.

Charge of blasphemy (Matt. 26:65; Mark 14:64). When Jesus acknowledged that he is the Son of God, the Messiah, he added a statement about the Son of Man sitting at the right hand of the Mighty One coming on the clouds (Matt. 26:64; Mark 14:62). This would have been recognized as a reference to Daniel 7:13–14 and Psalm 110:1–2, by which Jesus was making clear claims to being the Messiah.

Background Information

Gethsemane. The general location of the garden of Gethsemane is certain. It is on the lower western flank of the Mount of Olives just across the Kidron Valley from the Temple Mount. It drew its name from an oil press, which was there for harvesting the oil from the olive orchard that grew on the hillside. It would have taken Jesus and his disciples about fifteen to thirty minutes to walk from the Upper Room to the garden. Today the Church of All Nations commemorates one possible spot for the garden, and a grove of olive trees is continually maintained there. Some of the trees in the grove are over a thousand years old, but it is unlikely that any date back to the time of

Jesus. Another possible spot is about a hundred yards farther north along the flank where there are some caves that could have been used for the presses.

Cup. "Drinking a cup" was a figurative way of talking about experiencing something difficult (see Mark 10:38).

Caiaphas. Caiaphas was the high priest for eighteen years (AD 18–36). During this period, the office of high priest was political in nature because the Roman prefect made the appointment. It also took political savvy to hold the office, and, by all accounts, Caiaphas was a successful politician. His name is known from historians such as Josephus.

Sanhedrin. Based on the Judaism represented in the rabbinic writings that followed the destruction of the temple in AD 70, the Sanhedrin was a formal body that provided leadership for the Jewish people. It was not necessarily comprised of priests but of respected religious experts who made legal decisions, preserved traditions, and governed the spiritual and social life of the people. Though Pharisees, who were popular with the common people, were among the group, the Sadducees held the majority of the seventy-one seats. It is unknown whether the Sanhedrin in the New Testament was so formally institutionalized, though Josephus talks about the body meeting in council in the temple courts in the period before the temple was destroyed. The word can also refer to an ad hoc gathering of responsible people for decision making and may sometimes be used that way in the New Testament.

Trial regulations. There are numerous aspects of Jesus' trial that violate later rabbinic regulations, but there is no reason to think that those laws were in place at the time of Jesus' trial. It was out of the ordinary for the Sanhedrin to meet at night in the high priest's home. In later Judaism a capital case required a minimum of twenty-three members. The Sanhedrin viewed blasphemy as a crime deserving of death, but Roman law required something more political in nature for the death penalty, such as insurrection. Such a charge could have been brought against Jesus if it was determined that he was trying to raise a revolt against Rome.

Witnesses. Two witnesses were necessary to condemn a man to death.

Mistakes to Avoid

Jesus' prayers in Gethsemane are instructive in a number of ways, but the focus of the story isn't on how to pray. We can observe the humanity of Jesus as he prayed in the garden, and this should not be minimized, but it is not offered as proof of his humanity. Accusations concerning Jewish culpability in Jesus' death and resulting anti-Semitic sentiments ought to be carefully avoided, especially since Jews have so prominent a role in the founding of the Christian church. The Jews did seek to take Jesus' life and press charges in what could be considered a farcical trial. But it was also Jews who served as his disciples, followed him adoringly around the country, and became the core of the early church. Rejection of Christ is something we are all guilty of. The Jews were the target of Jesus' ministry because they were the covenant people of God.

129. The Trial before Pilate (Matthew 27:11–26; Mark 15:1–15; Luke 23:1–25; John 18:28–19:15)

Lesson Focus

After Jesus was condemned by the Jewish authorities, he was sent to Pilate, then to Herod (in Luke only), then back to Pilate, before he was sentenced to death. Pilate found little reason for execution and offered to release one prisoner; the Jews choose Barabbas.

- Jesus did nothing wrong but was executed for political and religious reasons.
- Jesus accepted the title of king but indicated that his kingdom was not of this world.
- God was fully in control of the events of the trial (see John 19:32).

Lesson Application

Jesus committed no crimes; he and his kingdom embody truth.

- We recognize the truth of the kingdom when we are confronted with it.
- We recognize Jesus as the true king.
- We understand that Jesus was not found guilty and, in fact, was without sin or guilt.

Biblical Context

The final events of Jesus' life are covered by all four Gospels and, as might be expected, follow in chronological order. Each writer offered slightly different wording and chose to omit or supplement according to his particular interests, and these individual aspects can be studied with benefit.

Interpretational Issues in the Story

Delivered over to Pilate (Mark 15:1). The Jews were prohibited under Roman law from carrying out a death sentence (John 18:31), so the Roman authorities were called upon to pass sentence. Rather than pressing the charge of blasphemy that the Jewish authorities had issued, which was not legitimate in a Roman court, the Jews claimed to Pilate that Jesus was guilty of subverting the nation (Luke 23:2).

"For this purpose I was born" (John 18:37). Jesus identified his mission as "to bear witness to the truth." The word "king" was Pilate's word, as Jesus indicated. For Jesus the keyword was not "king" but "truth," by which he meant the truth concerning God's kingdom and his own role in it, not truthful facts and ideas in general (John 14:6).

Background Information

Pilate. Pontius Pilate was governor (prefect) in Judea during the reign of Emperor Tiberius, from AD 26 to 36. His name has been authenticated from an inscription found at Caesarea Maritime, where his primary residence was.

Location of Jesus' trial before Pilate. It is not certain where Pilate's headquarters were in Jerusalem (see illustration p. 447). Options include the Herodian palace at the western edge of the city wall, which was built by Herod the Great near the modern Jaffa Gate; the old Hasmonean palace, which was rebuilt by Herod the Great over the earlier structure near the southwest corner of the temple mount just west of Robinson's arch; or the Antonio Fortress at the northwest corner of the temple mount. The first option is most likely. From the house of Caiaphas to the Herodian Palace is a ten- to fifteen-minute walk (depending on the exact location of the former).

Herod, tetrarch of Galilee. This was Herod Antipas, son of Herod the Great, who ruled in Galilee and Perea from 4 BC until AD 39. His ancestry was part Jewish. He is the same Herod who executed John the Baptist.

Location of Jesus' trial before Herod. Herod's primary residence was in the north, but as one who sought to be an observant Jew, he was in Jerusalem for Passover. He likely stayed at the Hasmonean palace when in town. It would take five to ten minutes to walk between the two palaces.

Release of a prisoner at the feast. Since ancient times, kings had followed the practice of releasing prisoners as a gesture of good will, either at the beginning of their reign or in connection with religious holidays. Many were imprisoned in the ancient world for debt rather than crime, so the release of a prisoner wasn't likely in many cases to endanger the public. There were also political prisoners, and that was likely the case with Barabbas. He is not identified as one of the Zealots, but Zealots were insurrectionists known to execute those they considered Roman sympathizers.

Praetorium. Technically the praetorium was the main residence of the Roman governor, but it could also refer to the headquarters of the Roman army. Most likely, however, the praetorium was at Pilate's headquarters at the western Herodian palace, which means that Jesus' torment took place in the same building complex as his hearing before Pilate.

Judgment seat at the Stone Pavement (Gabbatha). The judgment seat mentioned in several of the Gospels refers to the *bema* seat. It was the official bench used by a magistrate when making a ruling. It is said in John 19:13 to be located at the Stone Pavement, which some have identified with a stoned area from this time period excavated in what was the Fortress of Antonio. More often, however, it is identified as a large area connected with Herod's palace.

Mistakes to Avoid

When teaching the lesson, it is probably best to avoid seeking to place the blame for Jesus' death on specific people, such as Judas, the Jewish authorities, Pilate, Herod, or the Roman soldiers. The truth is that God's plan since the foundation of the earth was for Jesus to die. This does not remove blame from any of the parties, but if one group or person had not been involved, others would have been. Everyone was working from personal agendas and motivations, and since we cannot reconstruct or identify those with confidence, it is best not to try. Likewise, Pilate should not be the focus, creating from him an example of those who succumb to peer pressure.

130. The Crucifixion and Burial (Matthew 27:27–66; Mark 15:16–47; Luke 23:26–56; John 19:16–42)

Lesson Focus

Jesus died a painful death, suffering in his humanity and dying for us as the Son of God. Unnatural events accompanied his death, and he was buried in a nearby tomb.

- Jesus was the Son of God.
- Jesus suffered greatly.
- Jesus died.

Lesson Application

Jesus suffered and died for us.

- We should believe that Jesus truly suffered and died.
- We should accept Jesus' death as a substitute for our sin.

Biblical Context

The final events of Jesus' life are covered by all four Gospels and, as might be expected, follow in chronological order. Each writer offered slightly different wording or chose to omit or supplement according to his particular interests, and these individual aspects can be studied with benefit.

Interpretational Issues in the Story

Carrying the cross (Matt. 27:32). Those to be crucified were forced to carry the thirty- to forty-pound crossbeam to the site of their execution. It is understandable that this was beyond the physical capacity of someone who had been badly beaten. Both the flesh and the muscles of the back would have been torn.

"Today you will be with me in Paradise" (Luke 23:43). "Paradise" came into the Greek language from Persian, where it referred to a luxurious garden. It became a term to describe being in the presence of God after death.

Darkness over the land (Matt. 27:45; Mark 15:33; Luke 23:44). Passover was at full moon, so the darkness at the crucifixion cannot be a solar eclipse. Solar eclipses occur only at the new moon phase. It was an unnatural darkness, just as so much of what immediately followed. The following events are unnatural.

Curtain of the temple torn (Matt. 27:51; Mark 15:38; Luke 23:45). The text is not clear which curtain was torn. If it was the curtain visible from the temple courtyard, all could have seen the sign, but more likely the curtain was the veil hiding the Most Holy Place. The significance is either that God has left the temple or that access to God has been opened up through the death of Christ—or both.

Raising of the dead (Matt. 27:52–53). These brief verses that provide the detail of the dead coming out of their tombs leave many unanswered questions, but they indicate ripple effects of Jesus' victory over death.

Background Information

Flogging. Roman law called for flogging to precede execution, and there was no limit to the number of times the criminal could be flogged. The instrument used was a *flagellum* comprised of leather straps with pieces of bone and metal. Flogging, then, was not just a whipping; it flayed the skin. Many would die from the flogging itself.

Crown of thorns. There are many possibilities for the type of plant that was used for this makeshift crown.

Golgotha, Place of a Skull. The name is not attested in any ancient documents outside the Bible. It was located outside the city wall (by both Roman and Jewish law) and along a major roadway (by common practice) rather than in an isolated area or up on a hill. These conditions may be met at the traditional location known as Gordon's Calvary, where a rock formation that looks like a skull can be seen today. This has been a favorite spot for visitors since the nineteenth century. A longer running tradition places Golgotha at the Church of the Holy Sepulchre, which was built in the fourth century by Constantine. Both places are outside the second wall of the city, which was the outside wall at the time of Christ. The third wall was not built until the next decade.

Wine mixed with gall. It may have been common practice to offer a drink to the condemned, but mixing it with gall was no act of mercy. Gall refers simply to a substance of bitter taste. Mark 15:23 tells us that the substance was myrrh, which does have a bitter taste. It was not given as a narcotic to dull the pain; it was a prank to get Jesus to think he was going to receive refreshment.

Crucifixion. The skeleton of a man crucified during this period reveals that the feet straddled the upright beam and were nailed to the sides of it, but literary evidence suggests that a variety of postures were used. Arms were sometimes tied to the crossbeam but could also be nailed. The nails were possibly driven into the wrist or forearm rather than the palm (the Greek terminology supports any of these options). The victim was attached to the cross with no clothing to protect the wounds from abrasion or insects. Some victims died from loss of blood, others from suffocation when they no longer had the strength to boost up their bodies to allow them to take a breath. Exhaustion and exposure were also factors. Bodies were frequently left on the cross as birds devoured the remains.

Breaking victims' legs. This was a strategy to hasten death; once the legs were broken, the victim could no longer push himself up to catch a breath.

Pierced side. The "water" that flowed out of Jesus' side with the blood has been variably identified by physicians. The two main possibilities are that it was fluid from the pericardial sac and that it was fluid buildup between the body lining and the lungs resulting from traumatic injuries to the chest.

Location of the tomb. The rationale for Joseph's taking the body is that he had a usable tomb in the vicinity. That tomb cannot be what is today referred to as the Garden Tomb, since Joseph's tomb was new, and the Garden Tomb dates back to the eighth century BC. The Church of the Holy Sepulcher meets many of the requirements. There are quarries under the site that offered opportunities for tombs in the first century. According to burial customs of the day, bodies were laid out until only bones remained, then they were placed in an ossuary (bone box) for final burial.

Tomb with a rolling stone. Tombs of this period were cut into the rock, sometimes making use of natural caves or former quarries. The opening was covered by a large disk-shaped stone that rolled along a groove carved in the surface.

The day of Preparation. Most interpreters conclude that this refers to preparation for the Sabbath rather than for the Passover.

Seventy-five pounds of spices. This is an exorbitant amount comparable to that used for the burial of Herod the Great or the respected rabbi of the time, Gamaliel.

Mistakes to Avoid

This story is not easily distorted, since its teaching is so clear and central. It is understandable that teachers want to find creative ways to draw the students into the story, but care should be given so that creativity employed to make it fresh does not distract from the clear and obvious emphasis. Matthew 27 makes numerous references to Psalm 22; however, that does not mean that the psalmist was speaking of Jesus. By the end of Psalm 22 it is clear that the one suffering had been delivered. Still, some of the details of the psalm were clearly appropriated by Matthew and applied to Jesus. It would not do justice to the psalmist's context, however, to suggest to students that he was describing the crucifixion of Jesus.

131. The Resurrection (Matthew 28:1–10; Mark 16:1–11; Luke 24:1–12; John 20:1–18)

Lesson Focus

Jesus demonstrated by his resurrection that he is God.

- Jesus overcame the power of death by rising from the dead.
- Jesus is God.
- Jesus provides power over death.

Lesson Application

Jesus died for our sins and was raised to life again.

- We believe that Jesus rose from the dead.
- We believe that Jesus is God.

Biblical Context

The final events of Jesus' life are covered by all four Gospels and, as might be expected, follow in chronological order. Each writer offered slightly different wording or chose to omit or supplement according to his particular interests, and these individual aspects can be studied with benefit.

Interpretational Issues in the Story

Appearance of the angel (Matt. 28:2). The angel (Luke and John mention two angels) had the appearance of lightning and was dressed all in white. It is interesting that there is no mention of wings (a feature not mentioned about angels in any biblical passage). In earliest ancient religious texts, the gods are often portrayed as shining brightly, so this is typical of heavenly beings.

"Not yet ascended to the Father" (John 20:17). Jesus suggested that Mary should not hold onto him as if she would never see him again. He had not yet returned to the Father and intended to spend a little time with his followers first.

Background Information

Rolled back the stone. Stones cut into a disk shape were rolled in a track to cover the opening of the tomb. The sizes varied greatly, but clearly this one was large enough that the women did not believe they could move it.

Spices. The purpose of the spices was to cover the odor of decomposition, since friends and family would visit the tomb for several days. The spices the women brought are not identified in the text, but spices used for burial were myrrh and aloe (see John 19:40). Aloe is powdered sandalwood that was used as perfume. Myrrh was used in the embalming process in Egypt.

Women. Some of the women named here were present at the crucifixion and had observed the cleaning of the body to prepare it for burial. These include Mary, the mother of Jesus; Mary of Magdala; Salome, mother of the two disciples James and John; Mary, the mother of James, who was perhaps the disciple James the son of Alphaeus; and Joanna, wife of Chuza, who managed the household of Herod Antipas. Mary of Magdala had supported the ministry of Jesus ever since he had cast seven demons out of her (Luke 8:2).

The town of Magdala was on the western shore of the Sea of Galilee, seven miles southwest of Capernaum.

Mistakes to Avoid

Overemphasizing certain details or trying to read between the lines can get the story off track. Each Gospel writer has given particular details for his own purposes. We read against the text when we speculate about elements that the author has chosen not to include. The focus here is the resurrection of Jesus.

132. The Ascension (Matthew 28:16–20; Luke 24:50–53; Acts 1:1–11)

Lesson Focus

Jesus ascended to the Father with the promise that he will return, and in the meantime he commissioned his followers to make disciples throughout the world.

- Jesus remains alive in heaven—he did not die.
- It was not just Jesus' spirit that ascended to heaven; his body did also.
- Jesus' commission is to make disciples.

Lesson Application

We can know that Jesus is in heaven today, and we make disciples while we await his return.

- We live in light of the belief that Jesus is ruling in heaven.
- We live in light of the belief that Jesus will soon return.
- We make disciples.
- We believe that Jesus is with us.

Biblical Context

The ascension is the conclusion in the synoptic Gospels, and it is the introduction to Acts, where it begins the story of the development of the church. Jesus' life on earth has come to an end. The beginning of his kingdom through the church and his reign over the kingdom from the right hand of the Father has begun.

Interpretational Issues in the Story

Father, Son, and Holy Spirit (Matt. 28:19). Though there are few places in the Bible that mention all three persons of the Godhead together, each, like this one, is clearly in support of a triune God—one God in three persons.

"Restore the kingdom" (Acts 1:6). It is not a surprise that the disciples still thought in terms of the restoration of the political kingdom, for this had been the focus of many prophecies. It is interesting that this is the last question they asked before Jesus was taken up.

Background Information

Location. There are varying traditions about precisely where the ascension took place. Some guides show a supposed footprint in the rock inside the Church of the Ascension, which was built in the fourth century and rebuilt by the Crusaders, but, of course, we simply do not have the information to be precise. Luke tells us that it was in the vicinity of Bethany (Luke 24:50) and records that the disciples returned from the Mount of Olives (Acts 1:12).

Timing. Luke tells us that Jesus was with the disciples over a period of forty days (Acts 1:3). This means that less than two weeks passed between the Ascension and Pentecost.

Mistakes to Avoid

Despite Jesus' words that no one knows the time when the kingdom will be restored, too often God's people have become distracted with such speculation, which leads to much divisiveness and inattention to kingdom work here on earth.

133. The Widow's Small Coin (Mark 12:38–44; Luke 21:1–4)

Lesson Focus

As wealthy people gave impressive gifts to the temple, a poor woman gave a small offering, but Jesus commented that it was greater than the rest because it was all she had.

- God knows the sacrifices we make.
- God is impressed when we give sacrificially.

- God recognizes self-importance, vanity, and hypocrisy and condemns them.

Lesson Application

We should be willing to give sacrificially.

- We ought to think about our giving.
- We must not be overly impressed with those who make a show of their piety.
- We evaluate whether we practice hypocrisy or are guilty of vanity.
- Our attitude in giving should reflect our devotion to God.

Biblical Context

In both Mark and Luke, this story comes right after Jesus' comments that the teachers of the law were acting pompously and given much respect, though privately they oppressed the poor. Jesus indicated that the poor woman was more worthy of respect. In both Gospels the story of the gifts to the temple leads into a discussion of the imminent destruction of the temple as one of the signs of the end of the age.

Interpretational Issues in the Story

Widows (Mark 12:42). In contrast to the teachers of the law, widows were the people of very low status in Jewish society and often had no means of support.

"Devour widows' houses" (Mark 12:40). This accusation against the teachers of the law sets up a contrast between the widow's gift and the gifts given by the wealthy. While she gave all, they hypocritically were involved in activities or rulings that allowed the property of widows to be seized. Such acrobatic interpretations of law were clearly contrary to compassion and the spirit of the law that sought to protect the vulnerable.

Background Information

Offering box. Tradition indicates that a number of collection boxes were set up in the court of women so that all could have access for giving any one of the regular temple gifts.

Two small copper coins. Calculations vary but most say that the two coins were equivalent to what someone would receive for about ten minutes of work. Given a minimum wage today of eight dollars per hour, the two coins were the spending equivalent of less than two dollars in our relatively wealthy culture.

Mistakes to Avoid

The story is not designed to encourage people to give all they have. It is likely more about the hypocrisy and vanity of the teachers and the wealthy than about the widow herself and her giving practices. It is the contrast that is important.

134. John the Baptist (Luke 1:5–25, 57–80; 3:1–20)

Lesson Focus

John the Baptist was God's special messenger, and his job was to tell everyone that Jesus was the Messiah, the promised deliverer.

- God sent John to prepare the way for Jesus.
- God provides warning and forgiveness for his people.
- God accomplishes his work through faithful people.
- God unfolds his plan in the fullness of time.

Lesson Application

Jesus is the Messiah that John the Baptist talks about.

- Once we know who Jesus is, we will want to tell others about him.
- We must be faithful to God and be ready to be used in whatever way he chooses.
- We should be aware of our need for repentance and forgiveness.

Biblical Context

This story is found only in Luke's Gospel. Luke's interests were the saving acts of God and the way that Jesus fulfilled the historical kingdom of God begun in the Old Testament. John the Baptist served as the one who proclaimed this role of Christ and ushered in his ministry.

Interpretational Issues in the Story

Elderly barren woman (Luke 1:7). The motif of an elderly barren woman was recognized by all Jews (compare Abraham's wife Sarah). It served as an indication that a child would have a special role to play in God's plan.

"He must not drink wine" (Luke 1:15). The instructions for John's way of life marked him as a Nazirite, reminiscent of Samson and Samuel.

Filled with the Holy Spirit from birth (Luke 1:15–17). This is similar to the role of the Spirit in the Old Testament, when he gave revelation from God to prophets (the word of God came to John [Luke 3:2]) and empowered people with authority for specific ministry. Endowment with the Spirit in this way met the needs of the moment. This is not the indwelling of the Spirit that comes when believers are forgiven for their sins.

"In the spirit and power of Elijah" (Luke 1:17). The people compared John to Elijah because, by this point in history, Elijah was considered the model prophet, and John showed some similarity to him (compare Mal. 4:5–6).

"Turn many . . . children of Israel to the Lord their God" (Luke 1:16). John was going to fill the role of prophet as he warned the people and led them in a return to covenant faithfulness and observance of the law.

"Take away my reproach" (Luke 1:25) and "shown great mercy" (Luke 1:58). In both the Old and New Testament worlds, the ability to bear children was a gift from God and the inability was seen as God's judgment. Those considered under God's judgment were despised and avoided. Women who could not bear children lived in disgrace, so when Elizabeth became pregnant, it was viewed as the mercy of God.

Circumcision and naming (Luke 1:59). Circumcision was the sign of the covenant and initiated the child into the covenant community. It was generally performed by a priest in an official ceremony eight days after birth. Because of the high rate of child mortality, it was not unusual to delay the official naming until the time of the ceremony.

Zechariah's prophecy (Luke 1:67–79). Zechariah's prophecy, or song (NIV), reflects the motifs connected with John's role of announcing the Messiah, whose reign would bring to Israel deliverance from her enemies, faithfulness to the covenant, and forgiveness of sins.

"Baptism of repentance for the forgiveness of sins" (Luke 3:3). In this period baptism was an act of purification symbolizing cleansing from ritual and moral defect.

Message of judgment (Luke 3:7–9, 17). Like the prophets of old, John rebuked his audience for their sins and proclaimed the approaching judgment. He indicated that the Messiah would do the same. He also instructed them concerning the right path to follow.

Background Information

Time of Herod. John was born just a few months before Jesus was born, during the time of Herod the Great, who died about 4 BC.

Division of duty. The priests at this time were set into twenty-four divisions that rotated in performing service at the temple. Each had a one-week assignment twice each year. For the most prestigious jobs, lots were cast among those in the division to decide who would enjoy the privilege. The most coveted job was going into the antechamber of the temple to the altar of incense that stood right in front of the divider that cordoned off the Most Holy Place. Incense was offered twice each day.

Gabriel. Gabriel is known as one of the archangels and is one of only two identified by name in the Bible (the other is Michael).

Lived in the desert. Some have tried to associate John with one of the ascetic groups that lived in the wilderness, such as the Essenes or the Qumran community, but there is not enough information to be sure. John's food and clothing (Matt. 3:4; Mark 1:6) were reminiscent of Elijah and characteristic of those who dwelt in the wilderness. The camel skin cloak was waterproof and like sackcloth. John's diet was made up of that which could be gathered. Locusts (the insect, not the fruit of the locust tree as some occasionally suggest) were allowed in the Jewish diet (kosher) and were known to be eaten by the poor.

Date. Luke states that John was commissioned in "the fifteenth year of the reign of Tiberius Caesar, Pontius Pilate being governor of Judea, and Herod being tetrarch of Galilee" (3:1). This places the beginning of John's ministry in AD 27–28. Tiberius was the emperor in Rome; Herod the tetrarch was Herod Antipas who ruled in Galilee and was the son of Herod the Great; and Pilate was prefect (governor) from AD 26–36.

Mistakes to Avoid

Although the Bible designates John as John the Baptist, baptizing people was not his most important function. The Gospel writers present him as the one who proclaimed the coming Messiah, Jesus. His baptisms played a part in preparing people for the ministry of Jesus, but he was first and foremost a prophet.

135. The Angel and Mary (Luke 1:26–38)

Lesson Focus

God told of his plan to send the promised anointed one to Israel. Mary would bear God's son, Jesus.

- Jesus is the Messiah.
- Jesus is the Son of God.
- Jesus will bring salvation.

Lesson Application

We thank God that he sent his Son, Jesus, to be our Savior.

- We believe that Jesus is the Son of God.
- We acknowledge that Jesus is King.
- We trust Jesus for salvation.

Biblical Context

The angel visiting Mary is found only in Luke's Gospel. Luke's interests were the saving acts of God and the way that Jesus fulfilled the historical kingdom of God begun in the Old Testament. These elements are evident in the birth announcement in the proclaimed name Jesus, *Yeshua*, which pointed to God's salvation (1:31) and the Savior's intended role—reigning on David's throne in a kingdom that will not end (1:32–33).

Interpretational Issues in the Story

Descendant of David (Luke 1:27). Naming the ancestor of Joseph was important to establish that Jesus would be of royal lineage and would have legitimate claims as the Messiah.

Angel (Luke 1:28). Angels are messengers of God. They may or may not look different from regular people, and in fact people can also be designated as God's messengers. There is no reason to doubt that the angel in Luke 1 was a heavenly being, but notice that Mary was greatly troubled by his words rather than terrified at his appearance.

Birth announcement (Luke 1:31–33). Commonly, those who were to have an important role in God's ongoing plan had their birth announced by God or his messengers (cf. Isaac, Samson, and Samuel).

Born of the Holy Spirit as the Son of God (Luke 1:32, 35). The angel's announcement contains important theological facts concerning the very nature of Jesus. Without human father, he is both divine and human. Jesus is human in all the senses we are, including that he lived, suffered, and died, as we do. Jesus is divine because he is fully God; he is one with the Father. Jewish expectations concerning the coming Messiah did not include divinity, so the angel's revelation added to their understanding.

Background Information

Gabriel. Gabriel is known as one of the archangels and is one of only two angels identified by name in the Bible (the other is Michael).

City of Galilee named Nazareth. Nazareth was a small village of little importance. It was not on the major trade routes and it was never even mentioned in the Old Testament.

Virgin betrothed. Marriages were typically arranged by parents. Marriage arrangements were often made by formal contract between the couple's families when the children were young. Marriage often took place soon after the young girl became fertile, between the ages of twelve and fourteen. Mary was likely quite young.

Mistakes to Avoid

Do not speculate on the appearance of the angel and how astonishing it might have been to Mary. The text passes by all such information to focus on the message concerning the nature of Jesus, and the lesson should do the same. Likewise, we have little information about Mary and should be reserved with what we say. The text indicates that she was favored, but it gives no information about why she was favored. The favor might lie in the fact that she was chosen, without merit, as Abraham and Moses were, for a particular divine work. The point is that we should be reluctant to fill in gaps with our speculations about details. Discussions about the theological importance of the virgin birth and the significant role of Jesus as Messiah should be reserved for older children.

136. Jesus Is Born (Luke 2:1–7)

Lesson Focus

Jesus, the promised Son of God, was born.

- Complex situations came together to insure that Jesus was born in Bethlehem.
- Jesus was born in a humble rather than a luxurious setting.

Lesson Application

We thank God that he sent Jesus to be our Savior.

- We should recognize that God is in control of events and circumstances and that all is working out according to his plan.
- We should be aware that God will not always do things in the ways that we might expect.

Biblical Context

This story is found only in Luke's Gospel. Luke's interests were in the saving acts of God and the way that Jesus fulfilled the historical kingdom of God begun in the Old Testament. In this account we can see how events in the wider world have providentially led to the circumstances of Jesus' birth to a family in the line of David.

Interpretational Issues in the Story

"Wrapped him in swaddling cloths" (Luke 2:7). It was the practice at this time to wrap newborn infants in strips of cloth. It was believed that this would help their limbs to stay straight.

Manger (Luke 2:7). Archaeological finds from this period indicate that the manger was likely made of stone rather than wood. A stable is not mentioned but often inferred by teachers or in curriculum. If there was a stable involved, it was likely a cave (indicated in some of the earliest sources concerning the birth of Jesus) rather than an independent wooden structure. An alternative is that homes in this period sometimes used an area on the ground floor or in the courtyard for the keeping of a few animals, while the people lived upstairs or in surrounding rooms. With no rooms available in the living quarters, the area for the animals could have been used by Mary and Joseph. This would explain the mention of a manger with no reference to a stable. One other possibility is that in this time period there were buildings known as *caravanserai* that gave shelter to travelers, and these had mangers. Such shelters were more comparable to a modern truck stop or rest area along a turnpike than to a hotel or motel. So, the possible setting of the manger here was a rock-like cave-stable, a first floor or courtyard area of a private dwelling used for animals, or a caravansary.

Inn (Luke 2:7). The word sometimes translated "inn" generally refers to guest rooms in a house rather than to public commercial establishments. There was no innkeeper, but only those who lived in the house. The word for "inn" is the same Greek word used to describe the Upper Room where Jesus and his disciples had the Last Supper. Some modern translations reflect this: "No guest room available for them" (TNIV) and "No lodging available for them" (NLT).

Background Information

Caesar Augustus. Known as Octavian, he was born in 63 BC, and his rule began as part of a triumvirate (three rulers of equal authority) after the death of his great-uncle Julius Caesar in 44 BC. The next fifteen years saw struggles between the three rulers until Octavian emerged as sole ruler in 27 BC. He died in AD 14.

Registration. In the Roman Empire a census was taken every fourteen years and would have involved a tax being collected.

Quirinius, governor of Syria. From ancient sources, Quirinius was known as governor of Syria during the census taken in 6 AD (which Luke knew of and references in Acts 5:37), but the registration Luke mentions as occurring under Quirinius must have been an earlier census taken when Herod the Great was king. Herod died in 4 BC, so this census must have been earlier. It is confusing to think of Jesus being born in 6 or 5 BC, but the discrepancy is the result of miscalculations when the Julian calendar was instituted several centuries later.

Nazareth to Bethlehem. The distance between the two cities is approximately seventy miles. Walking took a week or two, depending on what pace they set. It is commonly assumed that Mary was riding on a donkey (unmentioned in the text), believing that Joseph would have been sensitive to her pregnancy, although that mode of transportation may have not been an improvement. We just don't know how they traveled; Joseph (a carpenter) may have made a pull cart of some sort.

Betrothed. Marriages were typically arranged by parents. Marriage arrangements were often made by formal contract between the couple's families when the children were young. Marriage often took place soon after the young girl became fertile, between the ages of twelve and fourteen. Mary was likely quite young. The pledge (NIV) refers to the fact that the families had sealed the agreement even though the marriage had not been consummated.

Bethlehem. A small town located about five miles south of Jerusalem, its claim to fame was that David had been born and raised there. Otherwise, it had no great significance. That was about to change. Luke was interested in more than simply giving a location or even in showing the fulfillment of prophecy (Mic. 5:2). A new David, the Messiah who is the ideal king from David's line, was being born in Bethlehem just as David had been.

Mistakes to Avoid

Stories as well-known as this are embellished by many traditions. In general, teachers should strive to keep to the details given in the text rather than adding to them with traditions or speculations. Some of the traditions come from Christmas carols, such as "Away in the Manger" with the lyrics, "No crying he makes," portraying Jesus as an extraordinary baby. He was a unique being, but he was fully human and in that regard would have acted like any other baby. There are many similar examples of such portrayals, and while teachers may not feel inclined to try to correct all these, they can avoid perpetuating them.

137. Christmas Shepherds (Luke 2:8–20)

Lesson Focus

The shepherds witness and proclaim the coming of the promised Savior.

- God brings deliverance and peace to his people through Christ.
- God's kingdom is for all people.
- God provides a Savior.

Lesson Application

We praise God for sending Jesus.

- We praise God and acknowledge who Jesus is.
- We accept that Jesus brought salvation.

Biblical Context

This story is found only in Luke's Gospel. Luke's interests are in the saving acts of God and the way that Jesus fulfills the historical kingdom of God begun in the Old Testament. Here, Luke demonstrates that the kingdom of God is for all the people, as the announcement of Savior and King is made to common shepherds. Luke's interests are shown in this story most strongly by the fact that Jesus is born in Bethlehem as a new David, the ideal King, the Messiah they have long awaited. The angelic announcement to the shepherds includes key terms on these themes such as "city of David," "Savior," "Christ" (Messiah), and "peace."

Interpretational Issues in the Story

"Glory of the Lord shone" (Luke 2:9). All the way back into ancient times, deity and the messengers of deity were portrayed as shining brightly, and that is the case here. It is this glory that terrified the shepherds. Later,

artists used the convention of halos to express this. No other distinguishing features are mentioned. There is no reason textually or historically to visualize these angels as dressed all in white (though some angels were, as at the garden tomb [Matt. 28:3; Mark 16:5; John 20:12; Acts 1:10]) or as having wings.

Angelic praise (Luke 2:14). God's glory extends from the heavenly realms ("in the highest [heavens]") to the earth. Other translations of the words vary—"good will toward men" (NKJV) and "peace to men on whom his favor rests" (NIV)—based on one Greek letter difference in the manuscripts. The text says that this was spoken by the angels, making the idea of an angelic chorus or angel song speculative.

Background Information

Shepherds. There is no reason to think of shepherds as worse than other people or lowlier, though later rabbinic literature suggests they were despised. In one sense they can be seen as part of the "David" picture, since he was taking care of sheep when chosen to be king. The announcement to shepherds also fits the profile of the humble circumstances of Jesus' birth and the focus of his coming to bring the kingdom to all. Finally, "shepherd" is a metaphor for leadership and kingship in the Bible, and Jesus will identify himself as the Great Shepherd.

Living out in the field. Some have suggested that the shepherds were watching sheep that belonged to the temple that were to be used for sacrifices. The proximity of Bethlehem to Jerusalem makes that a possibility. If so, it is possible that these sheep were kept out in the fields all year long, even during the winter rainy season. Indoor facilities could not provide enough space to accommodate large herds, and they had to graze.

Time of year. The choice of December 25 to celebrate Christmas was not made based on historical analysis of the text or traditions. It was selected in the fourth century to counter the pagan celebration of Saturnalia, which coincides with the winter solstice.

Good news of a Savior. A few decades earlier, the birth of Emperor Augustus, who was viewed as a god, had been declared as good news of a savior. The angel makes a similar claim for Jesus in relation to the Jewish expectation of Messiah (in Greek, Christ). Furthermore, Augustus was admired for having established the *Pax Romana*, a time of relative peace and security throughout the Roman world. The deliverance that Jesus came to offer his people is true peace, not just stability.

Mistakes to Avoid

Since the angels are referred to as "heavenly host," it is traditional to portray them as being in the sky. But the text suggests no such thing; angels appearing in the sky has no precedent. Angels are heavenly host because they come from heaven, not because they are seen in heaven. Since the most familiar stories in the Bible have had the most traditions grow up around them, it is important to keep the focus on the biblical details. Furthermore, emulating the shepherds is not the point of the lesson. We should recognize what God was doing, acknowledge Jesus, and tell others about him, but the point of the lesson is who God is and what he has done.

138. Anna and Simeon (Luke 2:21–39)

Lesson Focus

God revealed to Simeon and then to Anna that Jesus is the promised anointed one sent to redeem Israel. They thanked God.

- God provided a king.
- God provided a savior.
- God had promised to provide a savior, and he fulfilled his promise.

Lesson Application

We can believe what God says. God always keeps his promises.

- We believe that God will do all that he says he will do.

Biblical Context

This story is found only in Luke's Gospel. Luke's interests were in the saving acts of God and the way that Jesus fulfills the historical kingdom of God begun in the Old Testament. Both Simeon and Anna emphasize this aspect of Jesus' work. Notice particularly that Simeon includes both Gentiles and Jews in the salvation.

Interpretational Issues in the Story

Simeon (Luke 2:25). We don't know anything about Simeon except what is told here. We cannot assume that he was a priest just because he was encountered in the temple courts.

"Waiting for the consolation of Israel" (Luke 2:25). The comfort that

had been offered to Israel by the prophets (e.g., see Isaiah 40) had to do with the nation's restoration and had come to be associated with the expectation of a messianic kingdom.

Holy Spirit was upon him (Luke 2:25). This is similar to the role of the Spirit in the Old Testament, when he gave revelation from God to prophets and empowered people with authority for specific ministry. Endowment with the Spirit in this way met the needs of the moment. What occurred here is not the indwelling of the Spirit that comes when believers are forgiven for their sins.

"Revelation to the Gentiles" (Luke 2:32). In Christ there is not only the continuation of the kingdom of God but the expansion of the kingdom to the Gentiles.

"Fall and rising" (Luke 2:34). Jesus is both a stone of stumbling and a foundation for hope and deliverance.

Piercing sword (Luke 2:35). This anticipates the suffering of Jesus.

A prophetess (Luke 2:36). As an acknowledged prophetess, Anna's assessment of Jesus' destiny would have been taken very seriously.

"Did not depart from the temple . . . night and day" (Luke 2:37). This indicates Anna's constant devotion. People could not live in the temple courts, and if one fasted night and day, one would soon die.

"Redemption of Jerusalem" (Luke 2:38). This is a parallel to Isaiah 52:9: "The LORD has comforted his people; he has redeemed Jerusalem."

Background Information

Circumcision. Circumcision was the sign of the covenant and initiated the child into the covenant community. It was generally performed by a priest in an official ceremony eight days after birth. Because of the high rate of child mortality, it was not unusual to delay the official naming until the time of the ceremony.

Purification. The mother was ritually unclean from childbirth for forty days (seven days until the circumcision and thirty-three after it [Lev. 12:4]).

Present him to the Lord. As the text indicates (Luke 2:22), they presented him in this fashion because he was a firstborn child and had to be redeemed. This was not an act of devotion but a required ritual, nor was it a dedication to ministry or service.

Temple. Since Mary and Anna were present, the reference must be to the court of women.

Mistakes to Avoid

The point of the lesson is not that we are to be faithful and patient like Simeon or to tell others about Jesus like Anna but to give us an example of why we should have confidence that God will do what he says he will do. God has kept his promise to send a Savior, and we need to respond to him.

139. The Boy Jesus in the Temple (Luke 2:41–52)

Lesson Focus

Jesus showed his awareness that he was the Son of God, though he continued to develop as a normal child. His parents did not fully comprehend.

- Jesus showed early awareness of his identity and mission.
- Jesus demonstrated his wisdom at an early age.
- Jesus kept the law in ritual by attending the feast and in behavior by obeying his parents.

Lesson Application

Jesus is the Son of God.

- We acknowledge the developing credentials of Jesus.
- We believe that Jesus is the Messiah.

Biblical Context

This story is found only in Luke's Gospel. Luke's interests were in the saving acts of God and the way that Jesus fulfilled the historical kingdom of God begun in the Old Testament. Those elements are not accented in this narrative, but it illustrates Jesus' awareness of his mission as it characterizes him as a respectful prodigy.

Interpretational Issues in the Story

Passover (Luke 2:41). The Law of Moses required every male to come to the temple for Passover and the associated Feast of Unleavened Bread each year (Deut. 16:6, 16). Many did not make the trip. Joseph and Mary, however, were conscientious in their observance. Others were as well, and these annual pilgrimages were times for families to travel together. Jerusalem was always crowded on such occasions.

Teachers in the temple (Luke 2:46). The spacious temple courts with their shaded porticos were natural places for students and teachers to gather, formally or informally, to discuss the law and the Scriptures.

Amazed at his understanding (Luke 2:47). The Old Testament spoke of a Messiah who was filled with knowledge and understanding (Isaiah 11), and Luke presents Jesus as having just such qualities.

Background Information

Twelve years old. There is no evidence for *bar mitzvah* celebrations this early in history, but the mention of Jesus' age suggests Luke's emphasis on the fact that Jesus was not yet a recognized adult. This was not the first time Jesus visited the temple (2:41). The Gospels give us the impression that Mary and Joseph were observant Jews, which means that they would have made pilgrimage to the temple three times each year. This visit is significant because of the way Jesus impressed the rabbis.

Nazareth. Nazareth was a small village of little importance. It was not on the major trade routes and it is never mentioned in the Old Testament. Even though Nazareth was at a higher elevation than Jerusalem, they "went down . . . to Nazareth" (2:51) because their initial path led down from Jerusalem. The trip took four or five days each way traveling by foot.

Mistakes to Avoid

It may be appealing to teach children that Jesus obeyed his parents and therefore they should be like him in that way. One could hardly object to the truth of such a lesson, but we must ask whether Luke has told this story to urge children to obey their parents. We suggest that though we cannot go wrong when we seek to be like Jesus, Luke was not trying to urge his readers to obey parents any more than he was instructing them to go to Jerusalem when twelve years old or to make sure to ask questions of teachers. Luke notes that Jesus obeyed his parents so that we might understand the character of Jesus. Even that is a side remark, not the main point, which is Jesus' awareness of his mission.

140. Rejection in Nazareth (Luke 4:16–31)

Lesson Focus

Jesus read from the prophets in the synagogue at Nazareth and announced that the prophecy is being fulfilled. The people rejected him and attempted to kill him.

- Jesus is the Messiah.
- Jesus brought deliverance and the kingdom of God.
- Jesus was to be rejected by the Jews and the kingdom extended to the Gentiles.

Lesson Application

We should recognize that Jesus fulfilled prophecy by bringing deliverance as the Messiah.

- We acknowledge that Jesus is the Messiah.
- We accept his offer to become part of the kingdom of God.

Biblical Context

This story is found only in Luke's Gospel. Luke's interests were in the saving acts of God and the way that Jesus fulfilled the historical kingdom of God begun in the Old Testament. He put this narrative first in the reports of Jesus' ministry to draw out the basic theme of deliverance as prophesied in Isaiah 61:1–2. In this account Jesus gives hints that the kingdom of God is going to be opened to Gentiles when the Jews reject him—a universalistic theme common in Luke.

Interpretational Issues in the Story

"Today this Scripture has been fulfilled" (Luke 4:21). Luke was showing how the teaching of Jesus focused on the kingdom of God that was bringing deliverance to Israel. This deliverance was associated with the coming of the Messiah, so when Jesus identified the kingdom as having arrived, he was implying that he is the Messiah. The Scripture was fulfilled by Messiah initiating the prophesied program of deliverance.

"No prophet is acceptable in his hometown" (Luke 4:24). The people appear initially accepting (v. 22), but Jesus was aware of their underlying doubts and antagonism, which emerged when he addressed the matter forthrightly. It is worthy of note that the examples he gave do not just involve different Israelite towns but prophets going to Gentiles. So, even this early in his ministry, he was talking about rejection by the Jews and the offering of the gospel to Gentiles. This would explain why they reacted against him so strongly. Finally, there is an interesting wordplay not evident in translation. The last word of Jesus' reading from Isaiah (v. 18), "favor," is in Greek the same word that Jesus used when he says that a prophet enjoys no "favor" in his hometown (v. 24).

"Throw him down the cliff" (Luke 4:29). This was not necessarily a high precipice. In Jewish legal practice, someone executed by stoning was cast down by one of the witnesses over a precipice that had to be at least twice the height of the one to be executed. Large stones were thrown down on top of him, with the trial witnesses throwing the first ones. This was likely the intention of the crowd. If the event here was a prelude to stoning, we would not expect a high cliff. It would also indicate a radical response to Jesus, since Jews under Roman rule were not allowed to carry out execution in this period and usually would have been reticent to do so on the Sabbath.

Background Information

Nazareth. The first stage of Jesus' ministry is called the "Great Galilean Ministry" and here it reached his hometown of Nazareth. Luke placed this at the beginning of that stage, though his reference to the activities in Capernaum (4:23) indicate that Mark in his Gospel ordered his account more chronologically (see Mark 6:1–6). Though the period of the Great Galilean Ministry is characterized by Jesus' spreading popularity, the people of Nazareth were not so accepting. Nazareth was a small village of little importance. It was not on the major trade routes, and it is never mentioned in the Old Testament. It is located in the hills just west of Mount Tabor along the northern rim of the Valley of Jezreel.

Reading in the synagogue. Information about synagogue procedures and services is only available from later rabbinic literature, and it is unknown what practices were in place at this time. Readings from the Law and the Prophets were likely, accompanied by liturgical recitation of prayers. Since many were not fluent in Hebrew, explanation in Aramaic of the passages is presumed to have been common, which would lead into a homily of sorts. When Jesus sat, it did not mean that he was done but that the reading of Scripture had ended and the explanation was ready to begin; thus all eyes were on him.

Scroll. Scrolls were made of either papyrus or leather parchment sheets glued together. A scroll was typically about thirty-five feet long and maybe a foot wide.

Mistakes to Avoid

Teachers should be careful about how they talk about the issue of prophecy fulfillment. Jesus fulfilled many prophecies in many different ways. Some were traditionally associated with Messiah, and he fulfilled them in expected ways. Others traditionally attached to Messiah he fulfilled in unexpected ways, partially, or not at all. Still other prophecies that he fulfilled had not been associated with Messiah by any interperters. In many cases, identifying fulfillment was and continues to be a matter of interpretation, and differences of opinion are to be expected.

141. Jesus Anointed (Luke 7:36–50)

Lesson Focus

While Jesus was eating at the house of a Pharisee, a woman came and anointed Jesus' feet. He taught about forgiveness and forgave her sins.

- Jesus has the power to forgive sins.
- Jesus responds to love and faith.
- Jesus was sensitive toward sinners and did not ignore them.

Lesson Application

Jesus is willing and able to forgive our sins no matter how great they may be when we love him and have faith and ask.

- We respond to Jesus with faith and love.
- We believe that Jesus can and will forgive our sins.

Biblical Context

This story is found only in Luke's Gospel. Luke's interests are in the saving acts of God and the way that Jesus fulfills the historical kingdom of God begun in the Old Testament. This account is one in a series about how Jesus responded to people who were outcasts yet who showed faith. Jesus healed the Roman centurion's son (7:1–10), raised the dead son of the poor widow (7:11–17), and here forgave the sin of a woman known to be immoral. This helps show the nature of the kingdom of God and the salvation Jesus brings.

Interpretational Issues in the Story

Kissed Jesus and anointed his head with oil (Luke 7:45–46). These actions Jesus mentioned were not common amenities offered in hospitality; they were exceptional. Nevertheless, they pale in comparison to the lavishness of the woman's demonstration. If the host had gone to the extent of giving water for his feet, or greeting him with a kiss, or even so far as anointing his head with oil, he would have been considered gracious to a fault. But this woman provided the water of her own tears, anointed his feet with perfume, and washed his feet with her hair as she kissed them. Her actions should be noted as extraordinary rather than criticized.

Forgiveness. Forgiveness was offered by priests when sacrifices were offered in the temple. Here Jesus took on the role of priest and recognized the woman's act as an expression of remorse and her anointing with oil as a sacrificial act, so he forgave her sins. This should not be understood as the same type of forgiveness provided by Christ on the cross but the type that was available for restoration of relationship through the sacrificial system.

Background Information

Dinner setting. It was common for famous itinerant teachers to receive an invitation to dine with prominent citizens. The setting for the meal was open so that uninvited guests could easily drift in to listen. The guests reclined on their sides at the table with their feet extending out, away from the table. This would have given the woman access to Jesus' feet, though she might have preferred to anoint his head.

Hair. In order to use her hair to wipe Jesus' feet, she had to uncover and loosen it. Since the hair was considered part of a woman's sexual and social identity, this was a somewhat shocking act and could have been interpreted as risqué. Added to the woman's disreputable social status, it is no surprise the host was scandalized.

Mistakes to Avoid

Some details of the story are inappropriate for younger children, yet without them it is questionable whether they will understand the significance of it.

142. Good Samaritan (Luke 10:25–37)

Lesson Focus

A Samaritan traveler showed love to a Jewish man who had been robbed and beaten after two priestly travelers had passed him by and refused to help.

- God sees no limits to who should be considered our "neighbor."
- The law of love has priority over ritual law in the kingdom of God.

Lesson Application

We should show selfless love to all indiscriminately.

- We find our kingdom identity in how we love others.
- We are willing to treat anyone as our neighbor and therefore a worthy recipient of our love.

Biblical Context

This story is found only in Luke's Gospel. Luke's interests were in the saving acts of God and the way that Jesus fulfilled the historical kingdom of God begun in the Old Testament. The kingdom of God is more properly characterized by love than by its unswerving commitment to Jewish law.

Interpretational Issues in the Story

Jesus tested (Luke 10:25). Use of the word *test* suggests that opponents were giving Jesus difficult and controversial questions in an attempt to discredit or accuse him. If they could expose any flaws in Jesus, his popularity might diminish.

Parable focus. Parables are neither historical accounts nor allegories in which everything in the parable stands for something. Sometimes the people or situations are intentionally exaggerated to make a point. Many parables are about the nature of the kingdom of God. The principle in this parable is that we should not try to set limits on who counts as our neighbor. Here Jesus shows that our neighbor is anyone whom we can help.

Priest and Levite (Luke 10:31–32). By identifying the travelers as priestly personnel rather than simply as Jews, Jesus intended to expose which has the greatest value—law or love. The priestly personnel were concerned with ritual purity above all else. It is interesting to note, however, that the ritual experts were traveling away from the temple, not toward it.

Love command (Luke 10:27). The statement of the two great commandments is central to the teaching of Jesus and combines Deuteronomy 6:5 and Leviticus 19:18.

Eternal life (Luke 10:25). The lawyer asked Jesus about gaining eternal life. Because Jesus had not yet died and provided for eternal life as we understand it, he was addressing here the Jewish concept of eternal life, a common issue for theological debate. For Jews, eternal life meant enjoying life in the future world, which, in their view, was generally attained by faithfulness to the covenant. That is why the lawyer answered Jesus with the two great commandments. The conversation then turned to a question about how one should live out faithfulness to the covenant. Jesus was more interested in talking about the present kingdom of God than future eternal life, but faithfulness to the covenant is an important aspect of inheriting the kingdom of God.

"You go, and do likewise" (Luke 10:37). Jesus' words are not a directive to help injured people per se but to expand our definition of what love requires and who is our neighbor. We are called to have this sort of kingdom mentality.

Background Information

Jerusalem to Jericho. The seventeen-mile trip involved a descent of about 3,500 feet through barren wilderness that often provided refuge for robbers and opportunity for their villainy. Despite the desolate landscape, frequent traffic moved between the two cities, so it would not have been long before someone passed by to give help. A hearty traveler could make the trip in a day (especially downhill toward Jericho). But the inn located along the way could serve the needs of more casual travelers.

Corpse defilement. If the priest and Levite suspected that the beaten man was dead, they might have been concerned about the inconvenience of contracting an unclean condition if they were to touch him. Jewish law, however, required people to help someone whose life was in jeopardy or to bury a neglected corpse, even though such acts would render them unclean.

Samaritans and Jews. Samaritans were despised by the Jews as tainted and unclean. Samaritans were unable to worship in the temple in Jerusalem and had their own temple on Mount Gerizim. The mutual feelings of hate had at various times in history resulted in armed conflict.

Oil and wine for treating wounds. Oil and wine were used for washing and disinfecting.

Two denarii. This sum would have provided care for about two weeks.

Mistakes to Avoid

Those in God's kingdom will not exclude anyone from being considered a neighbor. The text does not go so far as saying that everyone is our neighbor, for we cannot help everyone. We also should not liken the Samaritan to Jesus as one who comes to our rescue in times of crisis. When Jesus instructed his audience to "go, and do likewise," he was not encouraging us to be like the Samaritan. The Samaritan is an illustration of a much larger principle: there are infinite ways that we can love our neighbor as ourselves. It should also be noted that the parable is not concerned with making sure that people love themselves but that they should love others as if they were ourselves. The parable is an elaboration of the golden rule and focuses on a selfless love. To make things understandable to children, teachers might explain eternal life as being citizens of God's kingdom rather than "live forever in heaven" or "live forever with God."

143. Mary and Martha (Luke 10:38–42)

Lesson Focus

Jesus showed Martha that listening to him is the most important thing a person can do.

- Jesus values attention to his teaching.
- Learning at the feet of Jesus is a higher priority than taking care of the details of life.

Lesson Application

Listening to Jesus and obeying him is more important than anything else we do.

- As disciples, we take time to learn from Jesus rather than getting caught up in the busyness of life.
- We seek appropriate priorities and balance in life as we serve God.

Biblical Context

This account is given only in Luke's Gospel and follows the parable of the Good Samaritan. It is in turn followed by Jesus' teaching on prayer. As such, it provides perspectives on true discipleship.

Interpretational Issues in the Story

Jesus and his disciples (Luke 10:38). The group is portrayed as traveling together, but the text mentions only Jesus coming to a village and Martha opening her home to him. This leaves it somewhat uncertain as to whether Jesus only was being shown hospitality or his entire troupe. We might assume that by inviting Jesus, his retinue was thereby included, with the singular pronouns indicating that Jesus was the focus. If all the disciples were included, it is easy to see why Martha was overwhelmed and even more shocking that Mary seated herself at Jesus' feet among the disciples.

Distracted by the preparations (Luke 10:40). This account serves as an interesting counterpoint to the story of the Good Samaritan, where assumption could be made that the priest and the Levite should have abandoned their perceived religious duties in order to serve the needs of another. Here Martha was working at serving the needs of others, as the Samaritan had done. She was not told to do otherwise, but neither was Mary condemned for the choice she made. Thus this narrative brings some balance to the previous parable.

Background Information

Location. We find out from other passages that Mary and Martha and their brother Lazarus lived in Bethany, just east of Jerusalem (the other side of the Mount of Olives).

Sitting at the Lord's feet. This expression is used to describe a disciple learning from a master (see Acts 22:3). As such Mary's behavior is unorthodox, if not shocking, since the disciples who attached themselves to rabbis in this period were consistently male. Women were not educated but taught the responsibilities of running a household, as Martha was doing.

Mistakes to Avoid

Notice that Jesus did not tell Martha that she ought to put aside her work and join Mary at his feet. He said only that what Mary had chosen would not be taken from her. Though Mary's choice was identified as "good," there is no suggestion that all should choose that. Though Mary had chosen something good and Martha was told not to worry so much, this is not about praising Mary or rebuking Martha. It is about the nature of discipleship and the role of Jesus as one who is worthy of having disciples.

144. The Rich Fool (Luke 12:13–21)

Lesson Focus

The rich man thought only about the good life his possessions could give him, and he gave no attention to God, which did him no good at all in the long run.

- God will judge those who trust in their wealth.
- God's kingdom is focused on spiritual wealth.

Lesson Application

We must not be greedy. Rather, we should love God and other people more than we love our things.

- Trust God rather than possessions.
- Avoid greed, for wealth is fragile and death can come unexpectedly.
- Set spiritual priorities higher than material ones.

Biblical Context

This story is found only in Luke's Gospel. Luke's interests were in the saving acts of God and the way that Jesus fulfilled the historical kingdom of God begun in the Old Testament. Luke has more parables than the other Gospels and shows some common themes. This is the first parable about money and greed, with others occurring in Luke 16. The parable is followed with admonitions not to worry.

Interpretational Issues in the Story

Parable focus. Parables are not allegories in which everything in the parable stands for something. Sometimes the people or situations are intentionally exaggerated to make a point. Many parables are about the nature of the kingdom of God. Here, the emphasis might be that it is better to think and plan for the kingdom of God than for our own kingdom. Wealth is neither the measure of our success nor the source of our security.

"Eat, drink, be merry" (Luke 12:19). The phrase indicates a particular view of ancient Greek life that emphasized the importance of pleasure and leisure activities.

"Fool!" (Luke 12:20). This word has not only intellectual overtones but also spiritual and moral ones.

Background Information

Divide inheritance. Sometimes brothers chose to live in community without dividing the inheritance left to them by their father. Other times the inheritance was divided and each went his own way. Perhaps in this parable the brothers disagreed on which option should be followed. Alternatively, the older brother as the executor of the estate might have been stalling in disbursing the inheritance share to his brother.

Judge. While official squabbles among the Jews could be taken to the Sanhedrin and Pharisees could offer rulings on principles of law, rabbis were often called upon to settle disputes.

Storing grain. The man speaks of storing rather than selling. One could store grain for family use, but one family could use only so much over the course of a winter. The grain could also be stored for seed for the next year's planting so that more could be grown and harvested. This insured prosperity in the future, as the rich man notes. An alternative to storing the grain was to use it to provide for the needy.

Mistakes to Avoid

The parable focuses attention on lifestyle and attitude and does not condemn building projects or planning for the future.

145. The Lost Son (Luke 15:11–32)

Lesson Focus

Jesus tells the story of two sons estranged from their father in different ways and the father, who had compassion on both.

- God has compassion on his estranged children.
- God shows grace to the repentant.
- The kingdom is characterized by repentance and forgiveness.

Lesson Application

We should believe that God welcomes repentant sinners.

- We welcome the repentance of others and celebrate it.
- We believe that God is ready to forgive.
- We repent of our waywardness and selfishness.

Biblical Context

This story is found only in Luke's Gospel. Luke's interests were in the saving acts of God and the way that Jesus fulfilled the historical kingdom of God begun in the Old Testament. Luke announces the arrival of the kingdom of God as occurring in the year of the Lord's favor (4:18–19)—the language of Jubilee (Leviticus 25), which had come to be associated with the messianic kingdom. It was a time of forgiveness, compassion, and recovering that which had been lost. These are the themes of the parables in Luke 15.

Interpretational Issues in the Story

Parable focus. Parables are neither historical accounts nor allegories in which everything in the parable stands for something. Sometimes the people or situations in a parable are intentionally exaggerated to make a point. Many parables are about the nature of the kingdom of God. The principle in this parable is that sinners should recognize their need for repentance and know that their repentance is accepted and celebrated by a compassionate God. The righteous should also welcome the repentance of sinners and be willing to join in the celebration.

Attitude of Pharisees (Luke 15:2). The series of Luke's parables about lost things follows from the muttering of the Pharisees. The Pharisees tended to be self-righteous. They believed that they understood the law and so meticulously that they had little for which to repent. Consequently, they generally believed that they were better than other people.

"Sinned against heaven" (Luke 15:18). Sometimes the word *heaven* was used as a synonym for *God* in an attempt to be cautious about using God's name.

Background Information

Inheritance and caring for parents. Part of the inheritance gained by sons was to be used for the care of their parents. This son instead took his share and left, thinking only of his own pleasure and success.

Caring for pigs. No employment was more despised by a Jew than taking care of pigs. Impurity resulted even from touching them.

Robe, ring, and shoes. The robe was one of status, probably the father's robe. The ring was a signet ring that gave the son the right to do family business. The shoes, or sandals, distinguished him from servants, who had none.

Fattened calf. Meat was not common in the regular diet and was used primarily at large celebrations or in religious rituals.

Mistakes to Avoid

Allegorical approaches of the past portrayed the younger and older sons as representing the Gentiles and Jews, with God as the father. Others have suggested that the parable is a picture of Israel's exile and return. Most frequently the parable has been understood as representing the unclean "sinners" mentioned in 15:1 and the Pharisees (the older brother). But parables do not give a picture of reality using a one-to-one correspondence. The Pharisees were rebuked for their uncharitable attitude toward repentance, but that does not mean that the description of the elder brother is supposed to match up with the Pharisees at every point. This parable makes frequent use of hyperbole. The extremes of the callousness of the younger son making his demands, his profligate lifestyle, the depths to which he fell, the father's watchfulness and forfeiture of his dignity, and many other features show that this account is constructed on details that are unrealistic and unlikely.

The parable shows how God compassionately accepts the repentant into his kingdom. It should not be interpreted theologically much beyond that. It offers no theology or model of repentance and no detailed idea of God's plan for welcoming sinners. We cannot arbitrarily pick out a particular behavior evidenced by a character in a parable and conclude that we are thereby called to imitate or avoid that behavior. So, for example, this is not a lesson about being careful with our money or obeying our parents. If behavioral change were the point of a parable, that would be made clear.

146. Ten Lepers (Luke 17:11–19)

Lesson Focus

Jesus healed ten men of their skin disease, but only one, a Samaritan, came back to thank him.

- Jesus has compassion on the sick and outcast.
- Often the most unlikely people responded to Jesus.
- Jesus brings not only healing but restores to purity.

Lesson Application

We should recognize the role of Jesus and respond to him.

- We are thankful for what Jesus has done for us.
- We have faith in what Jesus says.

Biblical Context

This story is found only in Luke's Gospel. Luke's interests were in the saving acts of God and the way that Jesus fulfilled the historical kingdom of God begun in the Old Testament. The narrative continues a theme of Luke's in which the most unexpected individuals are the ones who respond to Jesus. Jesus notes that faith is responsible for healing the man.

Interpretational Issues in the Story

"Jesus, Master" (Luke 17:13). The term translated "Master" is used only in Luke and equates to "lord" or "sir."

"Show yourselves to the priests" (Luke 17:14). The priests declared people "clean" and thus able to rejoin society and engage in rituals (see Leviticus 13–14). For eligibility for participation in temple rituals, the priests at the temple had to approve. Before someone could reintegrate into the community, a priest or Levite in the town had to be consulted. The Samaritans worshiped at a different temple, but it had similar regulations.

"As they went" (Luke 17:14). It is noteworthy that they were healed only when they acted in faith to go to show themselves to the priests.

"Your faith has made you well" (Luke 17:19). The Greek phraseology speaks of the man's faith saving him rather than making him well; however, Jesus is not talking about the man's being saved from his sins but about being delivered from his illness. In other instances of healing, mention is also made of forgiveness of sins, but that is not the case here. Even in those cases, the forgiveness of sins is comparable to that accomplished by the sacrificial system, not to what is offered by Christ after his death. "Saving" is a common theme in Luke's Gospel.

Background Information

Location. Along the border towns between Jewish Galilee and Samaria there were mixed populations. The text does not clarify what route Jesus took.

Leprosy. The term often translated "leprosy" is rarely, if ever, the modern form of leprosy known as Hansen's disease. The term used in the Bible refers to a variety of skin conditions, some mild, some serious. They were generally not life threatening but were significant because such conditions caused the afflicted to be cast out of society as unclean. People avoided the "unclean," not because the medical condition was contagious but because ritual impurity was. Such conditions were more devastating socially and ritually than medically. It is likely that these skin diseases were thought to make people unclean because death was unclean, and skin decay was characteristic of death.

Samaritan. The Samaritans were the descendants of those Israelites not deported to Babylon when Jerusalem was destroyed in the sixth century BC and of foreigners forcibly settled in Israel by the Babylonians. Intermarriage took place between these groups, and when the exiles returned from Babylon, they spurned those who had not been "purified by exile" and especially those who were now of mixed race. Thus, the Samaritans were considered unclean and Jews avoided any contact with them. Some even walked long distances to go around their territory instead of through it.

Mistakes to Avoid

One of the healed men went out of his way to come back and express his gratitude, but that does not mean that the focus of the story is about being thankful. It is at least equally important that the man was a Samaritan and that his return offered an opportunity to highlight his faith. The larger issue, then, is the importance of responding to Jesus in every way. The narrative offers insufficient evidence as to whether the healed man was spiritually transformed.

147. The Pharisee and the Tax Collector (Luke 18:9–14)

Lesson Focus

Jesus told a story about attitudes in prayer by means of a contrast between a proud Pharisee and a humble tax collector.

- God values the prayers of the humble.
- God is not impressed with self-righteousness.

Lesson Application

We should be humble before God and others.

- We must not look down on others.
- We seek God's mercy rather than try to impress him.
- We do good things as a response to a worthy God, not to impress him or others.

Biblical Context

This story is found only in Luke's Gospel. Luke's interests were in the saving acts of God and the way that Jesus fulfilled the historical kingdom of God begun in the Old Testament. The kingdom will establish justice for those whose cause is just (see the preceding parable in Luke 18:1–8). For those whose cause is not just and who are not characterized by justice (here, the tax collector) the kingdom is open to them if they come humbly before God and make known their requests for forgiveness and justice. In fact, it is open even to little children, which is the next topic in Luke.

Interpretational Issues in the Story

Parable focus. Parables are not allegories in which everything in the parable stands for something. Sometimes the people or situations in a parable are intentionally exaggerated to make a point. Many parables are about the nature of the kingdom of God. The principle in this parable is that humility before God is of higher value in God's kingdom than acts of piety.

The tax collector's prayer (Luke 18:11–12). Some translations say that he prayed *to* himself, but the whole point is that his prayer could be heard. In this time period people typically prayed aloud, not silently.

"Not like other men" (Luke 18:11). The primary fault of the Pharisee was not his extreme piety but his disdain for others.

Background Information

Pharisees. Pharisees were super-observant interpreters of the law and were highly respected by the Jews. Those listening to Jesus' description of the prayer of the Pharisee would not have reacted in a scornful manner but would have recognized features of extreme piety. Pharisees were often poor in material possessions but considered rich in spirituality, while tax collectors were often wealthy but considered morally destitute.

Tax collectors. Viewed as turncoats, tax collectors were despised by the population. Even the thought of one entering the temple was distressing. When people heard the prayer of the tax collector in the parable, they would have been surprised that he so readily acknowledged what was so obviously true and would not have expected the story to end up favoring the tax collector.

Praying at the temple. People could not go into the temple building even for prayer—only the priests were allowed inside. The Pharisee and the tax collector were in the temple court. Just as people come to the Western Wall in Jerusalem today to pray, people went to the temple complex to offer prayers.

Mistakes to Avoid

This parable is not intended to instruct in the posture of prayer, and there is no sense that either the Pharisee or the tax collector is presented for imitation. The Pharisee is not praying to show off to others around him, so no emphasis should be placed on praying aloud. Such was common practice. It is the attitude behind the words that needs to be stressed. It will be difficult for younger children to grasp the social dynamics necessary for understanding the story.

148. Zacchaeus (Luke 19:1–10)

Lesson Focus

Jesus showed Zacchaeus that he was loved even though he was a sinner.

- Jesus had compassion for the outcasts of society, whatever their crimes or economic station.
- The ministry of Jesus was to bring people to an understanding of the kingdom of God.

Lesson Application

Jesus loves us and came to save us, even though we are sinners.

- We recognize what we need to do to become participants in the kingdom of God.
- We respond to Jesus by repenting of our sinful ways.

Biblical Context

This story is found only in Luke's Gospel. Luke's interests were in the saving acts of God and the way that Jesus fulfilled the historical kingdom of God begun in the Old Testament. The story of Zacchaeus is found only in Luke, and its conclusion includes one of the most direct statements about Jesus and his mission—bringing salvation to the lost.

Interpretational Issues in the Story

"Half of my goods" (Luke 19:8). This is undoubtedly a significant gesture on the part of Zacchaeus, but without knowing how much he had, little more can be said. It is perhaps noteworthy that he indicated no intention to resign his position as chief tax collector.

"Restore it fourfold" (Luke 19:8). This amount became the common restitution for stealing, based on Old Testament law (Ex. 22:1).

"Son of Abraham" (Luke 19:9). Though in a general sense anyone born a Jew was a son of Abraham, those considered in violation of the covenant were also considered cut off from the benefits of the covenant; that is, they were no

longer accorded the status of full-fledged children of Abraham. Tax collectors fit easily in this category. Jesus reinstated him as a true son of Abraham in faith and practice.

"Son of Man" (Luke 19:10). This title is drawn from Daniel 7 and by New Testament times had come to be used as a title for the Messiah. Jesus often used it in reference to himself.

"To seek and to save the lost" (Luke 19:10). Throughout Luke, the concept of salvation has a focus on bona fide membership in the kingdom of God based on one's faith. The Gospel does not speak specifically of people's being saved from their sins by the atoning blood of Christ, which had yet to occur. In the aftermath of his death and resurrection, however, that would take its rightful place as integral to the understanding of the kingdom.

Background Information

Jericho. The Jericho of the New Testament was about a mile south of the Old Testament site and about seventeen miles from Jerusalem. It was an important customs station for those entering the territory from the east side of the Jordan River at the fords by Jericho and offered lucrative opportunities for tax collectors.

Chief tax collector. As chief tax collector Zacchaeus was a very important and wealthy person. He was in charge of appointing tax collectors for the region and received as commission a portion of all they collected. Tax collectors did much more than collect taxes from individuals' income or produce; they also collected tolls and customs from travelers and merchants.

Sycamore. Botanists specializing in studies of this region clarify that the tree Zacchaeus climbed was not the European or American sycamore but a relative of the fig tree that features low, wide limbs easy for climbing.

Tax collector and sinner. Tax collectors were easily identified as sinners because of the opportunities for abuse built into the system. They were also considered traitors because they profited from Roman rule.

Mistakes to Avoid

The point is not that we ought to be like Zacchaeus, but that we should understand the ministry of Jesus to the lost. We ought to be like Jesus in his compassion for the outcasts of society and to help them see their need for repentance. The lesson should not focus on the size of Zacchaeus—the text does not offer a lesson about overcoming particular obstacles or problems in order to see Jesus.

149. The Road to Emmaus (Luke 24:13–35)

Lesson Focus

Jesus showed that he had risen so we know he is God.

- Jesus rose from the dead and showed himself to people.
- It was necessary for Christ to suffer so that God's plan might be carried out.
- The Old Testament pointed to Jesus.

Lesson Application

Even though we cannot see Jesus as his friends did, we believe that he is alive.

- We believe that Jesus is alive.
- We believe that the suffering and death of Jesus was part of the plan of God.
- We believe that the Old Testament points to Jesus.

Biblical Context

Luke's interests were in the saving acts of God and the way that Jesus fulfilled the historical kingdom of God begun in the Old Testament. This account occurs only in Luke's Gospel and fits well with his overall purpose. It was necessary for Christ to suffer to bring salvation to the people, and this had historical roots in the Old Testament.

Interpretational Issues in the Story

"A man who was a prophet" (Luke 24:19). The description offered by the two walking on the Emmaus road is quite limited. They identified Jesus as a prophet and as one who spoke powerfully and did powerful deeds. They mentioned nothing about Jesus being Messiah or the Son of God.

"The one to redeem Israel" (Luke 24:21). Their comment suggests that their messianic hopes had been shattered by the crucifixion. It was not wrong to think that the Messiah was to bring redemption to Israel; it is clear, however, that they did not understand how that was going to happen.

"Was it not necessary that the Christ should suffer" (Luke 24:26). The tragic events of the last few days had not careened out of control; God's plan had been in action all along. The suffering of Christ was an essential part of this plan as Jesus died for the sins of all.

"He interpreted to them in all the Scriptures the things concerning himself" (Luke 24:27). Jesus was not suggesting that every Scripture directly foretold his coming but that hints are found throughout the Scriptures. The walk to Emmaus was not long enough for every part of Scripture to have been explained. Verse 44 does not suggest that every verse of Scripture had to be directly fulfilled by Christ but that everything that was written *about him* had to be fulfilled.

Background Information

Emmaus. The location of this village is unknown. Possibilities are known from other ancient literature but do not match the information given in Luke. Traditions identifying the site tend to be late (e.g., from the Crusader period).

Rose and returned. Assuming the two had left Jerusalem early in the morning soon after the news of the resurrection had been reported to the disciples, time for the seven-mile walk to Emmaus and the meal place the story at midday. The seven-mile return to Jerusalem would have been accomplished by dinner time.

Mistakes to Avoid

It might be tempting to try to identify the passages that Jesus expounded concerning himself, but doing so should be resisted. Certainly we know the Old Testament passages that formed the core of apostolic preaching in the New Testament, but those might not have been included in Jesus' discussion on the Emmaus road. The significance in this passage is not which passages were discussed but that Jesus identified the Old Testament as pointing to himself and his suffering, thus establishing his role in God's plan.

150. Doubting Thomas (Luke 24:36–49; John 20:19–29)

Lesson Focus

Jesus showed that he had risen so we know he is God.

- Jesus has risen from the dead.
- Jesus is God.

Lesson Application

Even though we cannot see Jesus as his friends did, we believe that he is alive.

- We believe that Jesus is risen.
- We believe that Jesus is God.
- We must not doubt, even though we have not seen Jesus.

Biblical Context

In John, this passage concludes with the identification of the purpose of his book. John has specifically written to give evidence that Jesus is God and that he rose from the dead. This is the climax—the appearance of the risen Christ. Jesus came in the flesh (John 1:14), and he was risen in the flesh. Luke's interests were in the saving acts of God and the way that Jesus fulfilled the historical kingdom of God begun in the Old Testament. His account records only the first appearance of Jesus to the disciples when Thomas was absent. Luke's emphasis was on the ways Christ fulfilled that which was written in the Scriptures.

Interpretational Issues in the Story

"Ate before them" (Luke 24:43). This is offered as evidence that Jesus is not just a disembodied spirit but has a body that is not only substantial (the touching of his hands and side) but functional.

Law, Prophets, and Psalms (Luke 24:44). These represent the three categories of the Jewish canon known at the time (the same books as the Protestant Old Testament). What we call the historical books were considered the "Former Prophets" by the Jews.

"Understand the Scriptures" (Luke 24:45). His teaching was not dealing with the meaning of the Scriptures in their context, but the way that the Scriptures were being fulfilled. The issues were the death and resurrection of Christ and the repentance and forgiveness that result.

"Promise of my Father" (Luke 24:49). This is a reference to the sending of the Holy Spirit that Jesus discussed with the disciples in the Upper Room (John 16:5–16).

"Receive the Holy Spirit" (John 20:22). This differs from what happened at Pentecost, which Luke references (Luke 24:49). What occurs here in John is similar to the role of the Spirit in the Old Testament when he came to empower with authority from God. This work of the Spirit would sustain the disciples until the endowment of the Holy Spirit at Pentecost fifty days later. This is similar to when Jesus received empowerment from the Holy Spirit for

his ministry at his baptism. Endowment with the Spirit met the needs of the moment. In John 20:22 this was not the indwelling of the Spirit that comes when believers are forgiven for their sins; it is the empowering that gave the disciples authority to forgive sins.

Power to forgive sins (John 20:23). The practice of baptism for the forgiveness of sins was a means of dispensing forgiveness. The apostles had the wherewithal to detect those who had not truly repented (see Acts 8:9–25). We might also see this as a transference of authority to the disciples in the newly forming Christian community, similar to how the Sanhedrin operated in the Jewish community. Just as God had given Moses the authority and insight to judge cases among the Israelites, the Spirit will enable disciples to act as judges in the Christian community. We see Peter playing this role in Acts 5:1–11.

Background Information

Evening of the first day of the week. This is the same day the women went to the tomb (perhaps twelve to fifteen hours have passed), and the same day that the risen Christ walked with the two on the road to Emmaus.

Thomas. The Aramaic name Thomas, like the Greek alternative, Didymus, means twin. Consequently, this may be more of a label or nickname than a personal name. Some early traditions give Thomas the name Judas, by which we might conclude that he went by the name Thomas so as not to be confused with Judas Iscariot (which also could explain why Judas was often identified by his second label, Iscariot). Some early church literature indicates that Thomas eventually worked in Parthia as the disciples spread around the Roman world. Other sources place him in India. Clement has him located in Alexandria. The name of Thomas is attached to several literary works in the centuries that followed, including the *Acts of Thomas* (third century), the *Gospel of Thomas* (Infancy Gospel, second century; Coptic Gospel, second century, with earliest copies from the fourth century) and the *Apocalypse of Thomas* (fourth and fifth centuries). These are all demonstrably late and have no claims to authenticity. The most controversial Coptic *Gospel of Thomas*, a collection of 114 purported sayings of Jesus, was rejected by the early church as heretical (third and fourth centuries).

Mistakes to Avoid

We should not be over-critical of Thomas. The other disciples had their doubts too, as do we all. Jesus' words imply mild rebuke but focus more on the need for all to set aside skepticism when confronted with the facts. Skepticism is easy, and belief does not always have the benefit of sight to support it. However, rather than make the lesson a negative one—"Don't doubt as Thomas did"—see the skepticism of Thomas as an occasion for an important teaching on the urgency of believing and the blessings that come to those who do.

151. Jesus Changes Water to Wine (John 2:1–11)

Lesson Focus

Jesus revealed that he is the Messiah by using his miraculous power to change water to wine. His disciples put their faith in him.

- Jesus responds to requests made in faith.
- Jesus responds to the ordinary needs of people.
- Jesus revealed his glory with the result that people believe.

Lesson Application

Jesus is the Messiah.

- We should not hesitate to put our requests to Jesus in faith.
- We must believe that Jesus is the Messiah and put our faith in him.

Biblical Context

The first part of John's Gospel (chaps. 1–10) is sometimes called the "Book of Signs." Signs served as a major part of John's case that Jesus is the Christ (John 20:31). Instead of asking the reader to start with Jesus the man and try to figure out who he is, the Gospel assumes a theological identification, "Christ (Messiah) the Son of God," and seeks to disclose who fills that role. Who has a claim to be the Messiah? Jesus does. Who can be identified as the Son of God? Jesus can. Jesus' turning water into wine and other signs are provided by John to reinforce Jesus' claim. Since the wedding story involves water for Jewish rites of purification, it subtly sets up the next story in John about Jesus cleansing the temple, where he reacted against misuse of what was meant to be pure.

Interpretational Issues in the Story

"They have no wine" (John 2:3). Running out of wine would have been humiliating to the host and the families of the bride and groom.

"My hour has not yet come" (John 2:4). In John's Gospel, this phrase typically refers to the time of Jesus' death. Here, Jesus had not yet done his first wonder—changing the water to wine— so he was indicating that it was not yet time for him to go public with his ministry. Nevertheless, he fulfilled Mary's request.

"Jewish rites of purification" (John 2:6). Water for Jewish rituals was stored in stone jars because pottery was thought to absorb impurities. The jars in this story were empty because water for rituals had to be "living" water, that is, moving water, gathered from a spring. Strictest Jewish regulation specified that water for purification could not be stored or even carried in jars, but that regulation was often not followed.

Background Information

Wedding. Marriages at this time were often arranged by the families of the bride and groom, and the wedding feast was the formal occasion celebrating the union of these families. Such ceremonies often lasted for a week. The master of the feast was an honorary position similar to a master of ceremonies today. One of his responsibilities was to oversee the levels of dilution for the wine. The feast was often held at the home of the groom, so he was the official host.

Cana. Cana was in the vicinity of Nazareth, but there is still some uncertainty about the site. It was undoubtedly in Galilee and within a day's journey of Nazareth.

Mistakes to Avoid

This can often be a difficult story to teach in churches where abstinence from alcohol is encouraged. Though at times wine was diluted with water to reduce its alcoholic content, that does not eliminate the fact that Jesus did indeed drink alcoholic beverages. The biblical warnings about alcohol pertain to excess, and abstinence is certainly one way to avoid drinking in excess, but students should not be given the idea that alcohol is intrinsically evil. To suggest that would compromise Jesus.

152. Nicodemus (John 3:1–21)

Lesson Focus

Recognizing that Jesus is from God, Nicodemus came to ask him questions. Jesus told Nicodemus how he could see the kingdom of God and how to be born again—by believing in Jesus, God's Son. Jesus came to give eternal life to those who believe.

- Jesus provides salvation for the world and eternal life to those who believe.
- God loves people so much that he sent Jesus to bring salvation.

Lesson Application

Jesus is God's Son and he came to give us eternal life.

- We must recognize who Jesus is and be born again.
- We should seek to enter the kingdom of God.

Biblical Context

The first part of John's Gospel (chaps. 1–10) is sometimes called the "Book of Signs." Signs served as a major part of John's case that Jesus is the Christ (John 20:31). Instead of asking the reader to start with Jesus the man and try to figure out who he is, the Gospel assumes a theological identification, "Christ (Messiah) the Son of God" and seeks to disclose who fills that role. Who has a claim to be the Messiah? Jesus does. Who can be identified as the Son of God? Jesus can. In this account, Jesus explains these things to Nicodemus, one of the leaders of the Jews.

Interpretational Issues in the Story

"Came to Jesus by night" (John 3:2). It is possible that Nicodemus came at night to avoid the crowd, but it is not as likely that he was being secretive or was afraid. Nighttime meetings or discussions were not unusual in the Judaism of the day.

"Rabbi" (John 3:2). Given Jesus' lack of formal training and Nicodemus's high position, Nicodemus was giving a high compliment by addressing Jesus this way—it was not a title given glibly. *Rabbi* was a term of honor typically used by a subordinate or student.

"Born of water" (John 3:5). When Gentiles converted to Judaism, they were baptized to remove their Gentile uncleanness. Nicodemus would have been startled to hear that Jews, and even Jewish leaders, had to convert and be baptized of the Spirit to enter the kingdom of God.

"That which is born of the Spirit" (John 3:6). Nicodemus would have understood Jesus as referring to the Spirit of God in an Old Testament sense, in other words, the Spirit's empowering individuals with a particular authority.

Entry into the kingdom of God (John 3:5). The Jews believed that they were the kingdom of God based on their ethnic heritage and the covenant made with their forefathers. In contrast, Jesus contended that one enters the kingdom by being born of the Spirit of God.

"Son of Man" (John 3:13–14). This is a title drawn from Daniel 7 and by New Testament times had come to be used as a title for the Messiah. Jesus often used it in reference to himself.

Background Information

Pharisees and ruling council. The ruling council of Judaism was the Sanhedrin, which was responsible for governing the people in Jewish matters and deciding cases of Jewish law. At this time, Caiaphas the high priest was presiding over the seventy-member group. Though Pharisees like Nicodemus were among the group, the Sadducees held the majority. Pharisees were experts in the interpretation of the law and were known for being pious to a fault. Their numbers were relatively few, but they were typically admired and respected by the people. Sadducees were wealthy and politically connected Jews who had control of the temple personnel. They had some theological differences with the Pharisees; most notably, they did not believe in the resurrection.

Contrasts. Jesus used several well-known Jewish contrasts: spirit/flesh, heaven/earth, and light/darkness. All these contained references to Jewish teaching and ideas with which Nicodemus would have been familiar. They are more than metaphors; they are also allusions to theological concepts. Even though it might seem obscure to us, Jesus was communicating with Nicodemus in ways that he could understand, though it is clear that Jesus' words were difficult for Nicodemus to grasp.

Mistakes to Avoid

It is important to convey to the students that being born again is not the end objective but the means of reaching the main objective. The main objective is taking one's place in the kingdom of God. Furthermore, we are called to believe in Jesus, who has died for our sin and thereby provided eternal life. Forgiveness, atonement, and eternal life are wonderful benefits available to us through grace, but we need to explain that though we receive these benefits, we enjoy them as members of the kingdom of God, which has its responsibilities and obligations. In being born again, we do not simply receive benefits; we commit to being productive members of the kingdom of God. Primary to the story is not what Nicodemus decided but the words that Jesus said to him.

Nicodemus appears again later as one who helped to bury Jesus, but that is immaterial to what the story here is about.

We are not being urged to be like Nicodemus, but to hear and understand the teaching of Christ. The spiritual status of Nicodemus when he left that night is not given and is irrelevant to the teaching of the story. Jesus made sophisticated and complex statements of theology in the story that would be difficult for children to comprehend. At the same time, his statements contain some of the most basic truths of Christianity. Teachers will have to consider carefully what elements of the text will be meaningful to students.

153. The Woman at the Well (John 4:1–42)

Lesson Focus

Jesus told a Samaritan woman that he was the promised Messiah. Many people in the town believed him.

- Jesus is the Messiah.
- God is to be worshiped in spirit and truth.

Lesson Application

Jesus is the Messiah, the Savior of the world.

- We believe that Jesus is the Messiah.
- Because Jesus is the Messiah, we spread the news.
- We worship God in spirit and truth.

Biblical Context

The first part of John's Gospel (chaps. 1–10) is sometimes called the "Book of Signs." Signs served as a major part of John's case that Jesus is the Christ (John 20:31). Instead of asking the reader to start with Jesus the man and try to figure out who he is, the Gospel assumes a theological identification, "Christ (Messiah) the Son of God" and seeks to disclose who fills that role. Who has a claim to be the Messiah? Jesus does. Who can be identified as the Son of God? Jesus can. John builds his case example by example. Here Jesus claims his title of Messiah, and the Samaritan woman believes who he is and proclaims it. This account is meant to stand in contrast to the previous one, where Jesus encountered first Nicodemus, of highest rank in Jewish perception, and then this Samaritan woman of lowest rank.

Interpretational Issues in the Story

"He had to pass through Samaria" (John 4:4). Technically Jesus did not *have* to go through Samaria, but it was the most direct route. The most fastidious Jews went considerably out of their way to avoid it.

Living water (John 4:10–14). When the Jews spoke of living water, they meant flowing water rather than collected water, which could stagnate. Living water was required for the cleansing process in preparation for participation in rituals. Jesus used this imagery to speak of a "spring of water welling up to eternal life" (v. 14). A well could not be a source of living water.

"I perceive that you are a prophet" (John 4:19). The woman tries to change the subject of the conversation with Jesus. Her inference that Jesus is a prophet was based on his obvious knowledge of the personal details of her life.

"Salvation is from the Jews" (John 4:22). Salvation was to come through the Messiah, and the Messiah was to come from the Jews.

"God is spirit" (John 4:24). This is not stated as though it was new information—everyone believed that God is spirit. Here it serves as the foundation of the following conclusion: he must be worshiped in spirit and truth.

"Told me all that I ever did" (John 4:29). The woman's account was not meant to persuade the people that Jesus is the Messiah but is evidence that he was extraordinary and so might be considered a candidate for Messiah.

Background Information

Samaria, Sychar, and Jacob's well. Sychar was in the territory of Samaria, but there is some dispute about its precise location. Jacob's well has been confidently identified with an ancient well situated in a valley between Mount Ebal and Mount Gerizim that is about 250 feet from the ancient site of Shechem (where Jacob lived for some time). The well is about one hundred feet deep and was identified as Jacob's well as early as the fourth century AD. This traditional identification is supported by Jewish, Christian, and Muslim traditions. The identification of the town of Sychar, however, became more complex when archaeological excavations demonstrated that Shechem was destroyed in the first century BC and was not occupied at the time of Jesus. The alternate identification of Sychar is modern Askar, about a mile away from the well.

Sixth hour at the well. The sixth hour (counting from the beginning of the day) was about noon. This was not a normal time to come to the well, not only because of the heat of the day but also because water was needed earlier in the day for cooking and cleaning.

Jews and Samaritans. The Samaritans were descended from the marriages between those Israelites not deported to Babylon when Jerusalem was destroyed in the sixth century BC and foreigners forcibly settled in Israel by the Babylonians. When the exiles returned from Babylon, they spurned those who had not been "purified by exile," especially those who were of mixed race. Thus, the Samaritans were considered unclean, and Jews avoided any contact with them. Some Jews even walked longer distances in order to go around their territory instead of through it. It would have been unusual for Jesus to speak to a Samaritan woman, but it would have been astonishing for him to accept water from her, since she was considered unclean. The shocking behavior continued as Jesus stayed (and undoubtedly ate) with the Samaritans for two days (4:40).

"This mountain" versus Jerusalem. The Samaritans were forbidden to worship in the temple in Jerusalem and had had their own temple, rituals, and traditions on Mount Gerizim, though the temple had been destroyed some centuries earlier and still stood in ruins.

Mistakes to Avoid

Though there are racial, ethnic, and gender elements to the story, its intent is not to encourage breaking down such boundaries. Jesus did so in the way he acted toward the Samaritan woman, which is worthwhile to observe, but the lesson should not be turned to that purpose. The point is that Jesus is the Messiah for everyone. We should be willing to share our faith with all sorts of people, but the story is not about evangelism techniques or who should qualify to receive the gospel. We are supposed to be considering Jesus' claims even as the woman does so, not thinking about whether we would share our faith with her.

154. Jesus Heals a Lame Man at the Pool (John 5:1–18)

Lesson Focus

Jesus healed a lame man at the pool of Bethesda.

- Jesus has the power to heal.
- Jesus showed that he is God.

Lesson Application

Jesus is God.

- We believe that Jesus is God.

Biblical Context

The first part of John's Gospel (chaps. 1–10) is sometimes called the "Book of Signs." Signs served as a major part of John's case that Jesus is the Christ (John 20:31). Instead of asking the reader to start with Jesus the man and try to figure out who he is, the Gospel assumes a theological identification, "Christ (Messiah) the Son of God" and seeks to disclose who fills that role. Who has a claim to be the Messiah? Jesus does. Who can be identified as the Son of God? Jesus can. This story continues the sequence of signs Jesus performed to show that he not only had power from God but also the right to claim to be the Son of God and equal with God.

Interpretational Issues in the Story

Stirring of the water (John 5:7). Pagans had various shrines designated for healing, and it is likely that the Jewish general populace treated the pool of Bethesda in a similar way, despite the syncretism involved. Verse 4 is considered by most scholars as a later addition, but the reference to the stirring of the waters in verse 7 is original. The waters were stirred as a result of the operation of the water system that fed the pools, a system not entirely understood by modern scholars. It appears that the water was brought into the pools through an aqueduct system from a reservoir farther north. It is deduced that periodically water was allowed to flow from one pool to the other so that the moving water made it usable for ritual purposes.

Water (John 5:7). John has been tracing a theme of water and purification (water to wine [2:6–9]; born of water [3:5]; living water [4:10]; and now healing water). In each case Jesus replaced the water with something that he has to offer.

Sabbath regulations and carrying a bed (John 5:9–10). The Old Testament law was not nearly so specific as to forbid a man to carry his bed, but Jewish legal experts such as the Pharisees attempted to regulate everything by their interpretations. Jewish traditions indicate that it was forbidden to carry an object from one domain to another. A bed with a person in it could be carried as an act of mercy, but an empty bed was another matter.

Sabbath regulations and healing (John 5:16). Physicians were restricted from healing on the Sabbath, yet no one could argue that works of God were forbidden. This left Jesus' healing in an ambiguous situation, depending on the opinion of the observer.

"Nothing worse may happen" (John 5:14). Jesus was probably not suggesting that further tragedies would befall the man if he continued to sin but that sin would lead to repercussions for the resurrection and afterlife.

"Equal with God" (John 5:18). Jesus was claiming a role in his Father's work and therefore sharing in God's prerogative to work on the Sabbath.

Background Information

Feast of the Jews. It is uncertain which feast this was, possibly the Feast of Tabernacles that took place in the fall after the harvest was complete. It was one of the three annual festivals for which all Jewish males were supposed to make pilgrimage to Jerusalem.

Pool of Bethesda. The extensive pools of Bethesda have been identified and excavated. They were located just north of the temple mount by Saint Anne's Church. Since it was by the Sheep Gate, it has been suggested that sheep were washed here before being taken into the temple area for sacrifice.

Mistakes to Avoid

We should remember that Jesus healed very selectively. Dozens of sick people were likely at the pool, yet for reasons unknown John recounts that Jesus dealt only with this man. For that reason and others, we understand that the point of the lesson is not about healing and praying to God when we are sick. Its focus is on Jesus doing God's work. He is God's agent and God's Son.

155. The Man Born Blind (John 9)

Lesson Focus

Jesus healed a man born blind. The man then testifies to the Jewish leaders concerning who Jesus is.

- Jesus is capable of healing even in the most difficult cases.
- Jesus showed that his power and authority were from God.

Lesson Application

Jesus is from God.

- We believe that Jesus received his power from God.
- We believe that Jesus can remove our spiritual blindness.

Biblical Context

The first part of John's Gospel (chaps. 1–10) is sometimes called the "Book of Signs." Signs served as a major part of John's case that Jesus is the Christ (John 20:31). Instead of asking the reader to start with Jesus the man and try to figure out who he is, the Gospel assumes a theological identification, "Christ (Messiah) the Son of God" and seeks to disclose who fills that role. Who has a claim to be the Messiah? Jesus does. Who can be identified as the Son of God? Jesus can. This extensive healing account is the climactic sign of the first section of the Gospel as it details a particularly extraordinary healing and includes lengthy discussion of the healed man with the religious leaders over the nature of Jesus, particularly the unlearned man's rebuke of the leaders.

Interpretational Issues in the Story

"Who sinned . . . ?" (John 9:2). It was common in the ancient world to believe that illness and disabilities were punishment for sin, but a person born blind presented philosophical challenges.

"But that the works of God might be displayed" (John 9:3). The question the disciples asked concerned cause—whose sin caused the man's misfortune? Jesus answered that it was neither the man's nor his parents' sin, thereby not identifying the cause, but he did identify the *purpose*. God did not make the man blind so Jesus could perform this sign, but since he was blind, whatever the cause, Jesus could use it to make a point about himself and the kingdom.

Blindness (John 9:2). This account is used to contrast the physical blindness of the man who was healed and the spiritual blindness of the Pharisees, who could not recognize the work of God when it was happening right in front of them.

Background Information

Pool of Siloam. The pool was at the south end of the city and fed by the Gihon spring. Since it was moving water ("living" water), it was usable for rituals of purification. Archaeologists have recently discovered the pool and excavated it.

Mud and saliva. In the pagan world, saliva was believed to have magical properties. Some traditions dating back to ancient Egypt indicate the belief that people were created from the spittle of the gods. It is not surprising then that the idea was condemned by the rabbis, and saliva was included among the bodily fluids that made one unclean.

Healed man brought to Pharisees. The man had not been ritually unclean and therefore would not have needed clearance by priests. But the Pharisees were not priests; they were the experts on Jewish law. Given the discussion that follows about the Sabbath, we can infer that the man was brought to the Pharisees for a judgment on the legitimacy of the Sabbath healing.

Sabbath. The fact that the healing was done on the Sabbath created a controversy. The "work" done by Jesus violated recognized standards, yet that might be overlooked if the healing was judged to be an act of charity.

The Jews. The Jews mentioned in 9:18 were not a group of the Jewish leaders but some of the neighbors who questioned the man's identity (see 9:8–9).

Put out of the synagogue. Expulsion from the community was a serious social consequence but not the same as excommunication. Being expelled did not keep one from worshiping in the temple, but such a one was excluded from participation in synagogue activities.

Son of Man. This is a title drawn from Daniel 7 and by New Testament times had come to be used as a title for the Messiah. Jesus often used it in reference to himself.

Mistakes to Avoid

We can admire the boldness of the healed man as he addressed the Jewish leaders, but the lesson of the story is not that we are to be bold in our testimony. It is about who Jesus is, not about what the healed man does. Additionally, if we emphasize the need to be thankful for all we can see, we miss the main point of the story. Rather than focus on the blessing of sight, focus on the power of Jesus.

156. Lazarus (John 11:1–44)

Lesson Focus

Jesus demonstrated that he is God by raising Lazarus from the dead.

- Jesus has the power to raise from the dead.
- Jesus is God.

Lesson Application

Know that Jesus is God.

- We accept that Jesus is God and place our belief in him.
- We acknowledge that nothing is too hard for Jesus.

Biblical Context

The first part of John's Gospel (chaps. 1–10) is sometimes called the "Book of Signs." Signs served as a major part of John's case that Jesus is the Christ (John 20:31). Instead of asking the reader to start with Jesus the man and try to figure out who he is, the Gospel assumes a theological identification, "Christ (Messiah) the Son of God," and seeks to disclose who fills that role. Who has a claim to be the Messiah? Jesus does. Who can be identified as the Son of God? Jesus can. The story of Lazarus is reported only in the Gospel of John. It stands at the hinge of the book as one of the major signs that Jesus performed and offers undeniable evidence that he is God. It ushers in the events of the last week of his life with a powerful indicator that death is no obstacle to him.

Interpretational Issues in the Story

Jesus' delay (John 11:6). Lazarus died soon after the messengers went to find Jesus. Jesus delayed his arrival so as to leave no doubt that Lazarus was dead. By the time of arrival, the body had been buried and had begun to decay. All this was essential for Jesus to display his power.

"If you had been here, my brother would not have died" (John 11:21, 32). Martha and Mary made similar statements. We cannot reconstruct their tone of voice, and there is little evidence to think that they represent different responses.

"Rise again" (John 11:23–24). Martha thought that Jesus was talking about the eventual resurrection of the righteous, but Jesus had something more immediate in mind.

"I am the resurrection and the life" (John 11:25). Here Jesus highlighted a truth that extends beyond his power to raise a person from the dead. The reason he has power over death is that he *is* the source of life. Life and resurrection find their definition in him.

"Jesus wept" (John 11:35). The weeping of Jesus was certainly not over the death of Lazarus, whom he knew he would raise from the dead, though the onlookers interpreted it as such. The text associates his weeping with his being "deeply moved in his spirit and greatly troubled" (v. 33). Such language typically expresses a harsh outburst rather than deep sorrow (see Mark 14:5). We might then conclude that his weeping was over the plight of humanity so overwhelmed by death and its apparent finality. His is a frustrated indignation that death should have such emotional power over people. Death is an offense to the Lord of life.

Jesus' prayer (John 11:41–42). He indicated in his prayer that he does some things for the benefit of those who are listening. Jesus was trying to provide an example for the people.

Background Information

Chronology. This event takes place mere days before the Triumphal Entry and the events of the death and resurrection of Jesus.

Location. Mary, Martha, and their brother Lazarus lived in Bethany (the other side of the Mount of Olives), just east of Jerusalem.

Four days. Determining physical death was more difficult in those days, so three days were allotted before doing so. By then, lack of water and nourishment would have ensured death. Burial usually took place the same day as the death, and bodies were interred in a cave, not buried under the earth.

Cave burial. Caves used for burial were typically rock-cut family tombs featuring numerous stone slabs on which bodies were laid while they decomposed. When only bones remained, they were gathered up and put in an ossuary—a stone box—which was placed in a hollowed-out tunnel, thus making room in the tomb for additional bodies.

Wrapped with strips of linen. These were used to enfold the body in spices.

Mistakes to Avoid

Attention should be focused on Jesus conquering death more than on Lazarus coming back to life, that is, on Jesus' power rather than on Lazarus, his family, or the mourners. We should not draw too much from Jesus' weeping. Every indication is that he was distraught over larger issues, not simply sad about the present circumstance or sharing in the sorrow of his friends. The story should not be used as a lesson about friendship, which would serve only to distract from the main point—Jesus is God and he has power over death.

157. Washing the Disciples' Feet (John 13:1–17)

Lesson Focus

Jesus taught humility by washing the disciples' feet.

- Jesus wants us to serve one another in humility.
- Jesus wants us to imitate him.

Lesson Application

We should imitate Jesus by serving one another in humility.

- We will look for ways to serve one another.
- We are to be humble even toward those who serve us.

Biblical Context

The first part of John's Gospel (chaps. 1–10) is sometimes called the "Book of Signs." Signs served as a major part of John's case that Jesus is the Christ (John 20:31). Instead of asking the reader to start with Jesus the man and try to figure out who he is, the Gospel assumes a theological identification, "Christ (Messiah) the Son of God" and seeks to disclose who fills that role. Who has a claim to be the Messiah? Jesus does. Who can be identified as the Son of God? Jesus can. The second part of John's Gospel (chaps. 13–21) is sometimes called the "Book of Glory," and it focuses on discipleship. The account of Jesus' washing the feet of the disciples provides a strong introduction to this theme.

Interpretational Issues in the Story

"Laid aside his outer garments" (John 13:4). A close-fitting, ankle-length, linen tunic with sleeves was worn next to the skin. On top of this was the cloak. On special occasions an additional robe was worn. Here, Jesus removed his cloak, the outer garment, which would have left him wearing only the tunic, the clothing of a working person. On top of this, he donned a cloth that wrapped around the waist and then up and over the shoulder. Such was the attire of a menial. Whether it was regularly used as a towel is unclear.

Background Information

Passover feast. The traditional Passover meal included lamb roasted over a fire, unleavened bread, a bowl of salt water, bitter herbs, a fruit dish (*harosheth*), and four cups of wine (one part wine to three parts water).

Foot washing. Foot washing was a standard part of hospitality in this dry, dusty region where people wore open sandals. There is evidence that foot washing was done only by non-Jewish servants. Generally the washing was performed by pouring clean water from a pitcher over the dusty feet into another basin. Then the feet were dried off. The act was performed either when guests entered or when they were reclining at the table. Here, the latter is suggested by verse 2—the meal was being served.

Mistakes to Avoid

Foot washing served an important role in the society of that time, but it no longer serves that role in our society. Teachers must therefore be careful not to make foot washing itself the issue but should seek out what actions might be comparable in today's society.

158. Pentecost (Acts 2)

Lesson Focus

After Jesus rose from the dead, he appeared to the disciples. He told them to wait in Jerusalem until they received the gift of the Holy Spirit, after which they would have power to do the job of telling everyone about Jesus. At Pentecost, this happened just as Jesus said. Many people repented and were baptized, becoming a part of the fellowship of believers.

- God gives his Spirit to empower his people.
- God can transform frightened and confused people into powerful witnesses to the gospel.
- God is the one who grew the church.

Lesson Application

God gave the Holy Spirit to lead his people when Jesus went up into heaven.

- We recognize that God can accomplish his work through us by the power of his Spirit.
- We believe that God gives his Spirit to advance the work of the kingdom.
- We acknowledge that the growth of the church in any age is the work of God, not the work of those he uses.

Biblical Context

Luke's first volume, the Gospel of Luke, documented the results of the coming of the Son. This second volume, the book of Acts, documents the results of the coming of the Spirit. Acts was not written to give specifics about the nature and operation of the church, nor is it simply a history of how the church started. Luke was making a case among his contemporaries that Christianity is a legitimate religion, despite opposition from the Jews and Romans, who were inclined to treat Christians as a group of lunatic troublemakers, fanatic followers of a crucified criminal. To the church today Acts stands as testimony to how God grew his church, primarily through the work of Peter and Paul. This account details the giving of the Spirit and the beginning of the growth of the church.

Interpretational Issues in the Story

Pentecost and the Tower of Babel (Acts 2:6). What happened at Pentecost is the reverse of what happened at the Tower of Babel (Genesis 11). When the Tower of Babel was built, God rendered people unable to understand one another's speech, and he scattered them. Here, people could all understand one another, and they become united in purpose—God's purpose.

Wind and tongues as of fire (Acts 2:2–3). Wind and fire were both manifestations of God's presence. Wind parted the Red Sea and brought to life the dry bones in Ezekiel's vision. Fire appeared in the burning bush and in the pillar of the Lord's presence as he led the Israelites in the wilderness.

Speaking in other tongues (Acts 2:4). The New Testament references the speaking of unknown tongues, but here the disciples were speaking in human languages that they had never uttered before and did not know, even as they spoke them.

Jews from every nation (Acts 2:5). After the destruction of Jerusalem by the Babylonians in 586 BC, many Jews were sent into exile and from them grew what is called the "diaspora"—Jews scattered around the world. Jews therefore lived in many parts of the world, and some made pilgrimage to Jerusalem for a major festival as they retained their Jewish identity and faith.

Day of the Lord (Acts 2:20). In Old Testament prophecy, the day of the Lord was the time when God's plans would fall into place—judgment on the wicked and blessing on the righteous, the people of God. People associated the day of the Lord with the coming of the Messiah and, as Joel 2:28 indicates, it was to be accompanied by mighty signs. Most important for Peter's use of Joel here in Acts 2 is the connection between the pouring out of the Spirit and the offer of salvation on the day of the Lord.

Salvation from sins (Acts 2:21). Pentecost is the beginning of the entire Christian system of salvation as we understand it. The death of Jesus in paying the penalty for sin and the Spirit indwelling the believer are new factors that have their origin at Pentecost. Neither was available in the Old Testament.

Background Information

Pentecost. This was a festival celebrated fifty days after Passover, and it coincided with the end of the grain harvest. It was connected with covenant renewal during the intertestamental period (as attested, e.g., in the Dead Sea Scrolls). The coming of the Spirit was an important component of the new covenant, so it is understandable why the Spirit's coming occurred at the time of the festival. Jerusalem would have been crowded with pilgrims, up to one million, according to some estimates.

Baptism. John had already been associating his baptism in the Jordan with repentance, and the baptism of Jesus showed an element of dedication. Peter combined both these as he called the people to a baptism for repentance of their sins (2:38) and commitment to Christ and the body of believers (2:41–42). Baptism had been known as a purification rite among the Jews for centuries. Here, the disciples were beginning to do what Jesus had commissioned them to do in Matthew 28:19.

Mistakes to Avoid

This was a great and unique day in the history of Christianity. The doctrine taught here is central to the passage, but the methods and results are not given as a pattern for all to follow. The passage gives no reason to think that preaching in tongues is necessary for all who are endowed with the Spirit. We should not expect that large numbers of converts will be the result of Spirit-filled teaching or that such numbers should be the gauge of success, nor should we strive to adopt the preaching content and style or interpretational methods of the apostles.

Nothing about the time, place, or method of baptism is prescribed, and there is no instruction to adopt the living style of the early church in Jerusalem as normative for Christian experience. This text is not here to provide a model for the church to follow; it is here to help us see that God was the one who got the church started. Some lessons focus on Peter, showing him as a powerful preacher, in contrast to his earlier denial of Jesus, and showing how God helps us overcome mistakes. If we plan to teach a series on Peter, these may be significant observations, but if the lesson is on the coming of the Holy Spirit, then focusing on Peter misses the point. We should be careful to note that receiving the Holy Spirit doesn't resolve all our problems. Our sin is dealt with in Christ, but problems will always be a part of life on earth.

159. Peter and John and the Lame Man (Acts 3:1–4:31)

Lesson Focus

Peter and John healed a crippled man by the power of Jesus through the man's own faith. Their continued preaching about the resurrection of Christ got them arrested. The Holy Spirit enabled them to speak boldly before the rulers. When Peter and John were released, they joined with the other believers in prayer. They were filled with the Holy Spirit and spoke the word of God boldly.

- The name of Jesus has power.
- God is able to give boldness to serve him.
- God gave his disciples opportunities to give the message for people to believe.
- It is better to obey God than people.

Lesson Application

The Holy Spirit gives believers power to speak boldly about Jesus.

- We believe that God will give us boldness to tell others about the kingdom of God.
- We keep alert to opportunities that God provides for proclaiming the gospel.
- We do not shy away from proclaiming that salvation comes only through Jesus.

Biblical Context

Luke's first volume, the Gospel of Luke, documented the results of the coming of the Son. This second volume, the book of Acts, documents the results of the coming of the Spirit. Acts was not written to give specifics about the nature and operation of the church, nor is it simply a history of how the church started. Luke was making a case among his contemporaries that Christianity is a legitimate religion, despite opposition from the Jews and Romans, who were inclined to treat Christians as a group of lunatic troublemakers, fanatic followers of a crucified criminal. To the church today Acts stands as testimony to how God grew his church, primarily through the work of Peter and Paul. This account details the giving of the Spirit and the beginning of the growth of the church. The healing in this account is important primarily because it is the event that got Peter and John before the Sanhedrin where they testified about Jesus. Pentecost brought the message of Jesus to popular attention, whereas this healing brought the message to the attention of the Jewish leaders.

Interpretational Issues in the Story

"Going up to the temple" (Acts 3:1). Some in Jerusalem would make their way to the temple when the daily sacrifices were offered. The sacrificial

offerings were followed by singing and corporate prayer. The second of these times was at three o'clock. The early believers likely continued these practices until such time as it became clear that the death of Christ made the temple and its rituals obsolete. The daily sacrificial rituals also provided a good opportunity for preaching at the temple, since there were more people around.

"Filled with the Holy Spirit" (Acts 4:8, 31). As with the work of the Spirit prior to Pentecost, people were endowed with the power of the Spirit to equip them for various tasks.

"There is salvation in no one else" (Acts 4:12). Salvation in Christ alone has always been a controversial issue, not least in today's world, which tends to be pluralistic. It is considered politically incorrect to insist that a particular belief is right and others are wrong. The power of Jesus' name brought salvation, or healing (the same Greek root), to the lame man. The point that Peter was making does not primarily concern being saved from sins or how one gets to heaven but that no name is as powerful as that of Jesus', and it is therefore appropriate that Jesus' name is the one that can accomplish any level of salvation—physical, spiritual, or national.

Background Information

Beautiful Gate. The location of the gate is disputed, but we do know that it was a gate into an area of the temple, not a gate into the city. Only Jewish males who met the criteria for purity, which excluded the blind and the lame, could pass through the entire series of gates into the inner court. The blind and the lame gathered near the gates to request charity from those entering the temple precincts.

Healing in the ancient world. Healers in the ancient world were typically exorcists who cast out demons believed to bring illness, often invoking words of power or names of power. In contrast, Peter and John simply commanded the man to rise up and walk in the powerful name of Jesus.

Solomon's portico. Porticos, or colonnades, surrounded the temple courts. The royal stoa stretched along the southern end, and Solomon's portico stretched the length of the eastern end, approximately three hundred yards (see illustration on p. 448).

Captain of the temple. The captain of the temple was a Jew under the control of the priests who enforced rules and decorum in the temple courts.

Sadducees. The first group of leaders the disciples encountered was the Sadducees, wealthy and politically connected Jews who had control of the temple personnel but were not themselves priests. One of the distinctive elements of their doctrine was a rejection of resurrection (see Acts 23:8), so the claim of the disciples about Jesus' resurrection would have caught their attention.

Put in custody in the evening. The disciples were to give account of themselves before the Sanhedrin, which would not gather until the next day.

Sanhedrin. In the Judaism represented in rabbinic writings after the destruction of the temple in AD 70, the Sanhedrin was depicted as a formal body that provided leadership for the Jewish people. Its members were not necessarily priests but respected religious experts who made legal decisions, preserved traditions, and governed the spiritual and social life of the people (note those mentioned in 4:5 who were convened by the high priest). Though Pharisees, who were popular with the common people, were among the group, the Sadducees held the majority of the seventy-one seats. It is unknown whether the Sanhedrin in the New Testament was so formally institutionalized, though the historian Josephus talks about it meeting in council in the temple courts before the temple was destroyed. The word *sanhedrin* can refer simply to an ad hoc gathering of responsible people for the purpose of making a decision.

Mistakes to Avoid

The healing is not the center of the story. It is merely a prelude that provides the opportunity for Peter and John to give the message of Christ to the people and then again before the Sanhedrin. The leaders of the early church exercised the power of Christ with boldness and spread the message despite the resistance. The story shows that the opposition to Christianity was not because of lawless acts by Jesus' followers. The text shows how the power of the Spirit grew the early church and does not present Peter and John as role models for us to imitate. The correct emphasis eliminates lessons that focus on helping those in need, being courageous in the face of opposition, and in any way encouraging us to be like people in the story.

Care must also be taken when dealing with Acts 4:19, one of the most familiar statements in the story, that it is better to listen to God rather than men. This verse does provide a basis for resistance against authority on moral or theological grounds, but the concept can be taken too far. It must be balanced against Paul's exhortation to live under authority (see Rom. 13:1–7; Heb. 13:17; 1 Pet. 2:13). As it stands, Peter and John's statement offers no guidelines about when it is appropriate to resist or what that resistance might look like. It does not advise Christians to rebel against parents or government.

Therefore, the application of this verse to particular situations today can be tricky and ought to be carried out with great caution.

160. Ananias and Sapphira (Acts 4:32–5:11)

Lesson Focus

The early church was characterized by certain values that it took seriously and lived out day by day. Ananias and Sapphira showed themselves hypocritical and dishonest and were punished severely.

- God is pleased when his people live out unity and love.
- God is pleased when his people practice self-denial.
- God is pleased when his people generously care for the needy.
- God holds us accountable for honesty.

Lesson Application

We should learn from the values of the early church and look for ways to cultivate the same values.

- As God's people we seek to be unified in love.
- As God's people we seek to free ourselves from the hold that possessions have on us.
- As God's people we seek out ways to be generous as we care for the needy.
- We should beware of hypocrisy, recognizing that we are accountable to God.

Biblical Context

Luke's first volume, the Gospel of Luke, documented the results of the coming of the Son. This second volume, the book of Acts, documents the results of the coming of the Spirit. Acts was not written to give specifics about the nature and operation of the church, nor is it simply a history of how the church started. Luke was making a case among his contemporaries that Christianity is a legitimate religion, despite opposition from the Jews and Romans, who were inclined to treat Christians as a group of lunatic troublemakers, fanatic followers of a crucified criminal. To the church today Acts stands as testimony to how God grew his church, primarily through the work of Peter and Paul. This story indicates that the growth of the early church was founded on values such as unity, self-denial, and caring for the needy. At the same time it shows that church members held one another accountable. Luke's portrayal is contrary to the accusations against Christians commonly made by Jews and Romans.

Interpretational Issues in the Story

Sharing possessions (Acts 4:32, 34, 37). The reference to their relaxed attitude toward ownership and sharing possessions stops short of indicating that all goods were held in common. The practice of selling property and donating the money to the cause is something that took place "from time to time" (4:34 NIV). Barnabas's contribution (4:36–37) is singled out as an outstanding example (rather than the norm), and it provides a contrast to Ananias and Sapphira. Liquidating assets and donating the proceeds to the church was not a requirement for being part of the church.

"Satan filled your heart" (Acts 5:3). Whatever role can be attributed to Satan here, Ananias is not thereby relieved of responsibility for his sin. This is similar to the statement made about Judas in John 13:27.

Lying to the Holy Spirit (Acts 5:3). In verse 9 the offense is further described as that of testing the Holy Spirit. Students might be concerned about committing such a crime themselves. Since the Holy Spirit is present in and represented by the church, lying to or testing the Holy Spirit occurs whenever someone lies to the representatives of the church who are acting in an official capacity.

Penalty of death (Acts 5:5, 10). The text stops short of saying that God struck them dead or that Peter called on God to strike them, though undoubtedly their deaths were viewed as God's punishment. This demonstrates that God is just as concerned about faithfulness in the New Testament age as he was in the time of the Old Testament. There is no hint of love and forgiveness being prioritized such that serious offenses are simply overlooked.

Background Information

Groups sharing possessions. In this time period there were other groups for which membership required one to forfeit possessions (such as the mystic Pythagoreans and the group whose writings are found in the Dead Sea Scrolls).

Levite. In the Old Testament. Levites were not given territory when it was distributed among the tribes. Instead, they lived in cities scattered throughout the land (see Joshua 21). By New Testament times, however, Levites did own land. It is possible that Barnabas viewed his act as a return to an older covenant ideal.

Kept back. The Greek verb for "kept back" is used only one other time in the New Testament (Titus 2:10) and only once in the Greek translation of the Old Testament (Josh. 7:1), where Achan kept back some of what had been taken from Jericho that belonged to the Lord. Achan was stoned to death for his betrayal. The connection suggests that the offenses of Achan and Ananias and Sapphira were in some ways comparable.

Mistakes to Avoid

This account of the early church is descriptive rather than prescriptive. It describes how the early church lived but it does not prescribe that all Christians ever after should live that way. Unity, self-denial, care for the needy, and accountability are good, and God's people should always strive to achieve them corporately and individually. But those values will not always take the same shape as they do in this story. Self-denial does not require communal living with pooled resources. Accountability will not necessarily lead to violators being struck down by God. Because of the death of Ananias and Sapphira, this story would not be appropriate for younger children. Rather than making this a lesson about not telling lies, focus on the fact that honesty is important to God. This puts the emphasis on God's character, which we should imitate, rather than on God's rules (or biblical rules), which never cover every circumstance.

161. Stephen (Acts 6–7)

Lesson Focus

Stephen was a Hellenistic Jew chosen for a position of responsibility in the early church. His zeal brought him into confrontation with certain Jewish leaders who accused him of blasphemy. When hauled before the Sanhedrin, he defended himself but so angered the Jews that he was condemned to death and executed.

- God grew his church despite persecution.
- God gave his people boldness and opportunity to speak.
- The church was faithful and upright but opposed by the institutions of the day.

Lesson Application

We should honor God in every situation, whether it brings praise and recognition or persecution and death.

- We honor God in faithfulness.
- We honor God in service.
- We honor God in boldness.
- We honor God with our words.
- We honor God in difficult circumstances.

Biblical Context

Luke's first volume, the Gospel of Luke, documented the results of the coming of the Son. This second volume, the book of Acts, documents the results of the coming of the Spirit. Acts was not written to give specifics about the nature and operation of the church, nor is it simply a history of how the church started. Luke was making a case among his contemporaries that Christianity is a legitimate religion, despite opposition from the Jews and Romans, who were inclined to treat Christians as a group of lunatic troublemakers, fanatic followers of a crucified criminal. To the church today Acts stands as testimony to how God grew his church, primarily through the work of Peter and Paul. The importance of this story is that it resulted in yet another opportunity for a Christian to speak publicly and officially before the Sanhedrin. Stephen's speech shows that his martyrdom did not come about because of criminal or rebellious behavior by members of the early church but because he spoke boldly about the faithlessness of the Jewish leaders, much like the prophets of old. So the antagonism grew between established Judaism and early Christianity.

Interpretational Issues in the Story

"Prayed and laid their hands on them" (Acts 6:6). Laying on of hands was evidenced in early biblical practice both in contexts of blessing (Gen. 48:14) and when authority was being passed on to someone (Num. 27:23; Deut. 34:9).

Charge against Stephen (Acts 6:11, 13–14). The charge of blasphemy in verse 11 is further defined in verses 13 and 14 as speaking against the law and the temple, both of which had attained a sacred status in Judaism. To speak disrespectfully about them was considered criminal. To suggest that the temple and the law were inadequate or would pass away was heresy. It was taken as strongly as someone today undermining democracy, freedom, or human rights.

Stephen's defense (Acts 7:2–53). Stephen's speech showed his respect for the covenant with Abraham, for Moses and the law, and for the tabernacle and temple; yet, in the process of speaking he denounced the historical unfaithfulness of the Jews. It was his accusation that, despite all that God had provided through the covenant, law, temple, and prophets, they had put to death the righteous one sent by God—Jesus. It was important for Luke to show that Stephen was executed based on false (unsubstantiated) accusations and his association with Jesus.

"Tent of witness" (7:44). This is a reference to the tabernacle built in the wilderness after the exodus. Sometimes the ark is called the "ark of the testimony" (Ex. 30:26) and Numbers 1:50 refers to the "tabernacle of the testimony," the place where the ark was housed.

Background Information

Hellenists (Grecian Jews). These were Jews who had adapted to Greek culture by adopting Greek as their first language. Many Hellenists had relocated to Palestine. In contrast, many of those whose families had been in Palestine for a long time continued to use Hebrew or Aramaic as their first language, though they could undoubtedly understand Greek.

Widows of Hellenists. Traditions in Judaism taught that it was advantageous to be buried in Israel, especially in Jerusalem. Eventually it was taught that those buried there would be resurrected first. As a result, there was a constant flow of elderly Jews resettling in Jerusalem, where they would remain until death. This, in turn, meant that there was an overabundance of widows to care for.

Synagogue of the Freedmen. The Freedmen were slaves who had gained their freedom. This synagogue was made up of those who had moved to Jerusalem.

Sanhedrin. In the Judaism represented in rabbinic writings after the destruction of the temple in AD 70, the Sanhedrin was depicted as a formal body that provided leadership for the Jewish people. It was not comprised solely of priests but of respected religious experts who made legal decisions, preserved traditions, and governed the spiritual and social life of the people. Though Pharisees, popular with the common people, were among the group, the Sadducees held the majority of the seventy-one seats. It is unknown whether the Sanhedrin in the New Testament was so formally institutionalized, though the historian Josephus talks about it meeting in council in the temple courts in the period before the temple was destroyed. The word *sanhedrin* can refer simply to an ad hoc gathering of responsible people for the purpose of making a decision and may sometimes be used that way in the New Testament.

Like the face of an angel. This reference in Acts 6:15 to a glowing face should be compared to the face of Moses, which shone whenever he had been in the presence of God (see Ex. 34:29). This provides a striking contrast to the fact that Stephen has been accused of blasphemy against Moses (Acts 6:11).

Stoning. In theory, only the Romans could pass down a death sentence, but here the crowd of leaders got carried away. Someone to be stoned was taken to an isolated place, stripped, and cast down by one of the witnesses over a precipice at least twice the height of the condemned man. Large stones were thrown down on top of him, with the trial witnesses throwing the first ones. In this mode of punishment, no one could determine which stone thrower caused the actual death, much like with more contemporary firing squads.

Mistakes to Avoid

We have to recognize that this story has not been given to us to urge us to be like Stephen, as admirable a character as he was. God was growing his church through people like Stephen, but God's work is the focus. There is a very thin line here, for, as we see in the points of application above, we are all called to be the kind of people that Stephen was. The difference is that we as Christians are called to emulate the exemplary qualities that Stephen possessed, not in an attempt to be like Stephen but to please God. God calls us as his church to honor him in every possible way. He has raised up his church for that purpose. Building a lesson around getting students to think about how they are persecuted may trivialize genuine persecution. Our inconveniences or mild discomforts cannot compare.

Additionally, to resolve the widows' dispute, the course of action decided on by the church is described, but there is no reason to think it was prescribed as a method for all churches to use. Finally, the character traits that Stephen evidenced are commendable but should not be used to derive a list of biblically mandated traits for leadership. This is a difficult story for young children and should be taught to older ages who can better understand issues of martyrdom.

162. Philip and the Ethiopian (Acts 8:26–39)

Lesson Focus

The Lord sent Philip to explain the good news about Jesus to an Ethiopian as the gospel continued to spread beyond Jerusalem.

- God puts his people in places where they can do his work.
- God finds inroads for the gospel to spread.
- God makes people receptive to the gospel.
- God expanded the church to include Gentiles.

Lesson Application

We should be sensitive to how God might grow his church through us.

- We keep alert for people who may be ready to hear the gospel.
- We acknowledge that God is the one who grows his church, so we faithfully do what he asks of us and leave the results to him.

Biblical Context

Luke's first volume, the Gospel of Luke, documented the results of the coming of the Son. This second volume, the book of Acts, documents the results of the coming of the Spirit. Acts was not written to give specifics about the nature and operation of the church, nor is it simply a history of how the church started. Luke was making a case among his contemporaries that Christianity is a legitimate religion, despite opposition from the Jews and Romans, who were inclined to treat Christians as a group of lunatic troublemakers, fanatic followers of a crucified criminal. To the church today Acts stands as testimony to how God grew his church, primarily through the work of Peter and Paul. This story shows how the gospel began to spread beyond the confines of Jerusalem through the ministry of Philip.

Interpretational Issues in the Story

Court official (Acts 8:27). It is significant that the gospel was readily accepted by a foreign VIP. This serves as evidence of two important points Luke wanted to make: (1) Christianity is not just something that attracts the uneducated, disaffected masses who will fall for anything and jump on any bandwagon that offers them hope; and (2) without the prejudices brought by the Jewish leadership and its stranglehold on the people, the gospel was perfectly sensible and intrinsically attractive. In this story, then, Luke shows evidence of the legitimacy of early Christianity, contrary to the claims of Jewish and Roman perceptions and accusations.

Come to Jerusalem to worship (Acts 8:27). The man is not Jewish but apparently fears God and desires to worship at the temple.

Isaiah 53:7 (Acts 8:32). The official was baffled by the prophecy he was reading, which is no surprise. God's timing was perfect, as the official's curiosity gave Philip the opportunity to explain how this prophecy had been recently fulfilled by Jesus. The contemporary Jewish audience would not have been easily persuaded by Philip's interpretation because most would not have considered Isaiah 53 to be a messianic passage. But the fact that Jesus was the fulfillment of many such passages was evident after his coming. For this reason, teachers might want to say that the passage was fulfilled by Jesus rather than saying that it referred to him.

Background Information

Road from Jerusalem to Gaza. Two roads went from Jerusalem to Gaza. The first went west to the coastal road, then south. The second, the desert road, went south first, then west.

Eunuch. Technically a eunuch is a castrated man. Important officials in the ancient world often were made eunuchs because, lacking descendants, they'd also lack ambition for the throne. Having eunuchs as officials was even more important when the chief monarch was a queen. As for the eunuch in this story, the official in charge of the royal treasury, he held an important position in the administration. Because he was a eunuch—and a Gentile—he was not able to participate fully in Jewish ritual, but he was accepted with open arms by Christians. It is of interest that in the very book of Isaiah he was reading, the Lord offers hope to eunuchs (see Isa. 56:3–7).

Ethiopia. The region known in the first century as Ethiopia is not today the country called by that name; rather, it coincides more closely with modern Sudan, just south of Egypt. The round trip would have taken the man three to four months. In ancient times the region was known as Nubia or Cush. Principal cities included Napata and Meroe. The inhabitants of this land were portrayed in Egyptian art as having very black skin. Some have tried to connect this man with a strong Christian community that grew up in Abyssinia (the Aksumite kingdom in the area today known as Ethiopia) in the fourth century AD. This cannot be the case because the origins of that community are well documented. Christian sources as early as the second century AD, such as Irenaeus, however, indicate that this eunuch became an evangelist himself and brought Christianity to his homeland, but the massive conversion of the kingdoms there to Christianity did not occur until the sixth century.

Candace. This is a title for the ranking female of the kingdom of Meroe (Ethiopia) rather than a personal name. Current scholarship favors it being connected to the queen mother. During this time period several different individuals carried the title. The current consensus pertaining to the identity of the one mentioned in Acts 8 is that she was Queen Nawidemak.

Chariot. The word here was used for a military vehicle in which the rider(s) stood, but it was also used for a wagon that had a seat (found in the Greek text of the Old Testament in Gen. 46:29).

Reading. In the ancient world people read aloud, not silently to themselves. Although the text says that the official was reading, it could just as easily be that a servant was reading to him. Literacy was common enough, especially among the upper classes, but even at this time information was often gained through hearing.

Mistakes to Avoid

Though the Ethiopian official might have been considered an outcast on several accounts (physically disabled, a Gentile, a "person of color") this story must not be turned into an account of how God accepts us for who we are (although he does). It is not about God accepting the eunuch, but about the eunuch accepting God. The story is also not given as a model for evangelism. Philip's method for evangelizing the eunuch worked because God was in it. God can work successfully through any method he chooses.

163. Saul's Conversion (Acts 9:1–19)

Lesson Focus

Jesus revealed to Saul that he is God. Saul the persecutor of the church converted to Christianity and became God's instrument for bringing the gospel to the Gentiles.

- God is able to change the life of even the most hardened skeptic.
- God chooses and recruits workers for his kingdom.
- God wants his church to grow beyond just one group to include the whole world.

Lesson Application

Believe that Jesus is God and that he will continue to grow his church through his people.

- We serve God in whatever capacity he asks of us.
- We recognize that God can bring even his greatest enemies to a place of belief.

Biblical Context

Luke's first volume, the Gospel of Luke, documented the results of the coming of the Son. This second volume, the book of Acts, documents the results of the coming of the Spirit. Acts was not written to give specifics about the nature and operation of the church, nor is it simply a history of how the church started. Luke was making a case among his contemporaries that Christianity is a legitimate religion, despite opposition from the Jews and Romans, who were inclined to treat Christians as a group of lunatic troublemakers, fanatic followers of a crucified criminal. To the church today Acts stands as testimony to how God grew his church, primarily through the work of Peter and Paul. This story introduces us to Saul (Paul) who would become God's instrument for taking the gospel to the Gentiles. The incredible account of the conversion of this staunch enemy and aggressive persecutor of the church demonstrates God's plan to grow his church even through difficult circumstances.

Interpretational Issues in the Story

Jews opposed to Christianity (Acts 9:1–2). The main problem Jews had with Christians was that Christians claimed, as Christ had himself, that Jesus is God. The Jews had long been looking for Messiah, but they had no expectation that Messiah would be God. For even the Messiah to claim to be God was a big problem to their theology since they believed there was only one God (they had had no revelation of a Trinity). As far as the Jewish leaders were concerned, the claim that Jesus is God was a major heresy and a threat to Judaism and had to be eliminated.

"The Way" (Acts 9:2). Early Christians referred to themselves by this term, "the Way," because Jesus had identified himself as "the way" (John 14:6). It is used several times in the New Testament.

Saul's conversion (Acts 9:13–19). Saul's conversion took place about AD 34–35. There has been some discussion about whether this should be called Saul's conversion or Paul's commissioning, but it need not be an either/or decision. The text emphasizes Paul's commissioning (9:15) but it is also clear that

Paul's mind has been radically changed about Jesus. He had converted from a persecutor of believers in Jesus to a believer himself. Nevertheless it should be noted that the early Christians did not consider themselves as having left Judaism. They still thought of themselves as Jews, but ones who believed that Jesus was Messiah and Son of God. Paul's commissioning as the apostle to the Gentiles served the same function as the commissioning of the prophets in the Old Testament (Isaiah 6; Jeremiah 1; Ezekiel 2–3).

Background Information

Damascus. The city was one of the Decapolis cities, one of ten free cities of the Roman Empire, and was ruled at this time by Aretas IV, a Nabatean king. A large Jewish population of many thousands lived in the city, so there were many synagogues there. As the hub of a number of international highways, the spread of the gospel was easily facilitated from Damascus, so it is understandable that Saul wanted to eliminate the presence of Christians there.

Road to Damascus. From Jerusalem to Damascus is about 135 miles and would have taken seven to ten days walking. The traditional site of Paul's experience is Kaukab, about ten miles southwest of Damascus. Remains of a Byzantine church have been found there, but evidence is too sketchy and traditions are too late to give any confidence that this was the location.

Street called Straight. Roman cities were often quartered by major roads running east-west and north-south. These roads contained the most important market districts, the Roman Cardo. The street called Straight was the major east-west street running through the city; its route has been preserved by the streets built over it throughout the centuries.

Mistakes to Avoid

We cannot turn Paul's commissioning story into a generic commissioning for all Christians. We are all called to do our part in God's kingdom, but different people have different jobs, and not all are called to preach the gospel. We should all be ready to give a defense of our faith, and we should all seek opportunities to tell others about it. But Paul was given his ministry as his vocation. We must not mistakenly teach that every kingdom role is the role of everyone in the kingdom (consider the diverse gifts of the Spirit in 1 Cor. 12:12–30).

We should also resist the temptation to turn this into a story about the particulars of Saul's conversion or about Ananias. Students can be asked to think about how it might have felt to be blinded and hear an invisible voice speaking or about how frightened Ananias would have been to go and see

Saul. But the lesson of the text is not about emotional responses and our abilities to overcome them. Boldness and obedience are important, but encouraging those virtues is not the point of the story. We certainly can mention them, however, while getting to the point the text is trying to make—God advancing the church as he recruits his team.

164. Dorcas (Acts 9:36–43)

Lesson Focus

The power of the risen Christ continued to be shown in the ministry of the disciples as Peter raised Dorcas from the dead. God was growing his church by showing that Jesus lives and that Peter was acting in his name.

- God has the power to raise from the dead.
- God often channels his power through his people so that their message about him will be believed.

Lesson Application

God is able to do acts of power through his followers as he deems fit to grow his church.

- We must not doubt God's power, though we must recognize that he exercises it in different ways at different times in wisdom in order to carry out his plan. (Many other faithful people died but were not raised from the dead.)
- We recognize that God, not we, is the one growing his church, but we keep alert to what role he wants us to play.

Biblical Context

Luke's first volume, the Gospel of Luke, documented the results of the coming of the Son. This second volume, the book of Acts, documents the results of the coming of the Spirit. Acts was not written to give specifics about the nature and operation of the church, nor is it simply a history of how the church started. Luke was making a case among his contemporaries that Christianity is a legitimate religion, despite opposition from the Jews and Romans, who were inclined to treat Christians as a group of lunatic troublemakers, fanatic followers of a crucified criminal. To the church today Acts stands as testimony to how God grew his church, primarily through the work of Peter and Paul. Peter's raising Dorcas (Tabitha) from the dead is the climax of the accounts displaying the power exercised by the apostles. From here the text turns to the Gentiles, first in the story of Peter and Cornelius and then in the ministry of Paul.

Interpretational Issues in the Story

Summoning Peter (Acts 9:38). It is clear that Peter had a growing reputation for acts of power and healing, but nothing recorded about him so far suggests that he might raise someone from the dead. Yet it seems that they had called him with the hope that he would do just that.

Peter's procedure (Acts 9:40–41). It is interesting that the text does not indicate what Peter prayed (e.g., that Jesus would raise the woman from the dead) and does not show her actually awakening in direct response to Peter's prayer. He simply finished praying and called her to get up. Unlike the magicians and sorcerers of the day, no incantations or rituals were performed. As seen explicitly in Acts 9:34, Christ did the healing, not Peter.

Background Information

Joppa. Joppa was a port on the coast just to the south of modern Tel Aviv. It was about eleven miles northwest of Lydda (Lod, Old Testament) where Peter was staying.

Processing the dead. The details given in the text reflect the practices of the day. Bodies were washed and anointed in a private area removed from living spaces, since contact with the dead rendered one unclean. In Jerusalem, burial usually took place the same day as the death, but in the rest of the country regulations were not as strict.

Widows. Widows are specifically mentioned here because they were among, and probably the majority of, the poor that Dorcas cared for. Widows had very low status and often had no means of support.

Tanner. The fact that Peter stayed with a tanner shows his lack of concern for common Jewish prejudices. Tanners dealt with dead animals all the time, so they were always ritually unclean, and the profession was considered demeaning. Visitors to Joppa today are shown the traditional site of Simon the tanner's house.

Mistakes to Avoid

There is a tendency to use the people in stories such as this as role models. Students might be urged to care for the poor like Dorcas, to pray like Peter, or to offer hospitality like Simon, but these are all incidental details. Certainly we do well if our lives are characterized by such behaviors, but when we consider this story and its place in the book of Acts, we see that these details are not the point, any more than "be a seamstress" (like Dorcas), "be a tanner" (like Simon), or "go find someone to raise from the dead." Such incidental details do not carry the force of the teaching or the authority of God's Word.

165. Peter and Cornelius (Acts 10:1–11:18)

Lesson Focus

God showed Peter that his church is to include all who believe the good news of Jesus, not just Jews.

- God intends his church to be of universal scope—he invites any and all to believe and receive forgiveness.
- God's covenant with the Israelites has been expanded through the work of Christ to provide for anyone to be in relationship with him.

Lesson Application

God's gift of salvation is for all who repent and believe.

- We must not think that God is only interested in certain groups of people.
- We understand that all stand equal in God's sight.

Biblical Context

Luke's first volume, the Gospel of Luke, documented the results of the coming of the Son. This second volume, the book of Acts, documents the results of the coming of the Spirit. Acts was not written to give specifics about the nature and operation of the church, nor is it simply a history of how the church started. Luke was making a case among his contemporaries that Christianity is a legitimate religion, despite opposition from the Jews and Romans, who were inclined to treat Christians as a group of lunatic troublemakers, fanatic followers of a crucified criminal. To the church today Acts stands as testimony to how God grew his church, primarily through the work of Peter and Paul. The story of Cornelius represents a key turning point in the book as the church is officially opened up to Gentiles.

Interpretational Issues in the Story

Cornelius (Acts 10:2). Cornelius is described as "a devout man who feared God," which shows that he had rejected Roman pagan beliefs and adopted the one God of Judaism (without becoming a proselyte). He supported and associated with the Jewish community.

"Gave alms generously . . . and prayed continually" (Acts 10:2–4). The angel indicates to Cornelius that his acts of devotion have pleased God.

Unclean food (Acts 10:14). Peter has this vision on the roof of the tanner's house where carcasses of unclean animals were processed all the time. Unclean animals are listed in Leviticus 11 and Deuteronomy 14, and Jews were forbidden to eat the meat from these animals. The fact that God here declares them clean demonstrates that the initial prohibitions were not for health or hygiene. Rather, these animals were unclean probably because they were associated somehow with death. Eating the meat from such animals rendered one unclean for participation in the rituals of Israel. Peter's vision prepared him to consider that the categories of uncleanness or impurity were about to change in other important ways—up until now, Gentiles had been considered ritually unclean. Though staying with a tanner may have stretched some of his Jewish sensitivities, entering the house of a Gentile was clearly prohibited by the Jewish law of the time.

Speaking in tongues (Acts 10:46). Since it is likely that Peter and his companions spoke the same language as Cornelius, it is unlikely that Cornelius was speaking in known languages. He was manifesting the gift of speaking nonhuman language.

Coming of the Holy Spirit (Acts 10:44). Peter is still speaking when the Holy Spirit came on Cornelius and his household. The text does not say they responded with acceptance of Peter's message, though we might assume that they mentally assented. This was remarkable to Peter and his entourage because these Gentiles were uncircumcised. For Gentiles to become proselytes, they typically had to be circumcised. From this we see that Peter still thought of Christianity as operating within Judaism.

Background Information

Caesarea Maritime. Located about thirty miles north of Joppa along the coast, the port of Caesarea was where the Roman governor of Judea had his main residence. Extensive excavations have been done at the site, and the palace of Herod Agrippa I (AD 37–44) has been located. This event probably took place about AD 40. The port city featured a large artificial harbor constructed by Herod the Great a generation earlier, as well as all the features of a Roman provincial center (hippodrome, theater, amphitheater, market center). The town had been named in honor of Caesar Augustus.

Roman centurion. The position of centurion was usually given to a competent soldier who had begun at a lower level in the army rather than appointed to a man on the basis of his aristocratic pedigree. Centurions each had charge of about one hundred men, and sixty such companies made up the Roman legion. Jews would have been prejudiced against Cornelius, not only because he was a Gentile but because he was a soldier of the despised Romans.

Italian regiment. This is a reference to the Italian cohort that dispatched to Syria when the Jewish revolt took place in AD 66. The centurion's company of one hundred was part of the larger cohort (regiment) of six hundred.

Caesarea to Joppa. This was a trip of about thirty miles.

Trance. In a dream one only sees things, in a vision one can converse, and in a trance one can act. A trance can also be described as a vision, but it is more than a vision.

Three times. The threefold repetition was a way of emphasizing the importance of what was being said.

Family baptized. In the ancient world and still to some extent in the Greco-Roman world, decisions about religious beliefs were made at the family or clan level, not at the individual level. In ancient times, for example, when a woman married into a new clan she automatically adopted the god or gods of that clan. Here Cornelius made a decision for his household, and they all followed his lead and accepted what he had accepted. The term translated "household" is more likely here than the translation "family" (NIV) because centurions were forbidden to marry. Cornelius's household would have consisted of retainers and servants (10:7; in 10:24 the reference is more to countrymen than to relatives).

Mistakes to Avoid

While this passage is about not discriminating between classes of people, we must be careful not to extrapolate beyond the bounds of the context. God does not discriminate regarding who can be admitted into his kingdom and who receives the gift of the Holy Spirit. Therefore, if we want to imitate God, we will not discriminate against one group or another. However, such an application stops short of guidelines about what constitutes discrimination and what policies might be set in place to prevent it. The lesson should focus on accepting all people as God accepts them. Younger children may find it difficult to understand the categories of Jew and Gentile.

166. Peter Released from Prison (Acts 12:1–17)

Lesson Focus

God answered the prayers of the believers, miraculously freeing Peter from prison.

- God is not hindered by chains and locked doors.
- God is able to secure freedom for those who serve him.
- God answers prayer.

Lesson Application

God has the power to do everything he has planned—more power than kings and soldiers. We should trust him.

- We recognize that nothing is too difficult for God.
- We accept God's answers, whatever they are.
- We stay be confident that God is able to do whatever it takes to carry forth his kingdom.

Biblical Context

Luke's first volume, the Gospel of Luke, documented the results of the coming of the Son. This second volume, the book of Acts, documents the results of the coming of the Spirit. Acts was not written to give specifics about the nature and operation of the church, nor is it simply a history of how the church started. Luke was making a case among his contemporaries that Christianity is a legitimate religion, despite opposition from the Jews and Romans, who were inclined to treat Christians as a group of lunatic troublemakers, fanatic followers of a crucified criminal. To the church today Acts stands as testimony to how God grew his church, primarily through the work of Peter and Paul. This account shows growing persecution, which resulted in Christians moving from Jerusalem, taking the gospel with them to their new places of residence.

Interpretational Issues in the Story

Herod (Acts 12:1). This is Herod Agrippa I, and it is the first time he is mentioned in Acts. Up to this point in Luke's story of the growth of the church, official opposition had come from the Jews, particularly the

Sanhedrin. Then Herod joined in the persecution as he attempted to curry favor with the Jews. This was much more dangerous, because he had the right to execute. The Sanhedrin did not—the execution of Stephen was a situation that got out of hand.

"Angel of the Lord" (Acts 12:7). When the angel of the Lord appears in the Old Testament, some wonder whether the angel was actually Jesus. The fact that the descriptive title "angel of the Lord" was used after the incarnation suggests that as a misidentification.

"His angel" (Acts 12:15). There are three possible interpretations of this phrase. (1) They thought that Peter's guardian angel was at the door; but if so, why would the angel have left Peter, and why would the praying people have paid no attention to it? (2) They thought Peter had been executed and become an angel, but there is little evidence that Jews of this time believed people became angels when they died. (3) They were simply using *angel* as another word for *ghost*. The last is the most likely, but the evidence for these two as synonyms is not strong enough for confidence.

Background Information

Herod Agrippa 1. This is the grandson of Herod the Great, who ruled at the time of Jesus' birth, and nephew of Herod Antipas, who mocked Jesus before his crucifixion (Luke 23:7–12). He grew up in Rome and was a childhood companion to Claudius, who would one day become emperor. When Caligula became emperor in AD 37, he appointed Agrippa king of the northern territories in Palestine. It was not until AD 41, when Claudius succeeded Caligula, that Agrippa gained control of all of Palestine. It is easy to see why this ruler, new to the throne, was interested in gaining favor with the ruling Jewish council.

Days of Unleavened Bread. This feast immediately follows Passover, so this is the same time of year that Jesus had been crucified about a decade earlier.

Imprisoned. Most likely, Peter was imprisoned in the Antonio fortress, the Roman garrison that was adjacent to the temple mount on the northwest corner. The house of Mary by its description was a large house with gated courtyard. It was most likely located in the elevated area to the southwest of the temple mount referred to today as Mount Zion. This is the area where the Upper Room was located, and some speculate it might be the same place.

Guarded by four squads. Luke shows his knowledge of how the military worked. The four squads took turns guarding throughout the watches of the night. The measures taken to secure Peter were heavy but not unusual.

Iron gate leading into the city. From the Antonio fortress, there was another gate that led into the temple precincts, but Peter was led out into the city.

Mistakes to Avoid

God answered the prayers of the believers and freed Peter from prison; he did not, however, answer their earlier prayers to free James, who was executed. Teachers should therefore be cautious in what they teach about prayer. It is God's place to determine how he will respond to prayers. It is important to point out that God answers prayers in keeping with the plan he is working out. Students must not be led to think that if only they can muster more faith, they will get what they want. Praying in faith is pleasing to God and therefore effective, but we need not try to muster up more faith in order to get a better answer. Prayer is not about getting what we want; it is about desiring God's kingdom to come and wanting what he wants, and all our prayers are answered in keeping with that. Prayer is more about who we are becoming than about what we are getting. Answered prayer shows itself not only in tangible answers but in the changes God works in us, which are primary.

167. Barnabas and Paul Sent from Antioch (Acts 13–14)

Lesson Focus

The Holy Spirit chose and equipped Paul and Barnabas to begin spreading the gospel throughout the Roman world. From Antioch their journey took them first to Cyprus, then into Galatia, a region of Asia Minor, where they made stops at Perga, Pisidian Antioch, Iconium, Lystra, and Derbe.

- God chooses the time and the people to use in the work of his kingdom.
- God works through those who are yielded to him and his work.
- God focuses his attention on those who are receptive to his work.

Lesson Application

We should recognize that even when God sends us, he does not necessarily make the job easy or successful in all ways we might imagine.

- Our responsibility is to be faithful; God determines the results.
- We recognize that God will not always work things out the way we expect he will when we begin a task.
- We must expect opposition to God's work.

Biblical Context

Luke's first volume, the Gospel of Luke, documented the results of the coming of the Son. This second volume, the book of Acts, documents the results of the coming of the Spirit. Acts was not written to give specifics about the nature and operation of the church, nor is it simply a history of how the church started. Luke was making a case among his contemporaries that Christianity is a legitimate religion, despite opposition from the Jews and Romans, who were inclined to treat Christians as a group of lunatic troublemakers, fanatic followers of a crucified criminal. To the church today Acts stands as testimony to how God grew his church, primarily through the work of Peter and Paul. As the church dispersed from Jerusalem under persecution, Antioch became a center for Christianity. This passage launches Paul, along with Barnabas, on what is known as the first missionary journey. As many Jews opposed them and rejected their message, the Gentiles were progressively more receptive. This ultimately brought a shift in Paul's ministry, a focus on the Gentiles.

Interpretational Issues in the Story

Message in Pisidia (Acts 13:16–41). Paul gave a brief synopsis on Israelite history, moving from Egypt and the conquest of Canaan to the covenant with David. From there he jumped to Jesus as the Son of David, Messiah, and Savior. He then reported the crucifixion and the resurrection. He concluded by noting the forgiveness of sins that is available through Jesus. It is likely that his audience was not familiar with the details about Jesus.

Jealousy (Acts 13:45). The jealousy of the Jews might have been motivated by the fact that Paul and Barnabas were drawing such wide interest and therefore threatening the power of the Jewish leaders in the town, or it might have been due to the Jews guarding their Jewish privileges and not wanting to see the Gentiles included. The text is inconclusive as to the source of the jealousy.

"Turn from these vain things" (Acts 14:15). It is natural that people try to fit new ideas into old systems. This had been true with the Israelites as they had trouble adapting to monotheism; it was true of the Jews and the Gentiles

as the church grew; it was true in Western Europe as Christianity spread; and it continues to be true today.

Stoned Paul (Acts 14:19). There is no reason to think that Paul was actually killed and raised from the dead, since the text says only that the mob thought he was dead. Yet it still must be considered stunning that he could walk and function. The heavy rocks that were used generally broke bones and crushed organs.

Background Information

First missionary journey. The journey of Paul and Barnabas took place in AD 46–48 and covered about 1,400 miles, half by sea.

Antioch and Seleucia. Antioch was about four hundred miles north of Jerusalem and was one of the largest and most important cities in the eastern part of the Roman Empire. Because it was located fifteen miles inland from the Mediterranean, it adopted the city of Seleucia as its seaport.

Cyprus. Cyprus is a large island in the Mediterranean about sixty-five miles from the coast of Syria. Though it is an island, it is roughly the same size as the land of Israel. It contained a sizeable Jewish population and was the homeland of Barnabas.

Synagogue. Synagogues are not to be confused with the temple. Synagogues were places where the Jews gathered to learn and pray, whereas the temple was the place where God's presence dwelt. Paul's strategy was to go to the synagogues first, because, at this time, Christianity was still largely a movement within Judaism. Paul, like Jesus, preached the God of the Jews and the kingdom promised through the Jews.

Pisidian Antioch. This was considered the most important Roman colony in Asia Minor. From Perga to Pisidia was about one hundred miles following the Cestrus River through the mountains, which took about a week to travel on foot.

Iconium. About ninety miles southeast of Pisidia, Iconium was not a major city like some of the places Paul had stopped previously. The small town had Phrygian ancestry (Phrygians were the Indo-Europeans who had inhabited the west central plateau since ancient times) and would have been home to some of the pagan Phrygian mystery cults.

Lystra. Lystra was a minor town only about twenty miles south of Iconium.

Zeus and Hermes. The chief god Zeus and his herald Hermes were worshiped at Lystra (as attested in reliefs found at the city). The first-century

Roman poet Ovid, in his work entitled *Metamorphosis*, told the story of Zeus and Hermes visiting the region of Phrygia in mortal form and finding no one who would offer them hospitality. They were finally taken in by an elderly couple, even though the couple didn't recognize Zeus and Hermes as gods. Because of the kindness of the couple, they were spared from judgment.

Derbe. Derbe, about sixty miles east of Lystra, was a small outpost town, which, unlike most of the other stops on Paul's journey, has not been excavated.

Mistakes to Avoid

Though the church at Antioch was successful, and the ministry of Paul and Barnabas was fruitful, these accounts are intended to show us what God did at that time and how he accomplished his purposes. It does not necessarily provide a model for how all churches of all times and cultures should work. In other words, it is descriptive rather than prescriptive. It may well be that a church today will want to follow the example of the church at Antioch in how its leadership works and how it sends forth missionaries. But we cannot say that the church today ought to conduct itself just as the church at Antioch did. These accounts in Acts should not be viewed as a how-to manual for churches.

Likewise, we cannot say that we must go about spreading the gospel the same way that Paul and Barnabas did. God works in many different ways through different people in a variety of times and circumstances. We must be cautious of making a model out of a description. Guard against role-model language: "Be bold and courageous like Barnabas and Paul," or, "Preach the gospel like Barnabas and Paul." We can encourage students to pray and ask God to give them courage and boldness to spread the good news of Jesus and tell them that God wants everyone to hear the good news of Jesus.

168. Lydia (Acts 16:6–15)

Lesson Focus

God continued to use Paul as his instrument through the Holy Spirit to expand the church into Europe beginning at the city of Philippi.

- God wants his salvation spread to the uttermost parts of the world.
- God is active through the Holy Spirit.

- God can use any class of people as his Word spreads—Jews, Gentiles, Ethiopians, Roman soldiers, political leaders, and women. It makes no difference—all are included and valued.

Lesson Application

We should note God's direct role as he carries out the expansion of his kingdom.

- We recognize the power of the gospel as we see it spread, not by conquest and forced conversions but by the movement of the Spirit and the persuasiveness of the message.
- When we obey, God does mighty things.

Biblical Context

Luke's first volume, the Gospel of Luke, documented the results of the coming of the Son. This second volume, the book of Acts, documents the results of the coming of the Spirit. Acts was not written to give specifics about the nature and operation of the church, nor is it simply a history of how the church started. Luke was making a case among his contemporaries that Christianity is a legitimate religion, despite opposition from the Jews and Romans, who were inclined to treat Christians as a group of lunatic troublemakers, fanatic followers of a crucified criminal. To the church today Acts stands as testimony to how God grew his church, primarily through the work of Peter and Paul. In this account the Macedonian vision was significant as it took Paul out of Asia and into Europe, where Lydia was the first recorded convert.

Interpretational Issues in the Story

"The Spirit of Jesus did not allow them" (Acts 16:7). We do not know if this was Paul's interpretation of an actual occurrence, such as opposition from people or difficulty of the journey. From Pisidia, instead of heading west toward Ephesus, he was apparently pushed northwest toward Mysia. From there he intended to head northeast toward Bithynia, but that option was also cut off, driving him to the coast at Troas (near ancient Troy). We do not know the circumstances that prevented him, but he took it as the leading of the Spirit. It is unlikely that the Spirit's leading was spoken communication, or he would have said so. The phrase "Spirit of Jesus" is rare (cf. Rom. 8:9 and 1 Pet. 1:11, "Spirit of Christ"; and Phil. 1:19, "Spirit of Jesus Christ") and demonstrates that the Holy Spirit *is* the Spirit of Christ.

Place of prayer by the river (Acts 16:13). Running water was considered ritually pure to the Jews, so if there was no synagogue building, the riverside would have been a logical place for them to meet because running water was considered ritually pure. Some interpreters point out, however, that the Greek terms recorded here were sometimes used by non-Jews to describe a synagogue. Alternatively, the fact that this mentions only the women suggests the possibility that the town did not have the requisite minimum of ten men needed to establish a synagogue.

"Worshiper of God" (Acts 16:14). This language describes Lydia as a Gentile who had rejected pagan gods and was in sympathy with the Jewish God.

Baptism (Acts 16:15). Lydia was most likely a widow and apparently the head of her household, whether that included children or just her domestic servants. Religious decisions such as this were often made by the head of household for the entire group.

Background Information

Second missionary journey. Paul and Silas covered about 2,800 miles on this second journey, which occurred from AD 49–52, much of it spent in Corinth.

Philippi of Macedonia. Paul quickly made his way to Philippi, a Roman colony and the most important city in the region, though Thessalonica was the capital. Macedonia was a region north of Greece and had been the homeland of Philip of Macedon and his famous son, Alexander the Great.

Seller of purple goods. Lydia was from Thyatira, a well-known center of purple-dyed cloth that was traditionally made using an extract from the murex snail. The fact that Thyatira was an inland city in western Asia Minor might suggest that the dyers' guild there was using alternative plant extracts for dye, but extracts from the shellfish could have been transported inland for the dyeing process. It was not unusual for women to be engaged in business or to be patrons of religion.

Mistakes to Avoid

What God was doing is more important than what Paul or Lydia were doing. We should not place too much emphasis on the European connection or the female connection, such as holding up Lydia as an example of a godly woman with business skills. The primary point of the lesson is that God accepts all, and all are invited for inclusion in his kingdom.

169. The Philippian Jailer (Acts 16:16–40)

Lesson Focus

Paul and Silas went about Philippi preaching Jesus as the way of salvation. When they were imprisoned for casting a demon out of a girl, God displayed his power in an earthquake. The jailer was filled with fear, and on hearing the way to salvation his whole family believed.

- God can protect his people in many ways.
- God can accomplish his purposes through circumstances that seem totally against him.
- God has power over spirits, government officials, and nature.

Lesson Application

When we are in difficult circumstances, we should realize that God can use them to glorify himself and bring people to faith in Christ.

- We can praise God whatever our circumstances and believe that he can work through them.
- We should not expect that God will always deliver us from difficult circumstances but have faith that he can accomplish much even through the worst times.

Biblical Context

Luke's first volume, the Gospel of Luke, documented the results of the coming of the Son. This second volume, the book of Acts, documents the results of the coming of the Spirit. Acts was not written to give specifics about the nature and operation of the church, nor is it simply a history of how the church started. Luke was making a case among his contemporaries that Christianity is a legitimate religion, despite opposition from the Jews and Romans, who were inclined to treat Christians as a group of lunatic troublemakers, fanatic followers of a crucified criminal. To the church today Acts stands as testimony to how God grew his church, primarily through the work of Peter and Paul. This narrative shows the power of God over spirits and how God can use even an earthquake to further his kingdom.

Interpretational Issues in the Story

Paul became annoyed (Acts 16:18). Though the woman was speaking the truth, she was not the sort of person Paul and Silas wanted their ministry and message to be associated with.

Exorcism (Acts 16:18). It was common for famous rabbis of the day to perform exorcisms. Here, the act of power testifies to the reality of the Holy Spirit, for Paul used no rituals or incantations.

Unlawful customs (Acts 16:21). Whether Paul and Silas were seen as promoting Judaism or Christianity, Gentiles who converted had to reject the imperial cult that involved the worship of the emperor. If that was the case here, the unlawful customs were associated with the worship of only one God. Claudius had recently expelled Jews from Rome because of disturbances related to the preaching of Christ.

"What must I do to be saved?" (Acts 16:30). It is possible that the jailer used "saved" as a theological technical term for being saved from sins. Paul might have conversed with him in the prison or perhaps he heard Paul's message as Paul spoke throughout the city. Alternatively, the jailer might have been referring more generally to deliverance from punishment from the authorities. Whatever his meaning was, Paul capitalized on the word choice to press his point home.

"You and your household" (Acts 16:31). In the ancient world and still to some extent in the Greco-Roman world, decisions about religious belief were made at the family or clan level, not at the individual level. In ancient times, for example, when a woman married into a new clan she automatically adopted the god or gods of that clan.

Background Information

Slave girl who predicts the future. She is specifically identified by the Greek text of Acts 16:16 as a having a "Python Spirit," which was associated with the oracle at Delphi, who predicted the future. There would have been some ambiguity in what she proclaimed because Zeus was sometimes referred to as the Most High God.

Magistrates in the marketplace. In Roman cities the agora (forum) was the public area where much business took place. Just as earlier kings held audience at the city gate, the officials of the city spent time in public judging cases.

Jews and Romans. The issue in cities other than Philippi was that Paul and his associates were Christians instead of Jews. The accusation in Philippi is that they were Jews advocating "unlawful customs" instead of being Romans. Though Judaism was a legal religion in the Roman Empire of this time, Tacitus commented about the Jews being hated.

Arrested, beaten, imprisoned. Paul and Silas could have been treated this way no matter the charges brought against them, were it not for the fact that they were Roman citizens. Public brutality for those deemed troublemakers was commonplace.

Inner prison and stocks. Inner prisons or cells were for dangerous criminals or people of the lower class. Stocks were designed not just to immobilize but to torment. Legs were put in gaps between metal rods and then a metal pole was fastened down over the ankles tightly enough to bring pain. This also prevented any change of position.

Jailor about to kill himself. The escape of the prisoners could have cost him his life, though exceptions were made in the case of an "act of God." Perhaps, however, in this case, the authorities were not inclined to be gracious in accepting such an assessment.

Baptism. In the ancient world and still to some extent in the Greco-Roman world, decisions about religious belief were made at the family or clan level, not at the individual level. In ancient times, for example, when a woman married into a new clan she automatically adopted the god or gods of that clan. The jailer was making a decision for his household, which followed his lead and accepted what he had accepted.

Privileges of Roman citizens. The law at the time prohibited beating Roman citizens or putting them in stocks without a trial.

Mistakes to Avoid

God does not always deliver his people from prison or other difficulties, so students shouldn't be led to believe otherwise. The fact that Paul and Silas were singing and praying testifies to their commitment to God, but it is fruitless to speculate about what they sang or to use them as models to encourage students to praise God in difficult circumstances. Such speculations risk missing the most important point, which is for us to see God's power at work.

170. Paul in Athens (Acts 17:16–34)

Lesson Focus

In Athens Paul entered the center of philosophical sophistication. He encounterd Greece's best thinkers and preached the message of the risen Christ to them.

- God has no needs.
- God wants people to seek and find him.

- God gives life to all.
- God wants us to repent.

Lesson Application

We should seek God and respond to him.

- We desire to know God as fully as we can.
- We recognize that God has made us, so we are his.
- We repent of our sins.

Biblical Context

Luke's first volume, the Gospel of Luke, documented the results of the coming of the Son. This second volume, the book of Acts, documents the results of the coming of the Spirit. Acts was not written to give specifics about the nature and operation of the church, nor is it simply a history of how the church started. Luke was making a case among his contemporaries that Christianity is a legitimate religion, despite opposition from the Jews and Romans, who were inclined to treat Christians as a group of lunatic troublemakers, fanatic followers of a crucified criminal. To the church today Acts stands as testimony to how God grew his church, primarily through the work of Peter and Paul. In past chapters Paul encountered Jews, Gentiles, and Romans. Here he encountered Greeks and debated them in philosophical terms.

Interpretational Issues in the Story

City full of idols (Acts 17:16). All cities had idols, including Tarsus, where Paul had come from, and Antioch, where his home base was. But the architectural glory that was Athens included a far greater density of idols and many pillars to Hermes lining the streets, which was overwhelming to Paul.

Altar to the unknown god (Acts 17:23). In the ancient world there were more supposed gods than could possibly be known; Assyrian literature had prayers addressed to "gods I know and gods I don't know." Difficult circumstances were commonly blamed on unknown gods since people did everything possible to please the known gods. That was likely the thinking behind this altar in Athens. Raising an altar to unknown gods was a way to thank or appease as necessary. If that was the purpose of the altar here in Athens, Paul was making use of its implications to introduce them to a God that they did not know.

Paul's message (Acts 17:22–31). Both Epicureans and Stoics would have agreed that God does not live in temples. Stoics would have affirmed Paul's statement, that God gives breath to all, but would have disagreed with how he understood it. By saying that God was near rather than far away, Paul opposed the Epicureans. The point is that Paul engaged the ideas of the people he was addressing. While they would have agreed with some of his basic points, Paul moved away from their ideas in dramatic ways.

Background Information

Distances. It was about one hundred miles from Philippi to Thessalonica. Berea was another fifty miles beyond Thessalonica. From Berea to Athens was about two hundred miles, but the text is unclear whether Paul traveled by land or sea (likely the latter). Paul arrived in Athens about AD 50.

Synagogues. The Jewish presence in Athens is attested by ancient historians, and Paul was able to go to the synagogue to preach the gospel. Jews and Gentiles who had rejected the pagan gods met there to learn and to pray.

Marketplaces. In Roman cities the agora (forum) was the public area where much business took place as well as discussion of news and issues.

Epicurean and Stoic philosophers. Epicureans considered God to be distant and uninvolved, and they focused their energy on habits of good living, health, and balance. They were materialists and hedonists who scoffed at the idea of resurrection. Stoics opposed pleasure and focused more on strict discipline and self-sufficiency. For them, matter was divine and reason originated from God and gave matter form. They believed in the eventual absorption of the soul into a great Oversoul, so they too denied resurrection.

Areopagus. This refers first to a group of people—the administration of Athens with regard to education and religion—and it is this group that Paul addressed. This was the Athenian equivalent to the Jewish Sanhedrin. The place where they met came to be called the *Areopagus*. It is a small outcrop west of the Acropolis where the Parthenon and other temples were located.

Mistakes to Avoid

The altar to the unknown god was not built for anonymous or secretive worship of the one true God. Though some interpreters have made that suggestion, there is no evidence for it, and it should not be taught. This is likewise not a story about idolatry, and to use this story as a way to direct students to identify personal idols is offbase. This is a very difficult lesson for younger children since there is no story to speak of. With older students, the lesson could be a launching place to get into detail about various philosophical schools of thought.

171. Aquila, Priscilla, and Apollos (Acts 18)

Lesson Focus

Aquila and Priscilla were tentmakers Paul encountered in Corinth. Paul worked alongside them as he served in Corinth, and they traveled with him to Ephesus where they met up with Apollos and instructed him about the death and resurrection of Christ.

- God continued to build the church through Paul and his acquaintances.
- God used the gifts of his people to spread the gospel.

Lesson Application

God is at work bringing people to the kingdom for his use.

- We must be alert to what we can do as God's instruments to build his church.

Biblical Context

Luke's first volume, the Gospel of Luke, documented the results of the coming of the Son. This second volume, the book of Acts, documents the results of the coming of the Spirit. Acts was not written to give specifics about the nature and operation of the church, nor is it simply a history of how the church started. Luke was making a case among his contemporaries that Christianity is a legitimate religion, despite opposition from the Jews and Romans, who were inclined to treat Christians as a group of lunatic troublemakers, fanatic followers of a crucified criminal. To the church today Acts stands as testimony to how God grew his church, primarily through the work of Peter and Paul, but this story adds coworkers to the account who played important supporting roles.

Interpretational Issues in the Story

Tentmaker (Acts 18:3). Paul worked with leather and likely other textiles, both in repair and manufacture. His skill could have been used in any town Paul visited, though we are not told how often Paul plied his trade while on his journeys.

"Claudius had commanded all the Jews to leave Rome" (Acts 18:2). A number of Roman emperors took official action against the Jews. According to the ancient Roman biographer Suetonius, Claudius banished them from

Rome in AD 49. The reason given was all the conflict surrounding "Chrestus," most likely Jesus.

"Reasoned in the synagogue" (Acts 18:4). Though formal services were sometimes held, particularly on the Sabbath, synagogues were places where people came together also informally for spontaneous prayer and discussion. Paul's rabbinic credentials would have given him an audience in any such context.

Background Information

Corinth. The city was strategically located at the western end of the isthmus between the Greek mainland and the Peloponnesus.The city of Paul's day had been built by Julius Caesar as a Roman colony and at that time served as the capital of the region. It was a city notorious for its immorality.

Synagogue ruler. Synagogues had rabbis to provide spiritual leadership but also had administrators, as a church today might have a chairman of the board.

Gallio, proconsul of Achaia. Gallio is well known from ancient literature and from an inscription found at Delphi. His brother was Seneca, a famous Stoic philosopher.

Ephesus. Though now inland, at the time of Paul it was a port city. Home to a quarter million people, it was one of the most prosperous and populous cities in the Roman Empire.

Mistakes to Avoid

The tent-making activity of Paul and Aquila and Priscilla is described, not prescribed. That is, the story does not teach us that we need to have a trade outside our ministry. In the world that Paul lived in, this was natural; there were no full-time ministry positions. But that does not mean that Christians of all time should follow that procedure. The story also does not claim that Christians ought to be evangelists like Aquila and Priscilla or Apollos. They are not in the text as role models but as illustrations of what God was doing as he built his church. We find a mandate for evangelism in the Great Commission of Matthew 28, not in the narratives of Acts. We must not attempt to derive normative, authoritative instruction from what the characters do. It is difficult to take a brief narrative such as this one and find a universal teaching. It is not an independent story with an independent lesson; it is part of the flow of Acts.

This is also the case with a number of Paul's associates. So, for example, we get a little of Timothy's background (2 Tim. 1:5), but that background is not given as part of the lesson of God's Word. It is information that serves as a backdrop for Paul's exhortation to Timothy as the leader of the church at Ephesus. It is not a lesson on the importance of godly families (though it illustrates that principle). There is no harm in mentioning such points, but they must not become the focus of a lesson that seeks to provide the authoritative teaching of Scripture.

172. The Riot in Ephesus (Acts 19)

Lesson Focus

Paul preached in Ephesus and did many acts of power. The success of the gospel was threatening to some who made their living from the worship of Artemis, so they sought to instigate a riot.

- God is greater than the spirits and the gods worshiped through idols.
- God grows his church despite opposition.

Lesson Application

We should recognize God's power.

- We must be careful not to misuse God's power for our own ends.
- We should expect opposition.
- We must not be surprised when the message we give gets twisted to make it sound wrong.

Biblical Context

Luke's first volume, the Gospel of Luke, documented the results of the coming of the Son. This second volume, the book of Acts, documents the results of the coming of the Spirit. Acts was not written to give specifics about the nature and operation of the church, nor is it simply a history of how the church started. Luke was making a case among his contemporaries that Christianity is a legitimate religion, despite opposition from the Jews and Romans, who were inclined to treat Christians as a group of lunatic troublemakers, fanatic followers of a crucified criminal. To the church today Acts stands as testimony to how God grew his church, primarily through the work of Peter and Paul. This account shows God's power over spirits and how the gospel threatened philosophies and religious practices of the Greco-Roman world. The perceived threat was rooted in ideology rather than in any disruptive behavior on the part of Christians.

Interpretational Issues in the Story

All heard the word (Acts 19:10). Because Ephesus was such an important city, the business of the region moved through it. What was taught in Ephesus gradually circulated around the rest of the province.

Seven sons of Sceva (Acts 19:14). Even among the Jews of the Roman world, exorcism of spirits was practiced as a demonstration of power. In exorcism, words or names of power were used to command the spirits, but exorcists would be in danger if they lacked the competence to control the power they sought to exploit.

The Way (Acts 19:23). Early Christians referred to themselves as "the Way" because Jesus had identified himself as "the way" (John 14:6). The term is used several times in the New Testament.

"Gods made with hands are not gods" (Acts 19:26). Paul taught this truth, but his opponents at Ephesus used it as an accusation against Paul to get the crowd angry at him. Similar things happen today when Christianity is ridiculed or opposed because we believe that Christ is the only way and that certain lifestyles are sinful.

Sacred stone that fell from the sky (Acts 19:35). In the ancient Near East a common belief was that the cult statue had a supernatural origin. Mesopotamians crafted images then threw their tools into the river and declared that the god had made the image. Such idols were referred to as "born in heaven, made on earth." This sort of claim gave spiritual credibility to the image.

Background Information

Journey. Paul had sailed to Ephesus after his stay in Corinth at the end of his second journey but had declined to stay long, as he headed back to Israel (18:18–22). After spending some time in Antioch, he began an overland trip that took him through Galatia and eventually back to Ephesus. This is called the third missionary journey and it covered about 2,700 miles. He traveled this time from AD 53–57 and spent more than half that time in Ephesus.

Synagogue. Though formal services were sometimes held in synagogues, particularly on the Sabbath, they were places where people came together informally for spontaneous prayer and discussion. Paul's rabbinic credentials gave him an audience in any such context.

Hall of Tyrannus. Despite widespread excavations at Ephesus, which have unearthed numerous public buildings, archaeologists have not yet been able to identify this hall.

Ephesus. Though now inland, at the time of Paul it was a port city. Home to a quarter-million people, it was one of the most prosperous and populous cities in the Roman Empire.

Books of magic arts. Ephesus was considered a center of magic and the occult. Documents, from small spells written on amulets to lengthy scrolls containing incantations and instructions for using them, were prevalent. Incantations, hexes, and numerous other powerful sayings were performed with rituals to exercise power over spirits, people, and circumstances.

Silverwork and Artemis. Artemis (Diana) was the most important deity in Ephesus. Her temple was considered one of the seven wonders of the ancient world, and it also served as a bank. Thus religion, economics, and politics were all here intertwined. Apparently, among the most popular products connected with the worship of Artemis were small silver sculptures that depicted her enthroned in her shrine.

Theater. The theater, which overlooked the harbor, has been excavated. It held up to 24,000 people.

Town clerk. The title of an elected official who served as the head of the city council.

Mistakes to Avoid

It is most important that we belicve the message of Paul rather than imitate the methods of Paul. While his methods may work well sometimes, they may not be best other times. His message, however, is always on target. This story would be inappropriate for younger children.

173. Paul on Trial (Acts 21–26)

Lesson Focus

Paul was arrested in the temple area and then went through several stages of defense. First he addressed the crowd gathered in the temple area, then he was brought before the Sanhedrin and confronted them. He was then taken to Caesarea where he defended himself before the governor, Felix. He was left in prison for two years and addressed Felix's successor, Festus. He then appealed to Caesar, and while awaiting transfer his case was heard by King

Herod Agrippa II. Finally he was shipped to Rome to stand trial. In all these situations, he gave account of the gospel and his ministry.

- God continued to grow the church by means of Paul's exposure to the highest officials.
- God uses even difficult circumstances to give us opportunities to serve the kingdom.
- God can use turbulent times to advance his kingdom.

Lesson Application

We should view difficult times as opportunities to serve God.

- We must always be ready to speak of our faith.
- We look at difficult times as opportunities.
- We trust that God is in control of circumstances.

Biblical Context

Luke's first volume, the Gospel of Luke, documented the results of the coming of the Son. This second volume, the book of Acts, documents the results of the coming of the Spirit. Acts was not written to give specifics about the nature and operation of the church, nor is it simply a history of how the church started. Luke was making a case among his contemporaries that Christianity is a legitimate religion, despite opposition from the Jews and Romans, who were inclined to treat Christians as a group of lunatic troublemakers, fanatic followers of a crucified criminal. To the church today Acts stands as testimony to how God grew his church, primarily through the work of Peter and Paul. Acts 21–26 details all Paul's opportunities to present the gospel message to high officials as he moved from one trial to another. The details show that Paul's adversaries were the ones causing the trouble because they opposed the gospel.

Interpretational Issues in the Story

Accusations against Paul (Acts 21:28). The initial accusations against Paul were made by Jews who had come after him from Asia and concerned teaching against keeping some aspects of the Jewish law and circumcision—important matters of Jewish identity. They also (falsely) accused him of bringing Gentiles into sections of the temple compound where they were not allowed, which carried a death penalty.

Speech to the crowd (Acts 22:3–21). Paul recounted his Jewish background and training as a Pharisee, his zeal in persecuting Christians, and his experience on the road to Damascus. He did not refer explicitly to his status as a Christian, for that was not a choice against his Jewish identity. The crowd was enraged when he told them of his call to preach to the Gentiles. For a Jew to recognize Jesus as the Messiah was not as objectionable as a Jew who reduced or eliminated boundaries between Jew and Gentile. The next day in the Sanhedrin, it was neither the identity of Jesus nor the mission to the Gentiles that caused problems but the question of the resurrection.

Speech before Felix (Acts 24:10–21). In this portion of the trial, Paul was accused of being a troublemaker who stirred up riots as a leader of the Christians (the Nazarene sect, v. 5). His opponents added the charge of desecrating the temple. Paul denied the charges (vv. 10–13, 18) but did identify himself as a Jew and follower of the Way. "The Way" was a description of followers of Christ.

Appeal to Caesar (Acts 25:11). Festus succeeded Felix and heard the same kinds of charges that his predecessor had heard two years earlier. Paul knew that Festus was currying favor with the Jews and that he might be inclined to turn Paul over to them, which would have been catastrophic. As a Roman citizen Paul had a right to appeal to Caesar, and he did so.

Speech before Agrippa (Acts 26:2–29). Again Paul recounted the details of his Jewish upbringing and training as a Pharisee. He told of his role in persecuting Christians, about his experience on the road to Damascus, and how he was sent to the Gentiles, stressing that they could receive forgiveness from sins. Nothing here indicates that he was making proselytes to Judaism, thus indicating that his message had nothing to do with Jewish law or circumcision. When he referenced Christ (v. 23) and his resurrection, Agrippa was astonished at the claim. Despite that, he was persuaded that the charges against Paul by the Jews were unfounded. This finding is very important to the case Luke has been making throughout the book.

Background Information

Sanhedrin. In the Judaism represented in rabbinic writings after the destruction of the temple in AD 70, the Sanhedrin was depicted as a formal body that provided leadership for the Jewish people. Its members were not necessarily priests but respected religious experts who made legal decisions, preserved traditions, and governed the spiritual and social life of the people. Though Pharisees, who were popular with the common people, were among the group, the Sadducees held the majority of the seventy-one seats. Paul exploited their differences of belief about the resurrection and thus gained support of the Pharisees (understandable since Paul was trained in that tradition). It is unknown whether the Sanhedrin in the New Testament was formally institutionalized, though the historian Josephus talks about it meeting in council in the temple courts in the period before the temple was destroyed. The word *sanhedrin* can refer simply to an ad hoc gathering of responsible people for the purpose of making a decision and may sometimes be used that way in the New Testament.

Caesarea. The port of Caesarea was where the Roman governor of Judea had his main residence. Extensive excavations have been done at the site, and the palace of Herod Agrippa has been located. The port city featured a large, artificial harbor constructed by Herod the Great a generation earlier, as well as all the features of a Roman provincial center (hippodrome, theater, amphitheater, market center). The town had been named in honor of Caesar Augustus.

Felix. Felix was the Roman procurator, which was the same office Pilate had held, from AD 52–59. As a slave, he had been a childhood friend to the young Claudius who became emperor. Felix was freed and given a high position but was unpopular and ineffective. He was deposed by Nero in AD 59 and replaced with Festus.

Festus. Porcius Festus was procurator from AD 59–62, his tenure cut short by a premature death. Little has been written about him, but it appears that he was respected and competent.

Agrippa. This is Herod Agrippa II, the son of the Agrippa who persecuted the apostles in Jerusalem in Acts 12. Agrippa I died in AD 44, but his son was judged as too young to succeed him. In AD 50 Agrippa II was given a position in the region of Chalcis (north of Palestine along the coast), and his domain gradually increased in succeeding years. He continued to rule through the Jewish Revolt and the destruction of the temple and Jerusalem in AD 70, all the way until AD 92.

Mistakes to Avoid

In this narrative, as throughout Acts, Paul testified to the power of God and was God's instrument to build his church. Luke does not present Paul as an authoritative model to show believers how they ought to act. Paul's behavior as a bold, faithful witness is commendable but not the primary point. We ought not to speculate about Paul's attitudes concerning his enemies—we don't know whether he loved them or prayed for them. Finally, we must not infer from the text anything about avoiding decision making, as Felix did. We want to teach from the lesson more about God than about the people involved. This lesson is too complicated for younger children.

174. Paul's Shipwreck (Acts 27:1–28:10)

Lesson Focus

Paul trusted the word of God, and God protected Paul's ship and its occupants through a terrible storm, delivering them safe to shore.

- God is able to protect those who are faithful to him.
- God preserved Paul because he still had work for him to do.
- God does not always prevent storms or other troubles but is able to see us through them.

Lesson Application

God is with those who trust in him.

- We trust God even in difficult circumstances.
- We keep alert to ways that we can serve and honor God—especially in difficult circumstances.

Biblical Context

Luke's first volume, the Gospel of Luke, documented the results of the coming of the Son. This second volume, the book of Acts, documents the results of the coming of the Spirit. Acts was not written to give specifics about the nature and operation of the church, nor is it simply a history of how the church started. Luke was making a case among his contemporaries that Christianity is a legitimate religion, despite opposition from the Jews and Romans, who were inclined to treat Christians as a group of lunatic troublemakers, fanatic followers of a crucified criminal. To the church today Acts stands as testimony to how God grew his church, primarily through the work of Peter and Paul. This account shows the Spirit's work through Paul as he gave advice to the sailors, encouraged the prisoners, had visions assuring their safety, and prophesied that none would be lost. Once on Malta Paul was protected from injury when bitten by a dangerous snake. All these incidents give evidence of the Spirit's protection of Paul and suggest that even in prison he would continue to have an important ministry.

Interpretational Issues in the Story

Took bread and gave thanks (Acts 27:35). This was the common practice at most meals, so we need not think of it as a celebration of the Lord's Supper. Few of those partaking were Christians.

Lightened the ship (Acts 27:38). The soldiers and crew knew they were sailing into shallow waters, and they hoped that by making the ship ride higher in the water, they could get closer to land before running aground.

Justice (Acts 28:4). Properly capitalized, the islanders use the word "Justice" to refer to a deity whose name meant "justice." Water "ordeals" were sometimes used as a way to judge someone's guilt or innocence, and the incident with the viper would have been viewed the same way. Luke uses these occurrences to add to the evidence already given by the various authorities proving that Paul was innocent of wrongdoing. This is important to the case Luke is making concerning the nature of Christianity.

Paul seen as a god (Acts 28:6). The superstitious islanders were used to hearing stories of gods roaming around in human form, and for someone to survive this sort of snakebite suggested to them the possibility that Paul was a god.

Background Information

Chronology. Paul was shipped to Rome in October in AD 59 where he remained under house arrest until about AD 62 and wrote the Prison Epistles (Ephesians, Philippians, Colossians, and Philemon). The book of Acts ends here, but it is generally thought that Paul was released and had a couple more years of ministry before he was imprisoned again and executed in Nero's persecution about AD 65. This was just before the beginning of the Jewish revolt against Rome that culminated in the destruction of Jerusalem and the temple in AD 70.

Ship's route. Ships regularly sailed along coastlines, always trying to keep land in sight. The route described in Acts 27 demonstrates that practice. They sailed north along the coast of Phoenicia and Syria then turned west along the southern shore of Asia Minor. Having reached the southwest corner of Asia Minor, they crossed over to Crete where, because of the winds, they sailed along its southern coast. From there the storm drove them out into the open waters of the Adriatic Sea (now called the Mediterranean Sea). They ran aground on the small island of Malta nearly sixty miles south of Sicily.

Mistakes to Avoid

God is able to deliver through trials, but students should be taught that God doesn't always deliver in the ways we hope. We cannot confidently derive promises for ourselves from the actual experiences of people in the Bible. Luke did not supply this story to offer Paul as a model for our own lives and ministries. Rather, his aim was to show how God preserved Paul and worked through him. As we teach the story, we do well to express admiration for God's work rather than Paul's. However, we can note Paul's faithfulness and point out that while everyone's circumstances are different, God expects us to be faithful to him. While older students might enjoy learning more about ships and shipping in the Roman world or tracing the ship's journey on a map, don't let them lose sight of the big picture. God is at work getting his servant, Paul, to Rome where he will share the good news of Jesus.

175. John's Vision (Revelation)

Lesson Focus

John addresses letters to seven churches of Asia Minor with admonitions and encouragement from Christ. These letters are followed by the extended report of a vision that tells of difficult times leading to the eventual establishment of the new heaven and new earth. The book of Revelation is intended to give hope and encouragement to Christians suffering persecution. The vision it contains depicts Christ triumphant, indicating that the present evil world will be replaced by the kingdom of God. Its intention is not to give a time line of events but to show that Christ and his saints will overcome all opposition. We should derive from it a sense of what it will be like rather than a confidence about how it is going to happen. The book should be read with eyes focused on Christ.

- God's plan includes times of persecution and trouble.
- God will judge the wicked.
- Jesus is coming again.
- Christ is worthy; he will overcome and be exalted.
- All will give praise to Christ.

Lesson Application

We should recognize God's control of history and see his plan for exalting Christ and establishing his kingdom in the new creation.

- We trust God and have hope in times of trouble.
- We exalt Christ at all times.

- We must have faith that God has history in his control.
- We look forward to the coming of Christ and the new creation.

Interpretational Issues in the Story

Satan's destiny (Revelation 20). The Devil will be thrown into the lake of fire at the end. He is not in hell now, and hell is his punishment, not his domain. He does not rule there; he suffers.

New creation (Revelation 21). The new creation is the new heaven and new earth, with a new Jerusalem. It is the climax of all creation and history in which all things have been made new with the effects of the fall and sin no longer in evidence. Though we can rightly talk about going to heaven when we die as believers, the Bible presents our ultimate destiny as being that of citizens of the new creation. In one sense, the new creation begins for us when we receive Christ (see 2 Cor. 5:17).

Background Information

Writing of the book. John was exiled to the island of Patmos where he received this vision, probably in the mid-90s during the persecution of Emperor Domitian.

Seven churches. The churches were all in western Asia Minor in the area of Ephesus where John had served. They formed a rough triangle that covered nearly 4,000 square miles (about half the size of New Jersey). The letters to the churches follow the pattern of prophecies in the Old Testament against foreign nations. They include the standard types of prophetic oracles (indictment, instruction, judgment, and encouragement or exhortation).

Apocalyptic visions. Apocalyptic visions are known as early as the later books of the Old Testament. They are a form of prophecy that use symbolism and often feature an angelic guide. The message of the vision is often unmistakable even though the symbolism is often obscure. The message is not the symbolism or the vision, which are merely ways to communicate the message. In Revelation the message has to do with the exaltation of Christ. This message can be recognized by the audience regardless of how it interprets the symbols of the vision.

Mistakes to Avoid

Whatever interpretation one's church or tradition might have about the timing and sequence of the end times, about whether the book of Revelation refers to our future or past, and about whether the book should be interpreted literally or figuratively, there are certain basics that all agree on, which are important to convey in the lesson. Teachers should resist replacing the theological teaching of the book with a system devised by interpreters concerning events of the end times. The book must not be used to frighten students with talk of Antichrist, tribulation, persecution, or the Beast. Its intention is exactly the opposite—to encourage and give hope. We are overcomers through Christ, whatever might come. Some lessons give the idea that, in heaven or in the new creation, we will walk and talk with God, such as in the garden of Eden before the fall, and that Jesus will be our friend. This undermines the transcendent deity and majesty of the King, Jesus, who is worthy of all honor, praise, and exaltation, as the book proclaims.

Resources for Further Study

Alexander, David. *Zondervan Handbook to the Bible*. Grand Rapids: Zondervan, 1999.

The best of the Bible handbooks. Covers each book of the Bible, its people, places, and events, as well as archaeological and historical information. Discusses how to interpret the Bible, how we got the Bible, manners and customs, and much more. Written by dozens of highly qualified biblical scholars and fully illustrated.

Arnold, Clinton, ed. *Zondervan Illustrated Bible Backgrounds Commentary: New Testament*. Grand Rapids: Zondervan, 2002.

A four-volume reference work that proceeds passage by passage through the New Testament giving information about background issues. Photographs, maps, and diagrams greatly enhance the value of this set.

Brisco, Thomas C. *Holman Bible Atlas*. Nashville: Broadman and Holman, 1998.

This atlas contains helpful maps and clear text that take the reader through Bible places and times.

Burge, Gary M., Lynn H. Cohick, and Gene L. Green. *The New Testament in Antiquity*. Grand Rapids: Zondervan, 2009.

An introduction to the New Testament literature that helps the reader to grasp some of the realities of the Greco-Roman period. Richly illustrated and clearly written.

Hill, Andrew E., and John H. Walton. *Survey of the Old Testament*, 3rd edition. Grand Rapids: Zondervan, 2009.

An introductory text to the Old Testament that proceeds book by book helping the reader to understand the most important aspects of the text.

Keener, Craig. *IVP Bible Background Commentary: New Testament*. Downers Grove, IL: InterVarsity, 1994.

A one-volume compendium by the premiere scholar on New Testament backgrounds. Particularly helpful in pointing the reader to Jewish, Greek, and Roman sources of literature that help illuminate the world of the New Testament.

Lawrence, Paul. *IVP Atlas of Bible History*. Downers Grove, IL: InterVarsity, 2006.

A helpful atlas with a comprehensive set of maps and engaging discussion of places and events.

Rasmussen, Carl. *NIV Atlas of the Bible*, 2nd edition. Grand Rapids: Zondervan, 2010.

This revised edition gathers the newest insights of one of the finest scholars of historical geography today. Fully redesigned maps and careful discussion of history and archaeology make this an essential resource for growing a library. Fully illustrated and beautifully designed.

Snodgrass, Klyne R. *Stories with Intent: A Comprehensive Guide to the Parables of Jesus*. Grand Rapids: Eerdmans, 2008.

A monumental scholarly treatment of the parables along with thorough discussion of each parable's history, background, and interpretation.

Walton, John H. *The Lost World of Genesis One: Ancient Cosmology and the Origins Debate*. Downers Grove, IL: InterVarsity, 2009.

An interpretation that reads Genesis 1 as an ancient text against the ancient Near Eastern world. Brings out theological depth not often recognized and offers a new path through the Bible and science debates.

________., ed. *Zondervan Illustrated Bible Backgrounds Commentary: Old Testament*. Grand Rapids: Zondervan, 2009.

A five-volume reference work proceeding passage by passage through the Old Testament. An international team of thirty specialists take the reader through the pages of the Old Testament giving information about archaeology, geography, history, manners and customs, ancient literature, and much more that brings the Old Testament to life. Features over 2,000 photos, maps, and tables.

Walton, John H., and Andrew E. Hill. *Old Testament Today: A Journey from Original Meaning to Contemporary Significance*. Grand Rapids: Zondervan, 2004.

An introductory text to the Old Testament that attempts to help the reader understand how to interpret all the types of literature found in the Old Testament. If you find yourself asking, "What is this stuff doing in my Bible?" or "How is this God's Word to me today?" this book is for you.

Walton, John H., Mark L. Strauss, and Ted Cooper. *The Essential Bible Companion*. Grand Rapids: Zondervan, 2006.

A slim volume presenting a two-page spread on each book of the Bible. A concise gathering of the important information about each book, including a discussion of the purpose of the book and its key themes.

Walton, John H., Victor Matthews, and Mark Chavalas. *IVP Bible Background Commentary: Old Testament*. Downers Grove, IL: InterVarsity, 2000.

A one-volume reference work that introduces readers to the background issues that illuminate the Old Testament.

Helpful Commentary Series

Muck, Terry, ed. *The NIV Application Commentary*. Grand Rapids: Zondervan, 1995–.

Children's Resources

Batchelor, Mary. *The Children's Bible in 365 Stories*. Tring, UK: Lion, 1985.

In our experience this is the best of the Bible story books for elementary school children. Stories are told in a straightforward manner without gimmicks and speculation. There is no attempt to *teach* the story—she just *tells* it.

Boyd, Charles F. *What God Has Always Wanted: The Bible's Big Idea from Genesis through Revelation*. Little Rock, AR: Family Life Publishing, 2006.

Helps elementary children to move beyond the stories to knowing God. This is the best book we know for giving the big picture of the Bible in one story.

Costecalde, Claude-Bernard, consulting ed. *The Illustrated Family Bible*. London: Dorling Kindersley, 1997.

One of the better books for upper-elementary-aged children. The stories are drawn mainly from the NIV. Throughout there are short sections for understanding the story, which are usually unobjectionable. The strength of the book is in the very helpful archaeological and cultural illustrations and information presented.

Helm, David. *The Big Picture Story Bible*. Wheaton, IL: Crossway, 2004.

Though occasional interpretations creep in that we disagree with, this is one of the best story books for preschool- and lower-elementary-aged children that tells the stories with a God focus rather than with a role-model or moralizing perspective, and without gimmicks.

Walton, John, and Kim Walton. *The Tiny Tots Bible Story Book*. Illustrator, Alice Craig. Elgin, IL: Chariot, 1993.

Fourteen Bible stories, mostly from the Old Testament, written for preschoolers. Bright illustrations, one line of text per page, and lessons focused on God in age-appropriate ways. Out of print but still available through the illustrator's Web site, http://www.aliceart.net.

________. *The Tiny Tots Jesus Story Book*. Colorado Springs: Chariot, 1996.

Seven Bible stories from the New Testament, written for preschoolers. Bright illustrations, one line of text per page, and lessons focused on God in age-appropriate ways.

Teaching Index

Topics Indexed by Lesson

Scripture Index

Indexed by Lesson

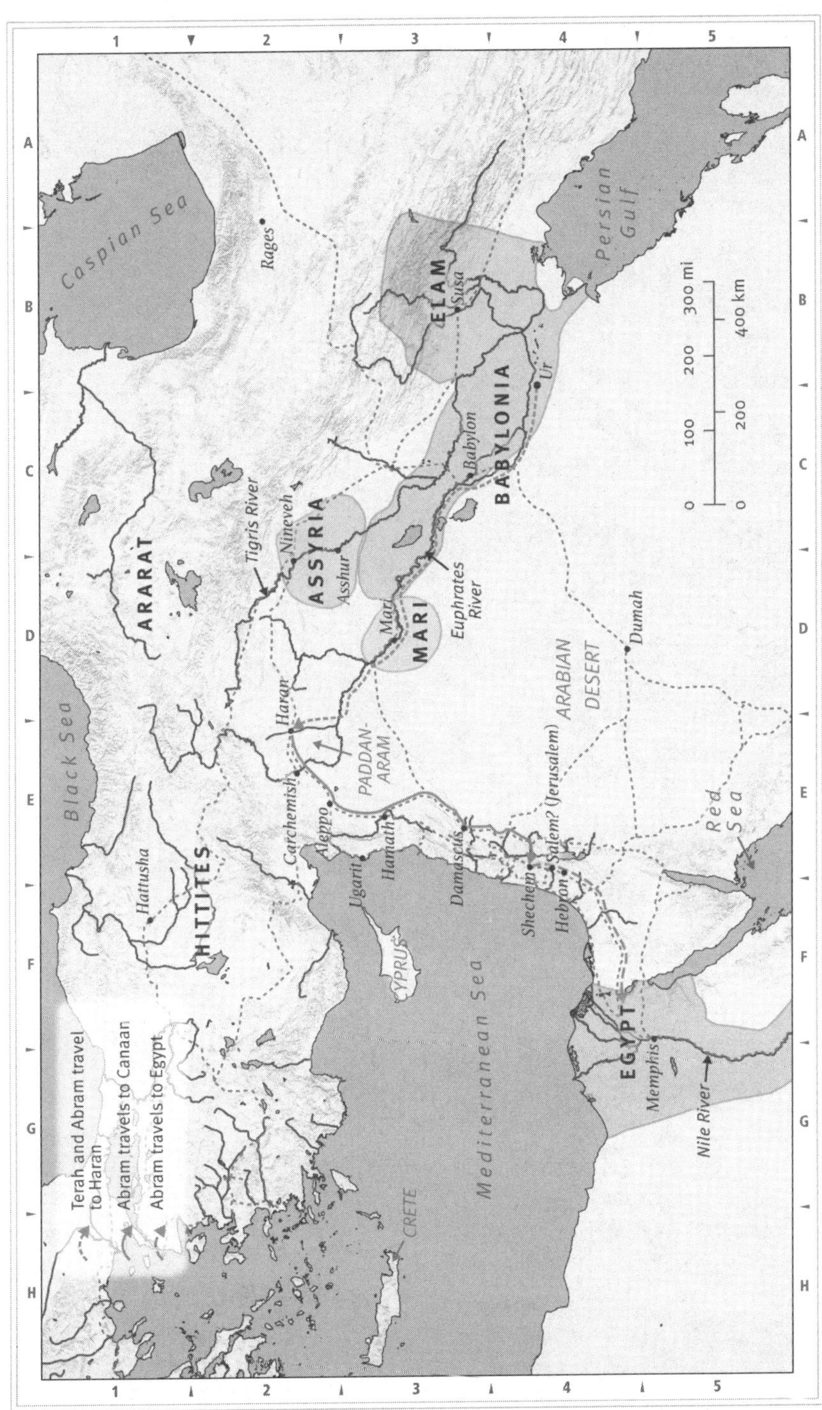
Caspian Sea
Black Sea
Mediterranean Sea
Persian Gulf
Red Sea
ARARAT
HITTITES
ASSYRIA
ELAM
BABYLONIA
MARI
PADDAN-ARAM
ARABIAN DESERT
EGYPT
CYPRUS
CRETE
Rages
Tigris River
Nineveh
Asshur
Susa
Babylon
Ur
Mari
Euphrates River
Haran
Carchemish
Aleppo
Hattusha
Ugarit
Hamath
Damascus
Shechem
Salem? (Jerusalem)
Hebron
Dumah
Memphis
Nile River
0 100 200 300 mi
0 200 400 km
Terah and Abram travel to Haran
Abram travels to Canaan
Abram travels to Egypt

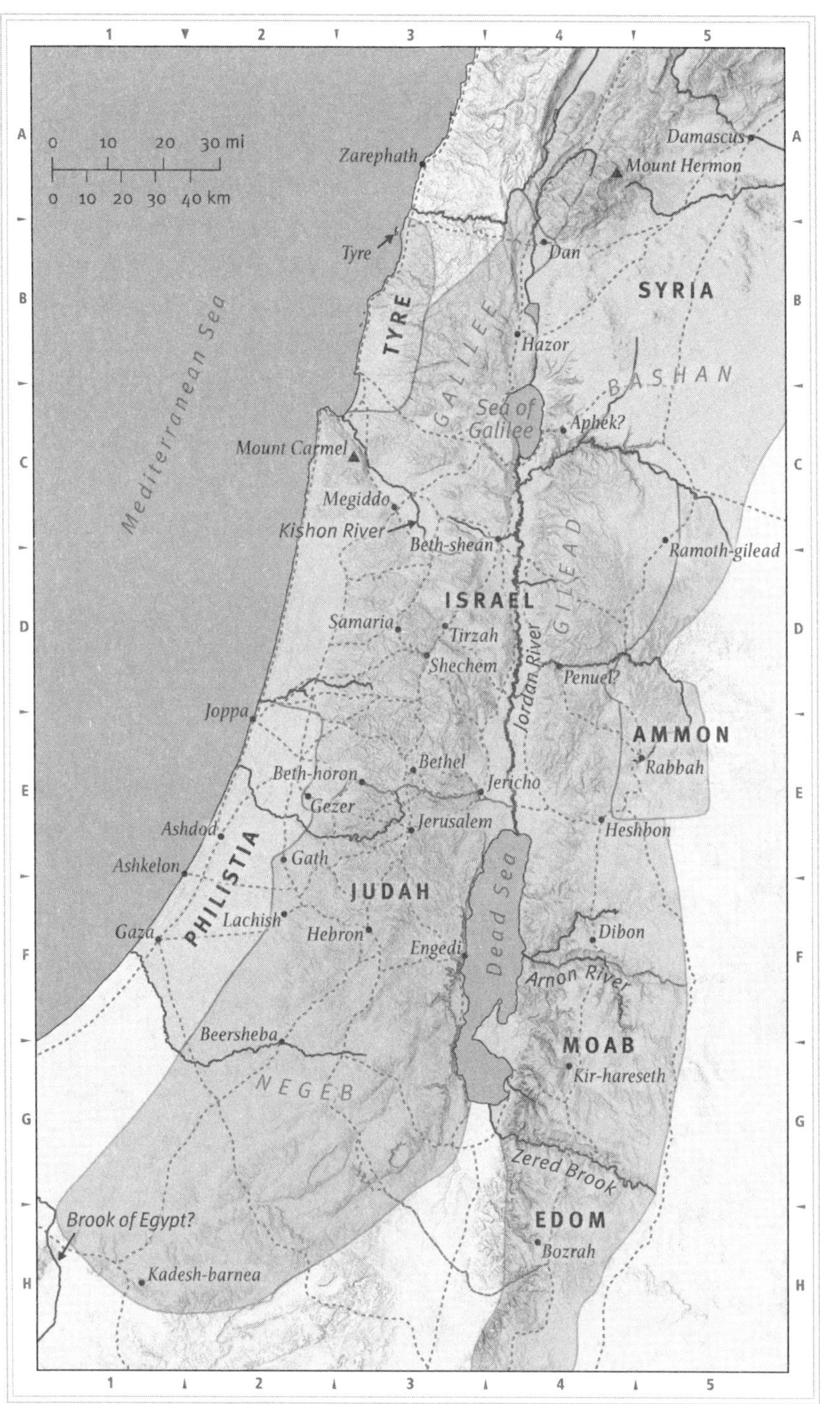

0 10 20 30 mi
0 10 20 30 40 km
Mediterranean Sea
Zarephath
Tyre
TYRE
Damascus
Mount Hermon
Dan
SYRIA
GALILEE
Hazor
BASHAN
Sea of Galilee
Aphek?
Mount Carmel
Megiddo
Kishon River
Beth-shean
GILEAD
Ramoth-gilead
ISRAEL
Samaria
Tirzah
Shechem
Jordan River
Penuel?
Joppa
AMMON
Rabbah
Bethel
Beth-horon
Jericho
Gezer
Jerusalem
Heshbon
Ashdod
PHILISTIA
Ashkelon
Gath
JUDAH
Dead Sea
Lachish
Hebron
Gaza
Engedi
Dibon
Arnon River
MOAB
Kir-hareseth
Beersheba
NEGEB
Zered Brook
EDOM
Bozrah
Brook of Egypt?
Kadesh-barnea

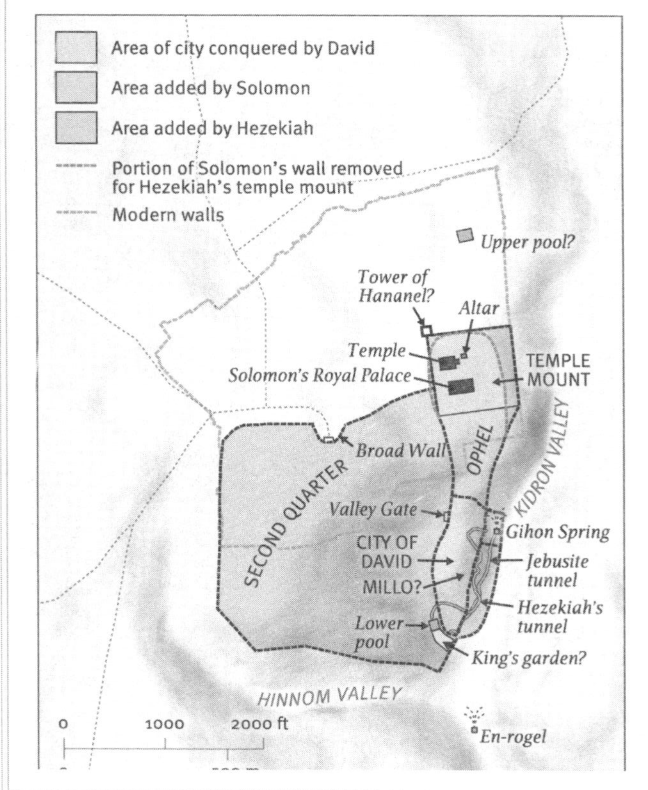
Area of city conquered by David
Area added by Solomon
Area added by Hezekiah
Portion of Solomon's wall removed for Hezekiah's temple mount
Modern walls
Upper pool?
Tower of Hananel?
Altar
Temple
Solomon's Royal Palace
TEMPLE MOUNT
Broad Wall
OPHEL
KIDRON VALLEY
SECOND QUARTER
Valley Gate
Gihon Spring
CITY OF DAVID
Jebusite tunnel
MILLO?
Hezekiah's tunnel
Lower pool
King's garden?
HINNOM VALLEY
0
1000
2000 ft
En-rogel

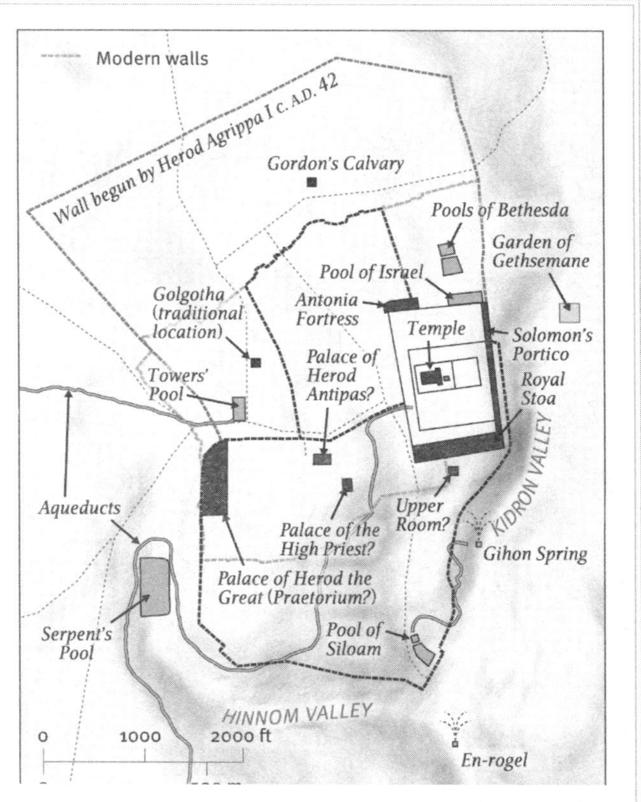
Modern walls
Wall begun by Herod Agrippa I c. A.D. 42
Gordon's Calvary
Pools of Bethesda
Garden of Gethsemane
Pool of Israel
Golgotha (traditional location)
Antonia Fortress
Temple
Solomon's Portico
Palace of Herod Antipas?
Towers' Pool
Royal Stoa
KIDRON VALLEY
Aqueducts
Upper Room?
Palace of the High Priest?
Gihon Spring
Palace of Herod the Great (Praetorium?)
Serpent's Pool
Pool of Siloam
HINNOM VALLEY
0
1000
2000 ft
En-rogel

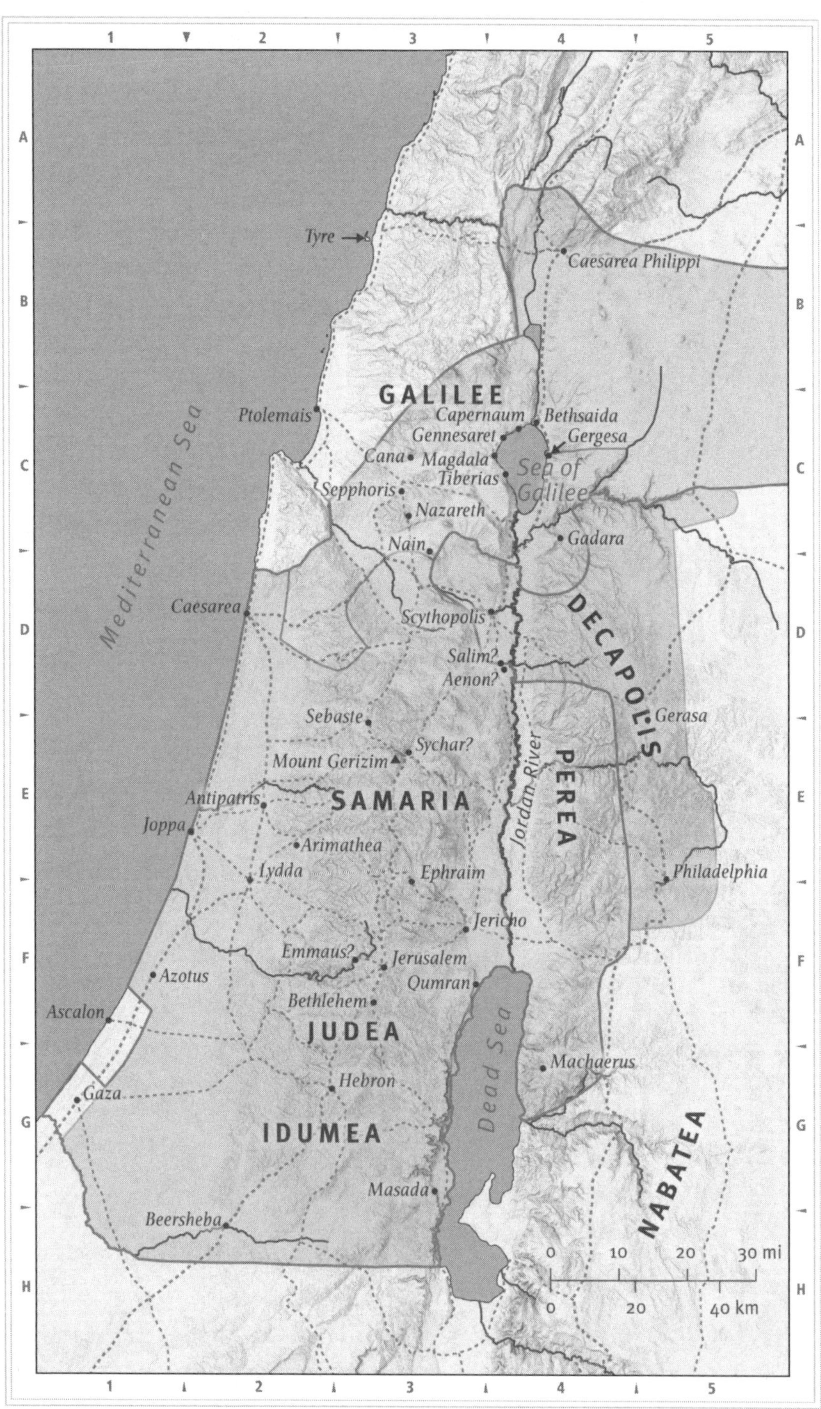

Mediterranean Sea
Tyre
Caesarea Philippi
GALILEE
Ptolemais
Capernaum
Bethsaida
Gennesaret
Gergesa
Cana
Magdala
Tiberias
Sea of Galilee
Sepphoris
Nazareth
Nain
Gadara
Caesarea
Scythopolis
DECAPOLIS
Salim?
Aenon?
Sebaste
Gerasa
Sychar?
Mount Gerizim
Jordan River
PEREA
Antipatris
SAMARIA
Joppa
Arimathea
Lydda
Ephraim
Philadelphia
Jericho
Emmaus?
Jerusalem
Azotus
Qumran
Bethlehem
Ascalon
JUDEA
Dead Sea
Machaerus
Hebron
Gaza
IDUMEA
NABATEA
Masada
Beersheba
0 10 20 30 mi
0 20 40 km

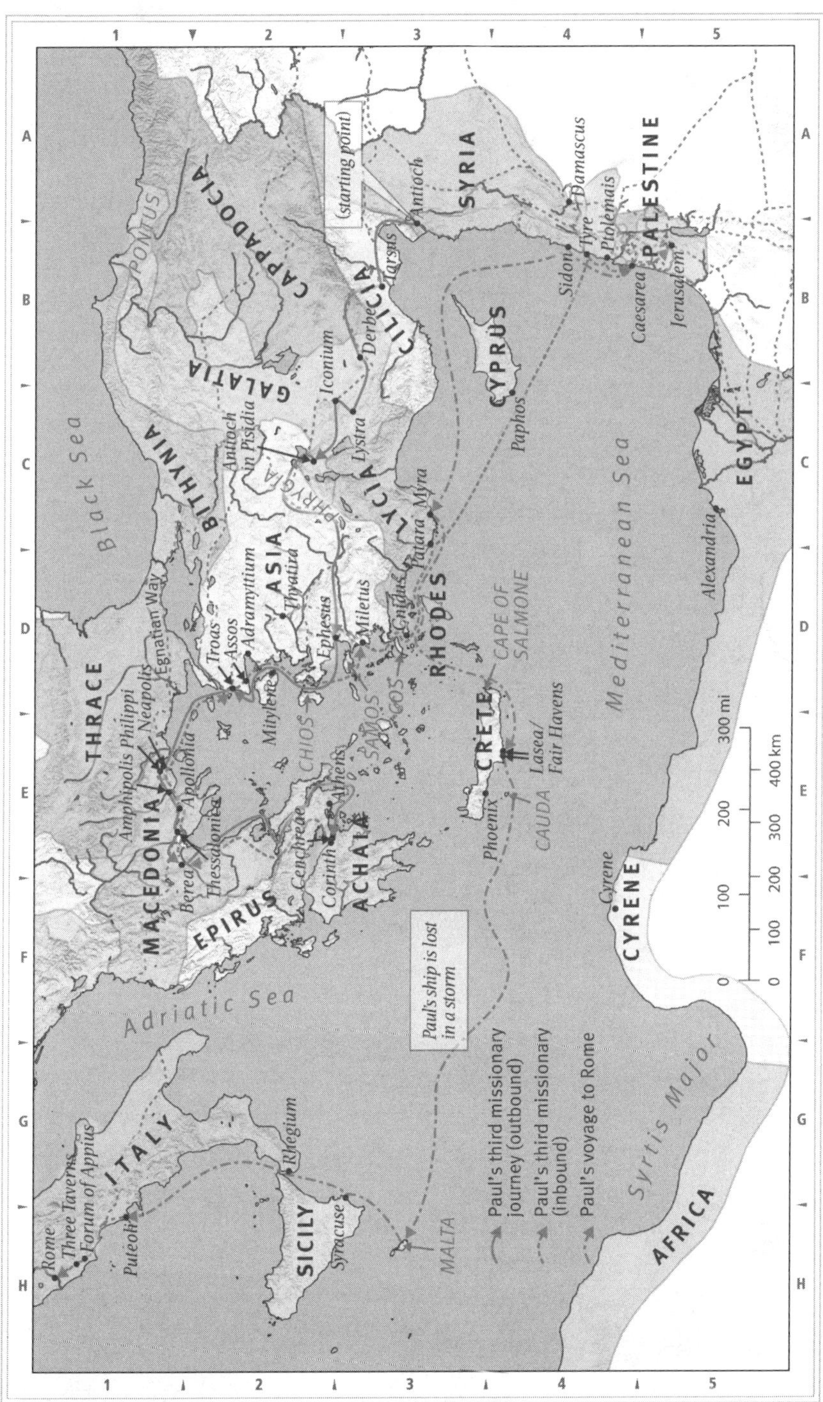

Black Sea
PONTUS
CAPPADOCIA
(starting point)
Antioch
SYRIA
Damascus
Tyre
Ptolemais
Sidon
PALESTINE
Caesarea
Jerusalem
CILICIA
Tarsus
Derbe
Iconium
Lystra
GALATIA
BITHYNIA
Antioch in Pisidia
PHRYGIA
LYCIA
Myra
Patara
CYPRUS
Paphos
EGYPT
Alexandria
Mediterranean Sea
ASIA
Thyatira
Adramyttium
Ephesus
Miletus
Cnidus
RHODES
CAPE OF SALMONE
Troas
Assos
Mitylene
CHIOS
SAMOS
COS
Egnatian Way
THRACE
Neapolis
Philippi
Amphipolis
Apollonia
MACEDONIA
Thessalonica
Berea
EPIRUS
Cenchreae
Athens
Corinth
ACHAIA
CRETE
Lasea/
Fair Havens
Phoenix
CAUDA
CYRENE
Cyrene
Paul's ship is lost in a storm
Adriatic Sea
ITALY
Rome
Three Taverns
Forum of Appius
Puteoli
Rhegium
SICILY
Syracuse
MALTA
Syrtis Major
AFRICA
Paul's third missionary journey (outbound)
Paul's third missionary (inbound)
Paul's voyage to Rome
0 100 200 300 mi
0 100 200 300 400 km

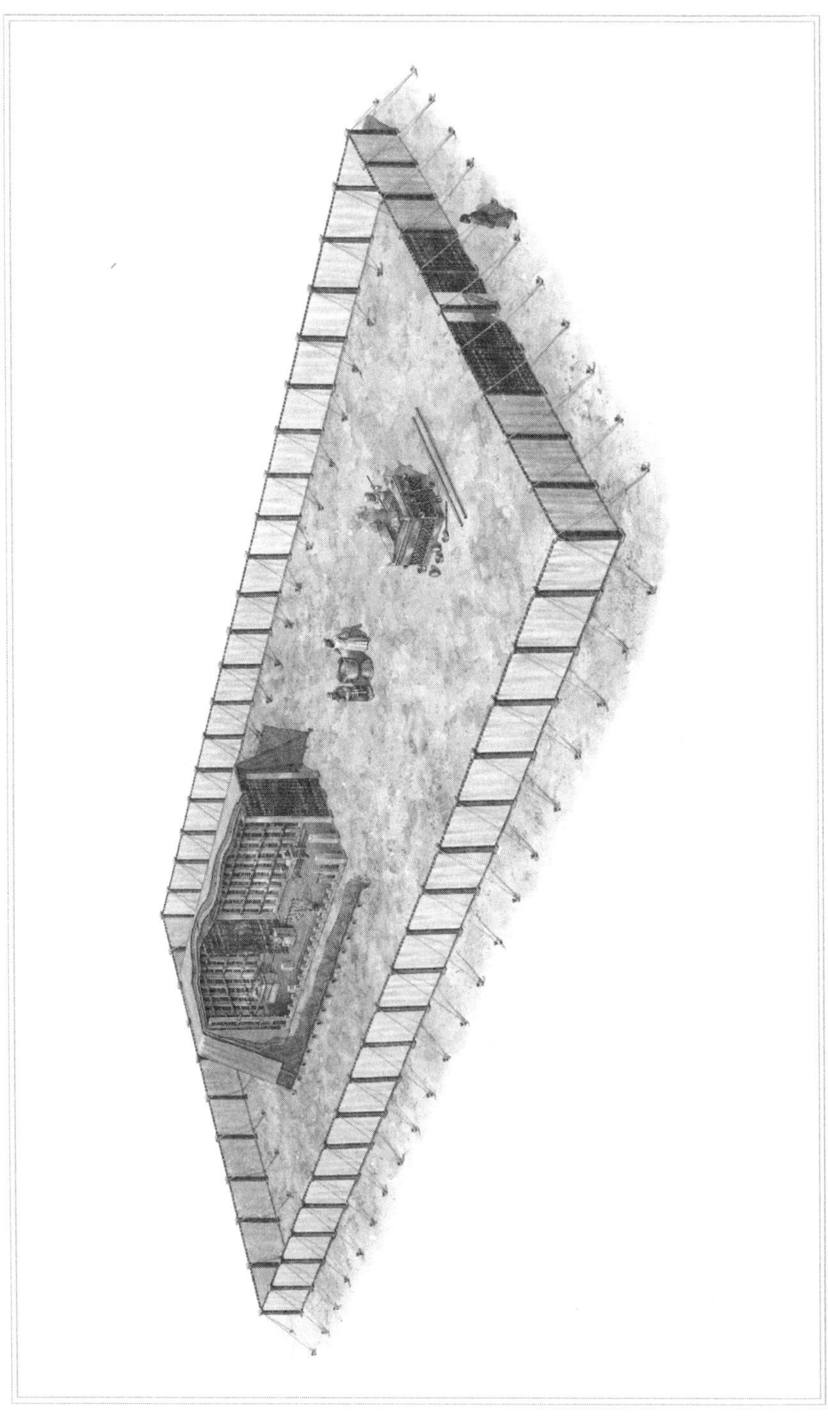

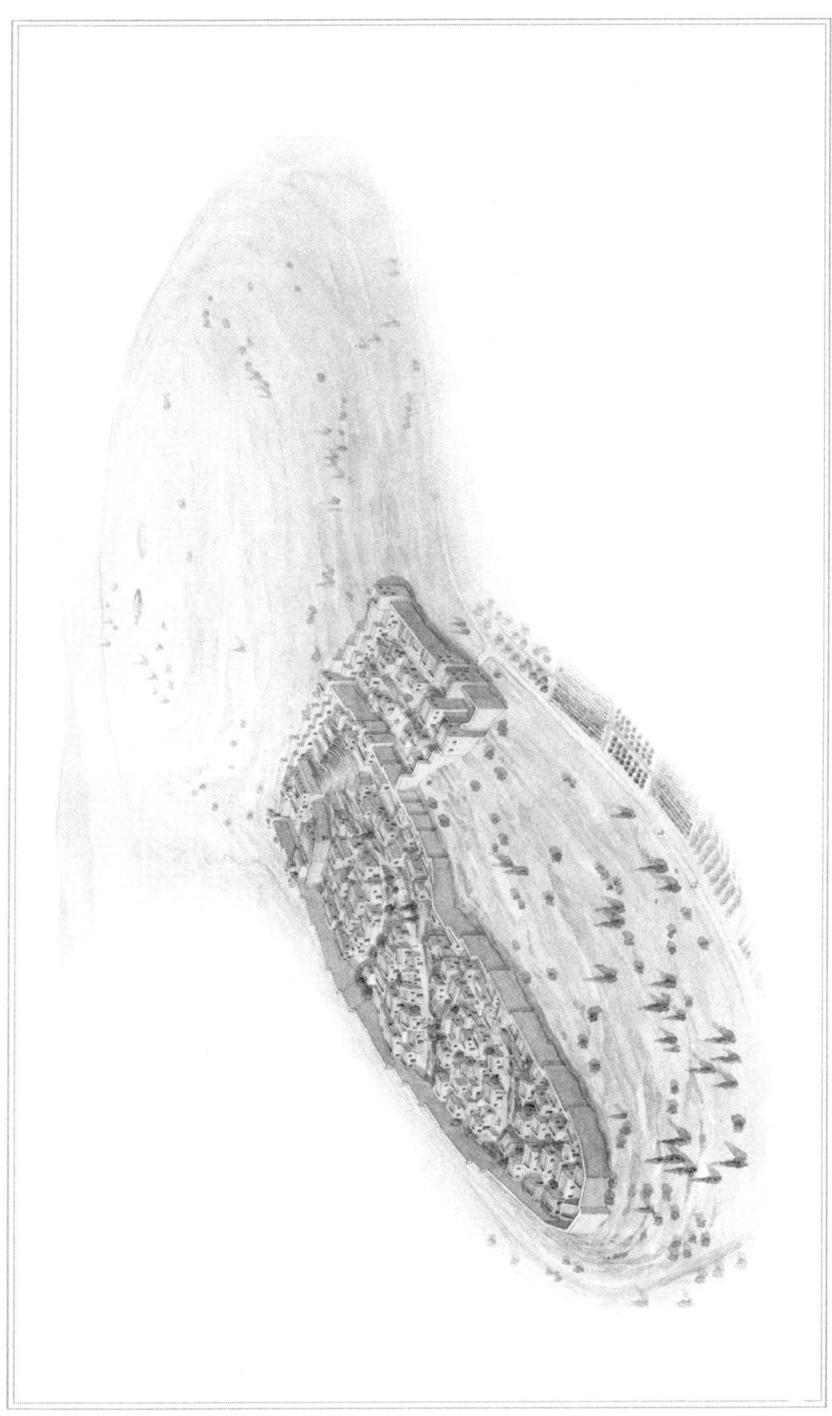

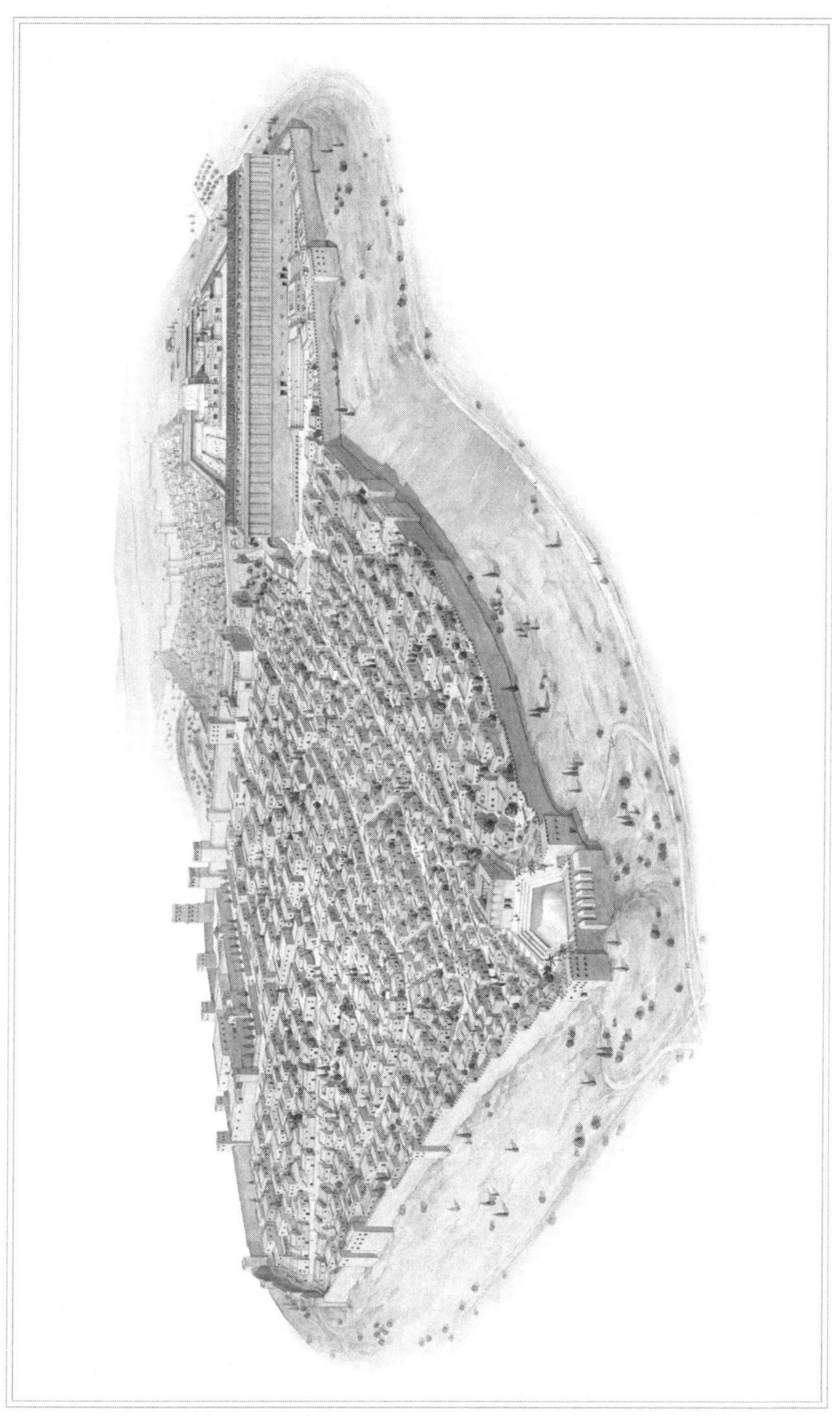

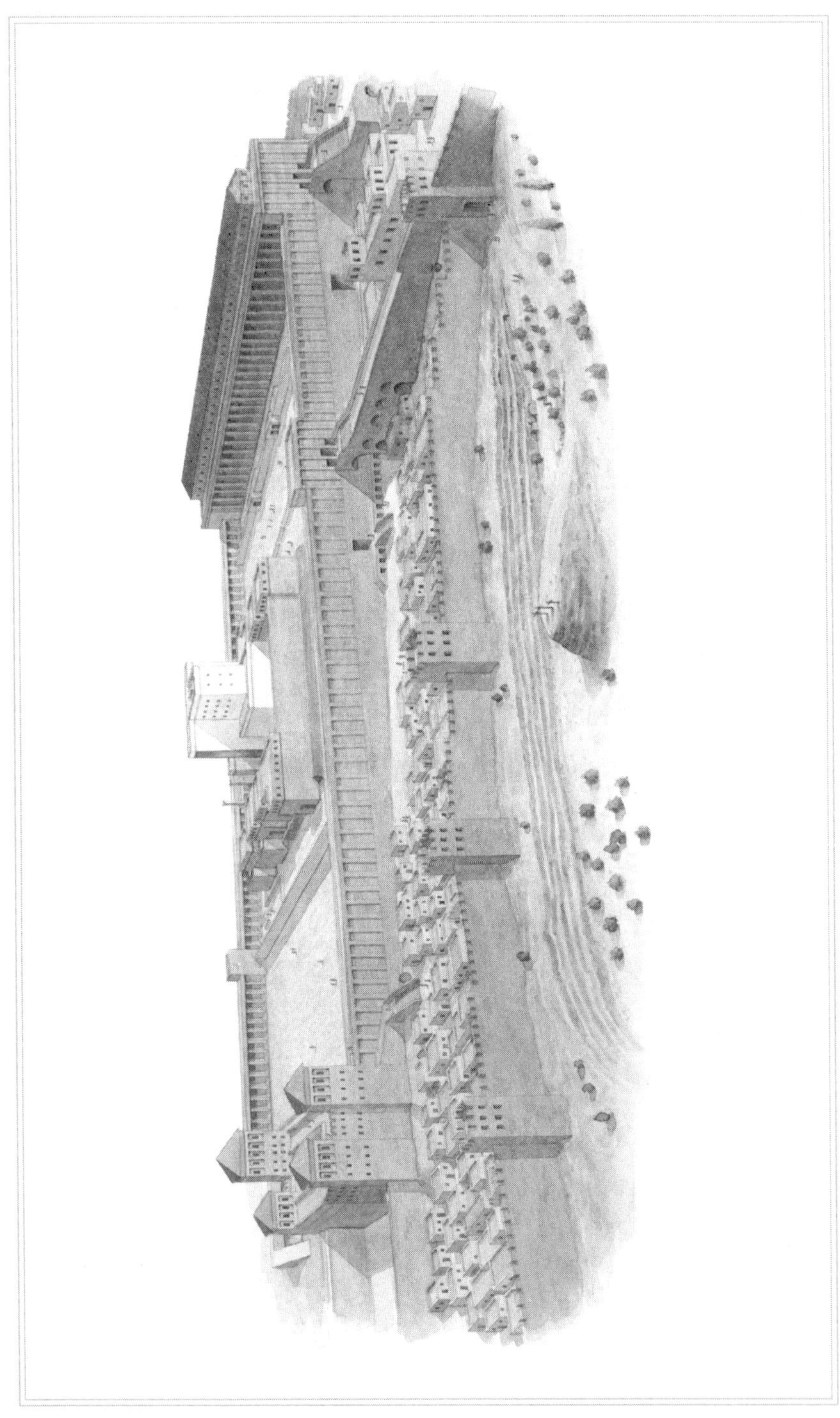